Follow the Leader?

Chicago Studies in American Politics
A series edited by Benjamin I. Page, Susan Herbst,
Lawrence R. Jacobs, and James Druckman

Also in the series:

Additional series titles follow index

Follow the Leader?

How Voters Respond to Politicians'
Policies and Performance

GABRIEL S. LENZ

THE UNIVERSITY OF CHICAGO PRESS   CHICAGO AND LONDON

GABRIEL S. LENZ is assistant professor in the Charles and Louise Travers
Department of Political Science at the University of California, Berkeley.

The University of Chicago Press, Chicago 60637
The University of Chicago Press, Ltd., London
© 2012 by The University of Chicago
All rights reserved. Published 2012.
Printed in the United States of America
21 20 19 18 17 16 15 14 13 12   1 2 3 4 5

ISBN-13: 978-0-226-47213-3 (cloth)
ISBN-13: 978-0-226-47214-0 (paper)
ISBN-13: 978-0-226-47215-7 (e-book)
ISBN-10: 0-226-47213-2 (cloth)
ISBN-10: 0-226-47214-0 (paper)
ISBN-10: 0-226-47215-9 (e-book)

Library of Congress Cataloging-in-Publication Data

Lenz, Gabriel S., 1975–
    Follow the leader? : how voters respond to politicians' policies and performance /
Gabriel S. Lenz.
        pages cm.—(Chicago studies in American politics)
    ISBN 978-0-226-47213-3 (cloth : alkaline paper)—ISBN 0-226-47213-2 (cloth : alkaline
paper)—ISBN 978-0-226-47214-0 (paperback : alkaline paper)—ISBN 0-226-47214-0
(paperback : alkaline paper)—ISBN 978-0-226-47215-7 (e-book)—ISBN 0-226-47215-9
(e-book) 1. Voting—United States. 2. Elections—United States. 3. United States—
Politics and goverment. I. Title. II. Series: Chicago studies in American politics.
    JK1965.L459 2012
    324.973—dc23

                                                                                2012002384

♾ This paper meets the requirements of ANSI/NISO z39.48-1992 (Permanence of Paper).

Contents

Acknowledgments

This book began as a PhD dissertation in the Politics Department at Princeton University. I had the good fortune to be advised by Larry Bartels, Tali Mendelberg, Martin Gilens, and Markus Prior. The dissertation examined a political campaign's ability to prime policy and performance issues. The topic was narrow, a fact I was slow to realize. The graduate school experience often leads us to focus on the parochial concerns of the existing academic literature, when we could focus on topics of broader importance; in my case, on central questions about democratic accountability. Early in the process, Larry Bartels commented that my dissertation would be primarily of interest to political scientists, a gentle put down. His comment and probing questions by my advisors, especially Tali Mendelberg, eventually led me to the broader questions about democratic politics I now address. I am so grateful to these individuals for their precious time and invaluable guidance. In graduate school, I was fortunate to have wonderful fellow students and visitors at the Center for the Study of Democratic Politics with whom to discuss the project, especially Jonathan Ladd, Tom Clark, Shana Gadarian, Amy Gershkoff, Matt Hindman, Karen Jusko, Chris Karpowitz, Hans Noel, and David Karol.

Much of the book was written, rewritten, and rewritten again while I was at MIT. I couldn't have asked for a more supportive department or a sharper set of colleagues, especially Stephen Ansolabehere, Adam Berinsky, Andrea Campbell, Jim Snyder, and Charles Stewart. I'm particularly thankful for Adam Berinsky's professional expertise and advice about book writing, not something taught in graduate school, as well as Jim Snyder's engagement with the project. I also benefited from wonderful colleagues in other subfields, especially Taylor Fravel, Jens Hainmueller, Orit Kedar, David Singer, and Lily Tsai. Finally, Charles Stewart funded and Adam Berinsky organized a book conference at an early stage in the writing. The participants—Matt Baum, Bob Erikson, Stanley Feldman, Sunshine Hillygus, John Patty, and Nick Valentino—generously gave up a day of their busy lives to provide helpful feedback at a critical point. At a later stage, Andrea Campbell assigned her graduate seminar to read the manuscript and write critical essays, and I'm especially thankful for the comments of Jeremy Ferweda, Krista Loose, Michele Margolis, Jennifer Pan, Mike Sances, and Vanessa Williamson.

With the help of Alan Gerber and Don Green, I was fortunate to spend two semesters at Yale University in the Center for the Study of American Politics and the Institution for Social and Policy Studies, where I benefited from discussions with them and with John Bullock, Dan Butler, Justin Fox, Michael Peress, and Ellie Powell.

As the book approached its current form, several individuals engaged the project with unusual depth. Richard Johnston provided lengthy comments and pushed me to think yet further about the implications for democracy, leading to substantial revisions. I am greatly indebted to him for his advice and his lifetime of work. John Zaller read the manuscript not once, but twice. His trenchant comments reshaped chapters and, ultimately, the conclusions. Dennis Chong's thoughtful comments helped transform the manuscript from a series of articles to a book. Paul Sniderman provided invaluable guidance about writing and publishing. Finally, I am forever grateful for Jamie Druckman's never-ending willingness to read and reread chapters. His tireless efforts made the book better at every level.

Over the years I have profited from comments and suggestions from many other colleagues, including Dong Ahler, David Broockman, John Geer, Stephen Goggin, Austin Hart, Matthew Hindman, Adrienne Hosek, Vince Hutchings, Karen Jusko, Aidan McCarthy, Marc Meredith, Joanne Miller, Andrew Owen, Christian Phillips, Markus Prior, Jasjeet Sekhon, John Sides, Byung Kwon Song, Rob Van Houweling, and Jeff Tessin. I also thank John Tryneski, Rodney Powell, Mary Gehl, and Dawn Hall at the University of Chicago Press for their professionalism and encouragement.

Mike Myers provided skilled research assistance, organizing data for my analysis. Monica Kahn, Peter Krzywicki, and Ilica Mahajan helped with everything from copyediting to fact checking. John Elder and Lisa

Camer McKay improved the book's style and readability, especially the more technical sections.

I benefited from the comments of seminar participants while presenting parts of this project at Columbia University, Duke University, George Washington University, Harvard University, MIT, NYU, Princeton University, University of Minnesota, University of Pennsylvania, and Yale University.

An early version of the analysis in chapters 3, 5, and 8 for a subset of the cases was published in the *American Journal of Political Science* in 2009 under the title "Learning and Opinion Change, Not Priming: Reconsidering the Evidence for the Priming Hypothesis," and won the best-article award in that journal for 2009.

Finally, I'm grateful to my family, especially for the love, support, and understanding of my wife, Erica Carlisle.

CHAPTER ONE

Rum Punch or Issue Voting?

In his long career as a public figure, James Madison lost only one election—his 1777 bid for a seat in the new Virginia House of Delegates. At the time, candidates for public office were expected to ply voters with liquor on Election Day; the favorite drink was rum punch. George Washington had supplied 160 gallons of alcohol to 391 voters for his successful 1758 election bid in Frederick County, Virginia (Labunski 2006). Madison, however, found this campaign tactic repulsive, "inconsistent with the purity of moral and Republican principles" (Labunski 2006, 32). Determined to introduce a "chaster" model of conducting elections, he refused to provide alcohol to voters in the 1777 election. His opponent, lacking such scruples, beat him.

Such apparently superficial judgments on the part of voters have always been one of the chief concerns with democracy. And even though most consider the worldwide spread of democracy since Madison's day a stupendous achievement, concerns about voters' judgments persist. Do voters still judge politicians on such irrelevant or superficial characteristics or do they vote on substantive matters?

In one view of democracy, elections are about substance; they are fundamentally about voters expressing their preferences on public policy (Dahl 1956; Pennock 1979). Voters judge, compare, and vote on candidates' policy platforms. (Political scientists call this *issue voting*.) The voter thinks: "This politician supports the policies I think are right and so I will vote for him or her." If this view is correct, politicians may generally reflect the will of the public. Citizens lead, politicians follow.

Other scholars consider the policy voting view unachievable. They see elections as periodic referenda on the incumbents or as a way of selecting candidates with the best character traits (Riker 1982; Schumpeter 1942). In this version of democracy, voters may focus on what I call performance-related characteristics, such as previous success in office and trustworthiness. The voter thinks: "This politician has the personal traits I think a politician should have. This politician has done a good job in previous political positions." In this view, citizens don't directly lead politicians on policy, but they do lead on performance, throwing out incompetent or corrupt incumbents.

We can also imagine a worst-case view of democracy, in which voters lack well-developed preferences about public policy and about politicians' performance and, instead, blindly follow the views of their preferred party or politicians. They judge, compare, and vote for candidates according to other matters—anything from rum punch and good looks to overblown gaffes and an ill-fitting tank helmet. In this view, politicians make policy with surprisingly little constraint. They must still win elections, but they win or lose on what Alexander Hamilton called the "little arts of popularity."[1] Voters, having decided they like a particular politician for reasons having little or nothing to do with policy, may simply adopt that politician's policy views. In this view, democracy is a farce. Politicians lead, citizens follow.

The main question I set out to answer is, which view of democracy best reflects modern reality? Do citizens lead politicians on policy? Do they judge them on performance-related characteristics? Or do they merely follow politicians?

To answer this question I administer a series of tests—some easy and some difficult—to assess citizens' judgments of politicians. To do so I analyze how citizens respond to major and minor political upheavals induced by wars, disasters, economic booms and busts, and the ups and downs of political campaigns. I focus on citizens' judgments of politicians who are holding or seeking the highest offices—president and prime minister—since if voters are going to pay attention to any political figures, it will likely be these.

I begin with what I argue is an easy test: do voters take into account factors that are relevant to a politician's future performance, such as his or her past performance (on say the economy) or character traits that are relevant to future performance (such as honesty or competence)? I then move on to harder tests, focusing especially on whether voters take into account a politician's policy views. Do voters decide which policies are best and then vote for politicians who support those policies?

The results paint a mixed picture of democracy. Voters do pass the relatively easy tests of judging politicians on performance. When people think a politician has performed well—perhaps by boosting economic growth or winning a war—they become or remain supportive of that politician. Likewise, when people perceive a politician as having desirable character traits relevant to performance, such as honesty, they become or remain likely to vote for that politician.

But voters fail the policy tests. In particular, I find surprisingly little evidence that voters judge politicians on their policy stances. They rarely shift their votes to politicians who agree with them—even when a policy issue has just become highly prominent, even when politicians take clear and distinct stances on the issue, and even when voters know these stances. Instead, I usually find the reverse: voters first decide they like a politician for other reasons, then adopt his or her policy views.

My results confirm the views of scholars who see democracy primarily as a means for voters to pass judgment on how well incumbent politicians have been performing rather than as a means for voters to express their own policy preferences. Although perhaps not everyone's ideal, democracy should therefore at a minimum select competent leaders over incompetent ones. Voters may even be exercising an indirect influence on politicians' policies by voting out leaders whose policies, in the voters' eyes, have not turned out well.

My results are likely to disappoint scholars who see democracy as a means for voters to express their policy preferences. In fact, my findings suggest that this idea of democracy has been inverted. Voters don't choose between politicians based on policy stances; rather, voters appear to adopt the policies that their favorite politicians prefer. Moreover, voters seem to follow rather blindly, adopting a particular politician's specific policies even when they know little or nothing of that politician's overall ideology. Politicians, these findings imply, have considerable freedom in the policies they enact without fear of electoral repercussions.

I.I The Problem: Observational Equivalence

After decades of research into electoral politics, how can such important behavior on the part of voters still be in question? Determining whether citizens lead their politicians or follow them turns out to be a lot harder than it sounds. In fact, to the student of democracy, the policy-voting view and worst-case view can look identical. To understand how that can

Excerpt from address by President Harry S Truman
Charleston, West Virginia, October 1, 1948

```
The Republicans ... led the country to depression, poverty, and
despair. ... The working men and women in this country could not
do much to help themselves, because the strength of their unions
had been broken by the reactionary labor policies of the
Republican administration. ...

-- There was no minimum wage to cushion the blow.
-- There was no unemployment compensation to carry the working
   man's family along.
-- There was no work relief program to help people through the
   crisis.
-- But the party of privilege was ready to carry big business
   through the crisis. It created the Reconstruction Finance
   Corporation for that purpose. The banks, the railways, the
   insurance companies -- they got relief, but not the American
   people.
-- For the unemployed, it was Hoovervilles and soup kitchens.
   Veterans were encouraged to go into business for themselves --
   selling apples.

That is the Republican record. Most of us well remember it. The
Democratic part of the record begins in 1933, when the Democratic
Party began to build prosperity for business, labor, and
agriculture.

-- We wrote into law the right of the working men and women to
   organize in unions of their own choice, and to bargain
   collectively.
-- We put a floor under wages.
-- We outlawed child labor. ...
```

FIGURE 1.1. Excerpt from address by President Harry S. Truman. Charleston, West Virginia, October 1, 1948.

be so, consider an example from a US presidential election in which it appears, at least at first, that citizens led their politicians on policy.

President Harry S. Truman's victory in 1948 was one of the great election upsets in American history. Long before the campaign started, journalists, pollsters, and pundits saw Truman's defeat as a foregone conclusion.[2] Nonetheless, Truman campaigned vigorously. He traveled the country by train to deliver his stump speech, excerpted in figure 1.1, in which he appealed to voters on public policy grounds. The Democratic Party, Truman told voters, had built prosperity for business, labor, and agriculture by enacting legislation that helped ordinary working men and women. Voters should vote for the Democratic Party because it supported the minimum wage, Social Security, and the right to organize unions and bargain collectively. "We put a floor under wages," Truman declared. "We outlawed child labor." On Election Day, Truman

[handwritten marginalia: Truman election]

defeated Thomas E. Dewey, the Republican candidate, by a respectable margin, with 49.6 percent of the vote to 45.1 percent (303 electoral votes to 189).

If the policy-voting view does accurately depict democracy—that the public leads on policy—then Truman's victory is likely attributable to the public's reasoned judgment of his policy stances. He won because his campaign brought his policies to the attention of voters, allowing them to choose based on their own policy views.

In a classic study of Truman's come-from-behind victory, Paul Lazarsfeld and his colleagues reach precisely this conclusion: "An impending defeat for the Democratic Party was staved off by refocusing attention on the socioeconomic concerns which had originally played such a large role in building that party's majority in the 1930s" (Berelson, Lazarsfeld, and McPhee 1954, 270). Are Lazarsfeld and his colleagues right? The evidence supporting their view primarily concerns one issue on which the candidates had clear and distinct positions: government policy toward labor unions. Before the election, the Republican-led Congress passed the Taft-Hartley Act, considerably restricting labor union organizing. Truman opposed the legislation, while Dewey supported it. If this issue did sway voters, we should find that union supporters tended to vote for Truman while opponents tended to vote for Dewey. And indeed, Lazarsfeld and his colleagues conducted a preelection survey in October 1948 that found that among those who said unions "are doing a fine job," about 60 percent intended to vote for Truman, but that among those who said the country would be "better off without any labor unions at all," less than 30 percent intended to do so.[3] Figure 1.2 shows this relationship, apparently confirming that voters—at least on this issue—did lead politicians, voting for the one who shared their policy views.

Unfortunately for democracy, there is also a less flattering interpretation of Lazarsfeld's survey results. Imagine a world in which voters in the 1948 election utterly lacked views about unions. Many voters, however, liked Truman for other reasons, especially the nation's robust economic growth, and intended to vote for him on those grounds.[4] In such a world, voters who had already intended to vote for him may have adopted his prounion policy view.[5] Likewise, voters who had already intended to vote for Dewey may have adopted his antiunion policy view. In such a world, Lazarsfeld's survey would have produced the same results and the election would have gone the same way. We are left with a dilemma. From the evidence presented so far—both Lazarsfeld's survey

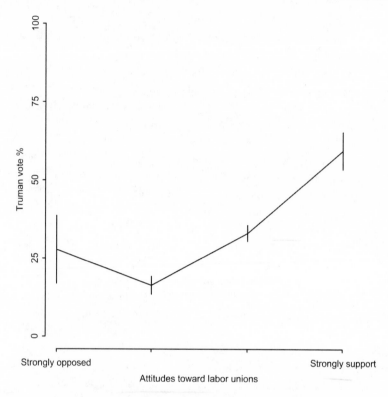

FIGURE 1.2. Leading or following on policy? Support for unions is positively associated with support for Truman (among those voting for Truman or Dewey) in the October interviews of a 1948 study—a pattern that could result either because union supporters voted for Truman because he shared their views (leading) or because Truman voters adopted his views on this issue (following). Error bars give 68 percent confidence intervals (one standard error). I show 68 percent confidence intervals whenever readers will want to compare means (checking whether these error bars touch provides a conservative differences-in-means test). Source: 1948 Elmira study (Berelson, Lazarsfeld, and McPhee 1954).

and the actual election—we cannot tell which came first, the voters' attitudes about unions or their choice of candidate, a problem researchers call *reverse causation*.

More generally, we cannot tell from such data—the correlation of policy views and vote choice—whether we are observing the policy-voting view of democracy, in which the people lead their politicians on policy, or a worst-case view, in which the people follow their politicians on policy. Like a bright star that is far away and a dim star that is near, these two conditions are very different, but we can't tell them apart without additional information. They are *observationally equivalent.*

1.2 The Literature: Lack of Consensus

Researchers don't give up easily. They have tried to overcome the observational equivalence problem with such social science tools as randomized experiments and structural equation modeling. These methods, however, have failed to settle the debate.[6] The result is that scholars have been unable to reach a consensus about whether citizens lead or follow, and several opposing schools of thought continue to flourish.

On one hand, some researchers believe democracy resembles the policy-voting ideal. According to this view, voters lead their politicians by selecting them on policy grounds, just as Lazarsfeld and his colleagues contend that voters chose Truman over Dewey because a majority agreed with Truman's policy views and disagreed with Dewey's.[7] (Although we know that voters are often surprisingly ignorant about politicians' policy views, they may rely on reasonable substitutes for direct knowledge—which researchers call heuristics—such as party identification [Popkin 1991]. That is, I may not know a particular Republican candidate's position on offshore drilling, but I know the Republican Party's position and I agree with that.) Since this line of scholars sees policy and performance judgments as the basis of a voter's choice, they would describe the reality of democracies as being close to the policy-voting view.

But another line of scholarship paints a much darker view. They see voters as being influenced by superficial or random factors, ranging from candidates' faces (Todorov et al. 2005) to the happenstance of natural disasters (Achen and Bartels 2004a) to the fortunes of a local sports team (Healy, Malhotra, and Mo 2010). This research could describe the reality of democracies as being closer to the worst-case view.

Of course, most schools of thought place democracies somewhere between the policy-voting view and worst-case view. A prominent school, exemplified by Angus Campbell and colleagues' *The American Voter* (1960), views party identification as the core of voters' political behavior. According to this view, people identify with political parties early in life and rarely, if ever, change. This identification typically develops from socialization through one's parents, though policy views and party performance may also play a role. Once identified with a party, voters pick that party's candidates and adopt that party's policy positions.[8] In this scenario, citizens primarily follow rather than lead their politicians, and democracy succeeds to the extent that the party elites act wisely.

Another group of scholars contends that voters vote primarily on performance rather than policy. Morris Fiorina (1981) exemplifies this view, claiming that many voters find direct judgments on public policy too complicated but are quite able to judge a politician's performance in office. For example, voters may be overwhelmed by the complexity of a health care policy debate, yet feel that they know whether or not the policy in place is working. In this view, citizens do lead, but only after the fact, throwing out incumbents who pursue failed policies.

Each of these views has been supported with evidence. The result is that we still do not know which view of democracy is correct.[9]

1.3 A Solution to Observational Equivalence

The cause must be prior to the effect. (Hume 1888, 173)

To overcome observational equivalence—to sort out cause from effect—this book brings together data with two crucial qualities. First, it uses surveys that reinterview the same person multiple times, which researchers call panel surveys. These help us sort out what is causing what because we can measure people's views *before* they experience the campaign or other political event that we think might have affected those views. We can then test whether they later bring their support for politicians in line with their earlier stated views; that is, whether they lead. We can also test for the reverse process: whether voters bend their performance assessments or policy views to match their party identification or candidate preferences; that is, whether they follow.

On its own, however, measuring the cause before the effect—measuring policy or performance views before measuring changes in vote or candidate evaluation—does not enable us to test whether these views really matter. We also need variation in the cause so that we can look for evidence of an effect. We need to observe, for example, voters becoming more liberal, because we can then test whether they also become more supportive of liberal candidates. Or we need to observe candidates gaining a performance advantage in the eyes of voters, because we can then observe whether such an advantage attracts votes. With shifts like these, we can use panels to help determine whether the public is indeed rewarding politicians for reasons of policy or performance.

The approach I adopt, then, is to use panels that span such shifts in voters' attitudes. Since political campaigns, wars, and disasters induce these kinds of shifts, the panels I analyze include such upheavals—some major, some minor. As I explain in the following sections, these upheavals induce three kinds of shifts in voters' thinking that have observable consequences for their voting decisions. The upheavals can (a) increase the salience of policy or performance issues (media priming), (b) change voters' own views about these issues (persuasion), or (c) increase voters' knowledge about politicians' policy positions (learning). By observing the consequences of these shifts—media priming, persuasion, and learning—I can test straightforward predictions about policy and performance voting.

Although panel surveys are still rare, their number is increasing. Analysis of individual surveys has yielded insights but has failed to generate a consensus about how much citizens lead and how much they follow.[10] This book contributes to the debate by bringing together, for the first time, many of these surveys, focusing on those spanning political upheavals. The cases come primarily from the United States, but also from Canada, Britain, and the Netherlands. In a few cases, previous research has already investigated similar questions with these data. I am indebted to these earlier works—especially Johnston et al. (1992); Johnston, Hagen, and Jamieson (2004); and Krosnick and Brannon (1993)—and build on their findings.[11]

Before moving on, it is worth briefly noting that, in drawing conclusions about democracy, my approach has limits.

If I find that these three shifts in voters' thinking—media priming, persuasion, or learning—lead to the predicted changes in votes or candidate/party evaluations, I can conclude that voters do judge politicians on policy or performance. This would be a reassuring conclusion, as it would indicate that voters are evaluating politicians on substantive grounds. But however reassuring, this conclusion would be limited in its scope. I can assess whether people do or do not so judge candidates, but I cannot ascertain whether they do so wisely. For example, voters may judge politicians on policy, but they may base their policy views on mistaken beliefs. Alternatively, the importance voters place on various policy issues could be manipulated by, for example, media priming. To the degree that these problems are real, any policy voting I observe may be far from ideal. I nevertheless focus on policy and performance voting because they are fundamental. If voters rarely vote on policy issues, then politicians cannot manipulate voters' choices through such issues anyway. I therefore test for the judgments themselves and leave questions about their soundness to other research.

1.4 Overview

Exploiting Priming on the Economy: An Easy Test

> Surely the most familiar fact to arise from sample surveys in all countries is that popular levels of information about public affairs are, from the point of view of the informed observer, astonishingly low. (Converse 1975, 79)

I start my search for substantive judgments with an easy test. Given the exceedingly low probability that a person's vote will ever be decisive, voters often lack incentives to learn about politics (Downs 1957). Most feel they have better things to do. They must earn a living, rear children, look after their parents, and enjoy life. The result, as Walter Lippmann put it, is that the political world often seems like a "swarming confusion of problems" (1927, 24). Since knowledge about politics is scarce (Delli Carpini and Keeter 1996; Zaller 1992), voters should find judging politicians on issues harder when those issues require more knowledge.

Lack of knowledge should make policy issues, such as labor or abortion law, more difficult for voters than performance issues. Consider public knowledge about the Democratic and Republican stances on abortion law. Even though this issue has divided the parties for at least thirty years, only slightly more than half of citizens appear to be aware of the parties' stances. For example, in the 2008 American National Election Study, only about 50 percent knew that the Democratic Party was more supportive of abortion rights than was the Republican Party. The percentage knowing the relative positions held by Barack Obama and John McCain was also about 50 percent.[12] Without knowing the candidates' positions, citizens could not determine which candidate they agreed with most. Even if a citizen held a strong opinion about abortion, he or she could not judge the candidates on this long-standing issue without knowing where they stood. For as many as half of the public, then, this lack of knowledge about policy stances renders policy voting impossible, even on the most prominent issues.[13]

[margin handwritten note: lack incentive to learn or engage in politics]

[handwritten: performance easier to assess than issues?]

Voters face less of a knowledge hurdle, however, with performance issues than they do with policy issues. On performance issues, voters need not know politicians' positions, since everyone generally agrees that economic growth and personal competence and honesty are desirable.

Performance issues may be less cognitively demanding than policy issues for a second reason. To judge politicians on any issue, voters must develop their own opinions about it. They must decide whether they support or oppose the right to unionize. They must determine whether the economy has grown or shrunk. Doing so may generally be harder on policy issues than on performance issues. With performance, individuals do not necessarily need to know anything about the particulars of public policy. Instead, they need only determine, for instance, whether their incomes are rising or falling. Performance judgments may also be cognitively easier because they are so familiar. In their everyday lives, people constantly judge family members, friends, and coworkers on criteria—such as job performance, competence, and trustworthiness—that are also relevant to success in public office. Since voters may more readily develop strong performance assessments than strong policy views, they may be more likely to judge politicians on performance issues than on policy issues.[14]

Given that performance issues seem easier for several reasons, I start my search for substantive judgments on the part of voters by examining these issues. In chapter 2, I ask whether voters judge politicians on a key *[handwritten: Ch. 2]* aspect of a politician's performance: the economy. For example, if voters perceive the national economy as faring well under a president, are they more likely to vote for him or her?

For many readers, this may seem like a settled question: of course, people judge the president on the economy, as numerous studies document (Erikson 1989; Fiorina 1981; Hibbs 1987; Kiewiet 1983; Kramer 1971; Markus 1988). But in fact, as I explain in the next chapter, we lack unambiguous evidence. We know that the economy affects elections and we know that people's economic perceptions correlate with their votes, but neither of these findings necessarily implies that citizens are judging incumbents on their own perceptions of the economy, and studies continue to raise doubts about such an explanation of election outcomes (e.g., Evans and Pickup 2010). *[handwritten: doubts about economic voting]*

To test whether people use their assessments of the economy to judge incumbents, chapter 2 exploits the first of the three shifts in people's thinking that I mentioned—a shift that political scientists call media priming (Iyengar and Kinder 1987; Iyengar et al. 1984). Media priming involves two steps. First, a campaign or the news media focus attention on an issue, which raises the salience of that issue for voters. Second, once the issue is "top of the head," voters place greater weight on it when they make their voting decisions, causing some voters to shift their support to politicians who are advantaged on the issue.[15] I therefore examine cases where campaigns and the news media dramatically raise the salience of the economy in US presidential elections. If voters do indeed use their perceptions of the economy to judge presidents, I should find them increasingly relying on these perceptions as the issue of the economy becomes more salient. If voters see the economy as strong, they should become more supportive of the president. If they see it as weak, they should become less supportive. To rule out the possibility of voters following rather than leading, I measure their assessments of the economy before the shift.

To conduct these tests I examine three cases in which the state of the US economy becomes a particularly prominent issue during presidential campaigns: the 1980, 1992, and 1996 elections. In all three cases, panel studies interview voters before and after the issue of the economy becomes prominent. I can therefore examine whether people's presidential approval subsequently changes to reflect their prior economic perceptions.

According to the results in chapter 2, voters do evaluate politicians on performance. As the economy becomes prominent in the news and campaigns, voters bring their support for the president in line with their prior economic perceptions. At least on this performance issue—a relatively easy one—they do lead.

Of course, the same media priming that brings important issues to the public's attention could also leave voters vulnerable to manipulation by causing them to give too much weight to one particular issue relative to other issues. Consequently, this finding is not unambiguously positive for democracy. It does, however, answer a more fundamental question about voters' behavior: whether they use their own performance assessments to evaluate politicians. I leave to other research the difficult question of manipulation.

Exploiting Priming on Policy Issues: A Harder Test

Chapters 3 through 5 continue the examination process with harder tests, assessing whether voters use their views about policy (in addition to their views about performance) to judge politicians. As I explained earlier, policy judgments are arguably more difficult for voters than performance judgments. To judge politicians on policy, voters must know politicians' positions and must form their own views about the policy. If voters pass this more challenging test, then democracy resembles the ideal policy-voting view some scholars espouse.

Chapter 3 applies the same media-priming test to ten policy-issue Ch. 3 cases, one of which is an experiment rather than a historical event. In all ten, the news media, the campaigns, or an experimental treatment raises the prominence of a policy issue. In all ten, panel surveys span a political upheaval, asking people about their views on these issues both before and after. In all but two, the parties or candidates take clear and distinct positions (I discuss the two exceptions shortly), allowing me to make clear predictions about how voters should change their votes—if they really are engaged in policy voting, that is. For example, I reopen the case of priming labor union views in Truman's dramatic 1948 election victory. With panel data from the Lazarsfeld study, I examine whether people really did shift their votes to Truman because of his views on this policy.

The ten policy cases analyzed in chapter 3 (and in subsequent chapters) span a wide range of issues—both new and long-standing—including redistribution of wealth, national defense, and national identity. One case explores what researchers call "activating fundamentals" by testing for the priming of overall ideology rather than a particular issue in the 1992 presidential election. Another case is an experimental study on the issue of health insurance for children in the United States, conducted as part of a national survey that interviewed the same people twice. As in the economic cases, measuring policy views beforehand allows me to exclude the possibility that people are following rather than leading their politicians.

As these issues become prominent, do voters increasingly judge politicians on policy grounds? Do they pass this harder test? In contrast with much research, I find little evidence that they do. When I measure voters' views on a particular policy before that issue becomes prominent, I do not subsequently—once the issue becomes prominent—find those voters shifting their support to politicians who share their views, nor away from politicians who oppose them. This finding holds whether voters are asked for whom they intend to vote, how favorable they are toward a particular candidate, or how favorable they are toward a particular party. Although I find that voters' economic assessments influence their support for politicians in all three economic-performance cases, I find their policy views having an influence in only one of the ten policy cases (defense spending).

These findings seem to be inconsistent with numerous other studies that not only find policy voting, but that also find media priming in particular. But these other studies—whether observational or experimental—generally measure policy views after the issues become prominent (posttreatment), so they could be getting the story backward. That is, they could be fooled by observational equivalence.[16] According to my results, which are not vulnerable to this alternative explanation, voters do not appear to be leading politicians on policy.

Exploiting Persuasion: Performance versus Policy

According to the results in chapters 2 and 3, voters appear to be rewarding or punishing politicians on performance issues, but not on policy issues. To examine whether these findings hold more broadly, chapter 4 exploits another shift in people's thinking: persuasion. By persuasion, I mean a change in a citizen's policy views or performance assessments between survey interviews. If voters do judge politicians on issues, then persuasion—a change in their own views—should lead them, all else being equal, to alter their votes accordingly. In these tests, instead of examining whether a voter's prior views become more important to his or her later support for a particular politician, as I did in the previous two chapters, I examine whether, when a voter *changes* his or her view on a particular policy or performance issue, that voter later *changes* his or her support for particular politicians who agree or disagree with his or her new policy view or performance assessment. Specifically, I examine whether policy or performance shifts between respondents' first and second interviews lead to vote shifts between the second and third. For example, when voters are persuaded that a candidate is dishonest (a performance issue), as many were with Al Gore in September during the 2000 US election, do they later become less supportive of that candidate?

With this persuasion test I can examine not only the three economic cases from chapter 2, but also three additional performance cases: Gore's honesty in the 2000 election, approval of George H. W. Bush's handling of the Gulf War in 1991, and Sarah Palin's fitness to be a vice presidential candidate in the 2008 election. I am also able to apply this test in six policy-issue cases.

Do the results of the persuasion test mirror the media-priming results, showing that voters pass the performance tests but fail the policy tests? That is exactly what we see. The results are surprisingly consistent. Voters pass all six performance tests and fail all six policy tests. When news stories persuade people to see Gore as dishonest (a performance issue), for example, they later shift to vote against him. In contrast, when the 1948 campaign persuades people to support unions (a policy issue), they do not later become more supportive of Truman, the candidate who supports unions. As before, these results hold whether we use vote choice or evaluations of candidate or party as the outcome variables.

Again, even the performance findings—where voters do seem to be judging politicians according to their own assessments—are not unambiguously positive for democracy. Voters were influenced by news stories claiming that Gore was dishonest, indicating that they evaluated Gore on this performance issue, but those news stories may have been misleading. Nevertheless, these analyses answer the more fundamental question: do voters use their own performance assessments and policy views to judge politicians?

Exploiting Learning on Policy: A Moderately Difficult Test

Chapters 2 through 4 suggest that, while democracy does not resemble the worst-case view, it does not resemble the policy voting view either. Chapter 5 refines this tentative finding. It administers a policy-voting test that is arguably easier for voters than the previous policy-voting tests, but harder than the performance tests. It investigates whether learning about candidates' positions on a policy leads voters to change their votes or their evaluations of presidents accordingly.

As noted above, the public is awash in ignorance about parties' and candidates' policy positions. Because of this ignorance, voters frequently support candidates with whom they disagree on policy issues— even the most prominent issues—without realizing it. When campaigns or political upheavals raise the prominence of an issue, however, voters often learn the politicians' positions (Ansolabehere and Iyengar 1995; Brians and Wattenberg 1996; Lang and Lang 1966; Trenaman and McQuail 1961). In the cases I examine, literally millions of voters do. When campaigns and the news media educate voters on candidates' policy positions, it should be easier for voters to vote on policy. But does it work out that way? With that knowledge barrier eliminated, do voters shift their support to politicians with whom they now know they are in agreement?

For example, during each US presidential campaign, millions of voters learn something they didn't know—that the Democratic Party is to the ideological left of the Republican Party.[17] In a seminal article, Andrew Gelman and Gary King (1993) argue that, by informing voters about these basic party orientations, campaigns and the news media fulfill their most important role in a democracy. Analyzing survey responses from the 1988 presidential election, Gelman and King find that this enlightening matters: voters align their votes with their self-reported ideology over the course of the campaign. Their results indicate that, when voters learn the parties' positions, they act on this information, shifting their votes accordingly. Put differently, Gelman and King find that voters pass this somewhat easier test. Given the requisite knowledge, citizens therefore appear to lead politicians on policy.

But Gelman and King's (1993) finding, like those of many policy-voting studies, can be interpreted in a less flattering way. They may have the story backward: instead of leading, citizens may just be following. When Democratic voters, for instance, learn that their party is ideologically liberal relative to the Republican Party, they may just become more ideologically liberal themselves. Instead of knowledge making it easier for them to lead, it may make it easier for them to follow.

To see if knowledge really does facilitate policy voting or whether it just looks that way, I reexamine the ideology case and six other policy cases in which panel surveys allow us to determine which voters learn politicians' policy positions and also to measure those voters' policy views beforehand. I then test whether this learning leads these voters to alter their support for the politicians whose views they now know.

Do voters pass this easier test? They do not. Even when they have just learned candidates' positions on the most prominent issues of the elections, they do not change their votes (or candidate evaluations) accordingly. When ideological liberals who approve of President Bush, for example, learn during the 1992 presidential campaign that Bush's party does not share their own ideology, they fail to shift against him; they don't decide to become Democrats despite having learned that the Democratic Party is more aligned with their own views, The six other cases reveal the same pattern. Many people learn, but they do not appear to act on this knowledge.

These findings—startling enough in their own right—also affect the way we view campaigns and the news media. Although campaigns and media provide information that could help voters pick the candidates who would further the voters' own policy goals the voters generally disregard this information. This puts democracy further away from the policy-voting view. At least according to these tests, voters do vote in accordance with their own views on performance issues but rarely do so on policy issues.

Voting on Easy Issues? Two Case Studies

Chapters 6 and 7 further refine our view of democracy and, to a degree, show it in a better light. Policy issues can be complicated and their implications remote. At times, however, they are straightforward and immediate in a way that captures the public's attention. In such cases, policy voting should be easier for voters (Carmines and Stimson 1989). Of the cases I examine, two arguably fall into this admittedly nebulous category: the issue of nuclear power in the 1986 Dutch election, right after the Chernobyl nuclear disaster, and the issue of defense spending in the 1980 US election, right after the Soviet invasion of Afghanistan and in the midst of the Iranian hostage crisis. In both cases, policy issues seize the public's attention to an unusual degree.

These two elections are part of the analysis in chapters 3–5, which found that voters did not judge the candidates on these issues. For a better understanding, I present in-depth case studies. Chapter 6 looks at the issue of nuclear power in the 1986 Dutch campaign and chapter 7 looks at President Jimmy Carter's attempt during the 1980 election to fend off charges that he was weak on national defense. These chapters reveal considerable evidence that voters did care about these issues yet end up confirming that in the end the issues did not influence vote choice or candidate and party evaluations.

Instead, these two cases suggest an important wrinkle. The two incumbents, facing widespread public concern over issues that put them at a disadvantage, responded strategically, adopting policy stances that mollified the public and thus ensured that voters did not actually cast their ballots on those issues. As in all the other cases in this book, we initially find opposing politicians maintaining opposing views on the policy in question. In these two cases, however, the incumbents change their positions, converging on their challengers' more popular views. In the Netherlands, the incumbent parties shift from supporting nuclear

power to opposing it within a week of the Chernobyl disaster and just
two weeks before Election Day. In the United States, President Carter,
despite some back-and-forth, ultimately shifts from being a defense dove
to being a defense hawk. In both cases I find that the public appears to
learn about and accept these dramatic shifts. It appears—although any
conclusions must be tentative—that voters fail to vote on either policy issue, not because of lack of interest or knowledge, but because the incumbents adopt more popular policy views, which neutralizes the issue because the candidates now hold the same position.

These case studies add further nuance to our view of democracy. It
may be that most of the time voters fail to judge politicians on policy. At
times, however, public policy does interest the masses. In these unusual
cases, politicians do appear to follow voters.

Following, Not Leading, on Policy

If citizens are generally not leading on policy in these cases, are they instead following? In chapter 8 I examine this possibility, and in case after case I find that they are. Instead of selecting candidates on the basis of policy, many voters apparently select them for other reasons, such
as performance advantages, party, or superficial traits such as appearance. Once decided on a candidate, voters often adopt that candidate's
policy views. This tendency to follow is particularly evident among voters who learn politicians' positions between panel interviews; this pattern emerges in every case of learning that I examine. When supporters
of George W. Bush, for example, learn that he opposes expanding a children's health care program (SCHIP), they too become opposed to the
expansion. The tendency even emerges for overall ideology. When supporters of a Republican president learn, for instance, that the Republican Party is on the ideological right, they shift their own reported ideology to the right. Instead of leading on policy, in case after case, citizens
follow.

This finding looks worrisome for democracy, but there are benign interpretations. People may follow a party or candidate on a specific policy because they see that party or candidate as sharing their own broader
policy outlook—their ideology. Thus voters may not be following blindly
so much as relying on cues from informative sources.

To investigate which interpretation is correct, chapter 8 submits voters to several more tests. Unfortunately for democracy, the results are

not reassuring. People who are ignorant about the parties' or candidates' general ideologies and therefore do not know which politicians share their broader policy outlook will nevertheless adopt the policy views of their preferred politicians. For example, supporters of George W. Bush adopt his view on investing Social Security funds even when they do not know that he is generally more conservative than Al Gore. Moreover, these less knowledgeable voters follow at similar or even higher rates than people who do know the politicians' ideologies. Several other findings suggest similar conclusions: not only do people fail to lead politicians on policy, but they appear to follow, maybe even blindly.

Implications for Democracy

Chapter 9 concludes the book by discussing the mixed picture of democracy that emerges from these results. Voters appear to rarely judge politicians on policy positions. Priming, persuasion, and learning on policy hardly ever change voters' votes or their evaluations of candidates. Instead of leading on policy—that is, choosing to support those politicians whose policy views agree with their own—voters follow rather blindly—forming attachments to politicians for various reasons and then adopting those politicians' policy views. At least on policy issues, democracy appears to be inverted: instead of politicians following the will of the people, the people seem to be following the will of politicians.

Not all the findings are unflattering however. I do find that voters reward politicians for performance advantages such as a strong economy. And as the case studies in chapters 6 and 7 illustrate, a lack of policy voting is not always a failure of democracy. When issues capture voters' attention to an unusual degree, politicians change their positions on the issue in accordance with the public's views. Thus, while we do not observe voters changing their vote, they do not need to—they have already successfully led the politicians on policy. Most often, however, voters do not appear to be voting on the basis of their own policy judgments, even when candidates maintain clear and distinct positions on the most prominent issues of the day.

Because my analyses overcome the problem of observational equivalence by taking advantage of panel surveys that span shifts in people's thinking—priming, persuasion, and learning—they arguably provide clearer tests of policy and performance voting than other analyses have done. They nevertheless have their limitations. In particular, although analyzing the consequences of these shifts allows me to overcome the observational equivalence problem, the resulting findings may not be fully generalizable, applying only to the kinds of individuals who experience these shifts. Other important limitations include the paucity of data on performance cases, the relatively short time between survey interviews, that most of the shifts occur during election campaigns, and the absence of policy issues relating to race (Hurwitz and Peffley 2005; Lee 2002; Mendelberg 2001) or social issues (Hillygus and Shields 2008). Chapter 9 elaborates on these and other limitations. Even so, the book's results make clear that, when research is designed to sort out what is causing what, evidence that voters' policy views influence their votes is sparse.

CHAPTER TWO

Rewarding Performance?
Priming the Economy

B ill Clinton, a newcomer to American politics at the national level, beat the better-known and more-experienced George H. W. Bush in the 1992 election. It is widely believed that he did so because voters cared more about the decline in the domestic economy than about Bush's success in foreign affairs.[1] Clinton won the election, but are we right to think that he did so because "it's the economy, stupid"? At least in the aggregate, the evidence that the national economy influences citizens is strong (Erikson 1989; Fiorina 1981; Hibbs 1987; Kiewiet 1983; Kramer 1971; Markus 1988). When the economy expands rapidly during election years, voters tend to reelect incumbent presidents. When it contracts, they do not. Studies at the individual level also find strong associations between economic perceptions and support for incumbents (e.g., Duch and Stevenson 2008).

All the same, we do not know with certainty that citizens use their own assessments of the economy to judge politicians. The aggregate relationships that have been observed could arise from indirect processes rather than from individuals voting on the economy. For example, the economy could influence elite behavior such as the willingness of donors to contribute to incumbents, the willingness of high-quality candidates to challenge incumbents, or the tone of news media coverage about incumbents. These factors, rather than the economy itself, could lead citizens to behave as if the economy had influenced them.

Similarly, the individual-level correlations between economic perceptions and votes, which researchers frequently report finding, could be a manifestation of the reverse causation I described in chapter 1; that is, a

citizen may support an incumbent politician for some other reason, such
as the politician's party or charisma, and then develop a positive view of
how the economy is doing under that incumbent (Bartels 2002a; Gerber
and Huber 2009; Sears and Lau 1983; Wilcox and Wlezien 1993).[2] Under
a Democratic president, for example, Democrats report seeing the economy as stronger than Republicans do. These studies raise the possibility
that voters don't decide how the economy is doing and then judge incumbent politicians accordingly, but rather the reverse.[3]

In this chapter I take advantage of three American presidential campaigns during which the economy became a prominent issue to test
whether citizens do indeed use their *own* perceptions of the economy to
judge an incumbent president. And here I find that they do. On the economy, at least, citizens appear to lead. (In chapter 3, we see what happens
with policy judgments.)

I begin with the role of the economy in Clinton's defeat of the incumbent Bush in the 1992 election. I then briefly examine two other
cases: the role of the economy in Bill Clinton's defense of his presidency
against Bob Dole in the 1996 election and the role of the economy in the
incumbent Jimmy Carter's defeat by Ronald Reagan in the 1980 election. While I would ideally apply this test to many more performance
issues—such as competence and honesty—and not just to the economy,
these were the only cases offering the particular type of survey information I need to overcome the problem of observational equivalence, which
I introduced in chapter 1.

2.1 Judging the President on Performance in the 1992 Election

In 1992 the media and the presidential campaigns of Bill Clinton and
George H. W. Bush relentlessly focused on the economy. Figure 2.1,
based on a content analysis of major newspapers for each quarter from
1990 through 1992, shows that during the 1992 campaign (the second and
third quarters of 1992), about a third of all articles containing the phrase
"President Bush" also mentioned either the economy or unemployment, whereas before the campaign, the figure was only about 15 percent.[4] Clinton's campaign ads also emphasized the economy. In fact, as
shown in figure 2.2, television ads from both campaigns were more likely
to mention the economy during this election than during any other election between 1960 and 2000.

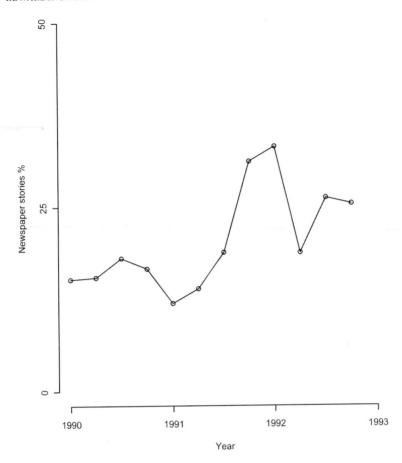

FIGURE 2.1. Newspaper coverage of the economy between 1990 and 1992. The figure shows
the percentage of all newspaper stories with the phrase "President Bush" that contain the
words "economy" or "unemployment." Source: newslibrary.com.

President Bush tried to neutralize the issue, arguing repeatedly that
the economy was not nearly as bad as people believed and attacking the
media for portraying it too negatively. In an interview with conservative radio talk-show host Rush Limbaugh, Bush said the economy was
"poised for a dramatic recovery" and maintained that most people believed otherwise because they were paying too much heed to the news
media (Wines 1992). At the same time, Bush attempted to blame Democrats in Congress for the poor economy. In his acceptance speech at
the Republican National Convention, he echoed a theme prevalent

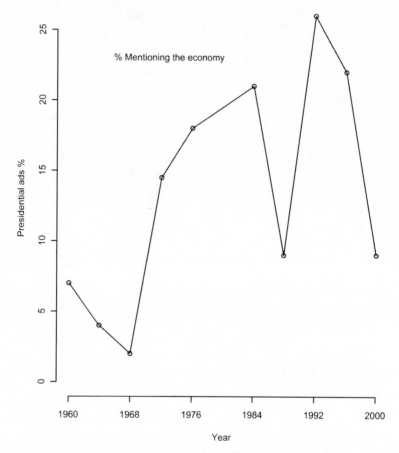

FIGURE 2.2. Campaign television ads and the issue of the economy, 1960–2000. Source: John Geer, Vanderbilt University (Finkel and Geer 1998).

throughout the convention: the Democratic-controlled Congress had blocked his economic growth initiatives. "I extended my hand to the Democratic leaders," he said, "and they bit it" (Toner 1992).

Several studies have found that, in spite of Bush's efforts, Clinton's campaign and the news media did indeed cause citizens to weigh the issue of the economy more heavily when judging the incumbent president (e.g., Hetherington 1996). The public undoubtedly saw the economy as poor throughout much of Bush's term. In the three waves of the American National Election Study (ANES) survey panel that cover this period, the percentage of respondents who said they saw the economy as somewhat worse or much worse than it had been the year before was 77 percent in 1990, 65 percent in 1991, and 72 percent in 1992. Despite such negative perceptions, Bush's approval soared in early 1991 around the start of the Gulf War. The war's halo, however, did not last long. As the media and rival campaigns turned their attention to the economy in 1992, Bush's approval collapsed, falling a striking thirty-two percentage points between the ANES's spring 1991 and autumn 1992 interviews.

Were voters turning against President Bush because the poor economy had convinced them that he was performing poorly as president? The survey data seem clear and the narrative plausible. But if voters were, instead, judging the state of the economy in accordance with the approval or disapproval they already felt for President Bush or candidate Clinton—the opposite of what we think we are seeing—the ANES surveys would show the same results. They are observationally equivalent. How can we tell the two explanations apart?

The Conventional Test

The purpose of this book is to address the question of whether voters judge politicians on performance or policy, or whether they instead align their views to match those of their preferred politician. In the next few pages, I explain several ways researchers approach this question with policy views or performance assessments, in this case, voters' perceptions of the 1992 economy. I focus on how to overcome the problem of observational equivalence due to of reverse causation. I explain these approaches in detail partly because these research methods are important to the argument of this book. Throughout the book, the reader will encounter the same terms and the same lines of reasoning, so it will be well to become familiar with them now. I present the techniques informally here and show the equations in the appendix (where I also show how they relate to a utility model of candidate preference).

ISSUE WEIGHT: HOW MUCH DOES AN ISSUE COUNT? Research on media priming (making an issue more salient to the voters through heavy coverage in the media)—like research on issue voting more generally— focuses on what are called "issue weights." For any particular voter, any number of issues may have some importance, but some will matter more than others; that is, some issues carry more weight in voter's approval or disapproval of a candidate and, ultimately, in how that voter decides to vote. As we will see below, political scientists calculate issue weights in order to understand when they change, to compare the relative importance of different issues, and to predict the effects different issues will have on a voter's evaluations and decisions. In the present case, we are interested in knowing the economy's issue weight; that is, how much did citizens' economic perceptions "count" when evaluating President Bush and deciding whether to vote for or against him. In particular, we want to determine whether this weight increased in 1992 after the news media and the Clinton campaign made the economy a more prominent issue.

In what I call a *conventional test* for media priming, an issue weight is assessed by how close an association there is between voters' attitudes about the issue and their approval or disapproval of a particular candidate. For example, people certainly have different attitudes about whether or not there is too much violence on TV, but these opinions would probably not line up with whether those same people approve or disapprove of the president. Violence on TV might be an "issue," but it doesn't have a high issue weight, at least not at the moment. As I write this in 2010, however, the issue of nationalizing health care would likely have a higher issue weight, that is, one's opinion about it probably would line up with one's approval or disapproval of the politician who had proposed it.

Returning to the case of 1992 election: researchers would assess the economy's issue weight by the strength of the association between people's perceptions of the economy and their approval of the incumbent President Bush. The more we find that voters' economic perceptions line up with their approval or disapproval of Bush, the larger the issue weight of the economy must have been.

CHANGES IN ISSUE WEIGHT.   The left side of figure 2.3 represents the issue weight for a hypothetical issue—America as the world leader in scientific research. Imagine that researchers ask a group of survey participants (a) whether they think America is leading the world in scientific research, and (b) whether they think the current hypothetical president is doing a good job or a poor job. The stronger the relationship between these attitudes, which is reflected in a steeper slope, the greater the issue weight. The "best fit" line doesn't have much of a slope on the left side of the figure, indicating that people who think America is leading the world in science don't approve of the president all that much more than people who think America is not leading the world in science. If scientific leadership is an issue at all, it isn't one that carries much weight when people judge the president.

Now let's imagine that soon afterward, something dramatic happens—none of the Nobel Prizes for physics, chemistry, or medicine go to an American scientist. The media make a big story of it—"What's happening to American science? Will the next Edison be Chinese?" The researchers then repeat their survey, as represented in the right side of figure 2.3. This time, the line representing the issue weight of American scientific preeminence has a steeper slope. Those who think America is not leading the world in science are significantly more likely to disapprove

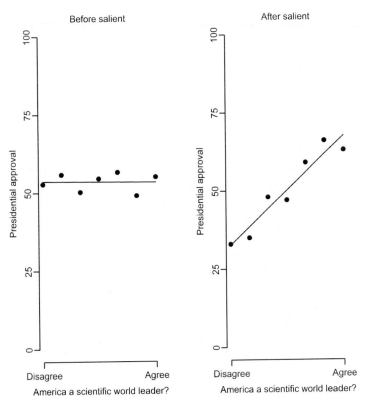

FIGURE 2.3. A hypothetical example of the public placing more weight on an issue after it becomes prominent. The slopes of these lines represent the weights people place on the issue when evaluating politicians—the issue weights. A steeper slope implies that the issue is more important to presidential approval; that is, the issue weight is higher. The change in the slopes from left to right shows the extent to which this issue becomes more important as it becomes prominent.

of the president than those who think America is leading the world in science. When people judge the president, this issue carries more weight than it did earlier—presumably because of the media attention.

Now we are ready to look at a real case. Figure 2.4 shows the results of a conventional test of whether the economy counted more as a factor in people's judgments of President Bush after the media and the Clinton campaign made a big issue of it. In the spring of 1991 (wave 1), a group of survey respondents were asked, on a 5-point scale, "How about the economy in the country as a whole, would you say that over the past year the nation's economy has gotten [much/somewhat] better, stayed about the same, or gotten [much/somewhat] worse?" They were also asked, on a 4-point scale, "Do you approve or disapprove of the way George Bush is handling his job as president?" The issue weight is shown by the slope of the line on the left in figure 2.4. During the following year and a half, the economy remained depressed. Then in the fall of 1992 (wave 2), the same group of respondents was asked the same two questions. The issue weight calculated from this repeat survey is shown by the slope of the line on the right in figure 2.4. The line is steeper this time, increasing from a slope of 0.45 to a slope of 0.69. That is, a feeling that the economy has gotten worse in the last year is now more likely to line up with disapproval of Bush's performance as president than it did a year ago. Presumably, this is the effect of the media priming.

This increase in slope (issue weight) according to the conventional test is large. Since this will be some readers' first encounter with issue weights, I briefly explain how to interpret them. Since I rescale both economic perceptions and Bush approval to vary from 0 to 100 for this figure, interpreting them is straightforward. In 1991, before the economy became salient, a shift from seeing the economy as "much worse" to "much better," a shift of 100 points, corresponds with a $(0.45 \times 100 =)$ 45-point increase in Bush approval. In 1992, after it's salient, the same shift corresponds with a $(0.69 \times 100 =)$ 69-point increase in Bush approval. Of course, few individuals shift the length of the scale. Since economic perceptions were originally measured on a five-point scale, a shift between responses (from say "much worse" to "somewhat worse") is the equivalent of 25 points on the 100-point scale. So, in 1991, for every 25-point increase in economic perceptions, there is a $(0.45 \times 25 =)$ 11.3 point increase in approval of President Bush. In 1992, this increases to a $(0.69 \times 25 =)$ 17.3 point increase.

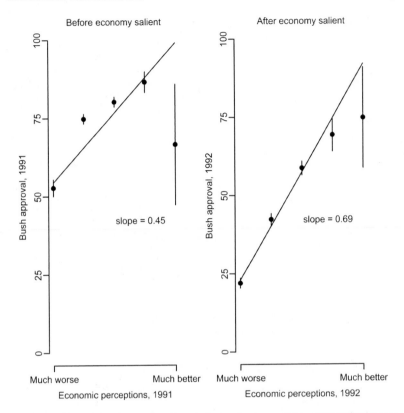

FIGURE 2.4. Conventional test of media priming on the issue of the economy in the 1992 election. Did campaign and media attention prime the economy in 1992, leading to the collapse in President George H. W. Bush's approval? The figure shows that economic assessments became more predictive (steeper slope) of Bush approval as the economy became prominent in the 1992 election. The slopes represent the issue weight on economic assessments, and the difference in the slopes is the priming effect (Δ_{it}) estimated with the conventional test (see equation 6 in the appendix). For the full ordinary least squares regression estimates, see table 2.1. This test is potentially biased by reverse causation; that is, its findings could be produced, not by economic assessments influencing presidential approval but by presidential approval increasingly influencing economic assessments. Error bars show 68 percent confidence intervals. Source: 1990–91–92 ANES panel.

In qualitative terms, the effect of the media priming is that the issue of the economy carries more weight in people's judgment of the president than it did a year ago. In quantitative terms, the effect of media priming is the difference between the two issue weights: 0.69 − 0.45 = 0.24. That's how much the issue weight increased. Much of this book is

TABLE 2.1. **Priming the economy in the 1992 election: The conventional test**

Dependent variable: Presidential approval	Wave 2 1991		Wave 3 1992	Dif. Δ_{ct}
Wave 2 Econ. assessments	0.45* (0.051)	Wave 3 Econ. assessments	0.69* (0.046)	0.24* (0.068)
n	956		956	
R^2	0.084		0.187	
SER	0.33		0.32	

Note: Ordinary least squares regression estimates with standard errors in parentheses. For ease of presentation, I code variables to vary between 0 and 100 in the figures. For statistical models, I code variables to vary between 0 and 1. Constant not shown. * $p < 0.1$.

about this key statistic: the change in issue weights from before to after an issue becomes prominent.

To summarize, the conventional test compares two issue weights:

- the effect of wave 2 policy views or performance assessments on wave 2 support for politicians (in this case, the effect of 1991 economic perceptions on 1991 presidential approval), and
- the effect of wave 3 policy views or performance assessments on wave 3 support for politicians (in this case, the effect of 1992 economic perceptions on 1992 presidential approval).

Researchers test for priming with the difference in these effects or issue weights. If the second effect is larger, it implies that citizens have changed the basis on which they evaluate the president, placing a heavier issue weight on the economy.

So that readers can understand this book's findings even if they know little about statistics, I present the main results visually. Since some readers will want to see the statistical models behind the figures, I include them either in the chapter or the appendix, but the results can be understood without them. In this case, table 2.1 shows the slopes using ordinary least squares regression models. These models allow us to assess whether the observed issue-weight differences could have arisen by chance. Based on the estimates in the table, the 0.24 increase is highly unlikely to arise from chance alone ($p < 0.001$, $n = 956$). For the sake of simplicity, these statistical models include no other variables.[5]

THE PROBLEM WITH THE CONVENTIONAL TEST. Over 150 published studies have used variations of this conventional test of change-in-issue-weight to detect media priming effects for a wide range of issues.[6] But as I pointed out in chapter 1, the conventional test has a serious drawback—it may get the story backward. People's views about an issue—such as how the economy is doing—may be a consequence of presidential approval or disapproval rather than a cause of it. That is, as the economy becomes a prominent issue during a campaign, people may adopt economic perceptions that are consistent with the approval or disapproval they already feel for the president. Several studies note or document this reverse process (Gerber and Huber 2009; Kramer 1983; Sears and Lau 1983; Wilcox and Wlezien 1993).

The reason why the conventional test cannot distinguish between real priming and the reverse-causal story is that the test measures economic perceptions and presidential approval at the same time, so researchers cannot be sure which is causing which.[7] Put differently, the conventional test cannot tell us whether citizens are leading their politicians or following them on the issue of the economy, since these two possibilities are observationally equivalent.

Overcoming Observational Equivalence: The Three-Wave Test

To overcome this drawback, I take an approach that is not as intuitively obvious as the conventional test. In a word, I do *not* assess changes in the relationship between economic perceptions and presidential approval measured at the same time; instead, I assess how well prior economic perceptions influence later change in presidential approval. Here is how the technique, which I call the *three-wave test*, is applied to the question of media priming before the 1992 election.

The ANES panel survey mentioned above was conducted in 1990 as well as in 1991 and 1992. Using survey results on Bush's approval gathered in the fall of 1990 and in the spring of 1991, I calculate the change in approval from 1990 to 1991.

The results of these first two waves of interviews are shown on the left side of figure 2.5. This is different from figure 2.4 in that we are neither comparing 1990's economic perception to presidential approval *measured at exactly the same time* nor comparing 1991's economic perception to presidential approval *measured at exactly the same time*. Rather,

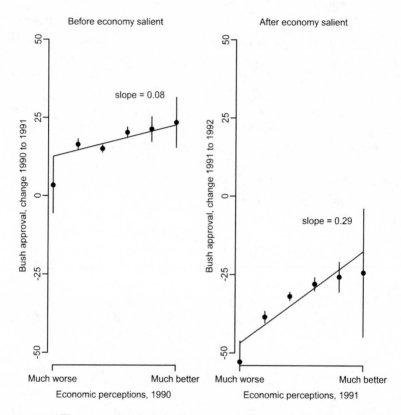

FIGURE 2.5. Three-wave test of priming the economy in the 1992 election. These plots show that prior economic assessments became more predictive of Bush approval (steeper slope) as the economy became increasingly prominent in the 1992 election. It visually represents the key results in table 2.2. The slopes of these lines represent the weights people place on the economy when they change their presidential approval—the issue weights. The difference in these slopes, ($\Delta_{3wt} = 0.29 - 0.08 =$) 0.21, represents the media priming effect. This test therefore confirms the conventional test's findings while ruling out reverse causation. The appendix presents the model behind these plots (equation 11) and explains how I create them. They are actually called partial residual scatterplots as they only show variation after accounting for control variables (that is, residualized variation). A quirk of them is that because of rounding residual economic perceptions, the number of points on the x axis does not necessarily correspond with the number of points on the original scale. Error bars show 68 percent confidence intervals. Source: 1990–91–92 ANES panel.

we are comparing 1990's economic perception to the *change* in presidential approval measured between fall 1990 and spring 1991. This is how I escape the chicken-and-egg problem of the conventional test: by not measuring cause and effect simultaneously, we are better able to tell which is which. Here, in the left side of figure 2.5, we see that the slope is only 0.08—not steep—implying that people's views of the economy in 1990 weren't a strong indicator of how much their approval of the incumbent president would go up or down by the spring of 1991. Figure 2.5 differs from previous figures as it is a partial residual scatterplot, which I explain soon.

The third wave of interviews took place in fall 1992. Between the second and third waves, the issue of the economy had been brought to the fore, both by the media and by the Clinton campaign. Now we can examine whether 1991's economic perceptions influence *change* in presidential approval measured a year later, in 1992. The results of the second and third waves are shown on the right side of figure 2.5. This time, the slope is steeper—0.29—indicating that the change in people's presidential approval had become more closely related to what their economic perceptions had been a year earlier. It appears that sometime between spring 1991 and fall 1992 the economy began to weigh more heavily in people's judgment of the president. In short, it appears that media priming did have an effect; the difference in the issue weights is 0.29 − 0.08 = 0.21. (This is similar to the 0.24 change found by the conventional test.) Because the changes in presidential approval were measured *after* measuring economic perceptions—not at the same time, as in the conventional test—this three-wave test more strongly indicates that it was people's economic perceptions that caused a change in their judgments of Bush, not the other way around. The two possibilities are no longer observationally equivalent and we can now better see which is real.

Figure 2.5 also reveals just how much Bush's approval collapsed in 1992 from its highs after the Gulf War. It also shows that economic perceptions only explain part of the collapse. Those who saw the economy as much worse in 1991 lowered their approval by almost 50 points on the 100-point scale. Those who saw the economy as much better still lowered their approval, but only by 25 points.

The three-wave test of priming is the primary test I use throughout the book. To summarize, this particular three-wave test compares two issue weights:

- the effect of wave 1 policy views or performance assessments on the change in support for politicians between waves 1 and 2 (in this case, the effect of 1990 economic perceptions on the change in presidential approval between 1990 and 1991), and
- the effect of wave 2 policy views or performance assessments on the change in support for politicians between waves 2 and 3 (in this case the effect of 1991 economic perceptions on change in presidential approval between 1991 and 1992).

If the second effect is larger, then the economy became more important to citizens' evaluations of the president. Again, I present this test informally here and show the equations in the appendix.

Of course, no test is perfect and there are other plausible ones. As I discuss in chapter 3, the results I find throughout this book hold, not just with the three-wave test, but across a wide variety of approaches.

Note that both the conventional test and the three-wave test found that there really was a media priming effect and that the effects they found were similar in magnitude—0.24 and 0.21, respectively. But the three-wave test rules out the reverse-causal story—a critical advantage over the conventional test. When a three-wave test finds that people increasingly judge a politician on a performance or policy issue—economic or otherwise—we can be sure it is not because they are changing their perceptions of the policy or performance to reflect their preexisting approval or disapproval of the politician.

HOW SURE ARE WE? THE TIME-LAG PROBLEM.   Since I use this test throughout the book, I briefly discuss questions about it that resurface every time I present its results. Although the three-wave test has an obvious advantage, that advantage comes with costs. I review these in detail in chapter 3 and in the appendix, but the most obvious problem is that it measures assessments of performance or of policy stances before these issues become prominent. By the time they do become prominent, people may have changed their original views. For example, I assess economic perceptions from the 1991 ANES interviews and explore the extent to which they predict change in people's approval or disapproval of President Bush over a year later. Yet they might not predict change in Bush's approval levels to any significant degree if something else had happened in between—a stock market surge or decline—that exerted considerable influence on economic perceptions.

I don't think this poses a serious problem for my examination of the 1992 election, or for the other cases I examine, for several reasons. In this particular case, attitudes about the economy happened to be surprisingly stable, at least in the aggregate, across all three interviews. As I noted earlier, people took a similarly dim view of the economy in the fall of 1990, late spring of 1991, and the fall of 1992. Although the time between waves is long in this panel, it is much shorter—only a few months or weeks—in many of the other panels I examine, so the time lag will be less of a concern.

There is also a more fundamental reason why this time lag is not a major problem for a three-wave test: time lags are more likely to mask the media-priming effect I am looking for than to exaggerate it. The more people change their economic perceptions over time, the harder it should be to detect media priming even if it really is happening. The fact that we detect it despite this methodological obstacle gives me more confidence that the effect is real.

HOW SURE ARE WE? CONFIDENCE INTERVALS.   I said that it is the difference between two issue weights—rather than the individual issue weights themselves—that interests us in this book. But not all such differences are equally informative. This is because the issue weights, like all statistical measures, have a degree of uncertainty. If, for example, the issue weight for the economy is measured during a particular survey as 0.5, statisticians would give a 90 percent range for the effect that it is between say 0.3 and 0.7. This range would be called the "90 percent confidence interval." What happens, though, if the difference between two issue weights is only 0.2 and the 90 percent confidence interval is between 0.8 and −0.4? That means we can't be sure that there's really any difference between them, at least not at the 90 percent level. Researchers would then say the effect of media priming lacked "statistically significant," meaning that the observed difference might have been due simply to chance rather than to any real cause and effect. To say that an estimate is "statistically significant" is to say that it is unlikely to arise from chance alone.

To make this point graphically, I use graphs such as the one in figure 2.6. This figure shows the issue weight of the economy in the 1991 and 1992 surveys, not as the slopes of lines but as points representing the slopes, each with a horizontal bar representing the 90 percent confidence interval. This figure also shows the difference—the change in the issue weight of the economy between the 1991 and 1992 surveys—as a point

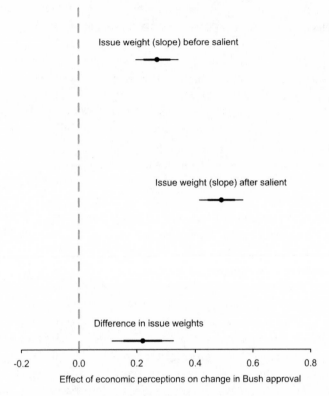

FIGURE 2.6. Three-wave test of media priming on the issue of the economy in the 1992 election. Did campaign and media attention prime the economy in 1992, leading to the collapse in President George H. W. Bush's approval? The figure visually represents the key results in table 2.2 and figure 2.5, showing that prior economic assessments became more predictive of Bush approval as the economy became prominent in the 1992 election. It also shows that this issue weight increase is statistically significant (the confidence interval does not overlap with zero). The estimates are from the three-wave test (see equation 11 in the appendix) with control variables. It confirms the conventional test findings by ruling out reverse causation. The thin and thick error bars show 90 percent and 68 percent confidence intervals, respectively. Source: 1990–91–92 ANES panel.

with a confidence interval. Since the bar representing this confidence range does not include zero, we can be more confident that the change in issue weight is real, not a product of chance.

HOW SURE ARE WE? RULING OUT OTHER POSSIBILITIES. We have seen that the three-wave test overcomes the thorny problem of reverse causation that bedevils research on issue voting. But this is not the only challenge researchers face. They must also rule out the possibility that something other than media priming might explain the changes in issue weights. A social scientist from Mars, for example, might note that as the temperature in New England drops people spend more money shopping. Our Martian might conclude that cold weather "causes" increased shopping, completely missing the real cause—the holidays. Similarly, the economy was a big issue in 1992, but not the only issue and conceivably not the issue that was making the difference. Maybe presidential approval was falling not because of the economy, but because Bush broke his promise not to raise taxes or because the media portrayed him as out of touch with ordinary voters' concerns (such as showing his surprise at seeing a supermarket barcode scanner, which he'd allegedly never encountered before). Or maybe the campaigns reinforced voters' partisan leanings, making voters more likely to view the state of the economy in terms favorable to their party's interests (rather than judging the incumbent in terms of the economy).

To help rule out such alternative explanations, researchers usually include control variables in their statistical models. That is, we explore whether other factors are having the influence we are provisionally attributing to the variable of interest. For example, if I think blood pressure is having a particular effect on the incidence of heart attacks, I would examine whether other factors—such as cholesterol levels or occupation—might be the real source of that effect.

With panel data, such control variables are potentially less important. By comparing the same people at different times, we are already holding constant the individuals. Of course, individuals may change. For example, a particular issue other than the one being studied may become more or less important between one survey and the next. I therefore statistically control for other variables, including party identification, approval of Bush's handling of foreign affairs, approval of his handling of the Gulf crisis, attitudes about defense spending, the 7-point ideology scale, attitudes about abortion, the government services and spending scale, attitudes about minority aid, and an index of moral traditionalism (see the appendix for details)—that is, for a number of factors that could also have influenced a person's approval or disapproval of President Bush. As with participants' economic perceptions, I measure these variables in the prior wave, so that cause and effect can be distin-

TABLE 2.2. **Priming the economy in the 1992 election: Three-wave test**

DV: Presidential approval	Wave 2 1991	Wave 3 1992	Dif. Δ_{3ct}
Prior economic assessments	0.08*	0.29*	0.21*
	(0.043)	(0.061)	(0.074)
Prior DV	0.34*	0.24*	
	(0.041)	(0.041)	
Prior party identification	0.13*	0.24*	
	(0.028)	(0.034)	
Prior Gulf Crisis handling approval	0.059	0.072*	
	(0.037)	(0.036)	
Prior foreign affairs approval	0.057*	0.046	
	(0.034)	(0.036)	
Prior defense spending	0.15*	0.16*	
	(0.042)	(0.045)	
Prior ideology scale	0.077*	−0.0068	
	(0.025)	(0.026)	
Prior abortion views	0.053*	0.053*	
	(0.025)	(0.030)	
Prior government services and spending	0.00097	0.12*	
	(0.039)	(0.068)	
Prior minority aid	0.12*	0.048	
	(0.034)	(0.038)	
Prior moral traditionalism scale	−0.053	−0.053	
	(0.045)	(0.053)	
n	956	956	
R^2	0.428	0.346	
SER	25.9	29.1	

Note: Ordinary least squares regression estimates with standard errors in parentheses. For ease of presentation, I code variables to vary between 0 and 100 in the figures. For statistical models, I code variables to vary between 0 and 1. Constant not shown. * $p < 0.1$.

guished.[8] (Table 2.2 presents the full statistical models behind the issue weights shown in figure 2.5.) In fact, figure 2.5 already controls for these variables and is called a partial residual scatterplot—residual because it only shows presidential approval and economic perceptions after removing variation accounted for by these controls. Given that the economy's issue weight increases even with these variables held constant, I conclude that the findings were not the result of these other factors and were, more likely, a real effect of media priming on the economy issue.

(Since I use these partial residual scatterplots throughout the book, they merit an explanation, which is unfortunately technical. Ideally, I would show plots of average approval by each level of economic perceptions, such as in figure 2.4, as these plots are easy to understand and show raw data with minimal processing. However, the three-wave test examines change in presidential approval, and while I could show the average change in approval by prior economic perceptions, a problem called "regression to the mean" may mask effects with this approach, that is, bias figures against finding priming [or persuasion or learning in future chapters]. By accounting flexibly for prior presidential approval [note the coefficient far less than 1.0 on "Prior DV" in table 2.2], this problem is minimized—a point I discuss in the appendix. Although the partial residual scatterplots also account for variation explained by other control variables, accounting for them leaves the results unchanged, and most other chapters have minimal control variables. The primary motivation for using partial residual scatterplots, then, is to account for regression to the mean.)

There is yet another pitfall to beware. We may be underestimating the true priming effect due to a problem that public opinion researchers often face—floor and ceiling effects. As with many questions asked in public opinion surveys, the prescribed range of answers only allows respondents to express so much approval or so much disapproval. Respondents in these ANES surveys were limited to a 5-point scale. Given the large overall shift against Bush between 1991 and 1992, we might suspect that people who already strongly disapproved of him in 1991 might have wished in 1992 that they could extend the scale to disapprove of him even further. Since we have postulated that media priming on the poor state of the economy would result in greater disapproval for Bush, using a scale that might not allow people to fully express that disapproval ("This scale doesn't go low enough!") could force us to underestimate how much media priming there really was.

To check for a floor effect, I examine the priming effect for each level of presidential approval in 1991 using the three-wave test. That is, I examine—using the 1992 survey results—how much the approval level had changed among those who had greatly approved of Bush in 1991, among those who had mildly approved, among those who had mildly disapproved, and so on. There turn out to be large differences. For example, among those who approved of Bush in 1991, the issue-weight increase is about 0.45 with controls ($n = 495$), twice the size as the estimate in the full sample (see the last column of table 2.2). Findings like this suggest that a floor effect is indeed causing us to underestimate the priming effect; we can see the full drop in approval for those who were initially approving, but for those who already disapproved, the full drop in approval likely goes "off the scale."

What the 1992 Election Tells Us about Issue Voting

Examining the 1992 election, I therefore find that people's attitudes about a substantive issue—how the economy is doing—really do play a role in their political judgments and choices. Between 1991 and 1992, citizens increasingly came to judge Bush on the basis of their own assessments of the economy. It seems that in 1991, voter's perceptions of the economy wouldn't have counted enough in their judgment of President Bush to sway an election, but by 1992, they did indeed count enough to do so. But is this example typical or is it an exception? To investigate this question, I briefly examine two more cases in which campaigns and the news media may have primed the same performance issue—the economy.

2.2 More Judgments on Presidential Performance

Reelecting President Clinton

During the election campaign of 1996, as during that of 1992, the media and the Clinton campaign made the economy more of an issue than it had been. This time, however, the economy advantaged the incumbent. Clinton campaigned hard on how much the economy had improved during his administration and he won the election. Did the former help bring about the latter? Did voters vote for Clinton *because* they judged his performance on the economy to have been good?[9]

In an ANES panel that reinterviewed the same respondents in 1992, 1994, and 1996, the public's assessment of the economy improved substantially, rising from 22 (on a scale of 0 to 100) in 1992 to 54 in 1994 to 58 in 1996. Clinton's reelection campaign attempted to capitalize on these perceptions of an improving economy. His campaign ads and speeches repeatedly emphasized the strong economy. The "Opportunities Spot," for instance, contrasted the economy's strength in 1996 with its weakness in 1992:

ANNOUNCER: Recession. Hard times. Bob Dole votes to deny families unemployment benefits.

BOB DOLE FROM 1992: "The economy was never that bad."

ANNOUNCER: [citing June 1992 statistic] Ten million unemployed, higher interest rates. Four years later unemployment, 7 year low. 10 million new jobs. We make more autos than Japan.

THE PRESIDENT: Growth and opportunity. Fifteen hundred dollar tax credit for college. A five hundred dollar per child tax credit. Expanded family and medical leave. A balanced budget. Building a bridge to the twenty-first century.[10]

At the same time, the news media also focused on the economy (Dover 1998). In September 1996 the Department of Labor released statistics showing that the annual unemployment rate had declined to 5.1 percent, the lowest in seven years. That statistic prompted a burst of

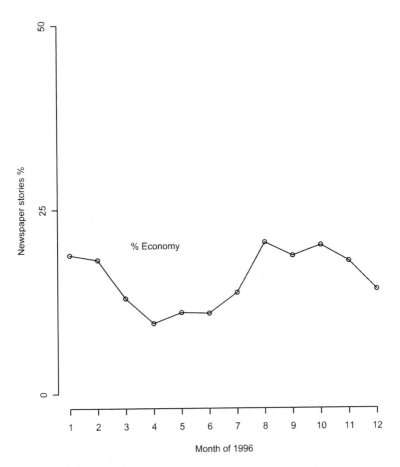

FIGURE 2.7. Newspaper coverage of the economy in 1996. This figure shows the percentage of newspaper stories with the names "Clinton" and "Dole" that also contain the words "economy" or "unemployment." Source: newslibrary.com.

television news coverage favorable to Clinton. NBC's *News at Nine*, for instance, commented that the unemployment rate had been 7.8 percent only four years earlier, when Clinton had first run for president (Dover 1998). Figure 2.7 shows that during the peak months of the campaign about 20 percent of all stories in major newspapers that mention Clinton and Dole also mention the economy.

Given all this attention to the issue of the economy, we might expect citizens to place greater weight on it in 1996. That is, we might expect a priming shift like that in the 1992 election. And indeed, Clinton's approval rose from 46 points in 1994 to 60 in 1996.[11] How much of this increase can be attributed to citizens increasingly judging Clinton on what they perceived to be an improving economy?

Clinton's opponent, Bob Dole, knew these positive economic perceptions threatened his candidacy. He was on the losing side of this issue and he tried to neutralize it, primarily by attempting to persuade voters that the economy was in worse shape than they thought. "The evidence for a weak economy is everywhere. Everywhere," Bob Dole said on the stump in late October (Nagourney 1996). He went on to attack the "false and empty talk about the so-called Clinton recovery," extorting the public to, "take off the mask—it's not Halloween—take off the mask! The economy is not good." Throughout the campaign, Dole continued to deride the economy, often saying it was "barely afloat" and repeatedly referring to the "Clinton recession." In part, he justified his 15 percent tax cut proposal—a principal theme of his campaign—by citing the need to get the economy moving.

To test more definitively for priming in this case, I again use the three-wave test (see equation 11 in the appendix). First, to establish a baseline, I examine the effect of 1992 economic perceptions on the change in Clinton's approval between 1992 and 1994. (I measure perceptions of the economy with the same survey questions used above to study the 1992 election.) Then I examine the effect of 1994 economic perceptions on the change in Clinton's approval between 1994 and 1996 and compare this effect to the baseline effect.

Of course, the economy was not the only issue in 1996. Several other issues may also have contributed to Clinton's reelection. For example, Clinton's campaign raised the fear of Republicans destroying Social Security. Clinton also shifted to the ideological center by cutting the deficit and enacting welfare reform, which he signed into law only a few months before Election Day. But Michael Alvarez and Jonathan Nagler (1998), in their analysis of the 1996 election, find little evidence that Social Security or Clinton's shift on welfare reform aided his reelection efforts. They do find, however, a strong association between abortion attitudes and Clinton support. To account for alternative explanations, I control for the following variables: attitudes about abortion, aid to minorities, government guaranteed jobs, government services and spending, the 7-point ideology scale, and party identification.[12] I measure these attitudes in the wave before I measure the level of Clinton approval. For example, I looked for an effect of 1992 attitudes about abortion on the change in Clinton's approval level between 1992 and 1994.

My analysis finds priming in this campaign, just as in the 1992 campaign. Figure 2.8 presents this result with a (partial residual) scatterplot from the three-wave test (for the full ordinary least squares regression estimates, see table 1 in the appendix). On the left-hand side, it shows that 1992 economic perceptions had no real influence on change in support for President Clinton between 1992 and 1994 (holding constant the control variables). If anything, the economy's issue weight (slope) is slightly negative, −0.04. In contrast, 1994 economic perceptions do appear to influence changes in Clinton approval between 1994 and 1996: the issue weight rises to 0.13. As the figure shows, individuals who saw the economy as much better in 1994 increased their approval by about 13 points on the 100-point scale, while those who saw the economy as much worse did not change their approval on average. The issue weight of the economy was thus higher in 1996 than it had been in 1994; the difference in issue weights is 0.13 − −0.04 = 0.17. The economy therefore counted for more in voters' judgment of Clinton's performance.

Defeating Carter

When Jimmy Carter ran for reelection in 1980, two issues were at the forefront: defense and the economy. Yet it seems to have been the economy—a poor economy, to be specific—that gained in issue weight and affected voters' judgments of Carter's performance and their choices to vote for Carter or for Ronald Reagan.

In the immediate aftermath of the Iranian hostage crisis in November 1979 and the Soviet invasion of Afghanistan in December of 1979, the public approved of Carter's handling of the presidency. According to the 1980 ANES Major Panel, 56 percent approved in the January wave—the first wave of the panel—despite a dismal economy with

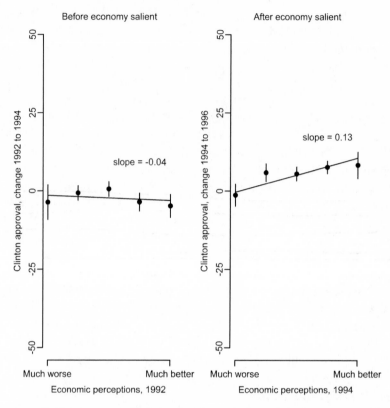

FIGURE 2.8. Three-wave test of priming the economy in the 1996 election—partial residual scatterplots. These plots show that economic perceptions became more important (steeper slope) after the economy became more prominent. They are called partial residual scatterplots because they only show variation after accounting for control variables (residualized variation). The difference in these slopes, $(\Delta_{3wt} = 0.13 - -0.04 =)$ 0.17, represents the media priming effect. The appendix presents the model behind these plots (equation 11) and the full ordinary least squares regression estimates (table 1). It also explains how I create residual scatterplots. Error bars show 68 percent confidence intervals. Source: 1992–97 ANES panel.

14 percent inflation, 18 percent interest rates, and high unemployment. It's not that citizens failed to perceive that the economy was bad; the public assessment of it was a dismal 19 points (on the 100-point perceptions scale) in January 1980. Yet the public seemed concerned with international issues (see the discussion in chapter 7) and apparently failed to consider the poor economy when evaluating Carter. Respondents who perceived the economy as much worse in this first wave of the panel were

only 10 points less approving of Carter than respondents who did not perceive the economy as much worse (their approval rates were 50 and 60 on the 100-point scale, respectively).

Over the course of 1980, Carter's opponents twice attempted to undermine his approval by priming the economy as an issue. The first attempt came from within the Democratic Party. Massachusetts Senator Edward Kennedy tried to unseat Carter for the Democratic nomination largely by linking Carter to the dismal economy. His ads showed Carroll O'Connor, who played Archie Bunker in the popular TV show *All in the Family*, declaring: "Carter equals Reagan equals Hoover equals depression" (Jamieson 1996, 388). During the primary season, Carter's approval plummeted. By June, when the ANES reinterviewed respondents, Carter's approval had fallen from 56 to 33 on the 100-point presidential approval scale.

Nevertheless, Carter won the nomination, and the second attempt at priming the economy came from the Reagan campaign. Compared to Kennedy's attack, Reagan's was more forceful and more national. As shown in figure 2.9, most of Reagan's general election television ads emphasized the economy: over 90 percent of the Reagan ads created in August and over 80 percent of those created in September. Much like Kennedy's ads, Reagan's attempted to make the economy a bigger issue in voters' minds and to blame Carter for the dismal unemployment and inflation rates. One of Reagan's ads asked,

Can we afford four more years of broken promises? In 1976, Jimmy Carter promised to hold inflation to four percent. Today it is 14%. He promised to fight unemployment. But today there are 8½ million Americans out of work. He promised to balance the budget. What he gave us was a $61 billion deficit. Can we afford four more years? (Jamieson 1996, 440)

The news media also shifted its focus onto the economy. In December 1979 and January 1980, only about 20 percent of stories in major news sources about Carter and Reagan mentioned the economy (see figure 2.10). By the late spring, this had risen to between 30 and 40 percent, where it remained through Election Day.

As in the 1992 case, the public's perceptions of the economy remained essentially unchanged, at least on average, in the January, June, and September 1980 interviews. (The postelection survey did not ask about the economy.) Using the same economy question, average perceptions were

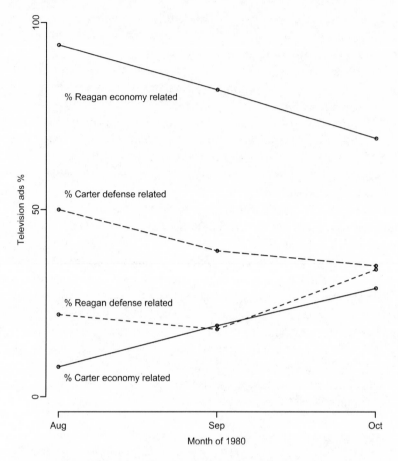

FIGURE 2.9. Carter's television ads emphasized defense, while Reagan's emphasized the economy. This figure shows the percentage of television ads created in each month of the 1980 general election campaign by Reagan and Carter mentioning a defense-related issue and mentioning an economy-related issue. Carter's campaign created twelve ads in August, thirty-one in September, and seventeen in October, while Reagan's created eighteen, twenty-two, and thirty-two, respectively. Source: John Geer, Vanderbilt University.

a dismal 19 points in January, 14 in June, and 20 in September (on the 100-point scale).

Did Reagan's ads and the news media coverage prime the economy as the campaign progressed? As before, I answer this question by first establishing a baseline: I examine the effect of January 1980 economic perceptions on the change in Carter's approval between January 1980

and June 1980. Then I examine the effect of June 1980 economic perceptions on the change in Carter's approval between June 1980 and September 1980 and compare this to the baseline effect. Ideally, I would have
tested for priming between June and Election Day, but the panel did
not ask about presidential approval in its postelection wave (and did not
ask about voter intent in June).[13] I measure perceptions of the economy
with the same set of survey questions used above to study the 1992 and
1996 elections. To address alternative explanations I include controls for
party identification, the 7-point ideology scale, attitudes about government spending and services, and about defense spending.

Once again, I find priming, just as in the 1992 and 1996 cases. Figure 2.11 presents this result with another (partial residual) scatterplot

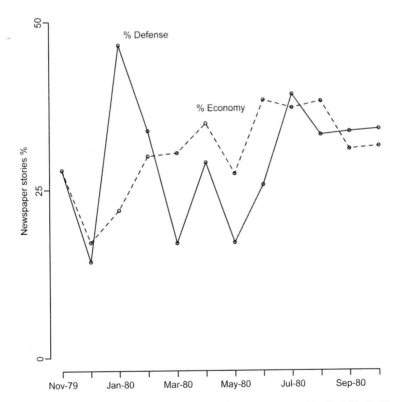

FIGURE 2.10. The issue agenda of major US news publications covered by LexisNexis. The
figure shows the percentages of all news stories mentioning Carter and Reagan that also
mentioned the economy or defense. For details, see the appendix.

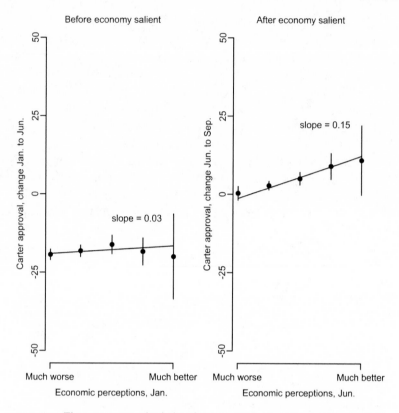

FIGURE 2.11. Three-wave test of priming the economy in the 1980 election—partial residual scatterplots. These plots show that economic perceptions become more important (steeper slope) after this issue becomes more prominent. They are partial residual scatterplots as they only show variation after accounting for control variables. The difference in these slopes, ($\Delta_{3wt} = 0.15 - 0.03 =$) 0.12, represents the media priming effect. The appendix presents the model behind the plots (equation 11) and the full ordinary least squares regression estimates (table 1). It also explains how I create partial residual scatterplots. Error bars show 68 percent confidence intervals. Source: 1980 ANES Major Panel.

from the three-wave test (for the model estimates, see table 1 in the appendix). On the left-hand side, it shows that January economic perceptions have no real influence on change in Carter approval between January and June (holding constant the control variables). As the figure shows, Carter's approval does drop considerably between these months, about 20 points on the 100-point scale, but does so equally among those who see the economy as getting much worse and among those who see it as getting much better. The issue weight in this period is only 0.03.

In contrast, June economic perceptions do appear to influence changes in Carter approval between June and September, as shown on the right side of the figure. The issue weight rises to 0.15. In fact, Carter approval rises among the few individuals who see the economy as getting better. The issue weight of the economy was thus higher in September than it had been in June; the difference in issue weights is $0.15 - 0.03 = 0.12$. The economy therefore counted for more in voters' judgment of Carter's overall performance.

A strange aspect of this result is that as Reagan's ads primed the economy Carter approval did not fall overall, but in fact rose, as is evident in figure 2.11. How is this possible? The answer is that something else was apparently driving up Carter approval between June and September. Apparently, priming the economy issue was enough to dampen this increase, but not enough to completely offset it. In other words, priming was taking place between June and September, but so was something else—something in Carter's favor. What that something else was, however, remains unclear.

2.3 Conclusion

Performance Issue Voting

This chapter has addressed a fundamental question about citizens' judgments of their political leaders: do citizens judge a politician according to their own assessments of his or her performance?

For some time, we have had ample aggregate-level evidence that American citizens do judge incumbent presidents on at least one performance criterion—the state of the economy. But we cannot tell whether these findings reflect voters' judgments or indirect processes such as the willingness of donors to contribute to incumbents, the willingness of high-quality candidates to challenge incumbents, or the tone of news media coverage about incumbents (e.g., Jacobson 1989).

We have also had individual-level analyses suggesting that American citizens judge incumbent presidents on the economy. But we could not tell whether citizens were judging politicians according to their *own* assessments of the economy or assessing the economy in accordance with their own preexisting approval or disapproval of the incumbent president. The two cases are observationally equivalent; one can't tell them apart without more information.

As I have argued, judging politicians on performance issues such as the economy should be an easy test for citizens. Performance issues are cognitively easier for citizens than are policy issues. People do not need to know a politician's positions—which may also be underreported or deliberately obscured—in order to judge him or her on performance issues. People may also have more practice forming opinions about performance issues than about policy issues; judging a person's performance is a part of everyday life.[14] If citizens pass the tests in this chapter—that is, if they do judge politicians on their assessments of the politicians' performance—then we at least know that democracy does not resemble the worst-case, rum-punch view of voters voting only for trivial or irrelevant reasons. Do the voters pass this beginner's test?

According to this chapter's findings, they do. As the 1980, 1992, and 1996 elections approached, voters increasingly changed their approval of the president based on their prior assessments of the economy. If they thought the economy had been faring well, they later became more approving of the president as the economy became more of an issue in the campaign. They judged the president on performance, just as citizens in a democracy are supposed to do.

Figure 2.12 sums up the findings for the economy shown separately in figures 2.5, 2.8, and 2.11. For each of the three elections, it presents only the difference in issue weight—the change in how much importance citizens attached to the economy issue when they judged the incumbent president (and eventually voted either for or against him). This is the key statistic examined throughout this book—it may help to remember that it is just the difference in slopes in the earlier figures. If this difference is positive, it indicates that the campaign and media coverage primed the issue.[15] In all three cases, we see evidence of priming: prior assessments of the economy always appeared to matter more as the economy became a more prominent issue in the campaign. The size of this effect is somewhat smaller in 1980 and 1996 than it was in 1992, but is still substantively significant.

The last estimate in figure 2.12 presents the average issue-weight difference across the three cases. Since I use these averages throughout the book, they need a brief explanation. They are called precision-weighted averages because they weight each effect by our certainty about it (how precisely we estimated it), so effects with smaller confidence intervals (more precision) count for more.[16] In this case, the precision-weighted average equals 0.17 and implies some confidence in an effect, as its

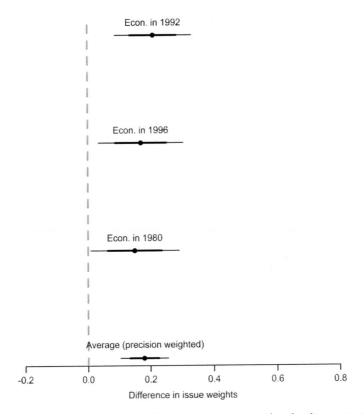

FIGURE 2.12. Summary of priming effects on the economy using the three-wave test. For each of these panel studies, this figure presents the difference in the economy's issue weight—the change in how much importance citizens attached to the economy issue when they changed their judgments of the incumbent president (before compared to after the issue became prominent). This is the key statistic examined throughout this book. If it is positive, which it is in all three cases, it indicates that this issue became more important after it became prominent. The difference in issue weights is calculated as the differences in the slopes from the three-wave tests shown in figures 2.5, 2.8, and 2.11 (it is calculated as $\Delta_{3wt} = \bar{b}_{w2} - \bar{b}_{w1}$; see equation 11 in the appendix). The last estimate presents the average issue-weight difference across the three cases. It weights each effect by our certainty about it (how precisely we estimated it), so effects with smaller confidence intervals (more precision) count for more. These ordinary least squares regression estimates include control variables, though the results remain essentially unchanged without these controls. The thin and thick error bars show 90 percent and 68 percent confidence intervals, respectively. Sources: 1990–91–92 ANES panel, 1992–97 ANES panel, and 1980 ANES Major Panel.

confidence interval is small. This 0.17 average effect implies that the increase in presidential approval caused by a shift from seeing the economy as much worse to seeing it as much better would be 17 points greater
(on the 100-point presidential approval scale) *after* priming had taken
place than it would be *before* priming had taken place. Put another way,
after priming has taken place, we get more presidential-approval bang
for our economic-perception buck.

These three cases do not provide ironclad evidence that when campaigns and the news media emphasize the economy, citizens give that issue greater weigh in their judgments of the president's performance and
their decisions to vote for or against the incumbent. Nevertheless, the
cases are strongly suggestive that such is the case, particularly in that
they avoid some of the pitfalls of previous studies.

Media Priming

Although my focus in this chapter is on evidence that voters make judgments based on performance, these findings also confirm previous work
on media priming. Earlier studies had found evidence of media priming
on the economy (Hetherington 1996; Iyengar and Kinder 1987; Kelleher and Wolak 2006; Mutz 1992; Sheafer and Weimann 2005), but without being able to rule out reverse causation; the analysis in this chapter
does rule it out.[17]

Media priming has interested scholars in part because of its potential for voter manipulation. It may imply that, merely by stressing one issue more than another, campaigns and the media can change people's
views about politicians or public policies, leading citizens to give some
issues too much weight and others too little. Did the campaigns manipulate citizens into placing undue weight on the economy in the elections
of 1980, 1992, and 1996?[18] The problem with inferring manipulation is
that we do not know what weight citizens would place on the economy in
the absence of media priming. In fact, some researchers see the greater
emphasis on the economy as a benefit rather than a problem. In Andrew
Gelman and Gary King's (1993) interpretation, campaigns and the media do not manipulate voters but rather help citizens think about which
issues are most important.

Although I have adopted the convention of referring to issue-weight
increases as the results of priming, these increases could also come about
because citizens are *learning* more about a particular issue. For example,

citizens would probably never see the economy as an unimportant issue, but they might well fail to place much weight on it because they have only a vague sense of how the economy is doing. During a campaign, however, they may become much more certain about their economic assessments and therefore allow them to count for more.

Given these ambiguities, we cannot be absolutely sure that campaigns and the media manipulated citizens in these three cases (or in the others I examine in this book). Consequently, my focus is not on priming or learning per se, but rather on using issue weight increases—whatever their source—to detect policy-related and performance-related judgments. On this arguably more fundamental question, the results are clearer. Citizens do appear to judge politicians on performance.[19] Citizens do sometimes lead.

CHAPTER THREE

Rewarding Policy Advantages?
Priming Policy

In April of 1999, Fred Steeper, longtime Republican consultant and pollster, was searching for new policy proposals for the Republicans to campaign on in the 2000 presidential election. As he examined survey responses to a variety of proposed policies, he was struck by the support for one in particular: allowing workers to invest a portion of their Social Security taxes in their own retirement accounts. "You could see that the results were overwhelmingly in favor of this," he recalled (Jamieson and Waldman 2001, 27). He found that the support was widespread across demographic groups; even those sixty-five and older favored it. Based in part on Steeper's findings, Republican presidential candidate George W. Bush campaigned on a proposal to invest Social Security funds in the stock market, running a television ad on this issue in June of 2000.

Fred Steeper was not the only pollster who thought this was a winning issue for Bush. The National Annenberg Election Survey, which interviewed about a hundred thousand people during the 2000 campaign, found large majorities supporting Bush's proposal throughout the election year (see below). As a result, the Democratic presidential candidate, Al Gore, faced a dilemma. He could adopt Bush's popular proposal on Social Security or campaign against it. In the end Gore took an opposing view, promising to protect Social Security by placing any surpluses in a "lockbox." As Bush and Gore stressed their differences, millions of citizens learned the candidates' distinct positions and in so doing became more aware of this issue.[1] By Election Day, investing Social Security funds in the stock market had become the dominant policy issue of the campaign.

In the previous chapter I found that when the economy becomes prominent citizens increasingly use their own assessments of the economy to judge the incumbent president. This encouraging evidence of *judgment based on performance* holds even when I measure economic assessments in one set of interviews and judgments of politicians in a later set of interviews, so that we can be more confident that assessments of the economy do indeed influence judgments of politicians. Performance judgments such as "how the economy is doing," however, are arguably much easier for voters to make than policy judgments such as whether or not investing Social Security funds is a good idea. Policy judgments require voters to know what positions various politicians have taken on a policy *and* to form their own views about that policy. Are voters up to this challenge? Do they judge politicians on policy issues such as the privatization of Social Security? Do they show any more than the minimal competence demonstrated in chapter 2?

To see whether they do, I administer chapter 2's three-wave media-priming test in ten policy cases; nine are historical events and one is an experiment. In all ten tests, something—campaigns, the news media, or a set of experimental conditions—raises the salience of a policy issue. In all ten, panel surveys span these changes in salience (whether genuine political upheavals or maneuvering by the experimenter). This allows me to gather people's views about each issue *before* it becomes more important, in order to exclude the possibility that people are simply following—adopting the policy positions of a politician they already like for other reasons—rather than leading—adopting their own policy views and then judging the available candidates accordingly. In eight of the ten cases, the parties or candidates take clear and distinct positions, so we can make straightforward predictions about how people should change their votes depending on their own views of the issue. (I discuss the two exceptions later.)

The ten policy cases analyzed in this chapter (and also in subsequent chapters) span a wide range of issues, some of long-standing concern to the public and some of only recent concern at the time. Most are from the United States, but there are also cases from Canada, the United Kingdom, and the Netherlands. The policies at stake include national defense, national identity, public works projects, and nuclear power. One case tests for the media priming of ideology—rather than for a specific policy issue—in the 1992 presidential election; this is what researchers call "activating fundamentals." Another case is an experimental study on the issue of health insurance for children in the United States.

As these policy issues become prominent, do voters pass this harder test by increasingly judging politicians on policy? I find little evidence that they do. When I measure people's policy views before the policy is made more salient, either by the media or by the campaigns themselves, I rarely find that people have either shifted their support to a candidate whose policy position agrees with their own views or withdrawn their support from a candidate whose policy positions do not agree with their own views. This finding holds when examining how citizens evaluate candidates or parties and how voters report voting. It also contrasts markedly with the previous chapter, where, in all three economic cases, we found people judging politicians on substance when it came to a performance issue. Here, in only one of the ten cases do we find them judging politicians on substance when it comes to a policy issue.

These findings are seemingly inconsistent with numerous studies, which not only find policy voting but media priming in particular. Whether observational or experimental, however, these studies generally measure policy views, not before, but at the same time as they measure vote choice or candidate evaluations, and so they could get the story backward. When we overcome this problem of observational equivalence by measuring them beforehand, evidence of policy voting mostly vanishes—citizens no longer appear to be leading politicians on policy.

3.1 Lockbox: Social Security in the 2000 US Election

> Al Gore: [interrupting debate moderator Jim Lehrer] Jim, may I just say that, in my plan, the "lockbox" would be used only for Social Security and Medicare. It would have two different locks. Now, one of the keys to the "lockbox" would be kept by the President; the other key would be sealed in a small, metal container and placed under the bumper of the Senate Majority Leader's car. (*Saturday Night Live*, 2000, Season 26, Episode 1)

It would be hard to overstate the emphasis that both the Bush and the Gore campaigns put on the issue of investing Social Security funds. The issue gained prominence on October 3, 2000, when Bush and Gore sparred on this policy during the first presidential debate (Hershey 2001). There were sharp exchanges during the third debate as well, and from that point on, both television news and campaign advertising focused on it heavily. Following the debates, 10 to 15 percent of network news statements about politics mentioned Social Security (Johnston, Hagen, and Jamieson 2004, 153–57).[2] The emphasis in television advertising was even heavier, with 40 percent of Democratic ads and 60 percent of Republican ads mentioning Social Security in the last week of the campaign (ibid.). A typical television station in media markets in which the campaigns advertised aired about 150 Bush spots and about sixty Gore spots mentioning Social Security that week (ibid.).

By devoting so much attention to this issue, both campaigns presumably intended to change votes. Did they succeed? Did they induce a media-priming effect?

Analyzing cross-sectional, time-series data on this election, Richard Johnston, Michael Hagen, and Katheen Jamieson (2004) conclude that the emphasis on Social Security did lead voters to increasingly judge Bush and Gore on this issue, partly explaining Gore's surge in the last few days of the campaign. Their test, however, could be misleading because of reverse causation. Their method doesn't rule out the possibility that voters first decide whether they like Bush or Gore and then adopt that candidate's policy.

As I did with the performance cases, I attempt to eliminate the bias due to reverse causation by testing whether people's attitudes about the policy of investing Social Security taxes (presented to them as a possible policy but not explicitly as something Bush supported and Gore opposed) increasingly explain later changes in their intended votes as this issue becomes prominent. I can apply the three-wave test, introduced in chapter 2, because the National Annenberg Election Study conducted several panel surveys, one of which interviewed the same respondents as many as four times. I use the July 21–August 13 interviews as wave 1, the August 4–27 interviews as wave 2, and the November 11–December 7 interviews as wave 3.[3] The issue of investing became prominent between wave 2 (before the debates) and wave 3 (after the election).

To assess citizens' views about the policy of investing Social Security taxes, the survey asked, "Do you personally favor or oppose allowing workers to invest some of their Social Security contributions in the stock market?" Respondents could answer "favor" or "oppose," which I code 1 and 0, respectively. Across these three waves, support for the investing policy varied from 68 percent favoring it in wave 1 to 69 percent in wave 2 to 63 percent in wave 3. As the dependent variable, I use vote intent ("Thinking about the general election in November, if you voted today . . . who would you vote for?") or reported vote choice after the election, coding a Bush vote 1 and a Gore vote 0. Among the 418 respondents who were interviewed in all three waves, the intention to vote for Bush falls from 63 percent in wave 1 to 61 percent in wave 2. Then in their postelection interviews (wave 3), 60 percent reported having voted for Bush.

Before applying the three-wave test, I first use the conventional test, which I introduced in the previous chapter and formally define in the appendix (see equation 6), to search for evidence of priming. That is, I replicate the Johnston, Hagen, and Jamieson (2004) finding with panel data. Of course, the conventional test is potentially misleading because of reverse causation, but it is nevertheless suggestive.[4] Confirming Johnston, Hagen, and Jamieson's (2004) results, I find that voters' attitudes about investing do become more predictive of their actual vote (at least, the votes they reported intending to make or having made). The media-driven and campaign-driven emphasis on this issue appears to have caused voters to take it more into account as they decided whom to vote for. To present this visually, figure 3.1 shows the issue weights (slopes) for attitudes on investing Social Security contributions.[5] The issue weight rises from 0.44 in wave 2 (predebates) to 0.59 in wave 3 (postelection), a highly significant increase.[6] Thus—at least according to this potentially biased test—the tremendous attention given to this issue produced at least the appearance of a priming effect. As the issue of Social Security became highly salient, citizens increasingly judged Bush and Gore on that issue.[7]

Now what will we find if we avoid the reverse causation bias by measuring investing attitudes in a prior wave—that is, by asking voters about this policy issue well before it became prominent and before citizens might have changed their votes because of the issue?

Figure 3.2 presents the three-wave test visually, examining whether views on investing underlie changes in vote.[8] In contrast with the conventional test, the three-wave test finds no evidence that citizens increasingly judged Bush and Gore on this issue. We can see that investing views did not drive changes in people's vote preference either before this issue became prominent (predebates) or afterward. The issue weights are small and drop slightly from 0.05 before the debates to 0.01 afterward, for a priming effect of -0.04. This means that a person who expressed support for the Social Security investment policy in wave 2 was only a percentage point more likely to be a Bush supporter by the time of wave 3—having presumably been subject to the flood of public attention on this issue—

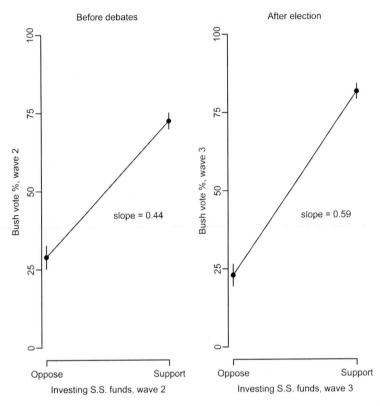

FIGURE 3.1. Conventional test of priming for Social Security in the 2000 election. Did campaign and news media attention to investing Social Security funds in the stock market prime this issue? This figure replicates previous findings showing an apparent priming effect. The slopes of these lines represent the weights people place on their views when determining their vote intents—the issue weights. The difference in these slopes, ($\Delta_{ci} = 0.59 -$ 0.44 =) 0.15, represents the media priming effect according to the conventional test, which is potentially biased by reverse causation. The appendix presents the model behind these plots (equation 6) and the full ordinary least squares regression estimates (table 2). Error bars show 68 percent confidence intervals. Source: 2000 National Annenberg Election Survey.

than he or she had been at the time of wave 1. Put more simply, the increase in media and campaign attention to this issue did almost nothing to make people whose position was the same as Bush's more likely to vote for Bush than they already were.

To provide a sense of our certainty about these estimates, figure 3.3 plots the issue weights (slopes) and their confidence intervals. We can

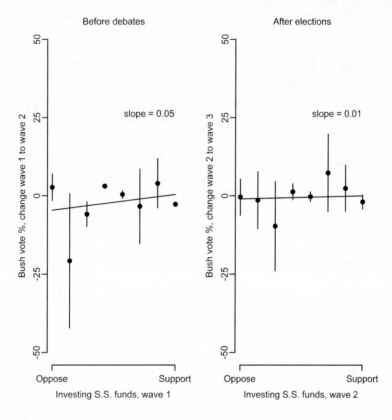

FIGURE 3.2. Three-wave test of media priming for the issue of investing Social Security in the 2000 election—partial residual scatterplots. In contrast with the conventional test, the three-wave test finds no evidence that citizens increasingly judged Bush and Gore on this issue. These plots show that prior views on this issue did not become more predictive of a Bush vote (steeper slope) after this issue became prominent. The slopes of these lines represent the weights people place on their views when changing their vote intents—the issue weights. The difference in these slopes, $(\Delta_{3wt} = 0.01 - 0.05=) -0.04$, represents the media priming effect. Figure 3.3 presents a test of whether the difference in the slopes is statistically significant. The appendix presents the model behind these plots (Equation 11), explains how I create them, and shows the full ordinary least squares regression estimates (Table 3). Error bars show 68 percent confidence intervals. Source: 2000 National Annenberg Election Survey.

see that they are precisely estimated, which means we are quite certain about the absence of an effect; that is, we can be certain that we really are seeing a failure of media priming to change voters' minds.

Social Security is just one of many issues upon which citizens could judge Bush and Gore. Maybe the campaigns did prime this issue but

only changed the votes of a small number of people for whom this issue was pivotal to their voting decision, too small a number to detect in
the panel survey. This is a real concern—one I address throughout the
book—but also one dismissed relatively easily. Even if media priming
changed few votes, it should still change overall evaluations of the candidates. Fortunately, the Annenberg National Election Study not only
asked about vote intentions and vote choice but also about favorability

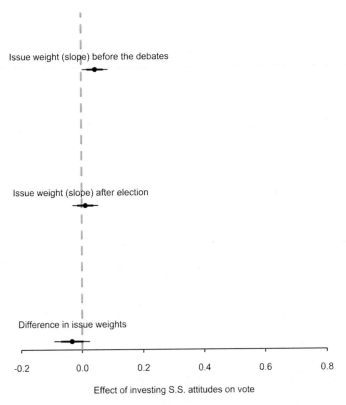

FIGURE 3.3. Three-wave test of media priming for the issue of investing Social Security in
the 2000 election. This plot shows the issue weights (slopes) from figure 3.2 and their confidence intervals. They allow the reader to see how precise the estimates of these issue
weights are and how sure we are about the difference between these issue weights. The difference between them, $(\Delta_{3wt} = 0.01 - 0.05 =) -0.04$, represents the media priming effect.
The appendix presents the model behind these plots (Equation 11) and the full ordinary
least squares regression estimates (Table 3). The thin and thick error bars show 90 percent
and 68 percent confidence intervals, respectively. Source: 2000 National Annenberg Election Survey.

ratings of Bush and Gore (e.g., "On a scale of zero to 100, how would you rate George W. Bush?"). When I replicate the analysis with these favorability ratings (Bush minus Gore) as the outcome variable, instead of vote, the results are the same as figure 3.3—they reveal no evidence that citizens changed their candidate evaluations to reflect their prior views on this issue (the difference in issue weights is 0.015, SE = 0.012, see the online appendix).[9]

This absence of an effect is robust. We can try looking at the same raw data using a variety of statistical models and we can try different ways to measure the variables—for example, we can control statistically for a host of other variables—but we keep finding that media priming about Social Security investment during the 2000 campaign did not cause voters to switch their support to whichever candidate agreed with their own position on that issue. Toward the end of this chapter, I discuss the numerous robustness tests that I apply to all ten cases we examine.

In the previous chapter we saw that the conventional test's finding—that voters did take economic performance into account in judging incumbent presidents—still held up when we eliminated the problem of reverse causation with the three-wave test. In this policy-issue case, however, the conventional test's findings do not hold up. Voters did not appear to be rewarding the candidates who agreed with them on this policy issue. They were apparently failing to lead.

3.2 Replicating: Nine More Policy Cases

Is this case unusual? Or is it generally true that as policy issues become prominent, voters fail to shift their support to candidates whose views they share? To find out I conduct similar analyses in nine more cases. As in the Social Security case, these all involve major increases in the prominence of an issue, changes that allow us to test whether that new prominence made a difference.

Since these diverse cases yield surprisingly similar findings, I summarize all the cases and then present the common results at the end of the chapter. If these descriptions seem a bit repetitive, it is for a good cause: the more cases we examine, the more confidence we can have in whatever common features we detect. For the first five cases, I apply the three-wave test. The next four had only two waves of interviews, so I have to use another approach.

3.3 Five Cases with Three Waves

Truman's Come-from-Behind Victory

President Harry S. Truman's election upset in 1948, which I introduced in chapter 1, is a good case to search for voters' judgment of politicians on policy issues. Lazarsfeld and his colleagues' classic study finds that Truman won by "refocusing attention on the socioeconomic concerns which had originally played such a large role in building that [Democratic] party's majority in the 1930s" (Berelson, Lazarsfeld, and McPhee 1954, 270).

To test for media priming in this case, I use the June interviews as wave 1, the October interviews as wave 2, and the November (postelection) interviews as wave 3.[10] To measure support for New Deal policies, I use the survey question in waves 1 and 2 about labor unions.[11] This question, discussed in chapter 1, asked respondents to agree with one of four statements that varied from "Labor unions in this country are doing a fine job" to "This country would be better off without any labor unions at all." To measure support for Truman, I use questions from wave 3 (postelection) about respondents' actual vote, coding Truman 1 and Dewey 0 and excluding respondents who did not report voting for either.

European Integration in the 1997 British Election

Although it has received little academic attention, the issue of European Union (EU) integration in Britain during the 1990s offers a fascinating opportunity to study citizens' judgments about politicians. Both the campaigns and the media ignored the issue of European integration in the 1992 British election, but emphasized it heavily in the 1997 election (Norris 1998). According to a content analysis of newspaper coverage, no front-page campaign article in a major newspaper mentioned this issue during the 1992 campaign, but 22 percent of such articles did so during the 1997 campaign, a far higher percentage than for any other policy issue (Butler and Kavanagh 1997, 175). The Conservative Party was partly behind this increase in attention. The party appealed to voters on this issue because, according to public opinion data, the public shared the Conservatives' opposition to EU integration. Campaign ads by the Conservative Party and other smaller parties appealed to voters with slogans such as, "With your support we can retain our nation's sovereignty." One ad even depicted Tony Blair as a ventriloquist's dummy on German Chancellor Helmut Kohl's knee. Did priming occur? That is, did all this media and campaign attention raise the "issue weight" for this particular issue?

Researchers have already found that it did (Andersen 2003; Evans 1999), but their studies relied on the conventional test and so may fall into the trap of reverse causation.[12] To test whether the campaign and media attention had caused this substantive issue to change the way people voted, I turned to the 1992–97 British Election Panel Study and measured support for European integration with a question that asked respondents on an 11-point scale whether they prefer seeking unity with Europe or protecting Great Britain's independence, with higher values indicating support for integration. For vote choice, I code Labour 0 and Conservative 1. I use the 1995 interviews as wave 1, the 1996 interviews as wave 2, and the 1997 interviews (postelection) as wave 3. Since the United Kingdom held no national elections in 1995 and 1996, the survey asked respondents who they would vote for "had there been an election." Given the tremendous attention the issue of European integration received in the 1997 election, we might expect this issue to become more important to citizens between the 1996 and 1997 interviews (between waves 2 and 3).

Public Works Jobs in the 1976 US Presidential Election

On September 23, 1976, Jimmy Carter and President Gerald Ford, the Democratic and Republican nominees for president, faced off in the first presidential debate since the Nixon-Kennedy debates in 1960. Seventy million households (53.5 percent) tuned in to watch Carter and Ford spar over the issue of public works projects (Kenski and Stroud 2005). Carter proposed initiating these projects to reduce the current high unemployment. Ford opposed them, preferring to address unemployment by stimulating the private sector, and had already vetoed several public works bills passed by Congress. During the debate, Carter criticized Ford's vetoes, and both candidates made the case for their positions on this issue (Abramowitz 1978).

The public may well have been more familiar with the long-standing issue of public employment programs than with some of the other policy issues at stake in these cases. Since the new deal era, the Democratic

Party had consistently supported such programs, while the Republican Party had generally opposed them. To analyze whether this debate and the subsequent media coverage of public works led citizens to increasingly judge Carter and Ford on this issue, I use the Patterson (1980) panel study, which interviewed representative samples in Erie, Pennsylvania, and in Los Angeles. Using a 7-point scale, it asked whether the government should directly provide jobs. I use the June interviews as wave 1, the August (predebate) interviews as wave 2, and the October (postdebate) interviews as wave 3. Finally, I code vote intent Carter 1 and Ford 0.

Defense and Reagan in the 1980 US Presidential Election

The 1980 US presidential election provides another important opportunity for the study of media priming. In chapter 2, I explored whether this election primed a performance issue—the economy. But a policy issue—defense spending—also became increasingly prominent during the primaries and the general election campaign. John Petrocik (1996) argues that the rise of this and other "Republican owned" issues helps explain Ronald Reagan's victory over Carter. Reagan and the Republican Party seized upon the Iranian hostage crisis in November 1979 and the Soviet invasion of Afghanistan in December 1979 "to help crystallize widespread disquiet about the United States' standing in the world, and turn that disquiet into a Republican campaign issue" (Bartels 1991, 459). The Carter campaign tried to turn this issue against Reagan, portraying him as trigger happy. In person-in-the-street ads, for example, the Carter campaign showed people making statements such as, "I think Governor Reagan in a crisis situation would be very fast to use military force" (Jamieson 1996, 407). Open-ended responses to an American National Election Study (ANES) question about the country's most important problem indicate that the issue became increasingly salient, with 12 percent of respondents mentioning defense as one of the country's most important problems in January, 16 percent in June, and 25 percent in November (Miller and Shanks 1982, 316).

To analyze this case, I use the 1980 ANES Major Panel and measure attitudes about defense spending with a 7-point question about whether respondents desire more or less defense spending. The panel interviewed respondents in four waves: January, June, September, and after the election.[13] Since the parties did not choose their nominees until after the first two waves of interviews, the vote intent question only becomes available in September. For the first two waves, then, I instead use feeling thermometers, which ask respondents to rate how warmly they feel toward particular politicians on a scale of 0 to 100. As I show in chapter 7, citizens did not appear to judge Carter on defense spending; attitudes about defense spending are unrelated to measures of Carter support in the panel's first wave and fail to become more related in the September wave. Support for Reagan, on the other hand, does become more related to defense spending attitudes. I therefore use people's ratings of Reagan on the feeling thermometer as the outcome variable and try to determine if media priming influenced that outcome. Because the study did not ask for feeling-thermometer ratings in the postelection wave, I use the January/February interviews as wave 1, the June/July interviews as wave 2, and the September interviews as wave 3.

Activating Fundamentals: Ideology in the 1992 Presidential Election

Scholars argue that campaigns not only change the salience of particular issues but also activate (or prime) "fundamentals." That is, they induce citizens to base their votes on fundamental variables such as the economy, race, and ideology (Gelman and King 1993).[14] In chapter 2 we observed priming for one of those fundamental variables, the economy. Another fundamental variable, ideology, shares similarities with the various policy issues at stake in this chapter. In particular, American presidential candidates hold distinct ideological positions; at least voters see them that way.[15]

Gelman and King's (1993) finding has spawned a growing literature on activating fundamentals (e.g., Andersen 2003; Andersen, Tilley, and Heath 2005; Bafumi, Gelman, and Park 2004). These research findings, however, have the same Achilles heel that the conventional test of priming has, because they measure ideology after it becomes prominent, so they could be wrong about what is causing what. Instead of people coming to support particular candidates on the basis of those candidates' ideologies during a campaign, already-committed Democrats and Republicans may simply be falling in line with their chosen party's ideology as the campaign heats up. I therefore use a three-wave test to examine whether or not citizens increasingly judge politicians on ideology as campaigns allegedly activate this fundamental variable.

To accomplish this, I need panel surveys that ask respondents about their own ideology both before and after the campaign. Few panel studies meet this requirement. Here, I examine the 1990, 1991, 1992 ANES panel, which is rare in that it surveys people in a nonelection year, 1991, and then reinterviews them during a presidential election year, 1992. The ideology question asked, "We hear a lot of talk these days about liberals and conservatives. Here is a 7-point scale on which the political views that people might hold are arranged from extremely liberal to extremely conservative. Where would you place yourself on this scale, or haven't you thought much about this?" The study also asked two other questions that tap general ideology: how warmly respondents felt toward "liberals" and how warmly they felt toward "conservatives," both on the 100-point feeling thermometer. To reduce measurement error, I create a scale of these three items, taking an (unweighted) average of them (Ansolabehere, Rodden, and Snyder 2008).[16] Unfortunately, the Democratic candidate, Bill Clinton, was still unknown to most citizens in 1991, so instead of examining intention to vote, I use approval for incumbent President George H. W. Bush as the dependent variable. I thus use the 1990 interviews as wave 1, the 1991 interviews as wave 2, and the 1992 (preelection) interviews as wave 3.

3.4 Four Policy Cases with Two Waves

The next four cases have only two waves of interviews, so I cannot conduct the three-wave test. I use a different test, which I discuss later in this chapter.

Chernobyl and Nuclear Power in the 1986 Dutch Election

In the 1986 general election for the Dutch parliament, the explosion and subsequent meltdown of a nuclear reactor in Chernobyl, USSR (now in the Ukraine), transformed domestic nuclear plant construction into a high-profile policy issue.[17] The accident happened to occur just three weeks before the election. Did it prompt Dutch citizens to judge their parties on this issue?

In the year before the campaign, the ruling coalition of Liberals and Christian Democrats had proposed constructing three nuclear plants. Their proposal generated opposition from the Labour Party and Social Liberals, the two major opposition parties, but passed anyway. About three weeks before the election, news of the Chernobyl nuclear accident reached the Netherlands. According to Wouter van der Brug (2001, 60), it "catapulted the nuclear power issue to the top of the public agenda" (see also Eijk, Irwin, and Niemöller 1986). Given the dramatic increase in the salience of this issue and the strong personal anxieties the accident generated for many people, Chernobyl seems likely to have primed attitudes about nuclear energy. Did it?

By chance, the Dutch Parliamentary Elections Study had almost completed the first of two waves of interviews when news of Chernobyl broke. Reinterviews began immediately after the elections of May 21. In both waves the study asked respondents to indicate on a 7-point scale their own position regarding nuclear energy, with the scale's end points labeled "The number of nuclear plants should be quickly increased in The Netherlands" and "No more nuclear plants should be built at all in The Netherlands." I code vote choice 1 for the two main opposition parties, who opposed nuclear power, and 0 for the two incumbent coalition parties, who supported it. I use the pre-Chernobyl interviews as wave 1 and the postelection interviews as wave 2. (I exclude respondents whose preelection interviews took place after news of the meltdown broke.)

The Free-Trade Agreement and the 1988 Canadian Election

One of the best-known examples of an apparent priming effect occurred in the 1988 Canadian election (Johnston et al. 1992). Prior to the campaign, the incumbent prime minister, Brian Mulroney of the Progressive Conservative Party, had negotiated a free-trade agreement with the United States that had yet to be ratified. The Liberal Party and the New Democratic Party, the main opposition parties, strongly opposed the agreement. Richard Johnston and colleagues (1992, 219–21) argue that the debate between the candidates, which occurred midway through the 1988 campaign, primed attitudes about this agreement. During this debate, the leader of the Liberal Party, John Turner, made the free-trade agreement even more central to the election, accusing the prime minister of selling out the country. Using surveys conducted by the Canadian National Elections Study (CNES), Johnston and colleagues (1992, 219–21) find about a 65 percent increase in the relationship between free-trade agreement attitudes and vote intent. The researchers conclude that the debate primed this issue; that is, it caused voters to place greater weight on their own opinions about the free-trade agreement when deciding how to vote. Johnston and colleagues estimate that the Progressive Conservatives lost between 1.5 and 2 percentage points to priming (Johnston et al. 1992, 224).

Although Johnston and his colleagues primarily used the CNES preelection survey (a rolling cross-section), the study does contain a panel consisting of preelection and postelection surveys, allowing me to test whether predebate attitudes about the agreement had become more predictive of vote choice when respondents were reinterviewed after the election. The question about the free-trade agreement asked whether respondents supported, opposed, or had no opinion on the agreement. For the dependent variable, I code Conservative vote 1 and Liberal or NDP vote 0. I use predebate interviews as wave 1 and postelection interviews as wave 2. I exclude respondents whose preelection interviews took place after the debate.

George W. Bush, Defense Spending, and 9/11

Although the issue of defense spending was central to American politics during the Cold War, it became less so when the Cold War ended in the early 1990s (Bartels 1994). The 9/11 terrorist attack and the war in Afghanistan, however, brought the issue back to prominence. In particular, President George W. Bush desired greater defense spending after 9/11—a clear policy position. News media coverage and the 2002 election campaign probably provided citizens with a great deal of information about this policy issue and Bush's position. Did hawkish citizens respond by favoring Bush? Did dovish citizens turn against him?

In a recent addition to the priming literature, Jonathan Ladd (2007) provides evidence that the 9/11 terrorist attack and its aftermath primed defense-spending attitudes, again making them central to American politics.[18] Using the 2000–2002 American National Election Study panel, he finds that defense spending attitudes became more predictive of presidential approval between 2000 and 2002, particularly among politically knowledgeable respondents. Unlike most previous work on priming, Ladd (2007) avoids the problem of observational equivalence by measuring defense spending attitudes in a prior survey interview. My analysis, therefore, merely replicates his findings. To do so, I measure defense-spending attitudes in 2000 with the standard ANES scale and measure support for Bush in 2000 and 2002 with the 100-point feeling thermometer. I use the 2000 preelection interviews as wave 1 and the 2002 post-election interviews as wave 2.

Bush Approval and SCHIP: A Survey Experiment

The last case I examine in this chapter is experimental. As the 2008 election approached, Democrats in Congress attempted to expand the State Children's Health Insurance Program (SCHIP). Created in 1997, SCHIP enables states to provide health care to children who have no health insurance. It covers uninsured children in families with incomes that are modest but still too high to qualify for Medicaid. In 2007, President George W. Bush, a Republican, and the Democratically controlled Congress battled over expanding SCHIP coverage from seven million people to about ten million, with Congress failing to override a Bush veto.[19]

I conducted a survey experiment intended to prime participants on this policy issue. I provide more details on this study in chapters 5 and 8 as well as in the appendix, but, briefly, the survey reinterviewed respondents who had first been interviewed, about six months earlier, for the 2007 Cooperative Congressional Election Study (Ansolabehere 2007). During the original interviews (wave 1), respondents were asked about their approval of Bush, their attitudes about SCHIP expansion, and numerous other issues. In my own study—the reinterviews (wave 2)—I had one group of respondents (the treatment group) read two short news stories about the SCHIP controversy as well as "neutral" stories on other issues and one group (the control group) read just the "neutral" stories. For reasons I explain in later chapters, this experiment also had another treatment group, which read the same stories about the SCHIP controversy, except that I had revised them slightly so that they did not mention Bush's or the Democrats' positions. I refer to the first treatment group as SCHIP info, because participants got information about these positions, and the second treatment group as the SCHIP no info. In this chapter, I only show the results for the SCHIP info group. After reading these stories, which should have primed attitudes about SCHIP, all respondents were asked a series of questions, including ones about their approval of Bush, their attitudes about SCHIP expansion, and their perception of whether or not Bush supported SCHIP expansion. To measure attitudes about SCHIP, I used the 5-point scale in the 2007 Cooperative Congressional Election Study.

3.5 Do Policy Issues Change Votes?

Priming Policy Issues in Ten Cases (Conventional Test)

In each of these ten cases, a policy issue—whether the government should pursue this or that policy—becomes prominent, and information about candidates' positions on the issue becomes available. In almost all, the parties or candidates take clear and distinct positions, so we can make straightforward predictions about how people should change their votes depending on their own views of the issue. The two exceptions are in the Chernobyl case and the defense spending in the 1980 election case, where the incumbents to some degree converge on their opponents' more popular positions (see chapters 6 and 7). Just as important for our purposes is that for each of these cases, there is a panel survey that asked people about their views on the policy issue both before and after it rises to prominence. We should therefore be able to determine whether, as these policy issues become increasingly prominent, voters increasingly take them into account when judging politicians and deciding which one to vote for. Table 3.1 lists the ten policy cases and their sample sizes.

In almost all of these cases, previous research had already concluded that voters did just that. But these studies could be wrong because they used the conventional test, which cannot rule out reverse causation.[20] Nevertheless, I begin by repeating the conventional test for each of these cases because it is undeniably suggestive and it is important to show that I can replicate previous findings. That is, the conventional test should at least show the same changes in the relationship between what voters think about a policy issue and what they think about a candidate, even if I come to an opposite conclusion about which caused which.

Figure 3.4 presents the conventional test for all ten cases. To summarize the results across these cases, it shows only the difference in issue weights for each one, which is just the difference in slopes between the panels of, for instance, figure 3.1. (For a formal definition of the conventional test, see equation 6 in the appendix. The appendix also presents the full models for all the estimates in this chapter.) To make the estimates comparable, I control only for party identification (measured in

TABLE 3.1. **The ten policy cases and their sample sizes**

	Issue	Country	Election/Year	DV	Panel obs.
1	Investing Social Security funds	US	2000	Vote Bush	479
2	Labor unions	US	1948	Vote Truman	577
3	Integration with Europe	Britain	1997	Vote Labour	847
4	Public works jobs	US	1976	Vote Carter	390
5	Defense spending	US	1980	Thermometer for Reagan	533
6	Ideology	US	1992	Approval of Bush	965
7	Nuclear power and Chernobyl	Netherlands	1986	Vote Inc. parties	785
8	Free-trade agreement	Canada	1988	Vote Conservative	511
9	Defense spending after 9/11	US	2002	Thermometer for Bush	710
10	SCHIP expansion	US	2008	Approval of Bush	446

a prior wave) and code all variables to vary between 0 and 1.[21] Consistent with previous research, the conventional test finds that in every one of these cases the policy issue does come to play a larger part in citizens' judgments about candidates in their interview after the issue became prominent (wave 3) than it did in their interview beforehand (wave 2). The issue-weight increases are moderate in size, averaging about 0.13. This implies that a citizen's shift from strongly opposing to strongly supporting a policy typically goes along with an increase in his or her approval of a candidate who supports that policy by about 13 points more on an approval scale or feeling thermometer of 0 to 100 (than it would've before the issue was salient). In vote choice cases, the same shift increases the probability of voting for a candidate by 13 percentage points more after it became salient compared to before. Based on findings like these, researchers have concluded that campaigns do prime attitudes on a wide range of specific policy issues, such as defense spending and integration with the EU, as well as activating fundamentals such as race or the economy. The key implication is that citizens do indeed reward politicians for holding policy views like their own. It would seem that citizens are judging politicians on policy, a potentially reassuring conclusion for democracy. But will three-wave (or two-wave) tests, which cannot be "fooled" by reverse causation, lead us to the same conclusions?

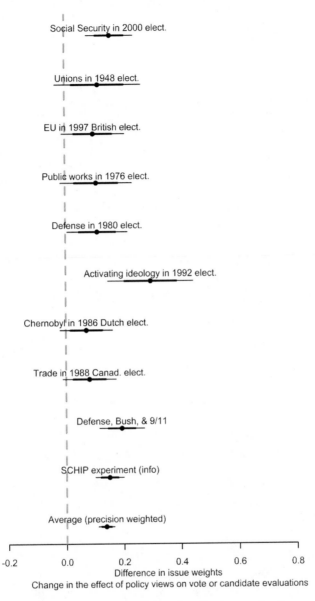

FIGURE 3.4. Summary of media priming effects on policy issues using the conventional test. This figure presents the difference in issue weights—the change in how much importance citizens attach to each issue when they judge politicians. The difference in issue weights is the difference in the slopes shown in, for example, figure 3.1 (it is calculated as $(\Delta_{ci} = b_{w3} - b_{w2})$, see equation 6 in the appendix). According to this test, citizens increasingly judged politicians on policy issues as these issues became prominent (media priming). This test, however, measures policy views after they become prominent, rendering it vulnerable to bias from reverse causation. The last estimate presents the average issue-weight difference across the cases. It weights each effect by our certainty about it (how precisely we estimate it), so effects with smaller confidence intervals (more precision) count for more. These estimates control only for party identification, though the results remain essentially unchanged without controls and with additional controls. The appendix presents the full ordinary least squares regression estimates (table 2). The thin and thick error bars show 90 percent and 68 percent confidence intervals, respectively.

Exploiting Priming Shifts in Six Cases (Three-Wave Priming Test)

I am able to study six of our ten cases using at least three waves of interviews, with the policy issue becoming prominent between waves 2 and
3, just as I did for the three economic performance cases examined in
chapter 2. This is not only arguably the best test with panel data, but it
also allows us to compare our policy-issue cases as closely as possible to
our performance-issue cases.[22] I explain the intuition behind this test in
chapter 2 and show the equations only in the appendix (equation 11).

Figure 3.5 presents the results for the first six policy-issue cases. Here
we see how issue weights change, controlling only for party identification.
Unlike the findings for the performance-issue cases and the potentially
misleading findings of the conventional test applied to these policy-issue
cases, the findings of the three-wave test here reveal no evidence that
citizens increasingly came to judge politicians on increasingly prominent policy issues. As the Truman campaign emphasized its support of
labor-friendly policies, labor union supporters were no more likely than
labor union opponents to shift their support to Truman. Similarly, pro-
ponents of the United Kingdom's further integration with Europe failed
to become more supportive of the Labour Party, which backed that policy. American defense hawks did not increasingly support Reagan, even
though he was on their side of this issue. Ideological conservatives failed
to become more approving of President Bush during the 1992 election;
in fact, they appeared to judge Bush less on ideological grounds as the
election approached.[23]

A few of the issue-weight increases are imprecisely estimated (there
are wide confidence intervals, indicating a significant possibility for error). It is therefore possible that they are consistent with modest policy
judgments. Averaging across the cases, however, suggests an absence of
such judgments; the precision-weighted average, shown at the bottom of
the figure, is tightly distributed around zero. And as in the Social Security investment case, the absence of effects is robust. Using a wide variety of models and using outcome variables other than the voter's vote—
all discussed in a later section—I still find that the public emphasis on
a policy issue failed to cause voters to shift their support to candidates
who agreed with them on that issue.

Thus, at least for these policy issues, the findings from the Social Security case appear to generalize. When we attempt to sort out what is
causing what, we find little evidence that citizens were judging politi-

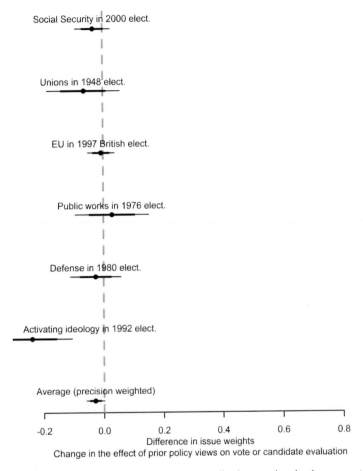

FIGURE 3.5. Summary of media priming effects on policy issues using the three-wave test. This figure presents the difference in issue weights—the change in how much importance citizens attach to each issue when they judge politicians. The difference in issue weights is the difference in the slopes shown in, for example, figure 3.2 (it is calculated as ($\Delta_{3wt} = \tilde{b}_{w2} - \tilde{b}_{w1}$), see equation 11 in the appendix). Although the conventional test generally finds priming in these cases (see the previous figure), when we test with policy views measured in a prior wave, we fail to find priming. According to this test, citizens were therefore not increasingly judging politicians on policy issues as these issues became prominent. These estimates control only for party identification, though the results remain essentially unchanged without controls and with additional controls. The comparison between the absence of effects in this figure and their presence in the economic cases (figure 2.12) is striking. The appendix presents the full ordinary least squares regression estimates (table 3). The thin and thick error bars show 90 percent and 68 percent confidence intervals, respectively.

cians on their actual positions. When these issues became prominent, citizens did not come to favor the politicians who agreed with them.

Exploiting Priming Shifts in Four More Cases
(Two-Wave Priming Test)

The results for the six policy cases are surprising. The same tests that found voters judging politicians on performance issues in chapter 2 now suggest that citizens do not judge politicians on policy issues. They also suggest that the conventional test may indeed get the story backward— that is, that voters actually begin by deciding which politician they like and then align their own policy positions with that politician's positions. I explore this possibility in chapter 8. What do we find by examining the four remaining cases, for which I had to adopt a two-wave approach?

In the two-wave test for priming, I estimate the wave 1 issue weight as in the conventional test, that is, I assess the strength of the relationship between wave 1 policy views and wave 1 evaluations or vote intentions *before* the policy has risen to prominence through the media or a campaign. I then estimate the wave 2 issue weight by estimating the strength of the relationship between wave 1 policy views (*before* the policy has risen to prominence) and wave 2 evaluations or vote intentions (*after* the policy has risen to prominence). I reuse the wave 1 policy views rather than using the wave 2 policy views because the latter could be influenced by reverse causation. (I present the two-wave test informally here and show the equations in the appendix.) To summarize, this two-wave test compares:

- the effect of wave 1 policy views on wave 1 vote or evaluations (pretreatment) with
- the effect of wave 1 policy views on wave 2 vote or evaluations (post-treatment).

Finally, I test for priming by taking the difference in these two issue weights. If the second issue weight is larger, it implies that citizens have changed the basis on which they evaluate the president or prime minister, granting more importance to the policy issue that has become more prominent. (Of course, issue weights can go down just as well as they can go up, but we have been concentrating on circumstances in which we expect them to go up.)

This approach is less desirable than the three-wave test because the "before" and "after" issue weights are computed differently.

In the end, the two-wave test finds the same general absence of policy judgments suggested by the three-wave test.[24] Figure 3.6 applies the two-wave test to all ten cases in this chapter, including the six for which we have already seen the results of the three-wave test. For those six, the two-wave test yields the same results as the three-wave test, finding no increases in issue weight. The six policy issues seemed to become more important, but in fact did not have any greater influence on how a voter judged various candidates.

Of the four cases for which I could only conduct the two-wave test, three—Chernobyl in the 1986 Dutch election, free trade in the 1980 Canadian election, and my 2008 SCHIP experiment—failed to show increases in issue weight. In these three cases, then, the conventional test appears to be wrong: voters were not using their policy views as a basis for supporting candidates who agreed with them. The absence of an effect in the Chernobyl case is especially striking. Scholars, pundits, journalists, and even the Dutch prime minister had thought that the nuclear power issue would hurt him in the aftermath of Chernobyl. Apparently, however, it did not. In chapter 6, I examine why.

In only one of these cases does the two-wave test suggest that voters *were* making policy-based judgments of their politicians. After 9/11 and the launching of the war in Afghanistan, defense hawks were more likely to become more supportive of Bush than defense doves were, implying that policy did shape their evaluations of Bush. Even in this case, though, the increase in the issue weight is not large. Imagine looking in on a passionate hawk and a passionate dove in 2000 and then again in 2002—after the 9/11 attacks, the US attack on Afghanistan, and Bush's strong support of increased military spending. After all that, the hawk's approval moved up only about 13 points more (on a scale of 0 to 100) than the dove's approval. But this case undoubtedly stands out—the only one of the ten in which we find voters increasingly judging politicians on policy grounds.

A More Sensitive Test: Priming among Those
Who Already Know Politicians' Positions

Political scientists generally test for priming among all voters in their samples. However, not all voters can be primed. In particular, many citizens remain unaware of the parties' positions on most issues. No matter

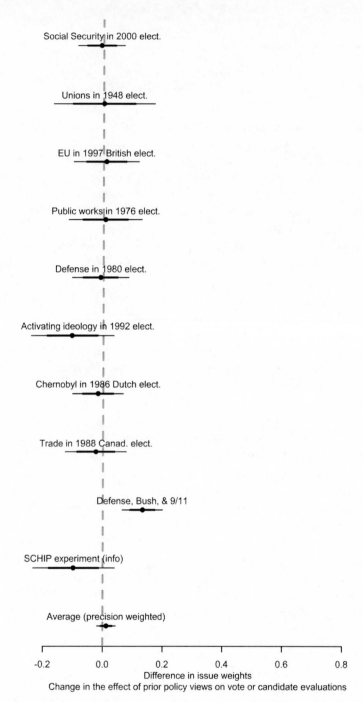

FIGURE 3.6. Summary of media priming effects based on the two-wave test. This figure presents the difference in the issue weights—the change in how much importance citizens attach to each issue when they judge politicians. (This difference is calculated as $\Delta_{2wt} = b'_{w2} - b'_{w1}$, see equation 14 in the appendix). As with the three-wave test, this test fails to find that citizens were increasingly judging politicians on policy issues as these issues became prominent. These estimates control for party identification, though the results remain essentially unchanged without controls and with additional controls. The appendix presents the full ordinary least squares regression estimates (table 4). The thin and thick error bars show 90 percent and 68 percent confidence intervals, respectively.

how salient the issue, a person cannot intentionally shift her vote to the party that shares her position unless she has some idea what that party's position is. Consequently, the analysis above, by testing among all respondents, could have failed to detect actual priming if the priming were rare enough that its effect was swamped by the "noise" of all the others among whom there was no priming. In fact, one could argue that comparing performance-issue and policy-issue priming in the full sample is unfair because citizens need to know the positions for the policy issues but not for the performance issues (everybody knows the president wants a stronger economy).[25]

To render these tests more comparable in this regard, I rerun them only for those respondents who already knew the parties' or candidates' positions before the issue came to prominence and still knew them afterward. Of the ten cases, six have questions that asked citizens to place parties or politicians on the same policy scale on which they place themselves. (For example, having asked, "On a scale of 1 to 7, do you agree or disagree with this position?" the survey then asked, "On a scale of 1 to 7, where would you place the Republican Party's position and the Democratic Party's position?") I determine who already knew these positions with an easy test—whether or not the respondent placed the parties or politicians on the correct side of each other before and after the issue became prominent (waves 2 and 3). In the European integration case, for example, I code individuals as knowing the parties' positions if they placed the Labour Party as more prointegration than the Conservative Party in 1996 and still did so in 1997.[26] One exception to this coding rule occurs in the Social Security case, where the survey only asked whether Gore and Bush favored or opposed investing. I code individuals as knowing Bush's and Gore's positions if they reported that Bush favored and Gore opposed the policy.

In the six cases with these questions, fewer than 50 percent of the respondents passed this easy test (see table 5.1 in chapter 5). I discuss the meaning of these results further in chapter 5, but it is clear enough that they show the public's startlingly poor knowledge of major candidates' and parties' public policy stances, even on the most prominent issues.

Do we find priming among those who did pass this test—the "knowers"? I search for evidence of priming again with the three-wave test but now only among the knowers. If priming does occur among this group, we should find larger effects than we did among the full sample (see figure 3.5). In all the cases, however, we again fail to find priming. That is,

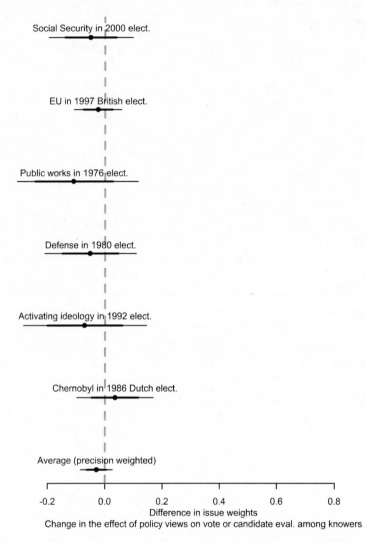

Social Security in 2000 elect.

EU in 1997 British elect.

Public works in 1976 elect.

Defense in 1980 elect.

Activating ideology in 1992 elect.

Chernobyl in 1986 Dutch elect.

Average (precision weighted)

-0.2   0.0   0.2   0.4   0.6   0.8

Difference in issue weights

Change in the effect of policy views on vote or candidate eval. among knowers

FIGURE 3.7. Summary of media priming effects on policy issues among those who know the candidates' or parties' positions (the "knowers") using the three-wave test. This figure presents the difference in issue weights—the change in how much importance citizens attach to each issue when they judge politicians. Searching for media priming among people who already know the positions provides a potentially more sensitive test, because citizens must possess some sense of these positions before they can bring their votes or candidate evaluations in line with their policy views. This figure, however, reveals no sign of priming among these knowers. The difference in issue weights is the difference in the slopes shown in, for example, figure 3.2 (it is calculated as $\Delta_{3wt} = \tilde{b}_{w2} - \tilde{b}_{w1}$, see equation 11 in the appendix). The appendix presents the full ordinary least squares regression estimates (table 8). Table 5.1 in chapter 5 shows the percentage of respondents who are knowers in each case. The thin and thick error bars show 90 percent and 68 percent confidence intervals, respectively.

the three-wave test generally fails to find policy judgments among those who possess the knowledge necessary to make them. Figure 3.7 presents these results. Given that I am only examining a subset of the full sample, the estimates are less precise (wider confidence intervals). The precision-weighted average, shown at the bottom of the figure, makes clear that the average effect across all the cases is close to zero.

I have replicated these results with the conventional and two-wave tests (see appendix table 5 and the online appendix), and they yield the same result: little or no sign of priming. I also get similar results when I measure voters' knowledge of party and candidate positions only before the policy issue becomes prominent. The failure to find priming in most of the policy-issue cases thus does not arise only because people don't know these positions. When we even the playing field between the performance and policy-issue cases by only examining those who know them, the results are the same.[27]

3.6 Alternative Explanations

The findings in this chapter contradict much of the political science literature. Voters are apparently not making the kind of judgments that in the policy-voting view are supposed to be the whole point of democracy. Can it really be true? One way political scientists try to make sure they have drawn the correct conclusions from their results is to test alternative explanations and see if they can explain the data just as well. I have explored numerous alternatives, which I describe below. Unfortunately, this requires a technical discussion. I include it because some readers rightly won't believe these findings without it and because I also apply the same robustness checks to the results in other chapters, so it is important to explain them at least once. For readers who haven't spent their lives studying research design or issue voting, this section can be skipped. The main takeaway point is that these findings cannot be easily explained away.

Effects Too Small to Detect

One concern is that media-priming effects may be occurring, but are too small to detect with samples of roughly 400 to 1,000 (see table 3.1). For several reasons, however, this seems unlikely. First, the issues I examine all received considerable attention. Several even received extraordinary attention, such as nuclear power in the 1986 Dutch election after the Chernobyl disaster, Social Security in the 2000 US election, free trade in the 1980 Canadian election, and defense spending in the 1980 US election. Although comparisons across cases are difficult, the prominence of these policy issues at these particular times seems likely to rival the prominence of the economy, if not in the 1992 election then at least in the 1996 election.

Additionally, the conventional test generally finds priming effects in the ten cases. Although not every case is statistically significant at conventional levels (as shown in figure 3.4), the results as a whole indicate that the increase in issue prominence was indeed large enough to have a discernable effect on citizens, though apparently not the one researchers expected.[28] And as I show in chapter 5, campaign and media coverage was also sufficiently intense to inform many voters about the candidates' or parties' positions.

Finally, in chapter 8, I show that the increase in prominence of these issues is associated with large effects of a very different sort: it leads many voters to follow—to adopt the policy positions of their preferred candidate or party. For all these reasons, it is hard to believe that media priming might have been there but was simply too small to detect in survey samples of admittedly modest size.

Bias Due to Prior-Attitude Substitution

Another concern is that testing with prior-wave attitudes may be overly conservative because it involves substituting those prior-wave attitudes for current attitudes. Since people's attitudes tend to change over time, earlier attitudes are certainly not perfect substitutes for later attitudes. In the 1948 election, for example, people may have changed their attitudes about unions in response to the campaign or to other intervening events, or they may simply have changed their minds with the passing of time. June attitudes about unions are therefore certainly not perfect substitutes for November (postelection) attitudes about unions. In general, the less accurate the substitution, the greater the bias *against* finding priming effects with the three-wave test. If attitudes are measured years earlier, the bias may be large.[29]

For several reasons, however, this conservative bias does not appear to be severe. First, despite the bias we do find priming effects in the three performance-issue cases discussed in chapter 2.[30] We also find them in one policy case—defense spending and 9/11—even though two years have passed between the waves of interviews. Yet in many of the cases where we fail to find effects, the time between waves is only a few months. It does not seem, then, that the lag in measuring attitudes is in itself a serious obstacle to detecting media priming.

Second, the effects fail to decline as the time between interviews increases, suggesting that this bias is not large (Lenz 2006).

Third, the failure to find effects holds even when I use an estimator, called instrumental variables, which is not vulnerable to this particular bias, although it is vulnerable to others.[31]

Fourth, as I have already noted, I also generally fail to find priming effects with the conventional test among those who already know the positions (shown in appendix table 5). This result is reassuring because the conventional test lacks the (potential) conservative bias as it does not use prior attitudes.[32]

All told, then, if there is a conservative bias due to the lag in measuring attitudes, it doesn't show any consistent tendency to keep us from detecting media priming.

Bias Due to the Particular Model of Judgment

Another concern involves correctly modeling citizens' judgments about politicians. Researchers have presented conflicting evidence on how citizens treat issues when judging politicians (Lewis and King 2000; Macdonald, Rabinowitz, and Listhaug 1998; Rabinowitz and Macdonald 1989; Westholm 1997). In this chapter, the statistical tests assume that citizens judge politicians in a particular way. Specifically, the tests assume that the more a citizen supports a policy, the more he or she supports a politician who supports that policy. An alternative view is that citizens judge politicians on proximity. That is, if you favor cutting defense spending, but not too much, while candidate A favors cutting it extremely and candidate B favors leaving it alone, it might make sense for you to vote for candidate B, whose defense budget would more closely resemble your own (an example of proximity), rather than for candidate A, even though candidate A is the one who is actually on your side on the principle of cutting the defense budget.

I model judgments as I do for several reasons. First, proximity models could be biased in favor of finding issue voting because citizens may project their own policy positions onto their preferred politicians (Brody and Page 1972; Markus and Converse 1979).[33] Second, with my approach, I can apply the same model in the policy and performance cases.

Nevertheless, in cases where respondents have been asked to place politicians' positions on multipoint scales, I can repeat these tests with proximity (or distance) models. When I do so—across a variety of proximity specifications—I continue to find the same results: no evidence that citizens increasingly judge politicians on policy.[34] See the online appendix for these and other robustness checks.

Bias Due to Lack of Controls and Interactions with Political Knowledge

In the ten policy-issue cases considered in this chapter, I only control for party identification. The absence of priming (or, in one case, its presence), however, is robust to numerous control variables and interactions between these controls and policy views.[35] For example, including political knowledge and interactions between policy views and levels of political knowledge leaves the results unchanged (these political knowledge interactions are generally small and not significantly different from zero).

Bias Due to Outcome Variable, Strategic Voting, and Third-Party Voting

Finally, many of these cases use vote as the outcome variable; they examine the change from how one had intended to vote before the issue became prominent (vote intent) to how one did vote after the issue had become prominent (vote choice). But given that the policies I examine are only one of many factors that could influence citizens' votes, the increased salience of these issues may not be enough to change many votes.

Put differently, priming may change citizens' views about the parties or candidates, but not enough to change their vote choice, which may be based on many considerations. Since the performance-issue cases all use presidential approval as the outcome variable, while some of the policy-issue cases use voting decisions, the disparity in these two sets of findings could have resulted merely from having used different outcome variables, one of which could be changed by priming and one of which could not. However plausible, I find no support for this contention. When I use feeling thermometers or party-favorability scales as my outcomes instead of using vote, I find exactly the same results: no evidence that citizens increasingly judged politicians or parties on policy issues. I find this result with the two-wave test, the three-wave test, and the conventional test among the knowers. Since these measures all contain more information than binary vote choice, and since they include larger samples of individuals (because nonvoters are included), these tests should be able to pick up smaller effects. Nevertheless, they still do not reveal media priming.[36] They therefore further support a general absence of policy judgments by citizens. These important robustness checks may also address concerns about strategic voting and third party voting.

3.7 Conclusion

When George W. Bush campaigned in 2000 on his proposal to invest Social Security funds in the stock market, he presumably hoped to gain the votes of voters who supported this proposal. As I showed in the first section of this chapter, however, his strategy apparently failed. Despite this issue becoming highly prominent, he neither attracted supporters of that policy (any more than he had already attracted them) nor repelled those who opposed it (any more than he had already repelled them).

Bush's experience appears to reflect a general pattern. Examining a broad range of policy issues on which candidates campaigned on opposing policies, I found little evidence that citizens altered their support for politicians in response to their own policy views (measured before the issues became prominent). That is, I found little evidence that citizens led on policy—that they rewarded candidates with whom they agreed on policy issues or punished candidates with whom they disagreed. While I found evidence for leading in all three performance-issue cases in chapter 2, I found it in only one of the ten policy-issue cases in this chapter.

Although the findings indicate that citizens rarely judge politicians on policy, it's premature to draw strong conclusions about democracy. Even the results we have seen so far indicate that in at least one case—defense spending between 2000 and 2002—citizens did appear to be judging politicians on policy grounds. And we have only reached the end of chapter 3.

The findings reported in this chapter raise a number of other issues that surface throughout this book. All along I have stressed the risk of pronounced bias from reverse causation in issue-voting studies. This chapter provides the book's first indication that such fears are justified. When we measure citizens' policy views only after the issues became prominent (the conventional test), as most observational and experimental studies do, we find that citizens increasingly judged politicians on these policy issues.[37] But when we switch to measuring citizens' policy views in prior waves, we fail to find this evidence. In chapter 8 I examine the tendency for people to follow their preferred politicians and show that it can generate biases large enough to explain these results.

Although my focus is on using media priming to detect policy judgments, not on media priming itself, the consistent absence of such priming is noteworthy. Research on priming revived scholarly interest in campaign and media effects and implied, according to some, that campaigns and the media can manipulate voters. The findings in this chapter suggest that such conclusions were premature, at least for policy issues. Campaigns and the media may lack the power scholars have thought they had to significantly affect elections by turning voters' minds to important (or seemingly important) policy issues. The bright side of voters' apparent indifference to policy issues is that they may not be as vulnerable to manipulation on these issues (at least not through priming) as scholars have suggested. Another implication is that setting a policy agenda need not be a candidate's first priority.

Finally, this chapter is the first of three that exploits shifts in people's thinking between panel waves to search for policy voting, while measuring their policy views in prior waves—the next two examine persuasion and learning about politicians' positions. This approach has a critical benefit: it allows me to overcome the problem of observational equivalence. But this benefit comes at a cost. I briefly noted limitations at the end of chapter 1, but it's worth reviewing them. In particular, the inferences I draw may be less general, applying only to the particular types of people who experience these particular types of shifts. I may therefore miss issue voting among people who, for instance, are immune to media priming because they already cared so much about Social Security policy before the 2000 campaign that the tremendous campaign and media attention failed to increase the salience of this issue.

Another limitation is that because of the available panel data, I search for effects only during election campaigns. It is possible that during a campaign, voters may be too swept up in partisan feelings to be willing to shift support to the other party even if its most prominent policy positions are closer to the voters' own. Perhaps voters are willing to change their assessments and judgments when the campaign and election are over. The absence of policy issues relating to social groups, such as race (Hurwitz and Peffley 2005; Mendelberg 2001) or social issues (Hillygus and Shields 2008), is another lacuna. Although several panel studies suggest that these policy views can matter (Carsey and Layman 2006; Tesler 2011), the evidence remains limited.

It's also worth noting that the failure to find policy voting in this chapter could have occurred, not because people just do not care about these issues, but for less troubling reasons, such as strategic behavior on the part of candidates. In the United States, we know that candidates from both parties tend to advertise on the same set of issues (Sides 2006). By bringing up competing arguments and frames (Chong and Druckman 2007), candidates may undermine citizens' confidence in their own views, making them unlikely to vote on an issue. In the 2000 campaign, for example, Gore strategists believed they neutralized any advantage Bush might have garnered from his popular Social Security proposal by raising doubts in supporters' minds about its financial feasibility (Jamieson and Waldman 2001, 173). Another strategic explanation, which I discuss in the conclusion, is that politicians may neutralize potentially damaging policy issues by adopting their opponent's more popular stances (before or during the campaign). Since candidates generally campaign only on policy issues on which they disagree with their opponents, they end up campaigning only on issues that interest the public little.

Chapter 9 elaborates on these and other limitations. Despite them, this chapter's results make clear that campaign and media influence is more challenging to detect than previously thought—at least through media priming. They also make clear that, when research is designed to sort out what is causing what, finding evidence that policy views influence votes is hard—much harder than cross-sectional studies imply.

CHAPTER FOUR

Changing Views, Changing Votes?
Performance versus Policy

In the 2000 US presidential election, Al Gore's character came under attack. The attacks came from many sides and hit on several aspects of his character, but they were mostly about his alleged lying and exaggeration. In the best-known example, journalists caught Gore lying about his mother-in-law paying three times as much for her arthritis medicine as Gore paid for the same medicine for his dog. As Richard Johnston, Michael Hagen, and Kathleen Hall Jamieson (2004, 129–43) have shown, the breaking of this story coincided with a considerable drop in evaluations of Gore's character and may ultimately have contributed to his defeat.

It would seem, from Johnston, Hagen, and Jamieson's account, that voters judged Gore on a character trait relevant to his potential performance as president: trustworthiness. If so, it strengthens the case made in chapter 2 that citizens appear to judge politicians on performance-related issues. In chapter 2, the issue was how the economy was doing—a possible outcome of the president's performance—while here it is personal character—an input into a potential president's performance.

Johnston, Hagen, and Jamieson's account also suggests another way we can try to detect whether voters judge politicians on substance. In chapters 2 and 3, I used instances of media priming—increasing an issue's salience—as opportunities to see if and when voters based their voting decisions and their judgments of politicians on substantial matters of policy and performance. In this chapter I take advantage of another kind of shift in people's thinking: *persuasion*. Persuasion shifts what people think about an issue; media priming shifts the issues that people are thinking about. I use instances of persuasion to examine whether, when voters change their views on a particular policy or a particular politician's performance, they subsequently change their support for particular politicians accordingly. This is what voters appear to have done in 2000, when some were persuaded that Gore was not as honest as they might have thought and subsequently shifted their support from Gore to Bush. If the findings from the previous two chapters are correct, we should find that persuasion on performance-related issues generally leads people to change their votes or their overall evaluations of politicians, but persuasion on policy issues does not.

(One might be wondering whether the news stories about Gore's alleged dishonesty could have induced priming in addition to persuasion. It likely did both—it persuaded people to see Gore as less honest and made the issue of honesty more prominent. These distinct effects can occur separately or together. If, for example, former President Bill Clinton were to run for office again, his opponents would try to raise the salience of his former marital infidelity but would be unlikely to persuade, since citizens already know about it. Since the allegations in Gore's case, however, were new to most voters, they likely did both. I focus on persuasion in this case because detecting media priming is difficult when people's attitudes are changing or are initially poorly developed.[1])

Although research studies have probed the causes of changes in policy views (Cobb and Kuklinski 1997; Sniderman, Brody, and Tetlock 1991), especially politicians' abilities to sway the public (Carmines and Kuklinski 1990; Iyengar and Kinder 1987; Kuklinski and Hurley 1994; Lupia 1994; Lupia 1995; Mondak 1993; Zaller 1992), surprisingly few have examined whether persuading people on the issues ultimately changes their votes or presidential approval.[2] In part, the lack of research stems from the paucity of panel surveys, without which the study of persuasion's effects is difficult.

Using instances of persuasion to study citizens' judgments of politicians is more difficult than using instances of media priming. With priming we can measure a person's policy-related or performance-related views in one set of interviews and his or her judgments of politicians in a later set of interviews. This allows us to be more certain that the view is the cause and that judgment of the politicians is the effect. We assume—rightly or wrongly—that people's views are not changing, but the salience of the issue is. With persuasion, however, we want to take advantage of changes in views, but that makes it harder to discern what is causing what.

To disentangle causation, I again try to separate cause and effect with time. I examine whether, when individuals change their policy or performance views between the first two panel waves, they then change their support for politicians accordingly by the third wave. For example, if a person is persuaded to view Gore as dishonest between her first and second interviews, is she more likely to shift her vote to Bush between her second and third interviews? Although this approach will miss shorter-term effects—an obvious disadvantage—it has a key advantage of being invulnerable to the problem of reverse causation; that is, it overcomes the problem of observational equivalence.

As we will see in this chapter, the results of this type of analysis turn out to be surprisingly consistent with those of previous chapters. That is, when people change their performance-related assessments—for example, seeing Gore as less honest—they do later change their support for politicians accordingly. When they change their policy views, however, they do not later change their support accordingly. Once more, we find citizens judging politicians on performance, but not on policy.

4.1 Honesty, Gore, and the Prior-Persuasion Test

Based on Johnston, Hagen, and, Jamieson's (2004, 129–43) content analysis of ads and network news during the 2000 campaign, the attack on Gore's character began in earnest with a barrage of Bush advertising in September 2000. Bush's ads interwove well-worn conservative slogans, statements about his personal commitment to widely shared values, and subtle reminders of the Clinton-Gore administration's failings. One ad quoted Bush saying, "I believe we need to encourage personal *responsibility* so people are accountable for their actions. And I believe in government that is *responsible* to the people. That's the difference in philosophy between my opponent and me. He *trusts* government, I trust you" (Johnston, Hagen, and, Jamieson 2004, 129).

These ads were followed by a series of news stories attacking Gore's character, including the one about the cost of medicine for his mother-in-law and dog. The news stories included claims that he was pandering to the public by calling for President Clinton to release oil from the strategic petroleum reserve, that he had lied about accompanying the Federal Emergency Management chief on tours of brush fires in Texas, that he was misleading the public about the size of his new spending plans, and that he had mischaracterized his own previous statements about Governor Bush.

Did this affect voters' assessments of Gore's character? Johnston and colleagues asked respondents how well the following traits describe Gore: "really cares about people like me" and "honest." The news stories coincided with a considerable drop in evaluation for both those traits, particularly for honesty. The researchers find no similar drops for other traits, including "inspiring," "knowledgeable," and "strong leader." Persuasion on Gore's character, they conclude, may have ultimately helped Bush defeat him.

Johnston and colleagues' careful analysis of television news, campaign advertising, and public opinion during this period is compelling and suggests that people do indeed judge politicians on performance assessments. Nonetheless, these researchers could have the story backward. Citizens could have decided to vote against Gore for other reasons and then projected their dislike onto their assessments of his character. They might, for example, have decided that Gore was too intellectual or too liberal and then simply gone along with the accusations of dishonesty when they arose, rather than being persuaded by them.

To increase our certainty about this finding, I reexamine this case, focusing on ruling out reverse causation. To do so I use what I call the prior-persuasion test. I examine whether persuasion between two earlier survey interviews leads to a change in vote or presidential approval in the next interview. Following Johnston and colleagues I analyze the 2000 National Annenberg Election Study—the same study used in the Social Security case in chapter 3. The *Boston Globe* broke the mother-in-law–versus–dog story about Gore on September 19. According to Johnston and colleagues' analysis, evaluations of Gore's character began dropping soon afterward. So I check whether people who change their minds about Gore's honesty between August (wave 1) and late October (wave 2) are more likely to change their minds about whom to vote for between late October (wave 2) and interviews conducted after the election (wave 3).[3] If they are, I contend that we have even stronger evidence that persuasion on honesty—a performance issue—matters.

The prior-persuasion test has advantages and disadvantages. Its main advantage is that it reduces concerns about reverse causation. Its main disadvantage is that it can miss the persuasion effects it is meant to detect. If the persuasion that takes place between waves 1 and 2 has already affected people's voting decisions by wave 2, then there won't be any change in voting decisions left to detect between waves 2 and 3—the change will already have happened and this test will miss it. The prior-persuasion test is therefore a conservative test of policy and performance judgments; it will likely underestimate any effect.

To measure perceptions of honesty, I use a survey question that asked, "Does the word 'honest' describe Al Gore (or George Bush) extremely well, quite well, not too well, or not well at all?" Coded to a 100-point scale, Gore's mean score was 49 in August but fell to 40 in October ($p < 0.001$, $n = 380$). In contrast, assessments of Bush's honesty on the same scale remained constant at about 60. Since different respondents might have interpreted the scales differently—some might just rate all candidates as less honest—I use the difference between the two measurements; that is, not how honest one thinks Bush is and how honest one thinks Gore is, but how much more honest one thinks one is than the other. A positive value for this "Bush-Gore honesty gap" indicates viewing Bush as more honest than Gore, while a negative value indicates viewing Gore as more honest than Bush. (The results are similar, though slightly weaker, if I just use Gore honesty instead of the honesty gap.)

Between August and late October, about 40 percent of panel respondents changed their minds and came to see Bush as more honest than Gore, while only 20 percent changed their minds and came to see Bush as less honest than Gore. The remaining 40 percent didn't change their minds at all about the candidates' relative honesty. Figure 4.1 presents this finding with a histogram of change in the honesty gap, showing the breakdown of shifts in views. Given its coding, change in the honesty gap can vary from -100 to 100, with 100 indicating a person who entirely reversed his or her perception in Bush's favor (which no one actually did).

Figure 4.2 presents this approach visually. (I show the equations and full models in the appendix.[4]) The horizontal axis represents change in perceptions about who was more honest—Bush or Gore—between waves 1 and 2 (that is, changes in the honesty gap, which is also what is represented in figure 4.1). The more to the right or left on the horizontal axis, the more one's opinion has changed (the more the honesty gap has widened) in Bush's or Gore's favor, respectively. The vertical axis represents change in the "feeling gap"—the difference in how "warmly" the respondent feels about Bush and about Gore—between waves 2 and 3, using

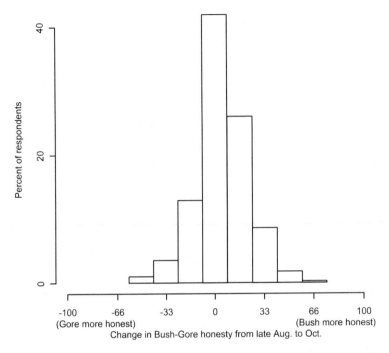

FIGURE 4.1. Histogram of persuasion on Gore's and Bush's honesty in the 2000 election. The public came to see Bush as more honest than Gore between the late August and October waves. To show this persuasion, I subtract late August Bush-Gore honesty gap from the October Bush-Gore honesty gap. Since both variables vary from 0 to 100, this *change in honesty gap* variable can vary from −100 to 100. As is evident, many maintain the same view of Gore's honesty relative to Bush's (0)—no change in the honesty gap—but many also come to view Bush as more honest than Gore, and fewer come to see Gore as more honest than Bush. Source: 2000 Annenberg Election Study, Multi-Reinterview Panel A.

the 100-point comparative feeling thermometer. To be clear, the horizontal axis is showing whether people changed their minds between August and October about which candidate was more honest, while the vertical axis is showing whether people changed their minds between October and November (postelection) about which candidate they liked better. And the big question is: does the former cause the latter? This is not a foregone conclusion. Voters might, for example, change their minds and decide that Bush is more honest than Gore but still intend to vote for Gore because they feel he is the more competent candidate or that he supports the right policies. If the two changes are related, then it suggests that honesty matters. Moreover, it does so while ruling out reverse causation.

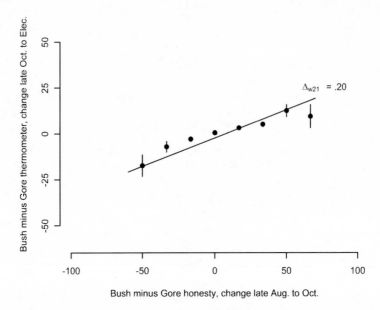

FIGURE 4.2. Prior-persuasion test on honesty and Gore in the 2000 election—partial residual scatterplot. This figure shows that people who came to see Bush as more honest than
Gore later came to like Bush more than Gore. It presents the residual change using the
comparative feeling thermometer (instead of vote) by partial residual change in perceptions of the gap in honesty between Bush and Gore. The partial residuals are calculated
from the model in column 4 of table 4.1, which controls for prior level and prior change on
numerous variables (Δ_{x21}, see equation 15 in the appendix). Error bars show 68 percent confidence intervals. Source: 2000 Annenberg Election Study, Multi-Reinterview Panel A.

In fact, figure 4.2 shows that persuasion on honesty did appear to matter. The degree to which it mattered is shown by the slope of the line. In
this case, the slope suggests a moderately sized effect of 0.20. Given that
both variables involve change, interpreting this slope is a tad awkward.
It implies that a shift of one position on the comparative honesty scale
(33 points) between waves 1 and 2 leads to a (0.20 × 33 =) 6.6-point increase in Bush support relative to Gore on the 100-point comparative
thermometer between waves 2 and 3. Prior persuasion on Gore's honesty, therefore, appears to cause a subsequent change in evaluations of
the candidates, supporting the Johnston and colleagues finding.

This figure shows the finding from using feeling thermometers, which
produce an eye-pleasing plot, but we get the same finding when we use
vote as the outcome variable; that is, if we look for how persuasion

changes (or fails to change) how a voter intends to vote rather than how much he or she likes one candidate more than the other (see table 4.1).

These results also account for a large battery of control variables, which help rule out alternative explanations. Readers unfamiliar with statistics can the skip the rest of this paragraph, a technical explanation of the controls I use. Since either vote or the comparative feeling thermometer in wave 1 (August) may influence change in honesty assessments and change in vote, I control for wave 1 vote (making this a model of change in vote)—I refer to this as controlling for the *prior level*. In case other variables predispose people to change their honesty assessments and their votes, I likewise control for other performance assessments and for policy views in wave 1 (see the appendix). But I have to worry not only about the level of the variables in wave 1 but also about change, which could drive later shifts in honesty assessments and vote. I therefore also control for change on vote between waves 1 and 2 on all the controls—I refer to this as controlling for the *prior change*. Since vote is a binary variable, it may not control with sufficient precision for prior level of candidate support and change in support, so I also control in the vote models for the wave 1 comparative thermometer and for change in the comparative thermometer between waves 2 and 3. To render the estimates comparable across cases, I use ordinary least squares.[5] Table 4.1 presents the full regression models, the last of which is used to produce the figure. Even with extensive controls, prior change in views about Gore's honesty relative to Bush's honesty appears to matter. The effects are not large, but this test probably underestimates the actual effect because of the time lag.

This finding is robust. It holds with and without controls for prior change on vote, feelings about the candidates, and the other variables. It also passes what is called a placebo test, which further addresses the concern that something other than persuasion could have led people to believe Gore was dishonest and to vote against him. This placebo test involves checking whether the same effect occurs with feelings about President Clinton as the outcome variable instead of vote. If the effect we see—subsequent changes in voters' intent—is actually a result of prior persuasion on Gore's honesty, we should *not* find that this persuasion also brings about a subsequent change in feelings about Clinton. If it does, it would suggest that other factors, such as a general anti-Democratic trend, are giving rise to change in voter intent (that is, a switch from supporting Gore to supporting Bush). Reassuringly, the effect is

TABLE 4.1. **Persuasion on honesty and vote in the 2000 election**

Dependent variable	(1) Vote w3	(2) Vote w3	(3) Comp. therm. w3	(4) Comp. therm. w3
Honest w2-w1 (Δ_{x21})	0.21*	0.13*	0.20*	0.20*
	(0.060)	(0.068)	(0.035)	(0.035)
Honest w2	0.22*	0.085	0.18*	0.17*
	(0.062)	(0.090)	(0.042)	(0.042)
Vote w2-w1	0.58*	0.52*		
	(0.042)	(0.044)		
Vote w1	0.87*	0.77*		
	(0.031)	(0.041)		
Comp. therm. w2-w1		0.16*	0.59*	0.54*
		(0.087)	(0.039)	(0.040)
Comp. therm. w1		0.073	0.87*	0.77*
		(0.092)	(0.038)	(0.043)
Party id w1		0.075		0.066*
		(0.046)		(0.020)
Party id w2-w1		0.12*		−0.0021
		(0.055)		(0.029)
Economy w1		−0.012		−0.0023
		(0.046)		(0.022)
Economy w2-w1		0.046		0.0096
		(0.049)		(0.025)
Tax cuts w1		−0.079*		−0.014
		(0.040)		(0.020)
Tax cuts w2-w1		0.027		−0.025
		(0.042)		(0.021)
Social Security w1		0.086		−0.0097
		(0.058)		(0.029)
Social Security w2-w1		0.054		0.024
		(0.048)		(0.025)
Liberal w1		−0.054*		0.0061
		(0.029)		(0.015)
Liberal w2-w1		0.0047		0.0063
		(0.031)		(0.016)
Conservative w1		0.030		0.029*
		(0.027)		(0.013)
Conservative w2-w1		0.026		0.013
		(0.028)		(0.014)
n	380	380	539	539
R^2	0.883	0.893	0.870	0.876
SER	0.17	0.17	0.10	0.10

Note: Ordinary least squares regression estimates with standard errors in parentheses. Constant not shown.
* $p < 0.1$.

absent on the Clinton thermometer (0.02, SE = 0.05), so we really do seem to be witnessing the effect of persuasion on a candidate's potential performance on voters' intent to vote for that candidate or for another.

These analyses provide further evidence that performance matters. Citizens who were persuaded during the campaign that Gore was less honest than Bush later appear more likely to shift their support to Bush. These findings may reflect positively on citizens, as they indicate that substantive issues matter to citizens. They are not, however, entirely reassuring. As commentators have noted, Bush made his own misstatements during the 2000 campaign and Gore's misstatements were not obviously worse or more frequent than Bush's, though Gore's received considerably more media coverage. So although the public may have judged Gore on a performance issue, it may not have done so wisely.

4.2 Persuasion on Six Policy and Six Performance Issues

Untangling causation with public opinion and voting data is extraordinarily difficult. The prior-persuasion test provides us with another tool to help sort out what is causing what. We can apply it not only to performance issues, such as honesty, but also to policy issues.

Consider again the case of the 1948 presidential election campaign. According to the previous chapter's findings, Truman's appeals to ordinary folk failed to prime views about the New Deal. Truman's appeals, however, may have influenced the election in a different way—through persuasion rather than through priming. Over the course of the campaign, Truman's rhetoric appears to have convinced many individuals not to place more importance on New Deal policies but to support those policies. As discussed in the previous chapter, the Elmira panel contains few questions about New Deal policies, but responses to its most relevant question—attitude about labor unions—suggest that Truman's rhetoric may have indeed been persuasive. Support for labor unions rises from 53 in June 1948 to 60 in October 1948 ($p < 0.001$, $n = 454$), the only waves in which the question is asked.[6] This shift, possibly reflecting a broader shift in support for New Deal policies, may have helped Truman come from behind to defeat Dewey.

To examine whether persuasion on policy also matters, I apply the prior-persuasion test to the Truman case and to those of the other policy-issue cases that have at least three panel waves: Social Security in the 2000 election, public works in the 1976 election, defense in the 1980 election, activating ideology in the 1992 election, and European integration in the 1997 British election.

To ensure that the performance results in the honesty case replicate, I also apply the test to a group of other performance cases: the three economic cases from chapter 2, all of which contain three waves, and two new performance cases, the 1991 Gulf War and Sarah Palin in the 2008 election. I now introduce these two new cases.[7]

Persuasion and the Gulf War

In the wake of the first Gulf War, approval of President George H. W. Bush's handling of the Gulf crisis (that is, Iraq's invasion and annexation of oil-rich Kuwait) rose dramatically. Bush's management of the multinational coalition and its victory over Saddam Hussein's armies led many Americans to change their approval of his performance on this issue. In the American National Election Study 1990–91–92 Panel, approval of his handling of the crisis rises from 58 prewar to 80 postwar (on a 100-point scale)—a large shift. In fact, more than 10 percent of the sample (122 of 939 respondents) shift the full length of the scale in a positive direction; that is, before the war, they strongly disapprove of Bush's handling of the Gulf crisis, but after the war, strongly approve of his handling of the crisis. Figure 4.3 presents a histogram of this change.

But did those who came to believe that Bush handled the crisis well also shift their overall approval of Bush? Jon Krosnick and Laura Brannon (1993) present evidence that they did. They find that about 80 percent of the increase in overall Bush approval arises from persuasion—being convinced that Bush had done a good job—while only 20 percent arises from priming—being made more aware of the job Bush had done.[8] Although their priming and persuasion findings suggest that citizens indeed judged Bush on his handling of the war, they could have the story backward. People could have come to approve of Bush overall in the Gulf War's immediate aftermath not because they approved of his handling of the war, but because they more frequently saw him looking presidential on television or because his opponents held back from criticizing the president during a war. Nevertheless, persuasion seems eminently plausible.

To examine this case, I again use the American National Election Study 1990–91–92 Panel, the same one used in the economy and ideology cases. I test whether citizens who were persuaded between 1990 (wave 1) and 1991 (wave 2) that President Bush had done a good (or bad) job handling the Gulf crisis were then more likely—on account of that persuasion—to approve more (or less) of President Bush between 1991 (wave 2) and 1992 (wave 3). Put differently, I examine whether we can still find traces of a 1991 Gulf War halo in the 1992 election.

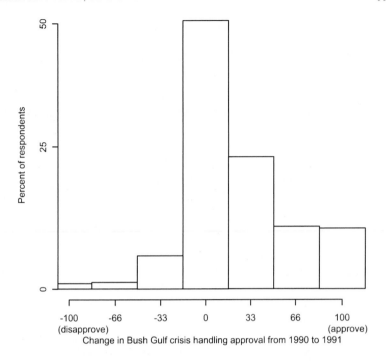

FIGURE 4.3. Histogram of persuasion on Bush's handling of the Gulf crisis. Becoming more approving of Bush's handling of the Gulf crisis in the wake of the war. To show persuasion, I subtract 1990 Gulf crisis handling approval from that of 1991. Since both variables vary from 0 to 100, this change variable varies from −100 to 100. Many people become more approving of Bush's handling after the war (1991), though about 50 percent maintain the same approval (whether high or low), and some become less approving. Source: 1990–91–92 ANES panel.

Sarah Palin

Changing views about Sarah Palin, the Republican Party's 2008 nominee for vice president, and the consequences for John McCain, its presidential nominee, provide another opportunity to search for performance judgments. In a series of interviews with CBS evening news anchor Katie Couric, Palin met with disaster. Her responses showed a lack of understanding of key national issues, including the constitutional right to privacy that forms the basis of *Roe v. Wade*. At times her responses were also incoherent. When asked about the Bush administration's proposed emergency bailout of financial institutions, Palin struggled to find an answer, meandering disjointedly from one unrelated topic to the next.

The interview train wreck, which followed a series of other missteps, coincided with a collapse in support for Palin—one that had obvious consequences for the decision to vote for or against McCain. Arguably, her collapse was due to concern about a performance-related trait—competency—which was particularly relevant given McCain's age. Moreover, by choosing her, McCain may have raised doubts about his own judgment. As McCain admits in his memoir, his decision making tends to be rash: "I make [decisions] as quickly as I can. . . . Often my haste is a mistake" (2002, 61). His last-minute decision to nominate Palin arguably exemplified this trait, one the public may find undesirable in a president.

According to Richard Johnston and Emily Thorson's analysis (2009), Palin's collapse coincides with a precipitous drop in support for McCain. To confirm Johnston and Thorson's findings, I examine this case using the prior-persuasion test. The American National Election Study 2008 panel asked about vote (McCain versus Obama) and support for Palin in September, October, and postelection. The question about Palin asked, "Do you like Sarah Palin, dislike her, or neither like nor dislike her?" A follow-up question asked respondents whether they like or dislike her "a great deal," "a moderate amount," or "a little." Ideally, it would have queried respondents about her competence. Since it only asked for overall assessments, aspects other than Palin's performance—anything from her conservative views to her hairstyle—could influence people's answers. I am therefore cautious about interpreting any effect as related to performance. To attempt to rule out such policy explanations, I control for economic perceptions, 7-point ideology, gay marriage, abortion, and an index of economic policy (see the appendix).

Figure 4.4 shows respondents liking Palin a bit less between September (wave 1) and October (wave 2). To see whether this shift hurt McCain, I examine whether it leads to vote change between October (wave 2) and Election Day (wave 3).

Persuasion Findings on Six Policy and Six Performance Issues

If the results from previous chapters hold, persuasion on performance-related issues (such as Gore's honesty and George H. W. Bush's handling of a crisis) should influence preferences about politicians, but persuasion on policy issues (such as defense spending, public works, and European Union membership) should not. This is precisely what I find.

Before presenting the results, I make three technical comments. First,

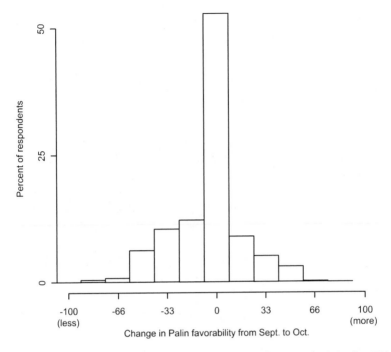

FIGURE 4.4. Histogram of persuasion on support for Sarah Palin in the 2008 election. This histogram shows support for Palin in October minus support for Palin in September. Since both variables vary from 0 to 100, this change variable varies from −100 to 100. Source: 2008–9 ANES panel study.

several of these eleven cases exhibit average change in views between waves 1 and 2—net persuasion, such as we see in the case of Gore's honesty in the 2000 election and the case of support for unions in the 1948 election—but not all do. In the case of the economy in 1992, for example, the average response to the economy question remains similar in waves 1 and 2. In such cases we may still observe considerable changes in people's opinions between waves 1 and 2, but some may be in one direction (the economy is getting better) and some in the other direction (the economy is getting worse), so that there appears to be no net persuasion.[9] The prior-persuasion test exploits this change.

Second, as I have already noted, the effects of persuasion may occur too quickly to be captured by panel waves that are often months or years apart. In the 1996 economy case, for instance, a person who changed her view about the economy between 1992 and 1994 may also have changed her view of the president by 1994 (if she changed it at all). If she has, this test would miss the effects persuasion had had on her. Prior-persuasion testing is thus likely to be biased against finding effects.

Third, I use the same outcome variables as in previous chapters with one exception. Since I have a policy and a performance case from the 1980 election—the economy and defense—I adopt the same outcome variable, approval of Carter, in both cases. The results are similar to those found with other outcome variables, including a Reagan feeling thermometer and the difference between a Reagan feeling thermometer and a Carter feeling thermometer.

Consistent with chapter 3's failure to find policy voting (as opposed to performance voting), the prior-persuasion tests also reveal little evidence of policy voting. Persuasion on policy issues certainly occurs but rarely, the test suggests, changes voters' judgments of politicians. In order to summarize the results across all the cases, I present only the key estimate of interest, which is the effect of change in policy view between waves 1 and 2 on change in vote or presidential approval between waves 2 and 3—e.g., the slope in figure 4.2 (Δ_{x21}, see equation 15 in the appendix). I use the same model I used in the case of Gore's honesty and thus control for voters' wave 1 vote intent and shifts between wave 1 and wave 2 vote (or other outcome variable).[10] So as not to bias the results against finding effects in the policy cases, the only additional control I include is party identification (both prior responses to party identification and prior change in party identification).

Figure 4.5 presents the prior-persuasion test for the six policy cases. To be clear about what these estimates capture, it might help to remember that they represent slopes like that in figure 4.2. The larger the estimate (the steeper the slope), the more prior persuasion on the policy issue leads to later change in vote or candidate evaluations. As the figure makes clear, we see little evidence that persuasion mattered on these policy issues. The estimates (slopes) are all close to zero and their confidence intervals all overlap with zero. These estimates imply, for example, that once people became more supportive of investing Social Security funds, an issue in the 2000 election, they did not later become more supportive of Bush, the candidate promoting that policy. Several are imprecisely estimated (they have wide confidence intervals, indicating uncertainty about the true effect sizes). It is therefore possible that they are consistent with modest policy judgments, such as with changes in attitudes about labor unions in the 1948 election. Averaging across the cases, however, suggests an absence of such judgments; the

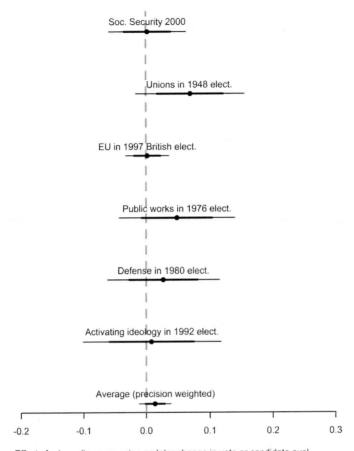

Effect of prior policy persuasion on later change in vote or candidate eval.

FIGURE 4.5. Summary of prior-persuasion test on policy issues. For each policy issue, it shows the effect of changes in policy views between waves 1 and 2 on changes in votes or approval of the president between waves 2 and 3 (Δ_{x21}, see equation 15 in the appendix). These estimates, it might help to remember, represent slopes like that in figure 4.2. The larger the estimate (steeper slope), the more prior persuasion on the issue matters. The figure reveals no persuasion effects on policy issues. The appendix presents the least squares regression estimates (table 6). The thin and thick error bars show 90 percent and 68 percent confidence intervals, respectively.

precision-weighted average, shown at the bottom of the figure, is tightly distributed around zero.

In contrast with the absence of persuasion effects on policy issues, the prior-persuasion test consistently finds effects in all six performance-related cases. Figure 4.6 presents these results, which control for many

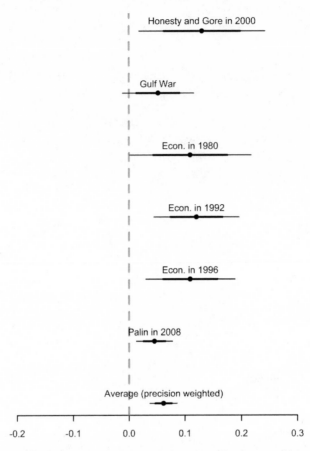

Effect of prior performance persuasion on later change in vote or candidate eval.

FIGURE 4.6. Summary of prior-persuasion test on performance-related issues. For each performance issue, it shows the effect of changes in performance assessment between waves 1 and 2 on changes in approval of the president between waves 2 and 3 (Δ_{x21}, see equation 15 in the appendix). The larger the estimate (steeper slope), the more prior persuasion on the issue changes the outcome variable. The appendix presents the least squares regression estimates (table 7). The thin and thick error bars show 90 percent and 68 percent confidence intervals, respectively.

other variables (prior level and change). In addition to the results on Gore's honesty, I find that those who changed their views about Bush's handling of the Gulf War or who changed their views about Palin or who changed their views about the economy in the 1980, 1992, and 1996 cases later changed their evaluations of politicians accordingly. Since the confidence intervals generally do not overlap with zero, we can be quite sure that these effects are not due to chance. The precision-weighted average, 0.06, suggests that being persuaded to shift the full length of the scale on a performance issue—for example, from seeing the economy as "much worse" to seeing it as "much better"—increased support for the president between later waves by about (0.06 × 100 =) 6 points on the 100-point scale. Although these effects are not large, this test probably underestimates the actual effect because of the time lag.

The two cases that took place in the 1980 campaign—the economy and defense spending—make for an especially telling comparison. They are from the same panel, use the same waves, have the same outcome variable (approval for Carter), and are estimated in essentially the same model, though the economy case includes additional controls. Nonetheless, I find that, when citizens were persuaded of Carter's performance on the economy, it affected their judgments of Carter himself, but when they are persuaded to change their position on defense spending, it did not affect their judgments of Carter, regardless of whether or not Carter's position on defense spending agreed with their own new position.

These positive performance findings and negative policy findings appear to be robust. The performance results show up regardless of whether the outcome is vote, as in the 2000 honesty case, or presidential approval, as in the 1992 economic case. They survive all the robustness checks outlined at the end of chapter 3. They hold with and without controlling for prior change on vote, prior change on feelings about the candidates, and prior change on the other control variables. They hold when I use party or candidate ratings as the outcome variable instead of using vote (in the three policy cases with vote outcomes). And finally, they hold when I conduct analyses only among the "knowers" (a group described in chapter 3) in the policy cases where knowledge measures are available.

4.3 Conclusion

Once again, citizens appear to judge politicians on performance but not on policy. When people changed their performance assessments, they later changed their support for politicians accordingly. When they changed their policy views, however, their support for politicians remained unmoved. The results are surprisingly consistent, with voters passing all six performance tests and failing all six policy tests. Put another way, they pass the easier tests, but fail the harder ones. Voters' behavior therefore does not resemble the worst-case view, outlined in chapter 1, that their political judgments are devoid of substance, but it also does not resemble the policy-voting view, where elections represent the will of the public on government policy.

Whereas in the previous two chapters I had to apply different methods depending on the available data (the two-wave or three-wave tests), here I was able to apply one approach uniformly across the cases. The results thus provide a more consistent basis for testing whether performance issues do indeed influence voters more than policy issues do. Consequently, they reassure us that the previous chapters' findings were not artifacts of different methods.

Nevertheless, it's worth recalling two limitations of my approach, which I briefly surveyed at the end of chapter 3. This approach involves exploiting shifts such as priming and persuasion and measuring views in prior waves, and, consequently, it has a critical benefit: it allows me to overcome the problem of observational equivalence. But this benefit comes at a cost. In particular, the inferences I draw from it may be less general, applying only to the particular types of people who experience these particular types of shifts. That is, I may miss policy and performance voting among people who care so much about a particular issue that it always has high salience for them and they are unlikely to change their opinion about it.

A second limitation I noted is that because of the available panel data, I search for effects only during election campaigns. It is possible that during a campaign, voters may be too swept up in partisan feelings to be willing to shift support to the other party even if its most prominent policy positions are closer to the voters' own. Perhaps voters are willing to change their judgments after the election.

To some extent the findings in this chapter should alleviate both these concerns because they both seem likely to apply to performance issues as well as to policy issues, yet I consistently find effects on performance issues and do not find them on policy issues. Other limitations, not so easily addressed, include a lack of policy cases relating to race or other social groups (Valentino, Hutchings, and White 2002) and social issues.

Although the findings in this chapter further confirm that citizens are judging politicians on their performance, it's worth noting again that this does not mean citizens are competent evaluators of performance. As

I've already noted, the news stories about Gore's dishonesty may have been misleading. Although limited, these analyses do answer a more fundamental question: whether or not citizens judge politicians on performance in the first place. The evidence suggests that they do. I leave to other research whether citizens use this capacity wisely.

CHAPTER FIVE

Learning Positions, Changing Votes?

In chapters 2 through 4, we found little support for the policy-voting view of democracy some scholars espouse. When I administered tests designed to sort out what's causing what, citizens appeared to judge politicians on performance, but they mostly failed to do so on policy. Specifically, neither priming nor persuasion caused people to alter their evaluations of politicians or to alter their votes in accordance with their own views on policy issues. Since our tests of policy voting so far appear to have been too difficult for the public, this chapter lowers the bar.

Much of the public does not know the parties' and candidates' positions, even on long-standing policy issues. In September and October of the 2008 US presidential campaign, for example, only about 60 percent of citizens saw the Democratic candidate, Barack Obama, as desiring a greater government role in providing health insurance than did the Republican candidate, John McCain, even though this issue was central to Obama's campaign and reflects a basic and long-standing difference between the two parties.[1] Because of this ignorance, citizens frequently support candidates with whom they disagree on policy issues without realizing it (Fowler and Margolis 2011). When campaigns or political upheavals raise the salience of an issue, some of these citizens finally learn their favored candidates' positions. (I call this "learning," as opposed to priming or persuasion.) In the cases I examine in this chapter, that happens to literally millions of voters. Learning that your candidate opposes you, which happens to many of these voters, ought to provide an even easier opportunity to change your mind about the candidate on policy grounds, as it eliminates the knowledge barrier to policy voting. Does this learning lead people to vote on policy?

Investigating learning, as opposed to priming and persuasion, also allows us to address an important question about the function of campaigns and the media in elections. "The most important role [of campaigns and the media], from this perspective," Andrew Gelman and Gary King write, "is to enlighten the voters—to give them sufficient information in a timely fashion so they can make up their minds relatively easily. . . . Information about candidates' positions on issues is therefore the most important role of the media" (Gelman and King 1993). We know from previous research that campaigns do inform citizens about politicians' positions (Ansolabehere and Iyengar 1995; Berelson, Lazarsfeld, and McPhee 1954; Brians and Wattenberg 1996; Lang and Lang 1966; Trenaman and McQuail 1961). In this chapter we ask, "Do citizens act on this information?"—a question that has received surprisingly little academic attention.[2]

This absence of research, like the equivalent absence of research on the effect of persuasion noted in chapter 4, stems largely from an absence of panel surveys. To study individual-level learning about politicians' positions outside of the lab, we need panel surveys that ask participants about their perceptions of these positions both before and after the campaign. Such surveys are rare. Of the research that has examined the effects of learning, that of Michael Alvarez's (1997) examination of the 1976 election most closely resembles my approach. Alvarez finds that citizens learn from the campaign and that this learning matters. I attempt to advance Alvarez's findings by ruling out reverse causation on policy views as an alternative explanation.

To see if new knowledge of positions really does facilitate policy voting, I reexamine the ideology case and six other policy cases from previous chapters. These seven cases have the survey questions I need to (1) sort out which respondents learn politicians' policy positions during the campaign and (2) to measure the learners' policy views beforehand. With both kinds of information, I am able to test whether this learning leads them to alter their support for particular politicians.

Do voters pass this easier test of policy voting? The results of these seven surveys indicate they do not. Even when voters have just learned candidates' positions on the most prominent issues in these elections, they do not change their votes or their candidate/party evaluations accordingly. When ideological liberals who approved of President Bush, for example, learned in the 1992 presidential election that his party did not share their ideology, they failed to shift away from him.

These findings have several implications that are worth previewing before we go over the cases themselves. First, they confirm that when we are careful about causation, finding evidence that citizens lead on policy is hard: the learning-induced association between policy views and votes—such as that found by Alvarez (1997)—vanishes. These findings also have ramifications for why policy voting is seemingly rare in that they suggest that lack of knowledge about candidates' positions is *not* what stands in the way. My findings also have implications for the way we conduct our political process. Although campaigns and the news media do inform citizens about political leaders' policy views, potentially helping them pick the appropriate candidates, the public generally disregards this information. For democracy, the key implication is that we are even further away from the policy-voting view than we seemed at the end of chapter 4. It seems that citizens do take a candidate's performance into account, but less often take policy into account, even when it should be easier for them to do so.

5.1 Surrendering to a Federal Europe

In the 1997 British general election, Prime Minister John Major and his Conservative Party campaigned on the issue of European integration. Using the slogan "true to Britain," Major promised voters that if reelected, he would protect Britain's independence by not ceding sovereignty to a European government. Speaking about a forthcoming European summit in Amsterdam, Major declared, "I will keep my feet on the brakes. Mr. Blair would go to Amsterdam and put his foot on the accelerator to a federal Europe" (Brown 1997).

The 1997 campaign marked a return to prominence for the issue of European integration (Norris 1998). Although long a part of British politics, it had played little role in the 1987 and 1992 elections. According to a content analysis of newspaper coverage, no front-page campaign article in a major newspaper mentioned this issue during the 1992 campaign, but 22 percent of such articles did so during the 1997 campaign, far more than for any other policy issue (Butler and Kavanagh 1997, 175). To the Conservative Party, this looked like a winning issue, as the public generally sided with them on Europe.

Given the tremendous focus on this issue in the 1997 election, citizens might be expected to give this issue greater weight in judging the parties.

But as we saw in chapters 3 and 4, they apparently did not. I found no evidence that people placed more importance on this issue and no sign that changing views about this issue led people to change their votes or even their sentiments about the parties. In other words, neither priming nor persuasion seemed to have any effect on voters.

There is one more way, however, in which this issue could have mattered. Instead of priming or persuading, the 1997 campaign may simply have informed the public about the parties' positions on this issue. Once informed, some individuals may have altered their votes accordingly.

Learning seems especially likely in the 1997 British campaign because the parties had recently switched sides on European integration. Even for politically aware voters, there was new information to absorb. As late as 1983 the Labour Party had advocated withdrawal from the European Community (which became the European Union in 1993), while the Conservatives supported further integration. By the late 1980s, the parties had more or less swapped positions (Evans 1998, 574). Although Major's cabinet was still divided over integration in the run-up to the 1997 election, Conservative MPs overwhelmingly opposed it (Butler and Kavanagh 1997).[3] Because of the parties' switching, much more of the public than usual may have been unaware of, or confused about, the parties' positions before the 1997 campaign.

Meanwhile, between 1992 and 1997, the British public had shifted away from supporting further integration with Europe and now sided with the Conservatives in opposing it. The shift was not large, but is plainly visible in figure 5.1, which shows mean responses to an 11-point scale with the end points labeled "prefer seeking unity with Europe" and "protecting Great Britain's independence" (the same question used in chapter 3). These data are again from the 1992–97 British Election Panel Study.

Through newspaper ads and speeches, John Major and the Conservative Party tried to benefit from their relative proximity to the public on this issue; they were, on the whole, closer to the public than Labour was. One newspaper ad, for example, warned,

> A single currency would be irreversible, would signal the end of sovereign Britain, would mean interest rates and mortgage rates set in Frankfurt, and would open the way to a federal Europe . . . Wake up to the facts Britain! Vote Conservative on May 1. (Guardian 1997)

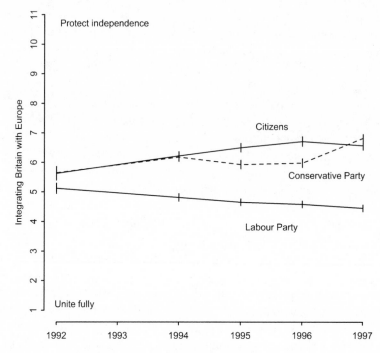

FIGURE 5.1. Citizens' views and their perceptions of the Labour and Conservative Parties' views on the 11-point European integration scale. Error bars show 68 percent confidence intervals (one standard error). Source: British Election Panel, 1992–97.

In the last days of the campaign, Major stepped up the attack on Labour, saying, "Labour would surrender to a federal Europe" (Freedland and White 1997).

Given the parties' relatively new positions and the absence of this issue in the two previous campaigns, it may have been during the 1997 campaign that many citizens learned that the Conservative Party opposed European integration while the Labour Party supported it. Did newly informed voters shift their votes accordingly? Did citizens who opposed integration and intended to vote for Labour, for instance, switch sides when they realized they were intending to vote for the wrong party?

Although the Conservatives apparently failed to benefit from their advantageous position on this issue (see chapters 3 and 4)—they also happened to lose the election—they may have benefited among the subset of people who learned during the campaign about the parties' positions. Figure 5.1 shows evidence of such learning; between 1996 and

1997, the public came to see the Conservative Party as more opposed to integration (and so, in fact, closer to itself).

To quantify this learning, I code a respondent as knowing the parties' positions if he or she places Labour as more pro-EU than the Conservatives.[4] I classify respondents into four categories, depending on their knowledge before the campaign (1996 wave) and afterward (1997 wave): those who (1) *knew before*, correctly placing the parties both before and after the issue became prominent; (2) *learned from*, incorrectly placing or failing to place the parties before, but afterward able to place Labour correctly relative to the Conservatives; (3) *never learned*, incorrectly placing or failing to place the parties both before and after the issue became prominent; and (4) *forgot*, correctly placing the parties before the issue became prominent but incorrectly placing or failing to place them afterward. In coding respondents into these categories, I treat nonresponses to the questions about the parties' positions as incorrect placements. Based on these definitions, about 44 percent already knew the parties' positions, 21 percent learned, 24 percent never learned, and 11 percent forgot. Thus the campaign and media emphasis on the issue of European integration did indeed lead some citizens to learn about the parties' new positions.

Did this learning change votes? If the issue of European integration mattered to voters, some among the 21 percent who learned should bring their votes in line with their attitudes about integration, or at least change their evaluations of the parties accordingly. (The EU issue might not be important enough to make a particular voter change a vote already based on even more important issues, but should still be important enough to change that voter's evaluations of the Labour and Conservative parties.) Voters who support unifying with Europe should be more likely to switch their votes to Labour or to continue intending to vote for it. Voters who oppose unifying with Europe should do the same for the Conservatives. As the reader may recognize, the behavior we expect to see with learning is the same behavior we expected to see with priming—both lead to increases in the strength of the relationship between policy views and votes or candidate evaluations.

To examine whether this learning-induced shift reveals evidence that policy matters to voters' judgments, I apply the same three-wave test (see equation 11 in the appendix) I have been using all along, but now only among the learners. I use the same variables as in chapter 3. To review, I measure European integration views with the 11-point scale, with higher values indicating opposition, and recoded to vary between 0 and 1. I use the 1995 interviews as wave 1, the 1996 interviews as wave 2, and the 1997 interviews (postelection) as wave 3. Since the United Kingdom held no national elections in 1995 and 1996, the survey asked for respondents' vote choice "had there been an election," which I code Labour 0 and Conservative 1. I control only for party identification, though the results are the same with and without controls.

Did this learning change votes? Figure 5.2 presents the findings.[5] To provide a baseline, the left-hand side of this figure ("Before learning") shows the effect of 1995 integration views on vote change between 1995 and 1996; that is, before the learning that took place during the campaign. In this baseline period, the learners did come to judge politicians slightly more on this issue (positive issue weight): those who wanted to protect Britain's independence became slightly more likely to vote Conservative between 1995 and 1996, while those who wanted to unite fully with Europe became slightly more likely to vote Labour. Although positive, the baseline issue weight is only 0.05, which is small and we can't be sure it is different from zero. Between the 1996 and 1997 interviews, as this group learned the parties' positions, the importance of this issue should increase (steeper slope) but it does not. In fact, it becomes slightly negative: −0.01. That is, as this group learned that the Conservative Party generally opposed integration, those who wanted to protect Britain's independence in 1996 became trivially *less* likely to vote Conservative, the party that actually supported their views. Likewise, as they learned that the Labour Party supports further integration, those who wanted to further integrate with Europe became no more likely to vote Labour between 1996 and 1997. Figure 5.3 presents the issue weight estimates and their confidence intervals.

Given that I failed to find an issue-weight increase among all citizens in chapter 3, I did not expect to find a large one among the learners (or I would have seen some sign of it in the full sample). Finding absolutely no effect, however, is surprising. Moreover, the absence of policy judgments among the learners is robust. It persists both without controls and with additional controls (see the online appendix). It persists when I switch to measuring learning based on placing the parties on the correct side of the scale (as opposed to the correct side of each other). It persists when, to reduce bias from random measurement error, I replace integration views in 1995 and 1996 with an average of integration views in 1994, 1995, and 1996. It persists when I use party-support scales instead of vote

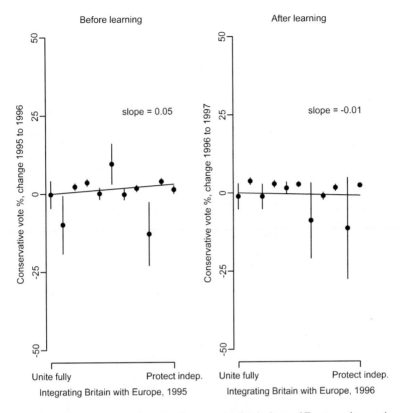

FIGURE 5.2. Three-wave test of the effects of learning for the issue of European integration in the 1997 British election—partial residual scatterplots. These plots examine only those who appeared to learn between 1996 and 1997 that the Labour Party was more prointegration than the Conservative Party ($n = 148$). They show that citizens who learned this information by 1997 did not subsequently judge the parties on this issue. The slopes of these lines represent the weights people placed on their views when changing their vote intents—the issue weights. The difference in these slopes, ($\Delta_{3wt} = -0.01 - 0.05 =$) -0.06, represents the effect of learning the parties' positions on vote change. Figure 5.3 presents a test of whether the difference in the slopes is statistically significant. The appendix presents the model behind these plots (equation 11) and the least squares regression estimates (table 8, column 2). Since the models control for party identification, the plots only show variation after accounting for party identification (that is, they show residualized variation). Error bars show 68 percent confidence intervals. Source: British Election Panel, 1992–97.

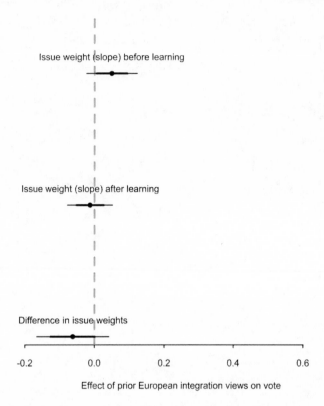

FIGURE 5.3. Three-wave test of effects of learning for the issue of European integration in the 1997 British election. This plot shows the issue weights (slopes) from figure 5.2 and their confidence intervals. They allow the reader to see how precise the estimates of these issue weights are and how sure we are about them and about the difference between them. They show the estimates only for those who appeared to learn between 1996 and 1997 that the Labour Party was more prointegration than the Conservative Party (n = 148). The difference in issue weights, $(\Delta_{3wt} = -0.01 - 0.05 =) -0.06$, represents the effect of learning. According to this test, citizens were not increasingly judging the Labour and Conservative Parties on European integration as they learned the party positions. The appendix presents the model behind these plots (equation 11) and the least squares regression estimates (table 8, column 2). The thin and thick error bars show 90 percent and 68 percent confidence intervals, respectively. Source: British Election Panel, 1992–97.

choice as the dependent variable. Finally, it survives additional robustness tests that I detail below.

For British citizens, this should be an easier test. As argued in the first chapter, lack of knowledge of the parties' or candidates' positions is a formidable obstacle to policy voting. In the 1997 British elections, the campaigns and the news media did much to remove this obstacle with respect to European integration, making it clearer where the parties stood, yet voters still failed to vote or to evaluate the parties on the basis of that issue. As we have seen before, they failed to lead.

5.2 Findings from Six Cases and an Experiment

The European integration findings confirm the results of previous chapters: citizens rarely appear to judge politicians on policy issues. To see if this pattern holds more generally, I replicate these learning tests in six other cases: Social Security in the 2000 election, public works jobs in the 1976 election, defense spending in the 1980 election, activating ideology in the 1992 election, Chernobyl in the 1986 Dutch election, and the SCHIP experiment. In each of these cases, the surveys asked about perceptions of politicians' positions on a policy issue before and after that issue became prominent. In each of these cases, campaign advertising, news media coverage, or—in the SCHIP case—an experimental treatment conveyed information about politicians' positions. In all but two of these cases, the parties or candidates took clear and distinct positions. (The exceptions are the 1986 Dutch election and the 1980 US election, which I explore in next two chapters.) And in each of these cases a considerable share of the electorate learned these positions.

Table 5.1 shows, for each case, the percentage of learners, knowers, forgetters, and never-learners. In the public works case, for instance, the attention this issue received in the 1976 election led 26 percent of the sample to learn that Carter supported and Ford opposed public works job creation programs. In contrast, only about 5 percent of the sample forgot these positions. Generally, I measure learning and knowledge about the issue as whether respondents place politicians or parties on the correct side of the issue in comparison to each other.[6] Ideally, the surveys would ask about candidates' positions and parties' positions, but they rarely do both, so I use whichever is available.

Of these cases the least learning occurs with ideology in the 1992 election, though even in that case the learning is substantial. Between 1991 and October of 1992, about 18 percent of the sample appeared to learn that the Republican Party was to the right of the Democratic Party, while 9 percent appeared to start out knowing it but then forgot

TABLE 5.1. **Learning about politicians' and parties' policy positions**

	Learners %	Knowers %	Forgetters %	Never Learners %	n
Social Security in the 2000 elect.	29	46	15	10	250
EU integration in the 1997 British elect.	21	44	11	24	706
Public works jobs in the 1976 elect.	26	45	5	24	308
Defense spending in the 1980 elect.	26	27	9	39	504
Activating fundamentals					
. . . Ideology in the 1992 elect.	18	47	9	26	940
Chernobyl in the 1986 Dutch elect.	17	44	15	23	785
SCHIP experiment	Info	No Info			
. . . Increase in % saying Bush opposed	17	7			446

Note: Percentages may not add up to 100% because of rounding error.

it. For the SCHIP experiment, this table presents the effect of the info treatment—news stories conveying information about Bush's and the Democratic Party's positions on SCHIP—on the percentage that knew about Bush's opposition to SCHIP expansion. Among the group that had received the info treatment, 62 percent knew that Bush opposed the expansion of SCHIP, while only 45 percent of the control group knew that ($p < 0.001$). A third group (no info treatment) was given news stories that were about the SCHIP controversy but that did not say anything about Bush's position (they were seven percentage points more likely to place Bush correctly than were those in the control group, a difference that could have resulted from chance [$p < 0.128$]).

To test whether this learning changes votes, I turn to the three-wave test where possible, which I now conduct only among those who learned the candidates' or parties' positions.[7] In the Chernobyl and SCHIP cases, which lack three waves, I use the two-wave test. As explained earlier, these tests examine whether policy becomes more important (larger issue weight) to citizens' voting decisions or to their views about politicians. To make the estimates comparable, I use ordinary least squares regression, code all variables to vary between 0 and 1, and control only for party identification (though the findings are robust to other specifications, as I detail later).

Figure 5.4 presents the learning findings, showing the three-wave and two-wave tests in the same figure (see appendix table 8 for the full model estimates). The figure shows only the difference in issue weights for each

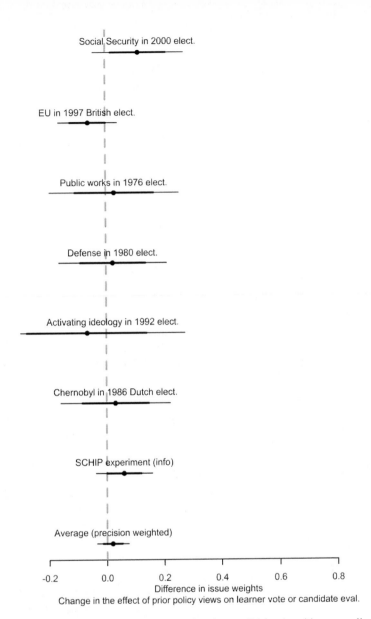

Social Security in 2000 elect.

EU in 1997 British elect.

Public works in 1976 elect.

Defense in 1980 elect.

Activating ideology in 1992 elect.

Chernobyl in 1986 Dutch elect.

SCHIP experiment (info)

Average (precision weighted)

-0.2   0.0   0.2   0.4   0.6   0.8

Difference in issue weights

Change in the effect of prior policy views on learner vote or candidate eval.

FIGURE 5.4. Summary of the effects of learning about politicians' positions on policy issues, using the three-wave and two-wave tests. This figure presents the difference in issue weights—the change in how much importance citizens attach to each issue when they judge politicians. The difference in issue weights is the difference in the slopes shown in, for example, figure 5.2. If learning these positions leads people to change their votes or their candidate evaluations accordingly, the importance of the issues should increase. The figure reveals, however, little sign of this behavior. The last estimate presents the average issue-weight difference across all the cases. It weights each effect by our certainty about it (how precisely we estimate it), so effects with smaller confidence intervals (more precision) count for more. Except for the Chernobyl case, the estimates are from the three-wave test (the differences calculated as $\Delta_{3wt} = \tilde{b}_{w2} - \tilde{b}_{w1}$ from equation 11 in the appendix). For the Chernobyl case, which has only two waves, the estimate is from the two-wave test (the difference is calculated as $\Delta_{2wt} = b'_{w2} - b'_{w1}$ from Equation 14 in the appendix). These estimates control only for party identification, though the results remain essentially unchanged without controls and with additional controls. The appendix presents the least squares regression estimates (table 8). The thin and thick error bars show 90 percent and 68 percent confidence intervals, respectively.

case—the change in how much importance citizens attached to each issue when they judge politicians. It might help to remember that the estimates are simply the difference in slopes in, for instance, figure 5.2.[8]
Across the panel cases and the experimental case, the estimates suggest
that citizens who learned the positions of the parties or candidates failed
to bring their votes in line with their own policy attitudes. When citizens
with conservative views, for example, learned during the 1992 campaign
that Republicans were more ideologically conservative than the Democrats, they did not become more supportive of Bush. When citizens
learned that Gore opposed investing Social Security funds and George
W. Bush supported it, they did not shift their vote to the candidate who
agreed with them on this issue. When supporters of SCHIP learned that
George W. Bush opposed the expansion and Democrats supported it,
they did not become less supportive of Bush.[9]

The ideology finding is particularly revealing. A person may care
about too many issues for learning on any one of them—no matter how
prominent—to change his or her vote or to shift his or her support for
a particular candidate by much. The ideology scale, however, is itself a
proxy for many issues. When people learned about parties' positions on
the ideological spectrum, we would therefore expect larger shifts in their
probability of voting for a particular candidate. Nevertheless, we failed
to find learning having that effect.[10]

Of course, the learners may not care about these particular policy
issues—or even about overall ideology—and may instead concern themselves with some other policy issue. Ideally, I would be able to examine
the effect of learning, not just among all respondents but among people
who are especially concerned with these particular issues and have developed strong attitudes about them. Conducting the media priming and
persuasion tests among such individuals would also be of interest. Unfortunately, researchers have yet to develop and implement reliable measures of issue importance or attitude strength—an embarrassment for
the field of survey research.[11] So this analysis is not possible, at least not
in a convincing fashion. Equipped with better measures, future research
will undoubtedly find policy voting among certain subgroups—such as
those few obsessed with European integration. Nonetheless, the main
thrust of this book is likely to be unaffected by such findings. Regardless of whether issue voting occurs among certain subgroups, the overall
influence of any particular policy on voters is probably small, or at least
smaller than indicated by cross-sectional studies.

As in the European integration case, the absence of policy judgments among the learners in all the other cases in this chapter is robust. It survives all the checks outlined at the end of chapter 3. It persists when I use candidate/party evaluations as the outcome variable instead of votes. It persists without controls and with additional controls. It persists when I switch to measuring learning based on placing the parties on the correct side of the scale (as opposed to the correct side of each other).[12] It persists when I use issue distance from the candidates or parties (proximity) instead of only policy views themselves. Finally, it persists when I use a technique called instrumental variables.[13] In all of these robustness checks, the precision-weighted average is close to zero and precisely estimated.[14]

The findings from the European integration case, therefore, appear to generalize. Even when citizens learned the parties' or candidates' positions, they failed to judge those parties or politicians according to their own prior policy views. In all seven cases, they failed what is arguably our easiest test yet of policy voting. For democracy, the key implication is that we are even further from the policy-voting view than it seemed at the end of the last chapter. At least according to these tests, citizens can handle performance issues but not policy issues.

5.3 Learning about Politicians Swapping Positions

Using panel data to exploit priming, persuasion, and learning, chapters 3 through 5 have searched for evidence that policy views and performance-related assessments matter to citizens. Although I easily found evidence that performance matters, the same tests rarely found that policy matters. As I have noted, however, there are of course potential limitations to my approach. In particular, to overcome the problem of observational equivalence, I only search for issue voting among voters who experience one of these three shifts—who change their minds about the importance of an issue, about their own position on that issue, or about a politician's (or party's) position on it. My results, therefore, may or may not generalize to individuals who do not change their minds in any of these ways. And these people might be different. For example, they may be more likely to care deeply about a particular policy and may already know the politicians' positions on it and be unlikely to change their own positions on it. Thus I may be failing to look for policy voting among a part of the population more likely to engage in it. Even so, the book's findings imply that campaigns do little to induce issue voting, even on highly prominent issues. That is, the only people voting on policy may be those who don't need a campaign to help them make up their minds.

Do my findings generalize to voters who are unlikely to experience these changes of mind? To shed light on this question, I briefly examine a type of shift that is not vulnerable to this generalizability concern. The shift occurs when politicians change positions. In particular, on the rare occasions when parties swap positions on a policy or diverge from previously similar positions, even voters who already care deeply about the policy have something new to learn. When they do learn, one would expect such voters to alter their support for a particular party accordingly. I therefore hypothesize that when people are learning about a real change in positions, learning should matter. In the absence of swapping or diverging by politicians, however, learning may be unlikely to change votes because those who are learning—who don't already know where the candidates and the parties stand—are the voters least likely to care about the issues. When politicians do swap or diverge in their positions, however, learning will be more likely to change votes as those who do care about the issue notice and respond. Thus by examining learning about changes in the candidates' or parties' positions, we have another chance to test whether policy-oriented voters do exist—voters whom the tests in the previous chapters may have missed.

As I mentioned earlier in the chapter, the issue of European integration in the United Kingdom provides us with one of these rare instances of parties swapping positions. Although learning the parties' platforms on this issue failed to change votes between 1996 and 1997, learning may matter earlier—in the first years of the 1990s—when the parties were in the process of swapping positions. Fortunately, the same British election panel interviewed citizens in 1992 and 1994; it may be that 1992 is early enough in the switching process to catch some of those who cared about this issue *before* they learned the parties' new positions. If so we have an opportunity to watch these voters learn about the switch in party positions and then see if they change their own voting intentions accordingly.

Between the 1992 and 1994 waves, voters did appear to learn about the switch. In 1992 about 46 percent placed the Labour Party as more prointegration than the Conservative Party. By 1994, this rises to 55 percent. This percentage then remains flat through 1996 and rises to 66 percent in 1997.

To test whether this learning actually changed votes, I use the two-wave test of learning effects. As the dependent variable, I use the vote question, which asked for hypothetical voting decisions in 1994; I examine only major-party voters.[15] Unlike other waves of this panel, the 1992 wave contains an eight-question battery about European integration. I create an unweighted index from these items (alpha = 0.75). This European integration index may provide a more reliable measure than the single item used above.[16] I control for an index of ideological views and an index of authoritarian views, also measured in 1992 (see the appendix).

Since I am interested in voters who learned about the swap, I examine individuals who placed the Conservative Party as more prointegration than the Labour Party in 1992 but placed the Labour Party as more prointegration than the Conservative Party in 1994. Out of 569 major-party voters in these two waves, only sixty-seven (11 percent) fall into this category.[17]

Figure 5.5 presents a (partial residual) scatterplot for these learners. It plots change in vote between 1992 and 1994 against European integration views in 1992, now measured with the eight-question battery. Learners appeared to change their vote based on their prior views. The estimate is large, about 0.28, and moderately statistically significant. It suggests that as these voters learned about the position swap between 1992 and 1994 they shifted their intended vote to the party that shared their position. I find no sign of a similar increase among other voters, nor do I find any effect using other definitions of learning; the equivalent slopes are all essentially zero (see the online appendix). In sum, these findings tentatively support the view that when citizens have something new to learn, at least some of those who acquire this knowledge do judge the parties on policy issues.

Some, but not many. So on the whole, these findings also bolster the conclusion that few voters judge parties or politicians or cast their votes on account of policy. Despite the Labour and Conservative Parties more or less swapping positions, only 11 percent of our voters learned about that swap. According to these findings, policy issues may matter, but only to a small subset. (In chapter 7, I present further evidence that at least a few citizens do judge candidates on issues when candidates diverge in their positions.)

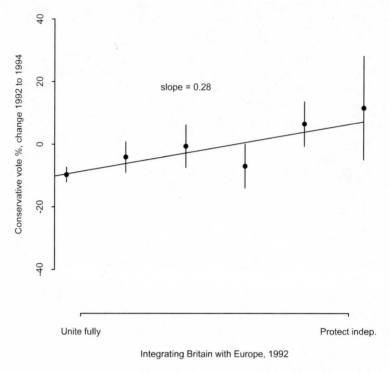

FIGURE 5.5. Did learning about the Labour and Conservative Parties switching sides on European integration change votes? Learning may matter in this earlier period, even though it did not later in the decade (see figure 5.2), because the parties swapped positions, giving people who already care about the issue something new to learn. The partial residual scatterplot shows the effects of an eight-item European integration index (measured in 1992) on the change in vote intent between 1992 and 1994. For the full model, see the online appendix. The error bars show 68 percent confidence intervals.

5.4 Conclusion

So far we have seen voters failing to change their votes in accordance with their own policy views when policy issues became prominent (chapter 3), when the voters' own policy views changed (chapter 4), and when they have learned the parties' or candidates' positions (chapter 5). Of these three tests—media priming, persuasion, and learning—voters should find the learning test easiest. As numerous studies have shown, voters are often unaware of long-standing party positions, even on the most prominent issues of the day. When campaigns and the media inform voters about the candidates' and parties' stances, this eliminates a barrier to policy voting. And yet lowering the bar doesn't seem to encourage more voters to jump—or just step—over it. The lack of policy judgments observed in this chapter takes us even further away from the policy-voting view of democracy.

These findings also say something about the way we view campaigns and the news media. Consistent with previous studies, these findings show campaigns and the news media fulfilling their role of informing citizens about politicians' policy stances, potentially helping citizens pick the right leaders. But they don't show that campaigns and the media are accomplishing anything by fulfilling this role. Rather, the campaigns and the media are providing a benefit from which almost no one apparently benefits.

Probably the most spectacular failure occurs with ideology. Gelman and King, in their seminal 1993 article, find that over the course of a campaign citizens increasingly bring their votes in line with their self-reported ideologies. As with most research on policy voting, however, the study measured self-reported ideology during and after the campaign; reverse causation is therefore a possibility. When policy views are measured *before* the campaign, as they are in this chapter, we find no support for Gelman and King's hypothesis. The voters are not leading candidates on ideology, but rather are following them, as I show in chapter 8.

Of course, these results do not imply that learning politicians' positions never matters. The same limitations I discussed in previous chapters also apply to this one: most of the learning occurs during campaigns, when partisan considerations may dominate, and none of the cases concern social groups such as immigrants (Citrin et al. 1997), or social issues, such as gay rights (Tesler 2011). People may identify with parties because of one of these policy issues and then follow on other policy issues (a possibility I discuss in the concluding chapter). Nevertheless, these findings suggest that learning about politicians' policy positions matters less often than we would expect.

CHAPTER SIX

Avoiding Political Meltdowns: Chernobyl

News of the Chernobyl nuclear accident frightened people the world over and had long-lasting political consequences for communist countries. Chernobyl's most immediate political consequence, however, was in the Netherlands, where the accident unnerved Prime Minister Ruud Lubbers and his center-right coalition of his own party, the Christian Democrats (CDA), and the Liberals (VVD). Not long before the disaster, Lubbers's coalition had enacted legislation to construct two large nuclear plants—at the time, one of the largest nuclear projects outside France (Raun 1986a). They had done so despite fierce resistance from the two major opposition parties, Labour (PvdA) and the Social Liberals (D66).

Given the Dutch center-right coalition's support for nuclear power, the Chernobyl meltdown would have been trouble enough. It was especially unsettling, however, because news of the meltdown broke just three weeks before the coalition faced voters in a parliamentary election on May 21, 1986. In the Netherlands, as in other countries, the accident "catapulted the nuclear power issue to the top of the public agenda" (Brug 2001, 60), undermining Lubbers and his coalition's electoral position (Brug 2001; Eijk, Irwin, and Niemöller 1986). Their pronuclear power policies were already out of line with popular opinion. Now, with Election Day almost upon them, they faced a dramatic increase in the salience of an issue that was straightforward and immediate (rather than complex and remote), that generated deep public anxiety, and on which Lubbers's coalition held a long-standing and now even more unpopular position.

In short, here was an issue on which it should have been easy for citizens to form their own opinions and judge the political candidates accordingly. As I noted in chapter 3, the meltdown seemed likely to
cause all three shifts I exploit in this book—priming, learning, and persuasion—all to Lubbers's detriment. Nevertheless, chapters 3 and 4
found no evidence that Dutch voters did judge their politicians on this
issue.

Or did they? This chapter and the next present case studies of two issues already examined in previous chapters. This one examines the 1986
Dutch election and the next examines the issue of defense spending in
the 1980 US election. In both cases, policy issues captured the public's
attention to an unusual degree, which should have made it easy for citizens to lead politicians on these issues. In both, however, citizens mostly
failed to lead on policy. These case studies attempt to understand why
these issues, despite extraordinary public interest, were nevertheless apparently irrelevant to vote decisions.

Both chapters focus on one explanation: in these unusual cases, policy issues fail to make the difference one would expect them to make because politicians are strategic. When caught holding unpopular views,
they try to neutralize the issues by adopting their opponents' more popular stances. In the other cases in this book, rival politicians maintain opposing views, but in these two cases, politicians on one side change positions, adopting those of their opponents. Lubbers, caught with a deeply
unpopular position, becomes antinuclear, and Carter becomes a defense
hawk. In both instances the public appears to learn about these sudden
shifts (no small thing, given the public's overall ignorance of politicians'
policy positions) and to accept them. Although any conclusions must be
tentative because we have only two such cases, it appears that citizens
failed to vote on either nuclear power or defense spending, not because
of lack of interest or knowledge, but because the incumbents changed
their own stances. And voters apparently bought these shifts, maybe too
readily.

These case studies add nuance to our view of democracy. Most of the
time, citizens apparently fail to judge politicians on policy, even when
opposing candidates take clear and distinct positions. At times, however, public policy does interest the masses. When it does, politicians appear to follow citizens. Consistent with theories about candidate strategy
(Downs 1957), Lubbers and Carter replaced their own long-standing
policy positions with positions much more in line with the public.

6.1 Radioactive Priming?

In the 1970s and 1980s, Dutch campaigns tended to be as flat as the land itself: low-budget and low-key affairs. Before the Chernobyl accident, the 1986 parliamentary campaign featured such riveting issues as the format of a proposed third television channel.[1] Prime Minister Lubbers's first term was generally viewed as a success. He lowered the budget deficit from 10.7 percent of national income in 1982 to 7.8 percent in 1986. Although the economy had at first contracted with his budget cutting, it grew a respectable 1.7 percent in 1984 and 2.1 percent in 1985. According to some accounts, the public saw Prime Minister Lubbers's budget-cutting austerity measures as having gone too far (Economist 1986). Despite economic growth, unemployment had failed to improve much, with a 14.9 percent unemployment rate in 1986. Before Chernobyl the opposition Labour Party primarily campaigned on a proposal to tackle unemployment by increasing job sharing and adopting a 32-hour workweek. On the long-standing issue of whether to deploy NATO's nuclear weapons on Dutch soil, the parties said remarkably little.

Occuring just three weeks before Election Day, the Chernobyl accident shook the Dutch campaign from its typical passionless state, becoming the focus of the media and the candidates. Until the disaster, Lubbers and his Liberal coalition partners seemed confident about maintaining their majority (Schuil 1986), though precampaign polls forecast a tight race (Eijk, Irwin, and Niemöller 1986, 294). Table 6.1 shows the distribution of seats before the election. The Chernobyl disaster revived Labour's flagging hopes of a return to government.

Lubbers and his coalition were rightly panicked by the meltdown. Three factors should arguably have facilitated media priming here: a rise in the prominence of the issue, the fact that the parties held long-standing positions on nuclear energy, and the ease with which typical voters could understand the issue.

Consider the first. The Chernobyl accident became the dominant news story in the days following the meltdown. The issue of nuclear power especially dominated the last few days of the campaign (Brown 1986a; Brown 1986b). In a televised debate on the eve of the election, Labour Party leader Joop den Uyl repeatedly attacked Lubbers for his support of nuclear power, while Lubbers tried to change the topic,

TABLE 6.1. **Dutch political parties before the 1986 election**

Party	Leader	1982 Election Results		
		%	Seats	
Labour (PvdA)	Joop den Uyl	30.4	47	Opposition
Christian Democrats (CDA)	Ruud Lubbers	29.3	45	Governing coalition
Liberals (VVD)	Ed Nijpels	23.1	36	Governing coalition
Social Liberals (D66)	Hans van Mierlo	4.3	6	Opposition
Other		12.9	16	Opposition
Total			150	

emphasizing the improving economy and the reduced budget deficit (Yekev 1986).

Priming also seems likely because the parties had long-established positions on nuclear power. Beginning in 1977 the Dutch Parliamentary Elections Studies have asked representative samples about their views on nuclear energy and what they perceive the major parties' stances to be on this issue. Throughout this period the surveys use a 7-point scale, with 1 labeled "No more nuclear plants should be built at all in The Netherlands" and 7 labeled "The number of nuclear plants should be quickly increased in The Netherlands." Respondents used this scale to report their views and their perceptions of the party positions. As figure 6.1 shows, the Dutch public viewed the incumbent parties, Lubbers's Christian Democrats (CDA) and the Liberals (VVD), as supporting nuclear power since at least the late 1970s and viewed Labour (PvdA) and, to a lesser extent, the Social Liberals (D66) as opposed to it since the early 1980s.

Priming also seems likely in this case because the issue of nuclear power seems easy to understand for most individuals, especially after Chernobyl. Citizens in the Netherlands faced daily stories about the potential—probably exaggerated—health consequences of the meltdown. The Dutch government, for instance, imposed a widely publicized ban on the outdoor grazing of dairy cows (Raun 1986b), as radioactive iodine fallout can spread to people via milk. Unlike policies involving complicated financial or regulatory issues, nuclear meltdowns were something citizens could immediately and unambiguously view as bad.

Priming an issue does not necessarily shift overall public support for the parties. For priming to alter election outcomes, voters must prefer one side of the issue over others. In this case a sizable majority of Dutch

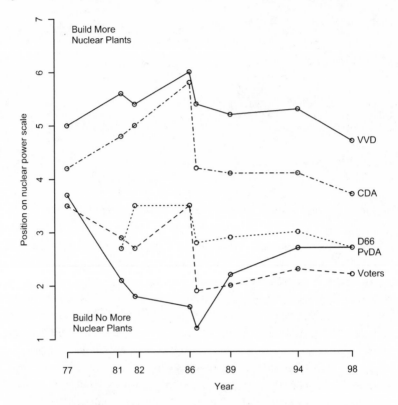

FIGURE 6.1. Citizens' views and their perceptions of parties' positions on nuclear power. Source: Brug (2001, 60) using Dutch Election Studies.

voters did oppose nuclear power. The panel data I use to analyze this case are from the 1986 Dutch Parliamentary Elections Study. In the interviews conducted immediately before Chernobyl, only about a quarter of respondents supported the construction of additional plants (see figure 6.2) and more placed themselves at the lowest point on the nuclear power scale than at any other point on the scale.

The governing parties were thus in a dire situation. They suddenly faced a dramatic increase in the salience of an apparently easy issue, one that generated deep anxiety among the public and one on which the incumbent parties' long-standing positions were further from the typical citizen than were the positions of the opposition parties.

As I showed in chapter 3, the tremendous media coverage and campaign attention failed to prime the issue of nuclear power. We can investigate that question with panel data because, through an extraordinary

stroke of luck, the Dutch Parliamentry Elections Study had almost completed the first wave of interviews for its two-wave panel when the Dutch
media reported the accident (April 30), with 1,293 pre-Chernobyl interviews. Reinterviews began after the elections of May 21. In both waves
the survey asked citizens about their views on nuclear power and where
they perceived the parties on this issue. They did so using the same
7-point scale described earlier.

To present the findings on priming from chapter 3 in detail, I show
them graphically. I use the same sample and variables I used in chapters
3 and 5: I analyze the 785 respondents who are interviewed and who express an attitude about nuclear power and a vote preference for one of
the four major parties in both waves of the panel *and* whose preelection
interviews occur before Chernobyl. I combine votes for the incumbent
parties—the Christian Democrats and Liberals—and for the major opposition parties—Labour and the Social Liberals, although the conclusions are not sensitive to these decisions.

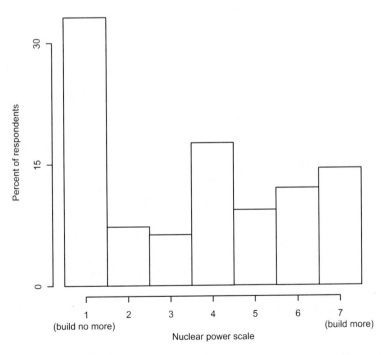

FIGURE 6.2. Citizens' positions on nuclear power pre-Chernobyl. Frequency histogram.
Source: 1986 Dutch Election Study.

Figure 6.3 presents the priming test. It shows the shift in vote for or against the incumbent parties by whether or not individuals want to build any more nuclear power plants (measured pre-Chernobyl). If the campaign and media response to Chernobyl primed attitudes about nuclear power, we should observe supporters and opponents of nuclear power diverging in their support for the parties. Citizens who oppose nuclear power should shift away from the incumbent parties between their pre-Chernobyl and postelection interviews (downward), while citizens who support nuclear power should shift toward the incumbent parties (upward), or at least not away from them. We should therefore see a plainly visible positive slope in this figure if Chernobyl primed attitudes with much force.

Consistent with the findings presented in earlier chapters, however, priming is not plainly visible; the figure reveals little overall pattern. The strongest opponents of nuclear power did not shift away from the incumbent parties, nor did the strongest supporters shift toward them. The slope of the line—the issue weight—is only 0.06, positive but small, which implies that shifting from being the strongest nuclear power opponent to being the strongest supporter leads to a mere 6 percent increase in the likelihood of voting for the incumbent parties. (For the model estimates throughout this chapter, I code the variables to vary between 0 and 1.) In sum, despite the tremendous media coverage of Chernobyl and the attempts by the opposition parties to exploit it to their advantage, we see little evidence of priming; the issue still didn't seem to have much sway over how the voters voted.

As with almost all the scatterplots I present, this one is a partial residual scatterplot; it already accounts for other variables. Since I find so little effect, I control only for pre-Chernobyl party identification and vote. (The appendix presents the model behind this plot [equation 10] and the online appendix shows the full ordinary least squares regression estimates.) Readers may have also noticed that this figure does not also show the relationship during the baseline period, as, for example, figures 3.2 and 5.2 do; it shows only one plot, not two. In the earlier chapters, showing a baseline period allowed us to assess the issue weight before the issue became prominent. Since the Dutch Parliamentary Elections Study only interviewed respondents twice, however, we lack the three waves necessary to do that here. But given that we don't find evidence of an effect, comparing it to a baseline is less important.

As noted in chapter 3, political scientists generally test for priming

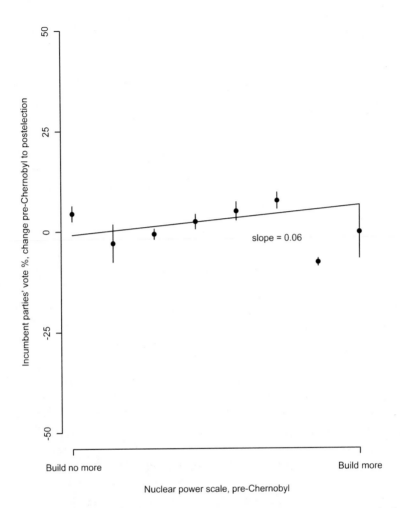

FIGURE 6.3. Did Chernobyl prime attitudes about nuclear power in the 1986 Dutch election? This figure presents the shift in vote for or against the incumbent parties by whether or not individuals wanted to build any more nuclear power plants (measured pre-Chernobyl). It shows a partial residual scatterplot controlling for pre-Chernobyl party identification and pre-Chernobyl vote. The appendix presents the model behind this plot (equation 10) and the online appendix shows the full ordinary least squares regression estimates. The appendix also explains how I construct partial residual scatterplots. For the model estimates throughout this chapter, I code the variables to vary between 0 and 1. Error bars show 68 percent confidence intervals. Source: 1986 Dutch Election Study.

among all citizens. Not all citizens, however, can be primed. No matter how salient the issue, individuals cannot shift their votes to the party
that shares their position unless they know at least some of the parties'
positions. Since a great many citizens are generally unaware of the parties' positions on most issues, the effect of priming on those who are
aware could go undetected in the test above, as in the tests in many other
studies. Figure 6.4 presents a more sensitive test. Using a similar scatterplot, it shows vote by attitudes on nuclear power, as above, but now
only among those who appear to have known the parties' positions before news of Chernobyl broke. As I do throughout this book, I measure
knowledge of the parties' positions by assessing the correctness of citizens' relative perceptions of these positions; that is, whether respondents
can place both incumbent parties as more supportive of nuclear power
than both major opposition parties. Since Dutch citizens must navigate
a multiparty system, I relax this measure somewhat by also including respondents who place only the party they vote for on the correct side of
the scale. According to this measure, about 44 percent of citizens correctly placed the parties both before Chernobyl and after the election;
I refer to these citizens as "knowers."[2] The rest either incorrectly place
some of the parties or fail to place them at all on the 7-point scale in one
or both waves (see table 6.2 in the next section). Figure 6.4 reveals little
sign of priming among these knowers. The slope is positive, but it's hard
to see a consistent trend. Those who opposed nuclear power failed to
shift their support to the opposition parties and those who supported nuclear power failed to become more supportive of the incumbent parties.

While my results do not show priming, they do reveal a striking
amount of sorting before Chernobyl. The figures do not reveal this pattern, but it's clear in the data. Prior to Chernobyl, almost 80 percent of
knowers who supported nuclear power (above the midpoint on the scale)
intended to vote for the incumbent parties, while only about 9 percent
of nuclear opponents intended to do so. Given that voters who knew the
parties' positions had already sorted themselves almost perfectly into
their respective camps before Chernobyl, priming among this group
seems unlikely.

These scatterplots confirm the results in chapter 3, which found no
evidence of media priming following Chernobyl. Of course, there are
other ways of examining these data. For example, one could examine
each party's votes, instead of combining votes for the incumbent and
opposition parties. One could also adopt other assumptions about how

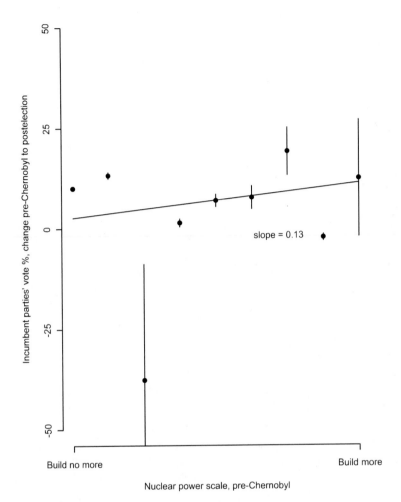

FIGURE 6.4. Did Chernobyl prime attitudes about nuclear power among voters who appeared to know the parties' positions (knowers)? This figure presents the shift in vote for or against the incumbent parties among knowers by whether or not they wanted to build any more nuclear power plants (measured pre-Chernobyl). It shows a partial residual scatterplot controlling for pre-Chernobyl party identification and pre-Chernobyl vote. The appendix presents the model behind this plot (equation 10) and the online appendix shows the full ordinary least squares regression estimates. Error bars show 68 percent confidence intervals. Source: 1986 Dutch Election Study.

people decide on their vote, such as proximity. I spare the reader the details, but I have tried numerous approaches, including those outlined at
the end of chapter 3, and always reach the same conclusion. The estimates of media priming (the difference in issue weights) center on zero,
with or without controls.

The literature on campaigns would lead us to expect media priming
in this particular case, especially given the parties' long-standing positions and the ease with which most citizens could understand this issue.
Nevertheless, I find no evidence of it.

6.2 Learning Which Parties Glow Green

If Chernobyl coverage did not prime the issue of nuclear power, it could
still have changed citizens' votes by informing them about the parties'
positions. The ruling coalition was especially worried about this possibility, in part because of the considerable potential for learning. Although
the parties held long-standing positions, only 44 percent of voters could
correctly place the parties before and after Chernobyl (the knowers), using the relaxed definition described earlier. Among all citizens, not just
voters, this falls to only 30 percent. So, much to the chagrin of the ruling
coalition, many potential and actual voters might have been learning for
the first time that it was the opposition parties that shared their opposition to scarier-than-ever nuclear power.

Did the Chernobyl media storm so inform voters? If it did, did this
learning change votes? Table 6.2 presents the breakdown of the panel respondents. About 16 percent failed to correctly place the parties relative
to each other (or did not place a party) in the first wave, but did do so in
the second. Thus media and campaign attention to Chernobyl appears to

TABLE 6.2. **Learning about Dutch parties' long-standing positions on nuclear policy**

	Placed the ruling coalition parties as more pronuclear power than the opposition parties?			
	Pre-Chernobyl	Post-election	n	%
Already knew (knowers)	Yes	Yes	348	44
Learned (learners)	No	Yes	129	16
Never learned	No	No	187	24
Forgot	Yes	No	121	15
Total			785	100

Note: These statistics are only for major-party voters. Source: 1986 Dutch Election Study.

have informed some voters about the parties' long-standing positions. But the net shift in knowledge of the parties' positions is almost zero because another 15 percent shifted in the opposite direction, correctly placing the parties' long-standing positions before Chernobyl but getting them wrong afterward. The lack of net learning probably results from Lubbers's attempt to change positions, which I take up later in this chapter.

Although there is little net learning about the parties' positions, the learning that did occur (the learners) could still have hurt Lubbers's coalition. Specifically, the nuclear opponents who had intended to vote for the ruling coalition might have realized their error and shifted their votes to the opposition. If they did, support for the incumbents should have shifted among the learners, depending on their support for nuclear energy: we should see supporters and opponents of nuclear power diverging in their tendency to vote for the incumbent parties as they learn the parties' positions. Figure 6.5 presents the (partial residual) scatterplot. As with priming, we see little evidence that learning changed votes. Nuclear opponents did not shift away from the pronuclear incumbents, nor did nuclear supporters shift toward them. The slope is positive, but just barely. So Chernobyl apparently failed not only to prime nuclear power but also to induce a learning effect, a finding that appears robust to numerous alternative specifications and codings (see the online appendix).

6.3 Persuasion

Not surprisingly, news of Chernobyl persuaded many people to oppose nuclear power. In fact, it persuaded more than half of all nuclear power supporters to become opponents, driving them from a 5, 6, or 7 to a 1, 2, or 3 on the nuclear power scale. In comparison, only 8 percent made the opposite shift. This corresponds with a mean shift on the scale from 3.6 pre-Chernobyl to 2.7 post-Chernobyl. As shown in figure 6.6, many respondents shifted to 1, the bottom point on the scale. Did this Chernobyl-induced policy persuasion lead to vote change; did persuasion actually produce a persuasion *effect*?

In chapter 4 I studied the effects of persuasion on policy and performance issues, but only with surveys that interviewed the same people three or more times. This allowed me to test the effect of prior persuasion and to rule out concerns that people were following rather than leading, that is, to rule out reverse causation. Since the present case only has two

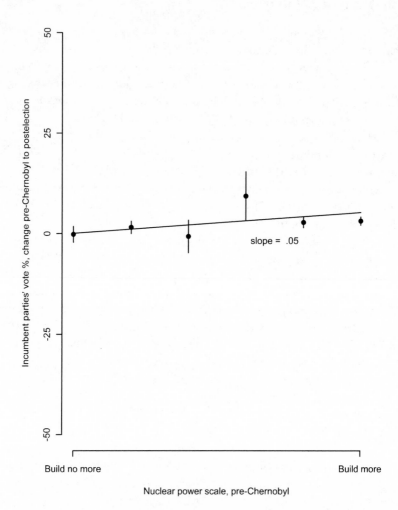

FIGURE 6.5. Did learning about the incumbent parties' positions because of Chernobyl lead citizens to vote against those parties? This figure presents the shift in vote for or against the incumbent parties among learners by whether or not they wanted to build any more nuclear power plants (measured pre-Chernobyl). It shows a partial residual scatterplot controlling for pre-Chernobyl party identification and pre-Chernobyl vote. The appendix presents the model behind this plot (equation 10) and the online appendix shows the full ordinary least squares regression estimates. Error bars show 68 percent confidence intervals. Source: 1986 Dutch Election Study.

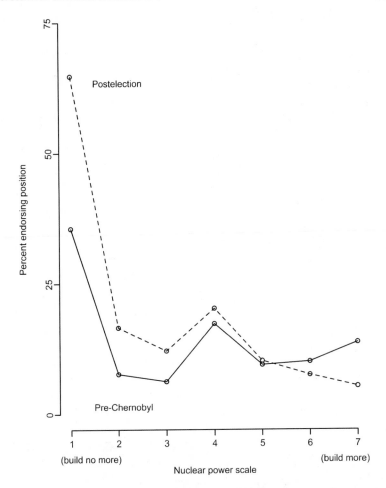

FIGURE 6.6. Changing attitudes about nuclear power. This figure presents the percent of respondents who placed themselves at each point on the 7-point nuclear power scale both before Chernobyl and when reinterviewed postelection. It shows the increase in opposition to nuclear power (the shift to 1) in the postelection interviews. Source: 1986 Dutch Election Study.

interviews, I cannot examine prior persuasion, so any findings could be due to reverse causation. I show the results using a residual scatterplot (the appendix presents the model behind this test [equation 16] and the online appendix shows the full ordinary least squares regression estimates).

Does this test reveal evidence that persuasion on nuclear power changed votes? As with priming and learning, the answer appears to be no, or at least not much. Figure 6.7 shows shifts by voters toward or away

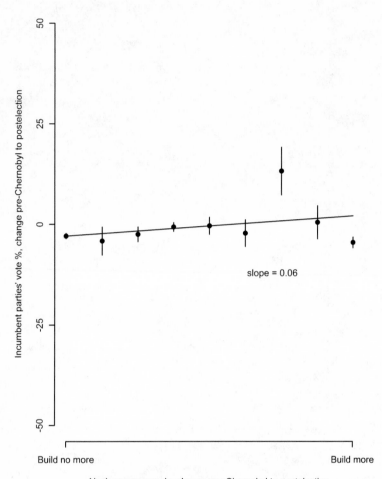

FIGURE 6.7. Did changing one's mind about nuclear power after Chernobyl change one's vote? This figure presents the shift in vote for or against the incumbent parties by whether individuals became more or less supportive of nuclear power between their pre-Chernobyl and postelection interviews. It shows a partial residual scatterplot controlling for pre-Chernobyl party identification and pre-Chernobyl vote. The appendix presents the model behind this test (equation 16) and the online appendix shows the full ordinary least squares regression estimates. The error bars show 68 percent confidence intervals. Source: 1986 Dutch Election Study.

from the incumbent parties by persuasion on the issue. The x axis in this figure represents the change in view on nuclear power between the pre-Chernobyl and postelection interviews. If persuasion on this issue changed votes, we should see a positive trend in the figure, with those who became opposed to nuclear power shifting toward the opposition (downward) and those who became supportive of nuclear power shifting toward the incumbents (upward). The figure shows a hint of this pattern. Those who became opposed did shift away from the incumbent parties, but only by about three percentage points, a small shift. The overall trend in the figure is consistent with persuasion having some effect on vote, but the effect is inconsistent and small. The slope is just 0.06, which implies that even for individuals switching from being the strongest nuclear power supporters to being the strongest opponents (from right to left), the likelihood of voting for the incumbent decreases by only six percentage points. Chernobyl did persuade people on the issue of nuclear power, but this simple test reveals little evidence that the persuasion translated into vote change, even though this test is likely biased in favor of finding such an effect because of reverse causation (as opposed to the prior persuasion test from chapter 4, which is likely biased against finding such an effect).

6.4 Neutralizing Nuclear Power by Switching Sides?

It is hard to believe that the Chernobyl nuclear disaster failed to influence vote choice. But that is the conclusion of these analyses. On Election Day, Chernobyl did not lead people to vote against the ruling coalition because of priming, learning, or persuasion.

The absence of these effects is consistent with the election results. Based on preelection polls, Lubbers and his governing coalition were bracing for defeat, that is, losing their majority (see table 6.3). Because of the Netherlands' unusual electoral system—proportional representation in a single, nationwide district—forecasting elections from polls is straightforward and had previously been highly accurate. Since the introduction of regular polling in the 1960s, polls had correctly predicted every election (Eijk, Irwin, and Niemöller 1986, 289). But in 1986, they were wrong. Lubbers's coalition maintained its majority of eighty-one seats (see table 6.4) and Lubbers's Christian Democrats gained nine seats.

Participants and journalists seemed puzzled by the failure of the polls

TABLE 6.3. **Polling forecasts and the actual election results for the number of seats each party holds in parliament**

		Forecast		
	1982 Result	May 7	May 17	1986 Result
Governing coalition	81	72	74	81
... Christian Democrats (CDA)	45		46	54
... Liberals (VVD)	36		28	27
Labour (PvdA)	47	54	54	52
Social Liberals (D66)	6		11	9

Note: May 7 poll is from Steele (1986). May 17 poll is from Raun (1986b). Excludes smaller parties, who won 16 seats in 1986. Seventy-five seats needed for a majority.

TABLE 6.4. **Dutch election results for 1982 and 1986**

	1982		1986		Change	
Party	%	Seats	%	Seats	%	Seats
Governing coalition	52.4	81	52.0	81	−0.4	0
... Christian Democrats (CDA)	29.3	45	34.6	54	+5.3	+9
... Liberals (VVD)	23.1	36	17.4	27	−5.7	−9
Labour (PvdA)	30.4	47	33.3	52	+2.9	+5
Social Liberals (D66)	4.3	6	6.1	9	+1.8	+3
Other	12.9	16	8.6	8	−4.3	−8
Total		150		150		

and especially by the failure of Chernobyl to hurt the governing coalition, which had been expected to lose from the "Chernobyl effect alone" (Anderson 1986). A journalist described Prime Minister Lubbers's own shock at the Christian Democrats' victory celebration:

> While his campaign workers celebrated with champagne and Dixieland Jazz, Ruud Lubbers self-consciously stroked his stubble. "I am a bit surprised," he said. "It's a very remarkable result." (Anderson 1986)

The Liberal Party—the other member of the ruling coalition—lost nine seats, but this was blamed on its unpopular leader, Ed Nijpels, not on its pronuclear stance. The opposition Labour Party managed to gain five seats, but since it had been expected to win, the election was seen as a loss. And its gains were not at the expense of Lubbers's coalition, but rather came from gobbling up left-wing fringe parties, with whom it could have potentially formed a coalition (Brown 1986b). In the end, Chernobyl and nuclear power—for all the impact they had had on the campaign—just didn't seem to have anything to do with the election results. How could this be?

One answer, consistent with much of this book's findings, is that issues just do not matter enough to citizens, even in these extraordinary circumstances. If so, these findings may represent a notable failure on the part of citizens. Even under conditions that should have greatly facilitated issue voting, they still failed the policy-voting test. This answer may indeed be right. There is, however, an alternative view: when an issue does capture the public's attention, politicians may follow citizens by changing their position, which is exactly what happened in this case.

In the week or so following the Chernobyl accident, Lubbers's coalition saw the first real evidence of electoral trouble with the publication of two polls (Steele 1986). The first showed a rapid rise in opposition to nuclear power. In Lubbers's Christian Democratic stronghold of Brabant, the poll revealed a jump in opposition to the nuclear construction plan from 48 percent six months prior to 63 percent. The other survey showed that Lubbers's coalition, which held eighty-one seats in the 150-seat Parliament, was now expected to lose its majority, winning only seventy-two seats (see table 6.3). The opposition Labour Party, which opposed nuclear power, was forecast to substantially increase its seats, from forty-seven to fifty-four, and so presumably would form a new, left-of-center would coalition.

Lubbers and his coalition, however, were not defenseless. Aware of the radioactive cloud literally hanging over their heads, they could try to change sides on the issue. Two weeks before Election Day, they did. They shelved plans for the new nuclear plants, hinted that the postponement was indefinite, launched reviews of existing plants, and implied that these plants might require dismantling (Steele 1986). For a timeline of events, see table 6.5. Initially, not all party members fell in with this strategy. The Liberal energy minister, Gijs Van Ardenne, caused a furor—not least in his own party—by dismissing Chernobyl as "a campfire in a forest" (Brown 1986a). But his fellow party members quickly silenced him (Eijk, Irwin, and Niemöller 1986, 294).

Did Lubbers's coalition actually succeed in changing voters' perceptions of its position? To see if they did, figure 6.8 presents perceptions of Lubbers's Christian Democrats on the 7-point nuclear power scale pre-Chernobyl and postelection. The shift in perceptions is surprisingly large. The bulk of voters moved from placing the Christian Democrats

TABLE 6.5. **Chernobyl in the 1986 Dutch election timeline**

First Dutch nuclear power plant	1969
Second Dutch nuclear power plant	1973
Governing coalition decides to build two large nuclear power plants	1985
Chernobyl nuclear accident begins	April 26, 1986
Soviets admit nuclear accident	April 28, 1986
Poll published showing public opinion moving away from nuclear power	May 7, 1986
Poll published showing governing coalition to lose majority	May 7, 1986
Prime Minister Lubbers postpones plans to build the new plants	May 7, 1986
Election Day	May 21, 1986

at the pronuclear side of the scale to placing them in the middle of the scale. This corresponds with a mean shift from 5.5 to 4.6. The shift in perceptions of the Liberals was less pronounced, from 5.6 to 5.2. Thus, at least in this case, the data indicate that candidates can quickly change perceptions of their parties' positions.

Although we cannot know for sure, these findings suggest that this radioactive issue failed to hurt Lubbers's Christian Democrats in the election in part because he changed voters' perceptions of his party's position.[3] As journalistic accounts put it,

> the surprising win by Prime Minister Lubbers' center-right coalition in May 21 elections can be attributed in part to the shrewd campaign decision to switch sides and join the nuclear-energy doubters. His Cabinet halted development of two nuclear plants that could have doubled Holland's electrical output. (U.S. News & World Report 1986)

Dutch scholars agree. Eijk, Irwin, and Niemöller (1986, 294) write,

> It seemed likely that "Chernobyl" would play into the hands of the opposition parties who had voted against the expansion of nuclear energy. However, a quick change of position by the government parties immediately defused the issue. . . . By the time the cows were again in the pasture, no substantial electoral gains could be made from this issue.

Before concluding that this is the most likely explanation, it is worth considering alternatives. One is that the public did judge the parties on nuclear power, but that the tests in this chapter are too weak to detect these judgments. Although that is always a possibility, we have an additional check in this case. If Chernobyl did indeed fail to induce such

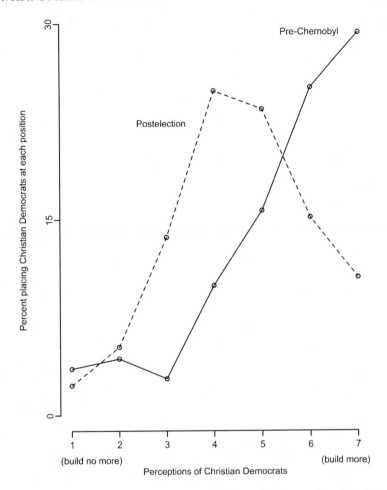

FIGURE 6.8. Shifting positions on nuclear power. This figure shows perceptions of the Christian Democrats on nuclear power pre-Chernobyl and postelection. Source: 1986 Dutch Election Study.

judgments, we should see no overall shift against the incumbent parties in the panel. This is precisely what we do find. In fact, consistent both with other polling and with the election results, respondents in the panel shifted toward the incumbent parties, not away from them: about 52 percent intended to vote for the incumbents pre-Chernobyl and about 55 percent reported having done so post-Chernobyl. Given that citizens, on net, shifted *toward* the incumbent coalition, it seems unlikely that these tests missed judgments that, on net, would have pushed them *away* from the coalition.

Another alternative is that nuclear power failed to capture voters' interest, even in the wake of Chernobyl. According to this view, Lubbers's switching sides did not neutralize the issue because there was never an

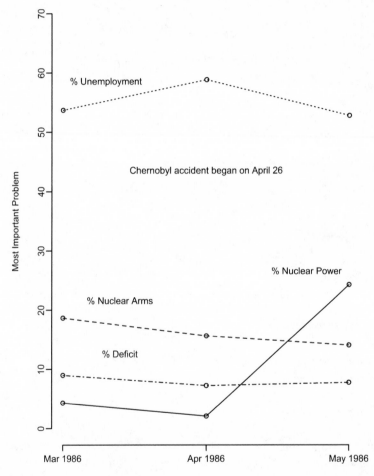

FIGURE 6.9. Monthly average of most important problems before and after Chernobyl. After Chernobyl, nuclear power became the second-most mentioned issue. Unlike most of the analysis in this chapter, here I use all respondents in the preelection wave, not just those who survive the panel, so as to maximize the number of post-Chernobyl interviews. In March, n = 489; April, 569; May, 48. For coding details, see the appendix. Source: 1986 Dutch Election Study.

issue to neutralize. Citizens would not have judged the parties on this issue even had Lubbers maintained his coalition's unpopular position because voters would have ignored the issue. Although we cannot rule out
this alternative with certainty, it seems unlikely. It would have been ideal
if the Dutch Parliamentary Elections Study had reinterviewed respondents in the week between the Chernobyl accident and Lubbers's switch,
allowing us to test whether the issue had begun to hurt the ruling coalition before the switch. Unfortunately, the Dutch study only conducted a
few dozen interviews between Chernobyl and Election Day and no reinterviews.[4] Without panel data covering the period during which the ruling coalition switched sides, the best evidence against this voter-indiffer-
ence alternative is the post-Chernobyl commercial polls I noted earlier,
which show shifts against nuclear power and against the ruling coalition,
even in regions usually considered safe for them—the same polls that led
Lubbers to switch sides.

Although the Dutch study reinterviewed few respondents between
Chernobyl and Lubbers's switch, it did interview several dozen between
Chernobyl and the election, and analysis of these interviews provides
further evidence that the media storm over Chernobyl did register with
the Dutch public. The preelection wave asked an open-ended question
about the most important problems facing the Netherlands. Respondents could mention up to five. As figure 6.9 shows, nuclear power was a
low-salience issue before Chernobyl—only 4 percent mentioned it as one
of the country's most important problems in March and only 2 percent
did so in April. After Chernobyl, however, 24 percent did so, making it
the second-most mentioned issue.[5] This finding reassures us that the nuclear issue did indeed matter to voters. It therefore bolsters the conclusion that Lubbers's switching sides made a difference, neutralizing the
issue and thus saving his party from defeat.[6]

6.5 Changing Policy Views, Not Votes

In the end, the Chernobyl meltdown apparently failed to influence vote
choice. It did, however, reshape public opinion about nuclear energy in a
partisan manner. In chapter 8, I find that as policy issues become prominent, people often adopt their preferred party's position, especially when
they learn where the parties or candidates stand. Instead of leading, they
follow. Chernobyl is no exception.

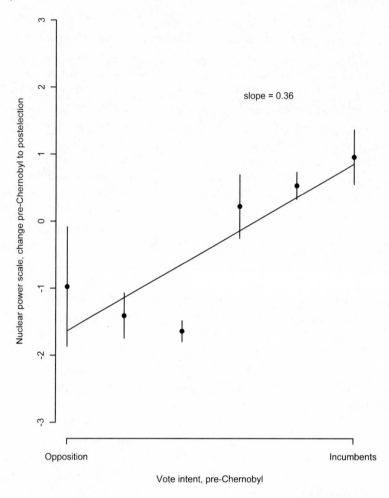

FIGURE 6.10. Holding onto your party's position despite a meltdown. When supporters of the incumbent parties learned that these parties were (or had been) pronuclear, they failed to be persuaded to oppose nuclear power. The appendix presents the model behind this test (equation 18) and the online appendix shows the full ordinary least squares regression estimates. Error bars present 68 percent confidence intervals. Source: 1986 Dutch Election Study.

News of Chernobyl persuaded many to oppose nuclear power, but not all. Among those who learned the parties' long-standing positions, supporters of Lubbers's coalition largely resisted this persuasion. Figure 6.10 presents this finding with a (partial residual) scatterplot (the appendix presents the model behind this test [equation 18] and the on-

line appendix shows the full ordinary least squares regression estimates). Those who, before Chernobyl, had intended to vote for the opposition parties became more opposed to nuclear power, shifting 1 to
1.5 points on the 7-point scale. In contrast, those who, before Chernobyl,
had intended to vote for the incumbent parties resisted the general shift
against nuclear power, continuing to support nuclear power at pre-
Chernobyl levels. Although news of Chernobyl failed to induce issue-
based vote change, it does appear to have induced vote-based opinion
change. When individuals learned where the parties stood, they adopted
their party's position.

6.6 Conclusion

Despite raising the salience of nuclear power three weeks before Election Day, despite the issue of nuclear power being easy for most citizens
to form an opinion on, and despite the parties holding long-standing positions on this issue, the Chernobyl nuclear meltdown apparently failed
to change votes by changing voters' attitudes toward nuclear power.
Confirming the analyses in chapters 3 and 5, I found no evidence that
the event led citizens to judge the parties on this issue. Although 16 percent of the public may have learned the parties' long-standing positions
following the accident, this learning did not lead those voters to change
their votes to the parties that shared their own positions. Although the
issue undoubtedly became more salient for millions, I found no evidence
that this increased salience increased the weight voters placed on this issue. Finally, although the meltdown persuaded many to oppose nuclear
power, I found no evidence that this persuasion ultimately changed votes.

At first glance, this appears to be a dismal failure on the part of citizens. On closer inspection, however, citizens probably failed to vote on
nuclear power not because of lack of interest or knowledge, but because
politicians responded to the citizens' policy preferences, moving toward
the median voter, as much theory predicts (e.g., Downs 1957). In a two-
week period, Lubbers's coalition changed public perceptions about its
position on nuclear power, convincing citizens that the coalition was on
their side. The failure to find that policy views directly influenced votes
is, therefore, not an indictment of voters or of democracy. In fact, it may
be a glowing example of democracy at its best: parties changing policy in
response to citizens' views.

A caveat to this rosy conclusion is that citizens may have reacted unwisely to the meltdown. Compared with Western nuclear power plants, Soviet plants had fewer safeguards and Soviet society lacked public interest watchdogs and a free press to help ensure nuclear safety (Rhodes 2007). Additionally, nuclear power—and nuclear radiation more generally—may be less dangerous than perceived (Ropeik and Gray 2002), and nuclear power does have distinct advantages, such as the absence of greenhouse gas by-products. Thus although the campaign may have forced Lubbers's coalition to better reflect public views—a victory for democracy—the public's judgment on this issue may have been less than wise.[7]

These findings also have implications for candidate strategy, indicating that candidates may be able to quickly change perceptions of their position, even when parties have long-established *and* recently reaffirmed positions on the issue. Of course, the 1986 Dutch election may be unusual. In particular, because the accident revealed new information about the dangers of nuclear power, the public may have found the sudden policy reversal reasonable rather than opportunistic. Several other factors may also have made the switch more credible. First, nuclear power may not have been a core issue for the incumbent parties' constituents as, say, abortion is to the Republican Party in the United States. Second, the parties switching sides were the incumbents and so were able to change actual policy, not just rhetoric, in advance of the election. In general, nonincumbents may be less able to convince the public that they have credibly changed sides because they are not in a position to put their words into action. Finally, the public may have found the switch credible in part because of Lubbers's strong personal reputation.

CHAPTER SEVEN

Fending off Swamp Rabbits: Defense and Carter

In the summer of 1979, a swamp rabbit attacked President Jimmy Carter while he was fishing in Georgia (see figure 7.1). His tepid response—splashing water on it—soon became a metaphor for his foreign policy toward the Soviet Union, which critics contended was not sufficiently forceful. Running for president in 1976, Carter had campaigned as a "dove" on defense policy, promising to "trim the fat" from the military budget. He and his chief advisers entered office in 1977 dedicated to reversing many of "the basic themes of American foreign policy during the Nixon-Ford era" (Burt 1980). Carter halted the development of the neutron bomb (Wicker 1980b), blocked construction of aircraft carriers, and vetoed a $2 billion military procurement bill, incurring the wrath of Democratic and Republican defense hawks in Congress (Kaufman and Kaufman 2006). Instead of building up the military, he stressed arms control, negotiating the SALT II accord with the Soviet Union. He also deemphasized the containment of Soviet expansionism, taking such steps as demilitarizing the Indian Ocean, placing restrictions on the exports of conventional arms (Morris 1997), and no longer using food (such as grain shipments) as a weapon in the Cold War.

Carter's dovish policies, however, increasingly came to haunt him as the 1980 election approached. At the end of 1979, two events—the Iranian hostage crisis in November 1979 and the Soviet invasion of Afghanistan in December 1979—reshaped public opinion on defense policy, rendering Carter's policies deeply unpopular. These events transformed the public into defense hawks, and the issue of defense spending captured the public's attention to an unusual degree, much as nuclear power

Weather

Today—Hot and humid, high in the low 80s. Fair tonight, low near 70. The chance of rain is 30 percent. Friday—Sunny and not humid, high near 80. Yesterday—3 p.m. high: 89; temperature range: 69-54. Details, D2.

The Washington Post

FINAL

Amusements F14 | Metro B 1
Classified C16 | Obituaries B16
Comics Weekly | Sports C 1
Editorials A22 | Style C 1
Financial D 1 | Style Plus F 1
Food B 1 | TV/Radio F15
Inside: The Weekly

102nd Year · · · · No. 268 | © 1979, Washington Post Co. | THURSDAY, AUGUST 30, 1979 | Metropolitan Home | 15c

U.S. Condemns Israel For Raids on Lebanon

By John M. Goshko
Washington Post Staff Writer

Outgoing U.S. Ambassador Andrew Young, treating a new U.N. bid to halt the Lebanese civil war, yesterday sharply criticized Israel's military incursions into Lebanon as "wrong and unacceptable to our government."

Young's statement at a U.N. Security Council meeting on Lebanon reflected mounting U.S. concern that the fallout from the fighting, pitting Palestinians and Lebanese Moslems against Israeli-backed Christian militias, could endanger the fragile Egyptian-Israeli talks on Palestinian self-rule.

"My condemns the policy of artillery shelling and preemptive attacks on Lebanese towns, villages and refugee camps which Israel said the overall Lebanese troops Israel expects have followed in recent months," Young said.

"Let there be no doubt or ambiguity about this: We cannot and do not agree with Israel's military policies in Lebanon. They are wrong and unacceptable to our government. They are

painfully at variance with the values which Israel has traditionally espoused."

Young was forced to resign as U.N. ambassador earlier this month after he violated policy instructions by secretly meeting with a representative of the Palestine Liberation Organization. He subsequently rebuffed publicly against most aspects of the Carter administration's Mideast policy as relating to deal with the PLO and not taking a firmer stance against Israel's attacks on Lebanon.

But, in yesterday's debate, he prefaced his remarks by stressing: "I speak with the full authority of the United States government."

He also had harsh words for those Palestinian guerrillas whose use of southern Lebanon as a base for terrorist raids into Israel triggered the Israeli retaliation. Young said:

"We condemn those who boast of the murder of an Israeli mother and her child, the attack on a bus filled with Israeli civilians, or the explosion of mortars and bombs in Israeli towns and cities."

Then, in a pointed reference to the

controversy kicked off by his own dealings with the PLO and last week's Security Council debate on Palestinian rights, Young added:

"If there is a strengthened understanding in my country of the importance of asserting that the legitimate rights of the Palestinians are included in a comprehensive settlement—and I believe there is—then it is time for the Palestinian leadership to recognize that their objectives cannot be achieved through violence and terrorism."

Despite this gesture toward even-handedness, the chief significance of Young's statement was the administration's acknowledgement that the United States—once again—is on record as condemning Israeli activities in Lebanon. It was a reiteration of a position that the United States has for some time been trying to enunciate and the Carter to the Mideast only caused by the Young-PLO incident and by a subsequent internal

See MIDEAST, A26, Col. 2

PLO leader, via congressman, suggests meeting with Young. Page A26

Vice President Mondale visits Peking's "Forbidden City" before visiting ancient capital of Xi'an. Story, A13.

Lebanese Border: A Free-Fire Zone

By Edward Cody
Washington Post Foreign Service

TYRE, Lebanon, Aug. 29—Five months of intensified Israeli air strikes against Palestinian guerrillas and relentless artillery pounding by Israel and its Lebanese Christian allies have devastated southern Lebanon, turning the rocky border hills into a virtual free-fire zone.

The concentrated attacks with 155mm and 175mm artillery, rockets and U.S.-supplied air fighters have taken a high toll in civilian Lebanese and Palestinian casualties. They have emptied many Lebanese towns, villages and farmland across a 10-mile-deep swath of Lebanese territory stretching along the border from the foothills of Mount Hermon to the Mediterranean Sea.

The flight of the civilian population, like that of the Palestinian and Lebanese Christian followers, have in effect

gained for the Israeli armed forces almost the same advantages as they were forced to give up in withdrawing from southern Lebanon three months ago. After their March 1978 invasion.

Despite the presence of United Nations peacekeepers, the border hills have been turned into the main battleground for the struggle between Israeli armed forces and Palestinian guerrillas, among the guerrillas that of Lebanon is afraid of along the Israeli border and reducing Palestinian guerrilla commandos to slip into Israeli settlements or shell them from nearby valleys points.

The Lebanese government estimates 175,000 Lebanese civilians have fled the fury of the border-area bombardments since Israel launched its policy of preemptive attacks against the Palestinians in April. In addition, the Palestine Liberation Or-

See LEBANON, A20, Col. 1

Soviets Amenable To SALT Shifts, Senators Infer

By Kevin Klose
Washington Post Foreign Service

MOSCOW, Aug. 29—Senior Soviet officials have indicated a willingness to consider "significant" criticals in nuclear weapons stockpiles in any future negotiations about strategic weapons, according to the head of a U.S. Senate delegation visiting here.

Sen. Joseph D. Biden (D-Del.) said he also detected both Soviet acceptance of more comprehensive "verification procedures than under the SALT II agreement, an attitude that could lead eventually to mutual inspection.

Biden and five other senators were briefed for possible Soviet attitudes toward prospective negotiations on a third strategic arms limitation treaty during three days of meetings with Soviet officials.

Biden added that Soviet officials, during four plenary sessions devoted almost exclusively to strongle arms matters, accepted without direct demur the senators' assertions that such powerful Soviet tactical nuclear weapons systems as the SS-20 and Backfire bomber must be specifically included in any accord to the SALT II agreement. SALT II was signed by President Carter and Soviet leader Leonid Brezhnev in June. The treaty has come under sharp criticism from some senators who are expected to vote on its ratification in early autumn.

According to one delegation source, the Soviets' attitudes were suggested as much by their silence as by specific Soviet reprise to the senators' assertions. Sen. Richard G. Lugar (R-Ind.) indicated this was notable especially to the Soviets responses to the senators' repeated assertions that the Soviets will require modifications or "reservations" into the pending SALT II.

The Soviets were said to have listened carefully to the senators' explanations of these proposals and repeatedly made known their desire to conclude SALT II quickly. This calls responses by the Kremlin groups.

See SOVIETS, A24, Col. 1

Challenge to Khomeini

The Kurdish uprising is posing the severest challenge Ayatollah Ruhollah Khomeini has faced since he was swept to power in Iran six months ago.

Details on Page A20

Pope Cancels Ulster Visit, Confirms Itinerary Here

By Christopher Dickey
and Marjorie Hyer
Washington Post Staff Writers

Pope John Paul II has canceled a plan to visit Northern Ireland because of the recent violence there, the Vatican announced yesterday.

A tentative decision to visit Ulster during the pontiff's upcoming 10-day trip to Ireland and the United States was received "with great regret," a Vatican spokesman said, "due to the brutal murders of recent days." On Monday, British war John Lord Mountbatten, members of his family and 18 British soldiers were killed by Irish Republican terrorist bombs.

The Vatican for the first time also officially confirmed previous reports that the pope will celebrate a mass for as many as 1 million people on the Mall while he is here.

The pope will arrive in Boston from Ireland early on the afternoon of Oct. 1, according to church officials here. He will fly to New York and address the United Nations Oct. 2, visit Philadelphia Oct. 3, and Des Moines, for a late lunch, on Oct. 4. He will spend two nights of Oct. 4 and Oct. 5 in Chicago and then arrive in Washington late in the morning of Oct. 6, officials said.

John Paul II will be the first pope

to visit the White House and is expected to celebrate a mass for as many as 1 million people on the Mall while he is here.

Father Maurice Fye, spokesman for the Washington archdiocese, said yesterday that detailed plans have not been worked out, but the hope also the trip scheduled to stay here and visit Andrews Air Force Base Oct. 7, then land at Andrews Air Force Base then to the residence of the apostolic delegate across from the Naval Observatory on Massachusetts Avenue NW, where he will spend the night.

At 8:30 a.m. on Sunday, Oct. 7, the pope will go to the National Shrine of the Immaculate Conception in Northeast Washington to address a group of nuns.

advancement political leaders from the major transfers of government. For the pope and as many as 5,000 people are expected to gather on the South Lawn for the occasion.

From the White House, the pope will go to the Organization of American States for about an hour to meet with members of the diplomatic corps, then to the residence of the apostolic delegate across from the Naval Observatory on Massachusetts Avenue NW, where he will spend the night.

He then will reach the Catholic University to speak to a convocation of the nation's leading Catholic academicians.

The papacy has a unique relationship to CU, the only university in this country originally chartered by a pope—Leo XIII, in 1887.

John Paul II also will address a gathering of ecumenical leaders from various protestant denominations at the university's Shrine Auditorium before returning to the apostolic delegate's residence at 12:30 p.m.

A motorcade will take the pope to the Mall at 3 p.m. Oct. 7, where he

See POPE, A17, Col. 5

Bunny Goes Bugs
Rabbit Attacks President

By Brooks Jackson
Associated Press

A "killer rabbit" attacked President Carter on a recent trip to Plains, Ga., penetrating Secret Service security and forcing the chief executive to beat back the beast with a canoe paddle.

The rabbit, which the president later guessed was fleeing in panic from some predator, swam toward a canoe from which Carter was fishing in a pond. It was hissing menacingly, its teeth flashing and nostrils flared, and making straight for the president, he said.

Carter was not injured, and reports are unclear about what became of the hapless bunny. But, fortunately for Carter's credibility, a White House staff photographer made a picture of the attack and the president's successful anti-defense.

It was fortunate because some of the president's closest staff members refused to believe the story of the aquatic attack rabbit when Carter related it to them later. Their skepticism arose despite Carter's strong and oft-repeated protests never to lie.

"You could see him in the canoe with his paddle raised, and you could see something in the water," the doubter said. "But you couldn't tell what it was it could have been anything."

So Carter ordered an enlargement made. "It was a rabbit, all right," said the staff member after seeing the blown-up photo.

No news photographers were allowed within camera range of Carter on the fishing trip April 20. The White House withheld pictures of the fishing trip and refused yesterday to make available pictures of the encounter with the rabbit.

"There are just certain stories about the president that must forever remain shrouded in mystery," spokesman Rex Granum said.

By William Crabtree for The Washington Post

Ex-Green Beret Is Guilty In Murder of His Family

By Adam Abrams
Special to The Washington Post

RALEIGH, N.C., Aug. 29—A federal jury, with some members in tears, took 6½ hours today to find former Green Beret Capt. Jeffrey R. Mac-Donald guilty of murdering his pregnant wife and two young daughters July 17, 1970.

MacDonald, 36, an emergency room physician in Long Beach, Calif., sat immobile as the jurors, four of whom were crying, were polled and pronounced him guilty of second-degree murder in the slaying of his wife, Colette, 26, and daughter, Kimberley, 5. The jury found MacDonald guilty of first-degree murder in the stabbing of his younger daughter, Kristen, 2.

U.S. District Court Judge Franklin T. Dupree Jr. sentenced him to three consecutive life sentences.

In his charge to the jurors, Dupree told they had three choices—to find MacDonald innocent or to find him guilty of first-degree murder or second-degree murder. Dupree told the jury that first-degree murder involved a defendant who "really deliberates or thinks the matter over" before acting and MacDonald should be found guilty of second-degree murder if jurors found that he killed his family but not acted without premeditation.

Before sentencing, MacDonald rose with the aid of his attorneys and spoke to the court. "Sir, I'm not guilty," MacDonald told the judge in a clear voice. "I don't think the court heard all the evidence. That's all I have to say."

Immediately after the verdict was announced, R. Mary's Medical Center in Long Beach announced that MacDonald had been fired.

MacDonald and his lawyers had previously indicated a belief by Dupree that the jury could not hear the truth story of any events the MacDonalds many of six persons who the jailed were told a former drug addict in the crime. At the time of the murders, MacDonald had been a doctor at Fort Bragg, N.C., whose MacDonald served as a Green Beret medical officer. One of his responsibilities was to conduct and treat drug abusers.

MacDonald has maintained since 1970 that his family was slain by four intruders who entered his home while he slept on a living room couch. He testified last Thursday that one of the intruders chanted, "Acid is groovy, kill the pigs" while struggling with him.

Assistant U.S. Attorney James Blackburn argued "murder that the stab, gestures and stab wounds Mac-Donald said he suffered in a fracas with the intruders were self-inflicted as part of a cover-up.

Shortly after beginning deliberations, the jury asked to see the pajama top MacDonald said he was wearing when he was stabbed. Jurors also asked for exhibits concerning the pajama top, blood-type charts showing places where blood was found, photos showing where the family members stabbed, "Acid is groovy, kill the pigs" still struggling with him, and others.

The pajama top saw a key piece of evidence for the government. Prosecu-

See MacDONALD, A3, Col. 1

FIGURE 7.1. Reprinted in *Washington Post*, August 30, 1979, A1.

did in the Netherlands after Chernobyl. Given such deep-seated public concern, judging a presidential candidate on the issue of defense spending should have been easy for most citizens. Nevertheless, the analysis in chapters 3–5 found little evidence that citizens actually did judge Carter on it. Even on this prominent policy issue, citizens apparently failed to lead.

As chapter 6 sought to understand how Dutch citizens could have failed to judge Prime Minister Lubbers on nuclear power, this chapter seeks to understand how American citizens could have failed to judge President Carter on defense spending. Lubbers defended his coalition, it appeared, by adopting his opponents' position. Could Carter do the same? Could he successfully neutralize this issue by shifting his position on defense spending? Ultimately, Carter lost the 1980 election to Reagan, but polls suggest that it was close until the end, and other factors, rather than his previously dovish stance, may explain his loss. In particular, Carter faced questions about his competency and, in the election year of 1980, presided over a dismal economy characterized by a debilitating combination of high inflation and high unemployment.

Like Lubbers, Carter tried to defend himself, but his response was uneven. Immediately following the November and December 1979 crises in Iran and Afghanistan, respectively, he adopted the vigorous prodefense policies the public embraced. In March of 1980, however, he retreated from these positions. He then shifted again, returning to a hawkish position in the summer. These three phases of Carter's response—hawk, dove, hawk—provide a unique opportunity to test for policy voting. If hawkish voters cared enough about defense spending to vote on it, then the issue might have done Carter no harm during his hawkish phase, harmed him during his dovish phase, and again done him no harm when he returned to the hawkish position the public embraced. This is precisely what I find. When Carter chose to neutralize the defense issue by becoming more hawkish, he succeeded. When he chose not to, he suffered. Carter therefore gives us a rare glimpse of the potential power of voters' judgments on policy issues, a power only visible when candidates adopt unpopular policy positions.

These findings, like those in chapter 6, paint democracy in a more positive light. Most of the time, citizens do not appear to lead on policy issues, at least not those upon which candidates campaign. When issues capture the public's attention to an unusual degree, however, voters appear to lead and politicians appear to follow.

7.1 The Threat: A Nation of Newly Minted Hawks

Carter faced two shifts in public opinion on defense spending, both to his detriment and both indicating heightened public attention to the issue. The first shift was a change in voters' positions on defense spending. As shown in figure 7.2, an overwhelming majority of the public came to prefer greater defense spending, marking one of the sharpest public opinion shifts in the history of polling on public policy, not unlike the

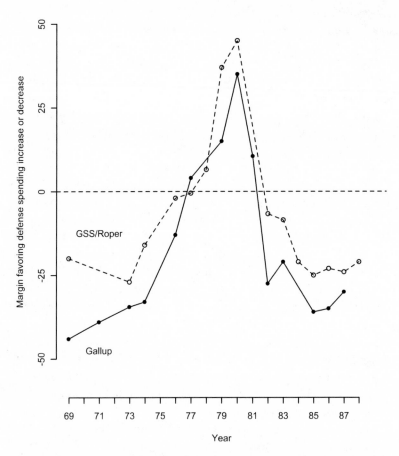

FIGURE 7.2. Margin favoring increased or decreased defense spending in public opinion polls, 1969–89. In the wake of the Iranian hostage crisis and the Soviet invasion of Afghanistan, Jimmy "the dove" Carter faced a public that overwhelmingly desired greater defense spending. Source: Bartels (1991).

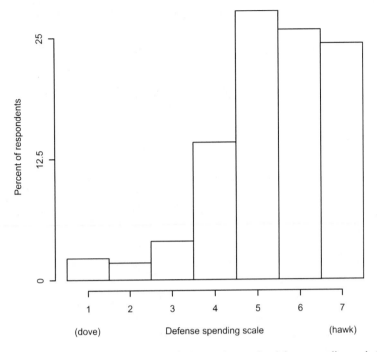

FIGURE 7.3. The distribution of public attitudes on the 7-point defense spending scale in January 1980 (histogram). Source: First wave of the 1980 American National Election Study (ANES) Major Panel.

changes in policy views induced by the Japanese attack on Pearl Harbor or 9/11 (Berinsky 2009). This strong support is evident in the January wave of the 1980 American National Election Study (ANES) Major Panel—the panel I use throughout this chapter. It asked respondents for their views about defense spending on a 7-point scale, with 1 indicating that they desire much less spending and 7 indicating much more. By January 1980, almost 80 percent of the public preferred greater defense spending, placing themselves at 5, 6, or 7 on the scale (see figure 7.3).

The second shift in public opinion Carter faced was an increase in the salience of defense policy. Citizens increasingly named national defense as the country's most important problem: 12 percent did so in January, 16 percent in June, and 25 percent in November (Miller and Shanks 1982, 316). Thus not only did citizens become more hawkish on defense spending, but they also became increasingly concerned with the issue as the 1980 election approached.

These shifts left Carter vulnerable to attack because of his dovish record on defense. Ronald Reagan and the Republican Party relentlessly exploited this vulnerability. They seized upon the Iranian hostage crisis and the Soviet invasion of Afghanistan "to help crystallize widespread disquiet about the United States' standing in the world, and turn that disquiet into a Republican campaign issue" (Bartels 1991, 459). Passages from the 1980 Republican Party platform illustrate the themes of the attack:

> The [Carter] Administration's neglect of America's defense posture in the face of overwhelming evidence of a threatening military buildup is without parallel since the 1930s. The scope and magnitude of the growth of Soviet military power threatens American interests at every level, from the nuclear threat to our survival, to our ability to protect the lives and property of American citizens abroad. . . . Despite the growing sentiment for a stronger defense, candidate Carter ran on a promise of massive cuts in U.S. defense spending, one promise he has kept. . . . We have depleted our capital and must now devote the resources essential to catching up. (*Congressional Quarterly* 1980, 75B–76B)

Combined with the growing public desire for increased defense spending, these political attacks seem likely to have induced priming, persuasion, and learning—all to Carter's detriment. If citizens ever judge politicians on policy grounds, they should have done so here. In a seminal paper on priming and issue ownership, John Petrocik (1996) argues that the rise of this and other "Republican owned" issues helps explain Ronald Reagan's victory over Carter. Is Petrocik right? Did the defense issue in fact hurt Carter? In particular, did the legions of newly minted hawks lower their approval of Carter because he was now too dovish for them? Did hawks—new or old—learn about Carter's dovish record and turn against him? Did campaign and media emphasis on this issue lead citizens to place more weight on defense spending and thus decide to oppose Carter?

7.2 The First Shift: Carter the Hawk, January 1980

Carter began his repositioning soon after the Iranian hostage crisis began. On December 13, 1979, in what the *New York Times* called "a major political move," Carter announced a U-turn in his foreign policy and particularly in military spending (Smith 1980). He called for nearly a $20 billion increase in the next year's military budget and 4.5 percent real increases in funding for each of the subsequent five years. Only three weeks later the Soviets invaded Afghanistan, and Carter shifted further, calling for an even larger 5.4 percent real increase in defense spending, including the addition of nineteen navy ships (Wilson 1980d).

In fact, Carter shifted so much to the right on defense that George H. W. Bush, who was campaigning for the Republican nomination, ran to Carter's left. In campaign appearances, Bush repeatedly criticized both Carter and Reagan for making warlike statements. "One of the problems with the Carter reaction," Bush said, "was there was too much talk of war" (McLeod 1980). Senator Edward Kennedy, who ran against Carter for the Democratic nomination, also criticized Carter on defense, calling him "a clone of Ronald Reagan" (Espo 1980) and saying "the Democratic Party cannot succeed by trying to out-Republican the Republicans" (Andrews 1980).

Did the public learn that Carter was now prodefense and change their support for him accordingly? Did the increased salience of this issue and the dramatic shift in public opinion induce priming and persuasion effects? Unfortunately, the first wave of the 1980 ANES Major Panel is the January one, after the shifts in defense opinion and after Carter adopted a prodefense policy. (This panel interviewed respondents in January, June, September, and postelection.) Consequently, for this first phase of Carter's response to the foreign policy crises, we cannot use the panel techniques used throughout this book. Nevertheless, the January 1980 interviews allow us to examine several simpler predictions.

For Carter's U-turn on defense policy to work, the public had first to take notice and then to change its perception of Carter. The evidence suggests that it did. Although the public saw Carter as a defense dove in the 1976 campaign, by January 1980, Carter was seen as a hawk (see figure 7.4).[1] In the January 1980 survey, almost 60 percent placed him above the midpoint on the 7-point defense spending scale described above (see figure 7.4). Almost no one placed him on the lowest two points of the scale. The most common placement for Carter was just above the midpoint, at 5, and a sizable number of respondents placed him at 6. (Of the 628 January respondents, only forty-seven failed to place him on the scale.) Figure 7.5 shows how these perceptions changed over the course of the campaign.

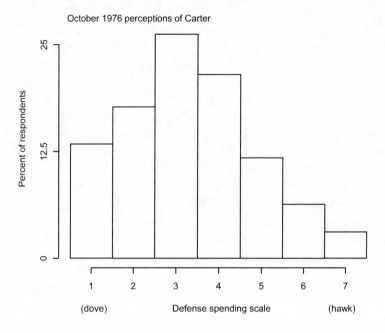

October 1976 perceptions of Carter

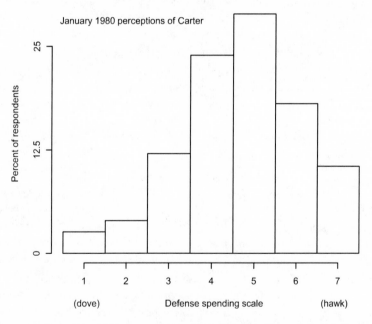

January 1980 perceptions of Carter

FIGURE 7.4. Perceptions of Carter on the 7-point defense spending scale in October 1976 and January 1980 (histogram). Despite having run as a dove in 1976, Carter convinced a majority of the public that he was prodefense by January 1980. Sources: Patterson 1976 panel and 1980 ANES Major Panel.

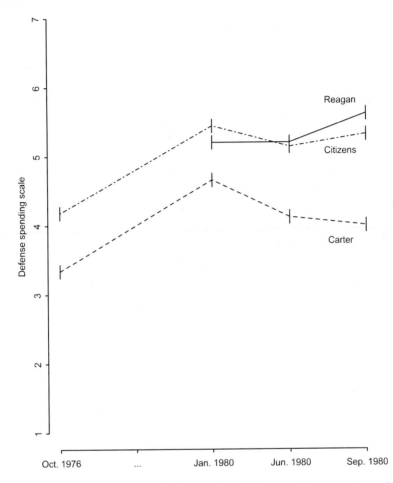

FIGURE 7.5. Citizens' positions and their perceptions of Carter and Reagan on the 7-point defense spending scale. In January of 1980, citizens saw Carter as a hawk. Error bars show 68 percent confidence intervals. Source: 1980 ANES Major Panel.

The second startling revelation in the January 1980 interviews concerns who most strongly supported and opposed Carter. If this sharp increase in the public's support for defense spending hurt Carter, the most prodefense citizens should have been the least supportive of him. However, as figure 7.6 reveals, the opposite was true. The most prodefense citizens were in fact the most supportive of Carter, not the least. As the figure shows, an increase from the least to the most prodefense attitude corresponded to about a 10-point increase on the 100-point Carter

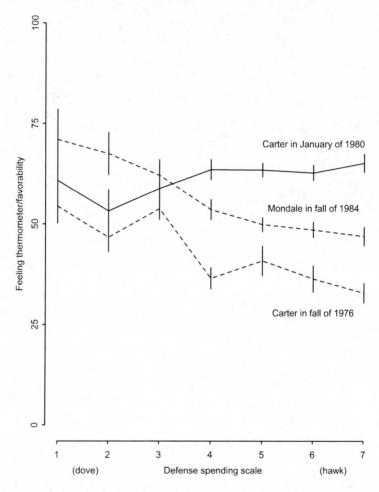

FIGURE 7.6. Support for Carter before and after he became a hawk by views about defense spending. The figure shows that in 1976, when Carter was a dove, hawkish citizens liked him less than did dovish citizens. In January 1980, however, after Carter became a hawk, this relationship reversed and hawkish citizens liked him most. It would appear from this figure, then, that the public bought Carter's hawkish shift on defense spending. To further show how unusual Carter's 1980 pattern was, the figure also shows this relationship for the Democratic nominee in 1984, Walter Mondale, finding that hawks again liked him least. Error bars show 68 percent confidence intervals. Source: Patterson 1976 panel, 1980 ANES Major Panel, and 1984 ANES.

feeling thermometer.[2] This is a reversal of the pattern for Carter in 1976 and a reversal of the standard pattern for Democrats more generally. To show this, figure 7.6 presents the same relationship for Carter in 1976 and for the Democratic nominee for president in 1984, Walter Mondale. As Carter had done in 1976, Mondale ran as a dove in 1984. In these two elections, we see the typical pattern: doves liked Carter or Mondale most, hawks liked them least. At least in January of 1980, then, Carter's prodefense repositioning worked: he appears to have convinced a nation of defense hawks that he was one of them.[3] These findings support the hypothesis that politicians can quickly change the perceptions of their positions in the eyes of voters.

7.3 The Second Shift: Carter the Dove, January to June

If politicians can defend themselves from attack by changing positions, then, for the most part, policy issues should neither hurt nor benefit them, even policy issues about which the public cares deeply. At least through January 1980, this appears to have been true for Carter with respect to defense. When voters care deeply about an issue, however, they should punish candidates who fail to follow their will. Given the overwhelming public demand for defense spending, one might expect Carter to have maintained or even intensified his hawkish position on defense. Instead, he retreated.

The retreat began in late March when Carter declared that, instead of supporting the 5.4 percent real increase in military spending he had promised in January, or even the 4.5 percent increase he had called for in December, he would support only a 3.0 percent real increase (Wilson 1980e). By opposing the larger increases, Carter put himself in direct opposition not only to the Republican presidential candidates but also to the Democratic-controlled House and Senate. In a string of prodefense votes, the House added billions to the Pentagon budget in the spring of 1980. Instead of supporting these defense appropriations, Carter fought them (Wilson 1980f). His opposition set off "a firestorm of Congressional criticism" (Weisman 1980b). Carter continued to stress the importance of military strength in his public statements but prioritized fiscal restraint over defense spending in his actions.

Given public attitudes about defense, these actions gave Republicans an opening that they eagerly exploited. In a series of campaign rallies,

Reagan repeatedly alleged that Carter's proposed increases were "not nearly enough" and that Carter's "actions do not match his new rhetoric" (Roberts 1980). In a key moment during that phase of the campaign, Carter and Reagan both gave speeches in Columbus, Ohio, on May 29, just days after Ford and Bush conceded the nomination to Reagan. The media labeled it "a debate," as Carter's and Reagan's rallies took place only six blocks apart. In his speech, Reagan took Carter to task for at first advocating increases in defense spending and then opposing such increases (Weisman 1980a). "Will the real Mr. Carter please stand up?" Reagan asked. Six blocks away, Carter vigorously defended his opposition to several military increases in the budget resolution now before Congress, saying they were no longer needed because "we have turned the tide in military strength" (Weisman 1980a).

Given Carter's reversals on defense, Reagan's allegations may have appeared credible to many citizens. Often Reagan's allegations originated with critics within Carter's own party and administration. On the same day as the so-called debate, for instance, Representative Samuel S. Stratton, Democrat from New York, called the Joint Chiefs of Staff to testify before the House Armed Services Investigation Subcommittee. Upset by Carter's retreat on the defense buildup, Stratton wanted to place the chiefs on record about how much defense funding is enough. Under questioning, the chiefs uniformly repudiated Carter, calling his proposed increases inadequate and describing the current military as "hollow"—like "a car running out of fuel"—and unable to meet the Soviet threat (Wilson 1980c).[4] The following day, newspaper readers were met with headlines about Reagan's allegations next to headlines such as, "Joint Chiefs Break with Carter on Defense Budget" (Wilson 1980c).

News stories at the time also portrayed Carter's actions on defense as deceitful, criticizing him for attempting to mask his retreat. In one instance, someone leaked a Defense Department memo describing budget chicanery that made military spending increases appear larger than they were (Wilson 1980e). Using what the *New York Times* described as the kind of arithmetic for which "a sixth-grade student would be accused of cheating" (Wicker 1980a), the administration was cutting military spending in the 1980 fiscal year to achieve a 3 percent real increase between 1980 and 1981 (Wilson 1980c). To justify his opposition to further military increases, Carter made arguments that many found dubious. In a letter to Chairman John C. Stennis (Democrat of Mississippi) of the Senate Armed Services Committee, Carter wrote that further military budget increases "could adversely affect today's military readiness by forcing offsetting reductions in the operations and personnel accounts" (Wilson 1980c). When asked during the House hearing about Carter's argument, the Joint Chiefs roundly denied its validity (Wilson 1980c).

Carter was not a fool; he had good reasons to retreat on defense. He faced a formidable challenge for the Democratic Party's presidential nomination from Senator Edward Kennedy, who ran to his left. And even after he had clinched the nomination, he may have hoped to bring Kennedy supporters back into the fold and prevent a rumored Kennedy run for president as an independent (Bartels 1988). Carter also hoped to limit government spending to counteract soaring inflation. Finally, given the severe recession in the spring of 1980, Carter prioritized unemployment relief over weapons. Given the overwhelming desire among the public for greater defense spending, however, Carter may have paid a high price for this retreat.

The 1980 ANES Major Panel reinterviewed its January respondents in June, two months into Carter's retreat, allowing us to examine whether this substantive issue hurt Carter. Of the three types of shift, his retreat seems likely to have induced at least two. The first is learning: defense hawks should have become less approving of Carter as they learned about his retreat, while doves should have become more approving. The second is a priming effect: the Reagan campaign's emphasis on the issue of military budgeting and Carter's battle with Congress over it made it a particularly prominent issue in May and June (see figure 2.10). Since defense spending was already a prominent issue by the time of the first wave of interviews in January, large priming effects seem unlikely between January and June, but smaller effects seem possible. In contrast, persuasion effects are unlikely, at least in net, because between January and June public attitudes on defense remained relatively stable in the aggregate (see figure 7.5). Do the results confirm these three predictions?

Learning and the Retreat, January to June

Carter's opposition to the defense appropriations and Republican criticisms of his "backsliding" were well publicized. Above I showed that, by January 1980, the public had come to see the previously dovish Carter as a hawk. For Carter's retreat on defense to hurt him, the public now had to notice. Table 7.1 shows that it did. Between January and June, 29 percent of the public came to see him as a dove. These individuals, whom

TABLE 7.1. **Awareness of Carter's retreat on defense spending between the January and June waves**

	Place Carter at the midpoint or below on the 7-point defense spending scale			
	Jan.	Jun.	n	%
Learned he was a dove	No	Yes	155	29
Already saw him as a dove	Yes	Yes	160	30
Never learned he was a dove	No	No	163	30
Learned he was not a dove	Yes	No	57	11

I classify as learners, initially placed Carter above the midpoint on the 7-point scale, but now placed him at the midpoint or below. In contrast, only about 11 percent made the reverse change, coming to see Carter as a hawk during this period.[5] The net result of these changes in perception is that, while almost 60 percent of respondents viewed Carter as prodefense (above the midpoint) in January, less than 40 percent did in June. As shown in figure 7.5, the average perception of Carter in June was still above the midpoint on the 7-point defense spending scale, but now only slightly above it. The shift in perception among the learners is large, more than two points in the dovish direction on the 7-point defense scale, from 5.5 to 3.4. The public noticed Carter's retreat.

This is an extraordinarily rare circumstance. Candidates rarely shift away from voters, especially during a campaign and on a highly prominent issue. To my knowledge this is the only instance in which panel data have captured such a shift, allowing us to observe its consequences. In these unusual circumstances, neither party strategy nor the tendency of people who care about an issue to already know the candidates' positions interferes with voters' policy judgments. Consequently, prodefense respondents who noticed Carter's shift should have lowered their approval of Carter compared to those with moderate positions. Using a (partial residual) scatterplot of change in Carter approval between January and June, the top half of figure 7.7 finds precisely this pattern. (Equation 10 in the appendix presents the model behind the scatterplot.) Those who most strongly supported military spending in January showed the biggest shift against Carter, their approval falling more than 50 points. In contrast, those who placed themselves at 4 (the midpoint) lowered their approval of Carter by only about 25 points. Unfortunately, there were too few respondents below the midpoint to draw inferences about them

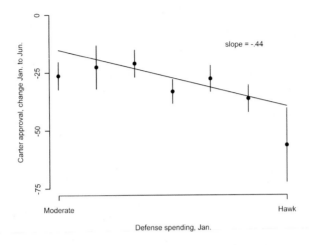

Learned Carter a dove (learning effect)

slope = -.44

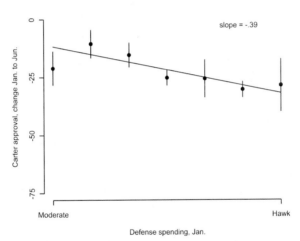

Already saw him as a dove (priming effect)

slope = -.39

FIGURE 7.7. Did Carter's retreat on defense spending between January and June hurt his approval ratings? This figure shows that those who were defense hawks in January became less approving of Carter between January and June. This group includes both hawks who came to see Carter as a dove during that period (top half) and hawks who already saw him as a dove in January (bottom half). Figure 7.8 provides significance tests using the two-wave test. For the learners, results are only for citizens who shifted from seeing Carter as a hawk (above the midpoint) in January to seeing him as a dove (midpoint or below) in June and who continued to see Carter as a dove in September. These figures are partial residual scatterplots and control for party identification, attitudes about government spending and services scale, perceptions of the national economy, and attitudes about reducing unemployment versus reducing inflation (all measured in January). The appendix presents the model behind these plots (equation 10) and the online appendix shows the full ordinary least squares regression estimates. Error bars show 68 percent confidence intervals. Source: 1980 ANES Major Panel.

(see figure 7.3). Since these doves are outliers, they have a pronounced influence on the estimates, so I exclude them from the remaining analyses in this chapter. In short, Carter's shift apparently hurt him through learning. Those who thought Carter was prodefense in January liked him most, but as they learned about his retreat, they judged him on this issue and came to like him least.

There is one complication here worth noting. Given that this learning should only have influenced people who cared about this issue and really did learn his position, it should only have emerged among those who noticed Carter's retreat on defense between January and June and who maintained that knowledge through the September wave of the survey.[6] This is precisely what I find. Of the 160 learners, ninety-five maintained their knowledge, and the learning effect only emerged among those ninety-five people. The remaining sixty-five do not appear to have shifted their approval of Carter as they came to see him as a dove. These sixty-five may only appear to have learned because of guessing or measurement error. It is also possible that they really did learn, but cared so little about the issue that what they learned did not change their view of Carter and had been forgotten by September.

Although figure 7.7 suggests a learning effect, there are several alternative explanations. For example, the same campaign communications that informed the learners about Carter's retreat may also have activated their partisanship, leading citizens to change their approval of Carter accordingly (and creating the appearance of a learning effect).[7] Numerous studies have found that campaign communications activate partisanship (Ansolabehere and Iyengar 1995; Berelson, Lazarsfeld, and McPhee 1954). In this alternative, the learning is real but inconsequential. Can we be sure that Carter's retreat hurt him among hawks more than it did among doves? That is, can we be sure of a learning effect?

To address alternative explanations, figure 7.7 already includes controls for party identification, attitudes about government spending and services scale, perceptions of the national economy, and attitudes about reducing unemployment versus reducing inflation (all measured in January; see the appendix). To confirm that this effect is statistically significant, figure 7.8 (top) presents the two-wave test of learning effects among the learners who retained their knowledge (see equation 14 in the appendix). It confirms the finding that learning hurt Carter. The prelearning issue weight among the learners was 0.17, indicating that hawks who had learned about his shift toward their position tended to support Carter in

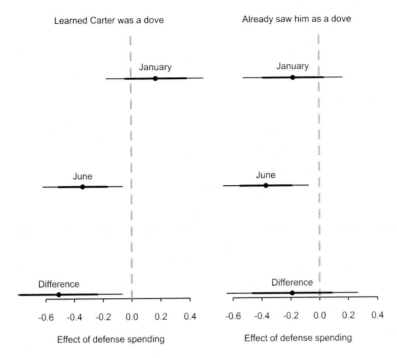

FIGURE 7.8. Two-wave test estimates of priming and learning, January to June. The effect of learning about Carter's retreat and defense-spending attitudes (left) and the effect of priming (right). All variables are coded to vary between 0 and 1. The appendix presents the model behind these plots (equation 14) and the online appendix shows the full ordinary least squares regression estimates. The thin and thick error bars show 90 percent and 68 percent confidence intervals, respectively. Source: 1980 ANES Major Panel.

January more than did defense moderates who had learned about it. By June, however, the issue weight had reversed direction to −0.34 (see figure 7.8), indicating that January hawks came to dislike Carter more than January moderates. Based on this change in the issue weight, the learning effect estimate is a whopping (−0.34 − 0.17 =) −0.51, an effect size consistent with the mean shift in figure 7.7. Thus learning about Carter's retreat appears to have led hawks to dislike Carter because they were hawks, not because they tended to be Republican or conservative or to see the national economy as poor.[8]

This is an exceptional finding. In chapter 5 I found that such learning rarely leads citizens to judge politicians. Learning may rarely matter, however, not because voters are inherently unable to be affected by it, but because candidates seldom shift away from public opinion on highly prominent issues. Carter's retreat on defense appears to have cost him, leading to a precipitous drop in support among defense hawks who had learned about his retreat. As I noted earlier, Carter may have benefited from his retreat in other ways, such as defeating Edward Kennedy's challenge. But he appears to have paid a price. Moreover, learning is only one of the shifts that could have hurt Carter. I now turn to the effects of priming.

Priming, January to June

The issue of defense remained prominent in the news between January and June of 1980, as shown in chapter 2's figure 2.10, and citizens increasingly named it as one of the most important issues facing the country (Miller and Shanks 1982, 316). Did this emphasis prime attitudes on defense spending? Testing for priming effects here is particularly tricky (as in the previous chapter) because perceptions of Carter are changing, making it difficult to distinguish between priming and learning effects. My approach is to test for priming among those who saw Carter as a dove both in January and in June. Since these individuals did not *learn* that Carter was a dove during that period, we can mostly rule out learning effects. But did these individuals come to place more weight on defense spending (an indication of priming) and consequently lower their evaluations of Carter? These data appear to suggest that they did. Among the 30 percent of the panel respondents who consistently saw Carter as a dove (see table 7.1), we do see evidence of priming. As shown at the bottom of figure 7.7, January defense-spending attitudes explain change in support for Carter between January and June among this group. And indeed, defense moderates do lower their evaluations of Carter, but defense hawks lower their evaluations even more. These findings thus suggest that between January and June citizens who already saw Carter as a dove came to place more weight on defense spending attitudes, indicating priming. Unlike the learning effect estimates, however, the priming findings could also be due to chance. The two-wave test suggests a smaller and statistically insignificant effect of -0.12 (see the right panel in figure 7.8).

So far I have only examined support for Carter. By June, however, Reagan's nomination was all but official. Although standard vote choice questions are not available until the September wave, we can look at the effect of defense-spending attitudes on a comparative feeling thermometer, which I code as Carter minus Reagan. These analyses fail to reveal evidence of learning or priming effects. Therefore at this early stage in the campaign, the learning that takes place between January and June hurts Carter but fails to directly benefit Reagan.

7.4 The Third Shift: Carter the Hawk, July through September

Carter's retreat on defense was short-lived. By late June he was once again vigorously pursuing prodefense policies. After fighting congressional demands to increase the defense budget more than 3 percent, Carter now supported 5 percent real growth (Wilson 1980b). After vetoing a weapons bill that authorized a nuclear aircraft carrier, "he signed the next, carrier and all" (Wilson 1980b). The draft of the 1980 Democratic platform drove home the point, claiming that Carter had undone the dovish policies of Presidents Nixon and Ford. It stated: "We had to reverse the steady decline in defense spending that occurred under the Republican administration" (Kaiser 1980). Of course, journalists quickly pointed out that the 1976 Democratic platform had stood precisely for a continuation of this steady decline, stating: "We believe we can reduce present defense spending by about $5 billion to $7 billion" (Kaiser 1980).

Not only did Carter readopt his prodefense policies from the spring, he also fought to bring Democrats along with him. A cornerstone of Carter's defense policy was the MX nuclear missile. One of many Cold War absurdities, the MX targeted hardened Soviet nuclear missile silos that targeted hardened American nuclear missile silos. Early in his term, Carter had slowed the pace of its development. By 1980, however, he was advocating a faster pace. In a handwritten letter to the Democratic National Convention delegates, he pleaded with them to back the MX, saying it was necessary to demonstrate that "we are committed to defending our country" (Wilson 1980b).

Besides changing course on many policies, Carter deployed another strategy to bolster his credentials as a hawk. His administration began leaking top-secret defense initiatives. In late July, for instance, Carter signed off on a nuclear policy, Presidential Directive 59, that embraced principles long advocated by hawks. The directive shifted nuclear targeting toward Soviet command-and-control centers and military facilities. Although secret, the directive was conveniently leaked to the *New York*

Times and *Washington Post* in early August (Wicker 1980b) and conveyed the impression that Carter was adopting tough measures against the Soviets.

Using the same strategy, Carter also ripped the veil of secrecy off the "invisible bomber." Reagan and other hawks had repeatedly attacked Carter for his cancellation of the B-1, a long-range nuclear bomber. By announcing the development of a stealth bomber, a technologically superior alternative to the B-1, Carter apparently aimed to reduce his vulnerability to this charge. The stealth bomber, however, was top secret for a reason; unveiling it during a campaign could appear unseemly. In a vain attempt to avoid opprobrium, the Carter administration leaked the stealth bomber to the *Washington Post* and received front-page treatment on August 14, 1980 (Wilson 1980a). A week later, Secretary of Defense Harold Brown held a press conference to respond to the leak (which he had presumably authorized), indicating that major technological advances would allow the United States to develop a bomber invisible to enemy radar. This development, he declared, would significantly alter the balance of power between the United States and the USSR (Shaw 1980). In response to questions, Secretary Brown insisted that he had come forward only because of leaks to the press, not to counter charges by Reagan that Carter had let the United States slip behind the Soviet Union militarily. Brown nevertheless used the occasion to assail "individuals (who) claim the United States is very weak." "That is incorrect," he said, "and I think it undermines our security by emboldening our potential adversaries, dispiriting our allies, and misleading the American people" (Shaw 1980). The news media criticized the Carter administration for the leak. According to the *New York Times*: "The stealth case ... is the second in a matter of weeks—since the general election campaign began—in which the administration could be plausibly accused of turning vital military information to Mr. Carter's selfish political purposes" (Wicker 1980b).

Reagan, of course, also repeatedly attacked Carter for the leak. But the dominant story was the development of the "invisible" plane, which television news devoured (Evans and Novak 1980; Nelson 1980) and which bolstered Carter's defense credentials.

Carter's renewed support for strong defense policies brought him back in line with public sentiment. Did it also stem the decline in his popularity? The panel reinterviewed respondents in September, allowing us to observe the effects of Carter's third shift. At first blush, his efforts appear to have stopped the public from increasingly seeing him as a defense dove. After shifting from 4.60 to 4.06 on the seven-point scale between January and June, average perceptions of him remained stable, falling only to 4.01 between June and September (where 4 is the midpoint; see figure 7.5). While perceptions of Carter remained stable, perceptions of Reagan's defense stance shifted somewhat toward the hawkish end during this period, from 5.10 in both January and June to 5.56 in September. So, at first blush, Carter's efforts appear to have paid off.

Underneath the stable average, however, considerable change occurred in perceptions of Carter on defense relative to perceptions of Reagan. Given that citizens in the summer months were presumably evaluating Carter in comparison to Reagan, I change how I code learning about the candidates' positions. Rather than measure how respondents see Carter's position on defense spending, I now measure how respondents see Carter's position relative to Reagan's. I code individuals as perceiving Carter to be a dove if they place him to the left of Reagan on the scale. Despite Carter's efforts to appear hawkish (and the stable average perception of his defense-spending stance), 24 percent of the public—a significant portion—came to see him as more of a dove than Reagan between June and September, while only 5 percent made the reverse shift, for a net increase in those seeing him as more dovish than Reagan of nineteen percentage points (table 7.2). Curiously, this seems to have occurred not because of shifting perceptions of Reagan, but because the learners were coming to see Carter as a dove. On average, these learners drastically shifted their perceptions of Carter, from 5.31 to 3.35, while they shifted their perceptions of Reagan only slightly—and, strangely

TABLE 7.2. **Carter's renewed support for defense spending policy between June and September failed to stop the shift in perception that he was a dove relative to Reagan**

	Place Carter to the left of Reagan on the 7-point defense spending scale			
	Jun.	Sep.	N	%
Learned Carter was more Dovish than Reagan	No	Yes	130	24
Knew Carter was more of a dove before	Yes	Yes	250	47
Never learned Carter was more of a dove	No	No	129	24
Came to see Carter as less dovish than Reagan	Yes	No	27	5

enough, in a dovish direction—from 5.55 to 5.39. Overall Carter perceptions remained stable, despite the shift, because of a countershift among
those who came to see Carter as a hawk relative to Reagan. So despite
Carter's efforts between June and September, the public came to see him
as less hawkish than Reagan.

Did this learning continue to lead hawks to shift away from Carter?
Although learning that Carter was a dove appeared to matter when
Carter really was becoming more dovish (January to June), learning
that Carter was comparatively more dovish than his opponent seems less
likely to have mattered when Carter was in fact shifting to a more hawkish position (June to September). The possible reason, which I spelled
out for the European integration case in chapter 5, is that individuals
who really did care about defense had, by September, probably already
come to a conclusion about Carter's position on defense—presumably
that he was less hawkish than Reagan. So individuals who were coming to see Carter as a dove during the summer were probably the kind
of people who did not care much about defense. The fact that they were
coming to see him as a dove during a time when he was actually becoming more hawkish makes it even more likely that they did not care much
about defense. Consequently, this learning seems unlikely to have affected their views about the candidates.

A similar argument applies to priming effects. By the summer, the
kind of person who cared enough about defense policy for it to influence
his or her vote had probably already determined an appropriate weight
to place on the issue and would no longer be likely to change it.

To test whether this learning mattered between June and September, figure 7.9 presents a (partial residual) scatterplot, showing change
in support for Carter and Reagan by June defense-spending attitudes.
(Equation 10 in the appendix presents the model behind the scatterplot.)
It does so for the 24 percent of the sample who, from June to September, came to see Carter as more dovish than Reagan. Since vote choice
is not available in the June wave, I instead measure support for the candidates in June and September using the comparative feeling thermometers (rescaled to vary between 0 and 100). As figure 7.9 shows, we see
no evidence of changing candidate evaluations among respondents who
learned that Carter was more dovish than Reagan; hawks did not become more supportive of Reagan versus Carter and defense moderates
did not become less supportive. In fact, the figure shows surprisingly little change in evaluations among any of the groups. A similar test that

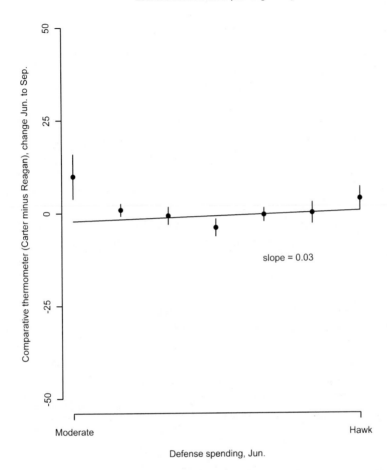

Learned Carter a dove (learning effect)

FIGURE 7.9. No learning effect as Carter returned to his prodefense position between June and September. Although almost a quarter of the public came to see Carter as more dovish than Reagan between June and September, the hawks among them did not shift their support away from Carter and toward Reagan, nor did defense moderates do the reverse. The comparative feeling thermometer (Carter minus Reagan) has been rescaled to vary between 0 and 100. Similar results hold among those who already saw Carter as more dovish than Reagan (that is, no priming effect). This figure shows a partial residual scatterplot and controls for party identification, attitudes about government spending and services scale, perceptions of the national economy, and attitudes about reducing unemployment versus reducing inflation (all measured in June). The appendix presents the model behind these plots (equation 10) and the online appendix shows the full ordinary least squares regression estimates. Error bars show 68 percent confidence intervals. Source: 1980 ANES Major Panel.

searches for priming effects, conducted only among those who already knew that Carter was more dovish than Reagan, likewise reveals no effect. Further analysis also fails to find these effects with the two-wave or three-wave tests. Contrasted with the presence of learning-induced judgments between January and June, the absence of such judgments between June and September is surprising. It is consistent, however, with the idea that such learning fails to influence people who learn late in campaigns, probably because they don't care a great deal about the issue. (If they did, they probably would have learned earlier.)[9]

The absence of priming or learning effects here is consistent with changes in average support for Carter and Reagan during this period. Figure 7.10 shows this with the average comparative feeling thermometer score and average vote choice, which becomes available in September. Between June and September, the public shifted slightly toward Carter and away from Reagan on the comparative thermometer, though still slightly preferring Reagan. On the 100-point scale, the mean in September was about 48, with higher values indicating support for Carter over Reagan; a mean of 50 indicates overall neutrality. Vote intent in September was a little less favorable for Carter, with 44 percent intending to vote for him (of those intending to vote for either Carter or Reagan).

7.5 September through Election Day

The panel provides us with one final period—between interviews in September and those after the election—in which to test whether defense hurt Carter. Although the panel respondents slightly favored Reagan over Carter in September, other national polls conducted in September found that the race was tied.[10] On Election Day, however, Reagan won a convincing victory. Defense spending appears to have hurt Carter when he retreated on the issue in the spring, but his efforts to neutralize it apparently succeeded between June and September. Did defense again hurt Carter between September and Election Day? Did his efforts to neutralize this issue fail after months of success, explaining Reagan's surge in the campaign's final days?

The campaigns and the media focused intensely on defense during the last two months of the campaign. As shown in figure 2.10 (in chapter 2), about 30 percent of all campaign-related articles in major news publications mentioned the issue in October, more than any other issue.

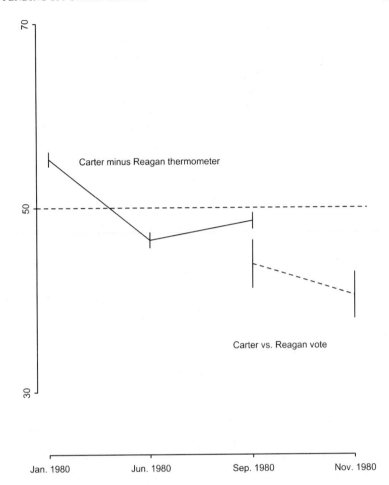

FIGURE 7.10. Support for Carter versus Reagan in the 1980 Major Panel. This figure presents the comparative feeling thermometer (Carter minus Reagan) and vote percentage for Carter versus Reagan for the months these are available in the panel. I rescale the comparative thermometer to vary between 0 and 100. On Election Day, Carter received 44.7 percent of the two-party vote. Error bars show 68 percent confidence intervals. Source: 1980 ANES Major Panel.

Carter and Reagan ran numerous television ads focusing on defense in September and October (figure 2.9). By October about 30 percent of new ads by both candidates mentioned defense-related issues.

Yet the tremendous emphasis on defense may not have ultimately led to Reagan's surge to victory, because Carter continued to defend him-

self on this issue. His ads, in particular, drove home his prodefense position. In the "commander-in-chief" ad, for example, the announcer states,
"when President Carter sits down at the White House with the Secretary
of Defense, he brings a hard, military professionalism to the meeting.
The president is an Annapolis graduate. He spent 11 years in the Navy.
And he knows what he's talking about" (Greenfield 1982, 252). While
the narrator speaks, the pictures portray President Carter as a modern-
day Patton, reviewing military exercises through his field glasses, while
explosions rip the earth, soldiers charge up a hill, tanks rumble across a
battlefield, missiles rise from their submarines, and aircraft carriers ply
the seas. As Greenfield describes (1982, 252–53):

> The ad ended with film of the Camp David peace accord with the announcer
> saying that "President Carter knows our final security lies not only in hav-
> ing a strong defense but in being willing to sit down and negotiate for peace,"
> but the pictorial thrust of the commercial was designed to rebut Republican
> charges that Carter had weakened America's defense posture. How, the ad
> seemed to ask, could any President surrounded by this much hardware be
> considered a softy?

As shown in figure 2.9, Carter's late-summer ads emphasized defense
much more than did Reagan's. Almost 50 percent of the ads created by
Carter's campaign in August mentioned defense-related issues, almost
40 percent did so in September, and 30 percent did so in October. In contrast, only about 20 percent of Reagan's ads did so in August and September, while just under 30 percent did so in October. This pronounced
emphasis by Carter revealed his campaign's concern with neutralizing
this issue.

Besides portraying Carter as tough, his campaign also attempted to
neutralize the defense issue by undermining Reagan's prodefense position, arguing that the Republican candidate was trigger-happy and likely
to lead America into war. The Carter campaign's person-in-the-street
ads, for example, showed people making statements such as, "I think
Governor Reagan in a crisis situation would be very fast to use military
force" (Jamieson 1996, 407). According to journalistic accounts, this was
Reagan's greatest vulnerability (Greenfield 1982).

By portraying Reagan as excessively hawkish, Carter may have further neutralized the defense issue. Instead of exploiting his apparent
advantage on this issue, Reagan had to go on the defensive, reassuring

Americans about his desire for world peace. During the October 27 debate, for instance, Reagan said, "I'm only here to tell you that I believe with all my heart that our first priority must be world peace, and that the use of force is always and only a last resort when everything else has failed" (Greenfield 1982, 235).

Did Carter's attempts to neutralize this issue continue to pay off in these last weeks? Alternatively, did the emphasis on defense again hurt Carter, leading to his defeat? Unfortunately, the panel conducted only a brief postelection interview that lacked questions about defense spending, the candidates' positions, Carter approval, or the feeling thermometers. This limits our ability to test for priming and learning effects. Nonetheless, we can test whether attitudes about defense measured in September became more important to vote choice between September and Election Day. Support for the candidates did not change much in the panel, with about 8 percent (31 of 378) changing their votes between September and Election Day. Nevertheless, the drop in support for Carter found in national surveys between September and Election Day still showed up in the ANES panel. In September about 44 percent intended to vote for Carter (of those intending to vote for either Carter or Reagan). After Election Day, only 40 percent reported having done so (see figure 7.10), less than the 44.7 percent he received in the general election.[11]

Was the defense issue behind this drop? The answer appears to be *no*. Given the surprising nature of this finding, I present the results in more detail here than I have in previous sections. Figure 7.11 begins by showing, not a (partial residual) scatterplot, but a simpler plot of the behavior of hawks and moderates (those at 7 and 4 on the defense-spending scale, respectively), based on their September responses to the defense-spending question. If defense hurt Carter, support for him should have dropped among hawks from September to Election Day, while support among doves should have dropped less, if at all. We see, however, no drop in support for Carter among hawks: 31 percent supported him in September and 31 percent reported having voted for him on Election Day. Instead, it is the moderates who shifted away; their support for him fell from 65 percent to 62 percent. Table 7.3 shows that this same pattern held for respondents at 3 through 7 on the defense spending scale. Less hawkish voters generally shifted away from Carter at higher rates than did hawkish voters. In fact, the largest shift away from Carter occurred among the most dovish citizens, those at 1 and 2 on the scale, but there were so few respondents at these two levels that the results can only be suggestive. At least according to this simple analysis, Carter's efforts appear to have prevented further damage from the defense issue in the weeks before Election Day.

Even though hawks didn't shift away from Carter between September and the election, figure 7.11 also shows that hawks were less likely

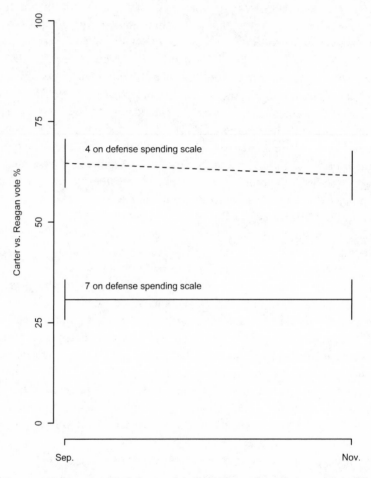

FIGURE 7.11. Defense spending fails to explain the shift away from Carter and toward Reagan between September and Election Day. Defense hawks (those who placed themselves at 7) remained consistently unsupportive of Carter, while moderates (4 on defense) shifted away from Carter, from 65 percent to 62 percent. See table 7.3 for a detailed breakdown of changes in support by defense-spending attitudes and the figure below for statistical tests. Error bars show 68 percent confidence intervals. Source: 1980 ANES Major Panel.

TABLE 7.3. **Defense-spending attitudes fail to explain the shift away from Carter and toward Reagan between September and Election Day.**

| Defense Spending Scale | Sep. | Carter approval | | n |
		Election Day	Diff.	
3	76.9	69.2	−7.7	13
4 (midpoint)	64.6	61.5	−3.1	65
5	46.6	38.6	−7.9	88
6	33.3	32.5	−0.1	114
7 (hawk)	30.7	30.7	0	88

Note: This table shows mean Carter approval by defense-spending attitudes in September, and supplements figure 7.11. Only five respondents placed themselves at 2 and five at 1.

to vote for Carter than were moderates in September (when vote is first asked), a stark reversal from January when hawks were more approving of Carter than were moderates. Since we lack vote-choice questions in the January and June waves, determining the source and timing of this reversal is impossible. With Carter approval and with the comparative feeling thermometer, which we have in the January, June, and September waves, we do not see this reversal. In fact, when controlling only for partisan identification, hawks were slightly more approving of Carter in September than were moderates, not less so. Something about voting decisions appears to have brought out hawks' support for Reagan over Carter, though the analyses throughout this chapter suggest it may not have been causal.

Although the failure of hawks to shift away from Carter between September and the election suggests that Carter prevented further damage to his campaign from the defense issue, there may have been a greater drop in support among prodefense citizens that was obscured by some other factor, possibly by something researchers call regression to the mean. To address this possibility I present a (partial residual) scatterplot, which holds September vote choice and other explanatory variables constant and tests whether defense-spending attitudes in September led to vote changes between September and Election Day. I code vote choice, reported after the election, as Carter 1 and Reagan 0. For prior vote intention, reported in September, I code undecided respondents as 0.5 in that wave (but exclude those who do not ultimately report a vote choice for Carter or Reagan in November). Because we now have three waves of defense-spending attitudes, I attempt to reduce measurement

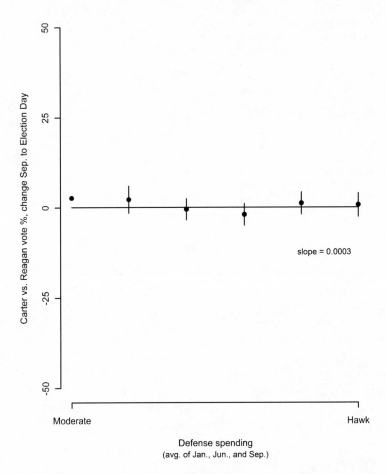

slope = 0.0003

Carter vs. Reagan vote %, change Sep. to Election Day

Moderate   Hawk

Defense spending
(avg. of Jan., Jun., and Sep.)

FIGURE 7.12. Defense spending fails to explain the shift away from Carter and toward Reagan between September and Election Day. This figure is a partial residual scatterplot and controls for party identification, the government spending and services scale, perceptions of the national economy, and attitudes about reducing unemployment versus reducing inflation. To reduce concerns about measurement error, I take the average response across all three prior waves (January, June, and September) on defense spending and the control variables. The appendix presents the model behind these plots (equation 10) and the online appendix shows the full ordinary least squares regression estimates. Error bars show 68 percent confidence intervals. Source: 1980 ANES Major Panel.

error by averaging these attitudes across all three prior waves (January, June, and September). Where possible, I also use the average response to the control variables over the three waves (see equation 10 in the appendix for the model and the online appendix for the full results).

Figure 7.12 presents the (partial residual) scatterplot, generally confirming the findings in figure 7.11 and table 7.3. On average, defense hawks were more likely to shift away from Carter than defense moderates were, but the effect was small. To further vet this finding, I have tried many other statistical models, but they all point to the same conclusion: defense spending contributed little to Carter's decline in vote share. In fact, the only variable that consistently predicts vote changes between September and Election Day is partisanship. A strong Democrat increased his or her average probability of voting for Carter by about 22 percent compared to a strong Republican.

Thus, at least in the ANES panel, we see little evidence that Reagan surged to victory between September and Election Day because of the defense issue. Carter's efforts to neutralize his dovishness appear to have worked, preventing further harm.

7.6 Conclusion

For voters, policy issues can be complicated and their implications remote, which may explain why I fail to find much policy voting in chapters 3–5. The last two chapters, however, have examined cases in which the issues were straightforward and immediate in a way that captured the public's attention, making policy voting easier. In both cases, citizens were choosing whether to reelect incumbents with major policy disadvantages on apparently easy issues. In both, the public suddenly and decidedly shifted its policy preferences away from the incumbents' position while the issue itself became increasingly prominent. In both, a share of the public learned about the incumbent's long-standing but now unpopular position on the issue. In both cases, this should have been a serious blow to the incumbent. Nevertheless, in both cases, rich panel data showed few signs that the issue hurt the incumbent, with the exception of a brief but revealing period during Carter's campaign. Despite what seemed like best-case scenarios for finding policy-based vote change, we saw little. Specifically, the attention paid by the media and by the campaigns to nuclear power in the 1986 Dutch parliamentary election and to defense spending in the 1980 US presidential election mostly failed to change votes through learning, priming, or persuasion effects. In both cases, substance appears not to have mattered, at least not directly. Citizens again appeared to fail easy tests of policy voting.

Why the failure? Why did nuclear opponents not shift away from Lubbers's coalition? Why did hawks, for the most part, not shift away from Carter? An answer consistent with much of this book's findings is that issues just never matter much to citizens, even under what seem like extraordinary circumstances. This chapter and the previous one, however, have pointed to an alternative view. When an issue does capture the public's attention, citizens may only *appear* to fail. Rather, when politicians face unusual public concern about an issue, they can act quickly to ensure that the issue doesn't hurt them by shifting toward their opponents' more popular positions. In sum, when an issue really captures the public's attention, citizens may be leading their politicians, even though it doesn't look that way.

Consistent with this alternative view, the incumbents in both of these cases attempted to neutralize their disadvantageous policy positions by changing them, adopting their challengers' more popular stances. Apparently, it worked. In the Chernobyl case, the Dutch public quickly changed its perceptions of Lubbers's coalition, coming to see it on the antinuclear side of the scale. In the 1980 US election, the public at first placed Carter on the hawkish side of the defense spending scale, despite his dovish record. By changing positions, both candidates appear to have successfully neutralized an issue that should have been detrimental to them.

Carter provided us with the best evidence that an issue could matter to the public, in this way revealing the potential power of policy issues to shape vote choice. When he briefly retreated from his prodefense position in the spring of 1980, I found evidence of learning effects and mixed evidence of priming effects. Hawks who noticed Carter's retreat shifted away from him, while doves shifted toward him. Citizens were indeed judging the candidate according to their own positions on what they considered an important policy. This chapter, therefore, provides evidence that policy issues can harm politicians when they fail to neutralize an important issue on which the public is significantly against them.

Of course, politicians do not necessarily serve their constituents' best interests by following the policies their constituents support. As noted earlier, the appropriate lesson from Chernobyl may not have been to stop constructing nuclear power plants, even though that was what the public wanted. Likewise, greatly increasing US defense spending may not have been the best response to the Iranian hostage crisis and the Soviet invasion of Afghanistan, even though that was what the public wanted. The public may have desired greater defense spending because defense hawks focused on an arguably misleading comparison of Warsaw Pact forces to US forces rather than to NATO forces, with which they were approximately balanced at the time (Posen and Van Evera 1980).

These two case studies add further nuance to our view of democracy. Most of the time, citizens apparently fail to judge politicians on policy. At times, however, public policy does interest the masses. In these unusual cases, whether for better or for worse, politicians do appear to follow citizens.

CHAPTER EIGHT

Following, Not Leading

Among the 100,000 Americans interviewed in the 2000 National Annenberg Election Survey was a man from South Carolina, labeled in the survey only as respondent #101104449653. But let us call him Joe. In the summer of 2000, Joe was a forty-four-year-old college-educated Democrat who intended to vote for Al Gore.

In the first of his interviews for the Annenberg survey, which took place in July 2000, Joe said he supported Bush's proposal to invest Social Security funds in the stock market. With an annual income over $75,000, Joe probably owned stocks that had appreciated considerably in the late 1990s, predisposing him to support Bush's proposal. Like much of the public, however, Joe apparently failed to realize that Gore, the candidate getting his vote, opposed the proposal. When reinterviewed in August, Joe still wrongly thought Gore supported it.

Joe's vote intent was thus out of line with his policy view on what soon became the most prominent policy issue of the campaign, as I discussed in chapter 3. In early October this issue took center stage when Bush and Gore repeatedly clashed over it during the presidential debates. They then both ran television ads on it. As a result, millions—Joe included—learned that Gore opposed investing. When he learned, Joe might have reevaluated his support for Gore, but he apparently did not. Consistent with chapter 5's findings about such learning failing to change votes or candidate evaluations, Joe did not switch his vote to Bush. He didn't even become more favorable toward Bush and less favorable toward Gore. Rather than leading on policy, Joe instead appears to have followed. By the time he was reinterviewed in late October, he had adopted Gore's opposition to investing. Thus for Joe, his vote came first and only later did he bring his policy view in line with his vote.[1]

In a policy view of democracy, as I described in chapter 1, citizens lead on policy and politicians follow. According to this book's empirical findings, however, citizens generally do not lead on policy issues—not when those issues became prominent (chapter 3), not when their own policy views changed (chapter 4), and not when they have just learned the party or candidate positions (chapter 5).

But failing to lead does not in itself imply they followed. That is what we study in this chapter. It examines whether people shift their policy views to be in line with their votes, candidate evaluations, or party allegiances. Researchers have long since noted the strong connection between people's partisanship and their policy views, a connection suggesting that people may adopt the views of their party (Belknap and Campbell 1951; Berelson, Lazarsfeld, and McPhee 1954; Campbell et al. 1960). Indeed, studies have documented such a tendency with both policy views and performance assessments.[2] Here I examine whether this tendency shows up across the broad swath of issues examined in this book. Using panel and experimental data, I find strong evidence that citizens follow; that is, they adopt the policy views of their preferred party or candidate. Like Joe, citizens appear to be picking candidates on some other basis, such as the candidate's party affiliation, performance advantages, other policy views, or superficial traits such as his or her appearance. Citizens then adopt that candidate's policy views, as Joe does on the issue of investing Social Security funds. This tendency is particularly evident among those who learn politicians' positions between panel waves; it shows up in every case I examine. When supporters of George W. Bush learned, for example, that he opposed expanding a children's health care program (SCHIP), they too became opposed to the expansion. The tendency even emerges for overall ideology. When supporters of a Republican president learned, for instance, that the Republican Party is on the ideological right, they shifted their own reported ideology to the right. Instead of politicians following the public will, the public appears to follow the wills of its politicians.

This strong tendency to follow helps explain why cross-sectional research often finds evidence of policy judgments when my panel analyses do not. Based on the findings in this chapter, it appears that such work can often get the story backward, interpreting correlations as evidence of policy voting, when those correlations actually reflect citizens following parties or candidates on policy. Media priming studies on policy issues seem especially vulnerable to this problem. In fact, the analysis in this chapter shows that a two-part process misleadingly gives rise to the appearance of media priming in every case. First, exposing citizens to campaign and media messages on an issue informs some of them about the parties' or candidates' positions on that issue. Second, these citizens, once informed, often adopt their preferred party's or candidate's position as their own. Given the strong tendency of people to follow on policy, particularly when they have just learned politicians' positions, this chapter's findings point to the tremendous inferential danger researchers face when analyzing data on public opinion. Reverse causation can often lead, not only to a wrong conclusion, but to the opposite of the correct conclusion.

Besides examining *whether* people follow, this chapter also examines *why* they follow. One perspective, called cue taking—relying on cues from informative sources—casts citizens' tendency to follow in a positive light (Levendusky 2010; Lupia 1994; Lupia and McCubbins 1998; Mondak 1993).[3] According to this view, learning and thinking about public policy takes time and energy, so citizens follow their party or preferred candidate as a reliable shortcut. Because citizens see their party as generally sharing their interests, taking cues from the party allows citizens to arrive, more often than not, at the same opinion they would have arrived at had they studied the issue, but without all the effort. If the tendency to follow actually reflects cue taking, then democracy stills falls short of the policy-voting view in which citizens vote on their own views, but it may be the best we can expect, especially given citizens' limited incentives to learn about politics.

Another perspective is less positive. People may follow their party, not because they are using party cues to make informed guesses, but because they are blindly following their "tribe." Numerous studies find a pronounced tendency to develop psychological attachments to groups, such as political parties (Green, Palmquist, and Schickler 2002; Hyman and Singer 1968; Miller 1976; Miller and Levitin 1976), and then take on the views of those groups (Mackie and Cooper 1984).[4]

My findings do not settle the question of whether citizens are following blindly or more reasonably, but they are more consistent with the view that citizens are blindly following their tribe. In particular, several tests suggest that when people learn their preferred politician's position on a particular issue they follow on that issue even if they know little about that politician (or that politician's party). For example, people who know little about politics, as measured by basic questions about government, are probably less likely to know which party shares their general political ideology; they are, so to speak, blind. All the same, I find that they are just as likely to follow as are politically knowledgeable people who probably do know which party or candidate shares their outlook. In several cases the surveys I analyze asked respondents about the parties' or candidates' general ideology, allowing for an even more specific test. Here, too, I find that citizens who seem to be ignorant of overall ideology—who cannot, for example, place Gore to the left of Bush in the 2000 election—nevertheless follow their parties and candidates at about the same rate as those who do know the candidates' and parties' ideologies.

All told, this chapter's findings are troubling. Democracy appears to be inverted. Citizens are not only failing to lead their politicians on policy, they are following their politicians. Moreover, they follow even when they know little about the parties' or candidates' broader policy orientations.

8.1 Voting for Gore, Liking Lockboxes

Despite Bush's and Gore's focus on the issue of investing Social Security funds in the stock market, citizens apparently did not come to judge them on this policy issue. As I showed in previous chapters, the campaign and media emphasis on this issue did not change votes through priming (chapter 3), through persuading citizens to change their views on this policy (chapter 4), or through informing the public about Bush's and Gore's positions on this issue (chapter 5).

The ads, news coverage, and *Saturday Night Live* skits, however, may have had another effect, one that could have created the appearance of priming or learning effects. They may have led millions of people to exhibit the same behavior as Joe; that is, to adopt either Bush's or Gore's position, depending on which candidate they already preferred.

To examine whether that happened, I again apply the three-wave test. In previous chapters I used this test to examine whether prior policy views influenced later changes in vote or in candidate evaluations. In this chapter I use it to search for the reverse process—whether prior approval of candidates or parties led to later change in policy views. For a formal presentation of this test, see the appendix (equation 19). To measure approval of Bush and Gore, I use a comparative approval scale (Bush minus Gore), which is the 100-point Bush approval scale minus the 100-point

Gore scale.[5] To assess citizens' views about investing, I again rely on the National Annenberg Election Survey's question, which asked, "Do you personally favor or oppose allowing workers to invest some of their Social Security contributions in the stock market?" Respondents could answer "favor" or "oppose," which I code 1 and 0, respectively.[6]

Did the increased prominence of this issue cause people to follow; that is, to adopt their preferred candidates' position on investing Social Security funds? Figure 8.1 presents the findings for all respondents, showing a (partial residual) scatterplot from the three-wave test. To provide a sense for how much people followed Bush or Gore on this issue before it became prominent, the left-hand side of this figure examines these relationships early in the campaign, before the candidates shifted their own attention to this issue. It shows the effect that the Bush-Gore ratings recorded in wave 1 had on the changes in views (on investing Social Security funds) that took place between waves 1 and 2. Both of these waves were conducted during the summer of 2000, before the issue became prominent.[7] Figure 8.1 shows that during this baseline period people did shift their attitudes about investing to bring them in line with their prior ratings of Bush and Gore, but the effect is not large. In previous chapters I referred to the slopes in these figures as issue weights. In this chapter I call them candidate weights; they indicate how important a voter's approval of a particular candidate is toward that voter's change of view about a particular policy. Before the issue became prominent, the candidate weight is positive, 0.22, which implies that a strong Gore supporter/Bush opponent's probability of changing her support for investing by adopting Gore's view is 0.22 greater than a strong Bush supporter/Gore opponent's probability of changing her support by adopting Gore's view. The increase is largely driven by Gore supporters rejecting Bush's view and adopting Gore's. Many Gore supporters started out supporting investing—as did the public in general, with almost 70 percent of respondents initially supporting it. Bush supporters, already more likely to support investment, were therefore less likely to need to change their own views in order to align with his.

What happens after the issue became prominent? In previous chapters I usually found nothing—prior policy views rarely predicted changes in vote or candidate evaluations before or after issues became prominent. But now that I am examining following, not leading, I not only find an effect, but also a large one. As this issue became prominent between wave 2 (August) and wave 3 (October), the tendency for people to follow

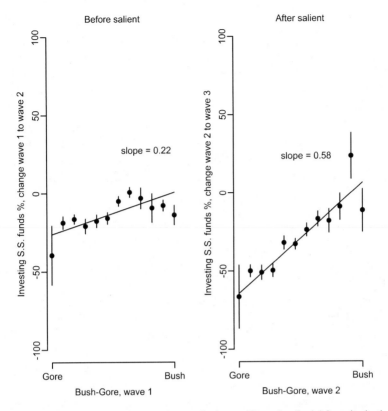

FIGURE 8.1. Three-wave test of following on the issue of investing Social Security in the 2000 election—partial residual scatterplots. Campaign and news media attention to the Social Security funds investment proposal led Americans to adopt their preferred candidates' position on this issue. Before the issue became prominent, prior Gore supporters/Bush opponents changed their views about investing, adopting Gore's position, but the effect was small. After the issue became prominent, they adopted Gore's view at higher rates. The slopes of these lines represent the weights people place on their ratings about Bush and Gore when changing their views on Social Security investing—I call them candidate/party weights. The difference in these slopes, (Ω_{3wt} = 0.58 − 0.22 =) 0.36, represents the degree to which those who learn their preferred politician's positions go on to adopt those positions. Figure 8.3 shows the slopes along with their confidence intervals and makes clear that the difference in the slopes is statistically significant. The appendix presents the model behind these plots (equation 19) and the least squares regression estimates (table 9). These plots only show variation after accounting for party identification (that is, they show residualized variation). The error bars show 68 percent confidence intervals. Source: 2000 National Annenberg Election Survey.

increased, as the right-hand side of figure 8.1 shows. The increase again appears to be largely driven by Gore supporters, who now adopt Gore's position on this binary policy question at higher rates. The effect of prior Bush-Gore support, the slope, increases from 0.22 to 0.58. The latter implies that a strong Gore supporter/Bush opponent's probability of changing her support for investing by adopting Gore's view is now 0.58 greater than a strong Bush supporter/Gore opponent's probability of changing her support by adopting Bush's view, a considerable effect. Thus the increased salience of this issue appears to induce following. The left panel of figure 8.3 presents the slopes (coefficients) and their confidence intervals, showing that the (0.58 − 0.22 =) 0.36 candidate-weight increase is indeed statistically significant.

This tendency to follow grows from large to massive among one group: those who, like Joe, learned Bush's and Gore's positions. Among these learners I consistently find a strong tendency to follow one's party or candidate in all the cases examined in this book. To measure learning in this particular case, I use the same variables and coding as in chapter 5. To remind the reader, the questions about the candidates' positions asked whether Bush supports and whether Gore supports investing Social Security funds in the stock market, "yes" or "no." I define learners as those who incorrectly answer one or both before the issue became prominent (wave 2), but correctly answer both afterward (wave 3). About 34 percent of respondents appeared to learn.[8]

Figure 8.2 presents the tests for following, but now only among the learners, not the whole sample. Before these respondents learned the candidates' positions, the pattern looks the same as it did for all respondents; that is, some evidence of following with a candidate weight of 0.22. As these respondents learned, however, the effect becomes much more pronounced, with the slope rising to 1.19. The increase again appears to be about Gore supporters, the strongest of whom now adopt Gore's position, when they learned what it was, with a probability of about 1.0— put differently, almost all became strong supporters of Gore's view. The increase in following induced by learning is thus (1.19 − 0.22 =) 0.97, a highly statistically significant difference in candidate weights, as shown on the right-hand side of figure 8.3.[9]

In contrast with the previous chapters' findings on policy issues, which generally found no effects, or at best anemic effects, these findings are striking. They suggest a tendency for Bush supporters to adopt Bush's

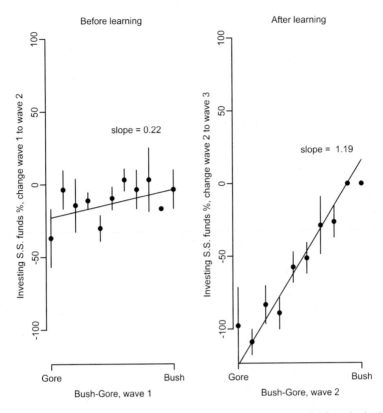

FIGURE 8.2. Three-wave test of following on the issue of investing Social Security in the 2000 election among learners—partial residual scatterplots. Learning about Bush's and Gore's positions on investing Social Security funds proposal leads Americans to adopt their preferred candidates' position on this issue. This figure shows the same relationships as the previous figure, but now only for the 34 percent of respondents who appeared to learn Bush's and Gore's positions on investing. Bush-Gore support is a scale of comparative ratings (Bush minus Gore). The slopes of these lines represent the weights people place on their ratings of Bush and Gore when changing their views on Social Security investing—I call them candidate/party weights. The difference in these slopes, (Ω_{3wt} = 1.19 − 0.22 =) 0.97, represents the following effect. Figure 8.3 presents a test of whether the difference in the slopes is statistically significant. The appendix presents the model behind these plots (equation 19) and the least squares regression estimates (table 10). These plots only show variation after accounting for party identification (that is, they show residualized variation). The error bars show 68 percent confidence intervals. Source: 2000 National Annenberg Election Survey.

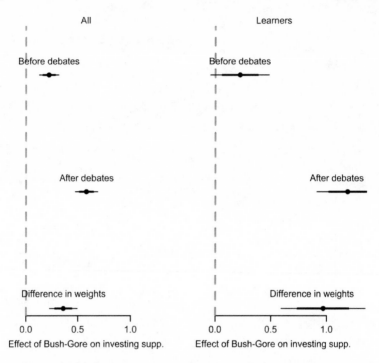

FIGURE 8.3. Three-wave test of following on the issue of investing Social Security in the 2000 election. Is the tendency to follow the candidates on investing Social Security funds, shown in figures 8.1 and 8.2, statistically significant? This figure examines our certainty about the effects in these previous figures by presenting their slopes (candidate weights) and confidence intervals. It then presents the difference in these weights and the confidence interval on the difference, which is the key test of whether increased salience or learning increases following. The appendix presents the model behind these plots (equation 19) and the least squares regression estimates (column 1 of tables 9 and 10, respectively). The thin and thick error bars show 90 percent and 68 percent confidence intervals, respectively. Source: 2000 National Annenberg Election Survey.

policy of investing, and, especially, for Gore supporters to adopt Gore's lockbox policy.

Like the findings in previous chapters, these are robust to alternative specifications. They hold when I substitute vote intent for Bush-Gore support; when I use a much larger, two-wave Annenberg survey (see Lenz 2009); when I control for demographics that could be relevant to Social Security views, such as age, age squared, income, marital status, gender, and employment status; and when I control for self-reported ideology. Learners thus appear to be adopting Bush's or Gore's position, not because their candidate preferences are associated with demographic, partisan, or ideological differences, but because they like their candidate.

As noted above, researchers have long since observed the strong connection between partisanship and policy views. In this analysis, however, I examined the influence of candidate preference, not party identification. I did so in part because the Republican and Democratic Parties lacked long-standing positions on investing Social Security funds. Moreover, the surveys I use asked for people's perceptions of the candidates' positions, not the parties' positions. Substituting party identification for candidate preferences, however, produces similar findings. I return below to the question of whether people are following parties or candidates.

In sum, although the tremendous campaign and media attention to this issue of investing Social Security funds failed to change citizens' votes (see chapters 3–5), it apparently did cause people to learn Bush's and Gore's policy positions and then adopt their preferred candidate's position as their own. It did not cause them to lead, but to follow.

8.2 Learning and Following in the Other Cases

The findings we just saw among the learners in the Social Security case are notable for their magnitude, but they may be unusual because the issue was new and technical. Does learning positions more generally lead people to follow their preferred candidate or party?

To see whether it does, I apply the same three-wave test to all the cases where we can measure learning. These are European integration in the 1997 British election, public works in the 1976 election, defense spending in the 1980 election, ideology in the 1992 election, Chernobyl in the 1986 Dutch election, and finally the SCHIP experiment. As I showed in chapter 5 (see table 5.1), between 17 and 29 percent of respondents appeared to learn the parties' or candidates' positions as the issues became prominent (between waves 2 and 3). I therefore examine whether these learners also follow their preferred party or candidate, as the learners did on the issue of investing Social Security.

Before showing results, I make several technical remarks. Since I am interested in the total effect of party or candidate preference on policy views, I do not control for variables that help explain party or candidate preference, though including the controls generally leaves the results unchanged. I include the SCHIP case (info condition), but explain the analysis of this experiment in the next section. As in the Social Security case, I measure prior candidate or party preference with questions asking people about the degree of their support: I use Labour Party minus Conservative Party support in the European integration case, Carter minus Ford support in the public works jobs case, the Reagan thermometer in the defense case, and Bush approval in the activating ideology case. The results hold with vote, though the effects are about 20 percent smaller.[10] I use a 7-point party identification scale in the Chernobyl case (incumbents versus opposition). Where possible I use these continuous measures instead of vote because they provide us with more information about candidate or party support.[11]

Figure 8.4 shows that the Social Security results for the learners replicate in all seven cases. It summarizes the results by showing only the difference statistic; that is, the increased importance of prior candidate or party support on *change* in policy views from before people appeared to learn to after they did; these are the same statistics shown at the bottom right of figure 8.3. Figure 8.4 shows that when people appeared to learn the candidates' or parties' positions, they tended to adopt the position of their preferred candidate or party. They did this whether the policy issue was public works projects, national sovereignty, defense spending, nuclear power, or health insurance for children. (For the percentage of learners in each case, see table 5.1.) The effects, although not as large as in the Social Security case, are substantial.

Citizens tended to follow, not only in their policy opinions, but also in their overall ideologies. Between the 1991 and 1992 waves of the ANES survey, citizens who learned that Democrats were more liberal than Republicans changed their self-reported ideology depending on their prior approval of President Bush. If they approved of Bush in 1991, they became more conservative. If they disapproved of Bush in 1991, they became more liberal. A person who strongly disapproved of Bush became about 4 points more conservative (on the 100-point scale) than a person who strongly approved of Bush *before* they both learned where the parties stood ideologically. After learning that, the strong Bush supporter became about 18 points more conservative, for a net difference of (18 − [−4] =) 22 points, which corresponds with the 0.22 difference shown in figure 8.4. The fact that Bush supporters started out becoming less conservative than Bush opponents certainly seems odd, but the 4-point shift is not statistically significant.[12] The point here is that wherever the Bush supporters started, they were about 22 points more conservative (on the

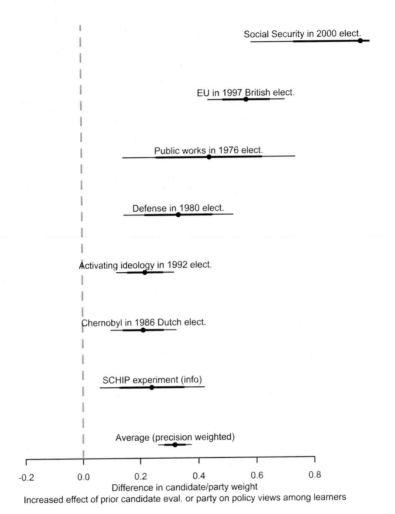

FIGURE 8.4. Summary of following effects among those who learned the candidates' and parties' positions. This figure shows that learning about the candidates' and parties' positions led people to follow their preferred candidate or party. It summarizes the results by showing only the difference statistic, that is, the increased importance of prior candidate or party support on change in policy views from before to after people learned—the same statistic shown at the bottom right of figure 8.3. The difference in weights is the difference in the slopes shown in, for example, figure 8.2 (formally, it is $\Omega_{3wt} = f_{w2} - f_{w1}$, see equation 19 in the appendix). The last estimate presents the average issue-weight difference across the seven cases. It weights each effect by our certainty about it (how precisely we estimate it), so effects with smaller confidence intervals (more precision) count for more. The appendix presents the least squares regression estimates (table 10). The Chernobyl case uses the two-wave test. The thin and thick error bars show 90 percent and 68 percent confidence intervals, respectively.

100-point scale) after learning that Republicans were generally more conservative than they would have been had they never learned that.

The consistency of this pattern throughout these cases is striking. Regardless of whether the policy is old or new, domestic or foreign, we find the same behavior. When people learned the positions of their preferred political leaders, they followed.[13]

As noted earlier, I usually test whether people follow candidates, not parties, even though most research on cue taking focuses on parties. I do so because the questions about positions are mostly about candidates, not parties. Since party identification likely influences candidate choice, these findings do capture people's tendency to follow parties but also appear to reflect more than just the effect of parties. In fact, additional analyses indicate that individuals appear to cue off candidates as much, or more, as they cue off parties. When I control for party identification in the five cases where I use candidate evaluations (Social Security, public works, defense, activating ideology, and the SCHIP experiment), the effect of candidate evaluations is statistically significant and larger than that of party identification in the first three, while in the last two cases, party identification is larger and candidate evaluations are not statistically significant.[14] At least to some degree, finding that people follow candidates as much, or more, than parties may imply a less informed kind of cue taking. People may have years to learn about the parties' constituencies and the general interests they reflect and therefore have a better chance of discerning which party best represents their own interests. With candidates, people may often have much less history and so can less plausibly discern which candidate best represents their interests.[15] Apparently, however, this does not stop them from following their favorite candidates.

8.3 The SCHIP Experiment

As the 2008 election approached, Democrats in Congress placed President Bush in a politically unpalatable position. They attempted to embarrass the president by forcing him to veto popular legislation, a commonly used strategy (Cameron and McCarty 2004; Groseclose and McCarty 2001). As noted in chapter 3, they passed a bill expanding the State Children's Health Insurance Program (SCHIP). President Bush had to either sign it, which was unpopular with Republicans, or veto it, which would allow Democrats to criticize him for callousness. Bush chose the latter, vetoing an expansion of coverage to an estimated four million children.

The findings in the previous section indicate that people follow politicians on policy, especially when they learn their preferred politician's stance. Nevertheless, those findings are observational, not experimental. As described in chapter 3, I conducted a panel survey with an embedded experiment about the SCHIP expansion, which allows us to test these claims experimentally.[16] To review, the panel interviewed respondents in November 2007 (wave 1), where I measured prior SCHIP support and Bush approval, and again in July 2008 (wave 2), where I administered the treatments and then remeasured SCHIP support and Bush approval.[17] The embedded SCHIP experiment in wave 2 had two treatment groups. The first read two stories about the SCHIP debate that contained no information about Bush's or the Democrats' positions on this issue, a treatment I call SCHIP no info. The second treatment group, which I call SCHIP info, read identical stories except that I changed the language of the first story so that it explicitly conveyed Bush's and the Democrats' positions. Figure 8.5 presents the story with the position cues underlined. The control group saw neither of these stories but read neutral stories shown to all groups.

Despite the attention this issue received in late 2007 and in the spring of 2008, respondents were still largely unaware of Bush's opposition in their second interviews. In the control group, about 45 percent correctly reported that Bush opposed it, about 49 percent say they were "not sure," and 6 percent erroneously reported that he favored it, as noted in chapter 5. In the info treatment group, the news stories conveyed information about Bush's and the Democratic Party's positions on SCHIP, which increased the percent saying Bush opposed the expansion of SCHIP by 17 percentage points, from 45 percent (control group) to 62 percent ($p < 0.001$). (Knowledge of Bush's position on SCHIP among those who received the no info treatment was 7 percentage points higher than it was for those in the control group, a difference that could have resulted from chance [$p < 0.128$]).

In previous chapters I showed that the SCHIP treatments failed to influence Bush approval, even though they raised the issue's salience and, in the info condition, informed participants about Bush's opposition. This failure to find media priming and learning—the finding that neither the increase in salience nor the new information had any effect—provided an important experimental confirmation of the observational

No info treatment	Info treatment
Congress Fails to Enact Expansion of Children's Health Insurance	**Bush's Second Child Insurance Veto Stands in House**
Washington Post (summary)	*Washington Post* (summary)
The House of Representatives failed for the second time in nearly four months to pass with a sufficient margin a proposed $35 billion expansion of the State Children's Health Insurance Program (SCHIP). Supporters argued that expanding a program that provides subsidized health insurance to children of the working poor is especially important during these times. Opponents argue that it is too costly. The 260 to 152 tally left backers of the legislation about 15 votes short of the two-thirds majority of lawmakers necessary.	House Democrats failed for the second time in nearly four months to override President Bush's veto of a proposed $35 billion expansion of the State Children's Health Insurance Program (SCHIP). Democrats argued that expanding a program that provides subsidized health insurance to children of the working poor is especially important during these times. Republicans argued that it is too costly. The 260 to 152 tally left backers of the legislation about 15 votes short of the two-thirds majority necessary to override the president's Dec. 12 veto.

FIGURE 8.5. The SCHIP treatment news story with and without party cues. The underlined words are those that differ in the info treatment; they convey Bush's and the Democrat's positions on this issue. In addition to this story, the SCHIP treatment groups also read a second story about problems California would face if Congress fails to reauthorize SCHIP. This second story was identical for both conditions and conveyed no information about Bush's and the Democrats' positions. The control group saw neither of these stories, but read neutral stories shown to all groups.

findings in chapters 3 and 5. I now examine whether the SCHIP experiment also confirms the findings about citizens following politicians on policy, which we have already seen in this chapter. Did the treatments cause people to adopt Bush's view if they approved of him or reject his view if they disapproved of him?

Given my findings in this chapter, we would certainly expect the SCHIP info treatment to have this effect because it informs people about Bush's position. It should therefore increase the percentage of people whose views about SCHIP match their prior Bush approval or disapproval; that is, it should cause some of those who approve of expanding health insurance for poor children but also support a candidate who opposes that policy to change their own minds, not about the candidate, but about expanding health insurance for poor children.

To analyze the data, I use an approach similar to the two-wave test except that the control group takes the place of the baseline estimate. That is, for both the control group and the info treatment group, I model wave-2 SCHIP views as a function of wave-1 Bush approval and wave-1 SCHIP views. I then see whether wave-1 Bush approval influences SCHIP views more in the info treatment group then in the no info treat-

ment group or the control group. (Table 8.1 shows the full model results
and the appendix presents the test formally in equation 25.)

As usual with statistics, this sounds technical but is easily understood visually. Figure 8.6 shows (partial residual) scatterplots of the key
relationships—change in investing views by prior Bush approval—for the
control group (left side) and for the info treatment group (right side). In
the control group, Bush supporters became somewhat more opposed to
SCHIP expansion—they adopted his view—between the two waves. The

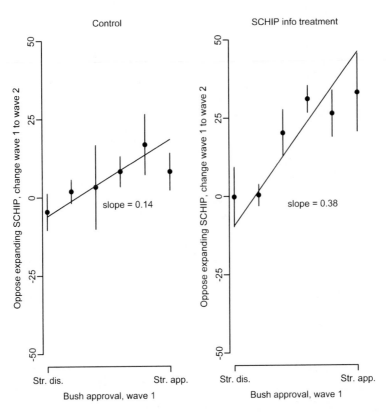

FIGURE 8.6. Did informing citizens about Bush's and the Democrat's positions on SCHIP
expansion lead Americans to adopt Bush's or the Democrat's position on this issue? This
figure suggests that it did. Citizens in the info treatment hold views more consistent with
their prior Bush approval than do citizens in the control group. For the least squares models, see table 8.1. The no info treatment, which does not contain cues about Bush's and the
Democrat's positions, fails to produce a similar effect (as shown in the left panel of figure 8.7). The thin error bars show 68 percent confidence intervals. Source: 2007–8 SCHIP
Experiment.

effect is small, just 0.14. It implies that a strong Bush approver became about 14 points (on the 100-point scale) more opposed to SCHIP expansion than a strong Bush disapprover between waves 1 and 2. Given the attention this issue received during this period, this tendency probably resulted from events and media coverage. As expected, the info treatment markedly increased this tendency to follow, with the effect rising from 0.14 to 0.38. This effect implies that a strong Bush approver became about 38 points (on the 100-point scale) more opposed to SCHIP expansion than a strong Bush disapprover. Although this effect is smaller than that found in some of the previous cases, keep in mind that the info treatment only increased knowledge of Bush's position by 17 percentage points (from 45 percent to 62 percent). In the other cases, 100 percent learned (or at least appeared to learn) by definition.[18]

The left panel of figure 8.7 presents the slopes (coefficients) and their

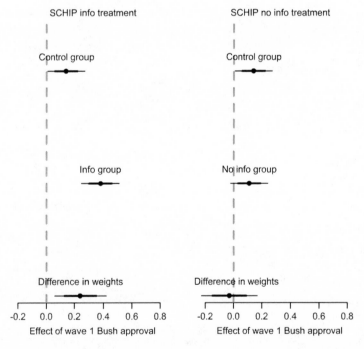

FIGURE 8.7. Experimentally induced learning leads people to adopt or reject Bush's position on expanding SCHIP, depending on whether they previously approved or disapproved of his performance in office. For the full models for the left panel, see table 8.1, and, for the right panel, see the online appendix. Source: 2007–8 SCHIP Experiment.

TABLE 8.1. **Experimentally induced learning leads people to adopt or reject Bush's position on expanding SCHIP, depending on whether they previously approved or disapproved of his performance in office.**

DV: SCHIP expansion	(1) Control	(2) Info treat.	(3) Diff.
Prior SCHIP expansion	0.74* (0.06)	0.49* (0.07)	
Prior Bush approval	0.14* (0.08)	0.38* (0.08)	0.24* (0.11)
n	155	146	
R^2	0.576	0.543	
SER	0.289	0.309	

Note: Ordinary least squares regression estimates with standard errors in parentheses. All variables coded to vary between 0 and 1. Constant not shown. * $p < 0.1$. Constant not shown.

confidence intervals, showing that the $(0.38 - 0.14 =) 0.24$ increase in candidate weight is indeed statistically significant. Given that the no info treatment did not provide party cues, we would not expect it to induce a similar effect, which is confirmed in the right panel. Thus this study confirms in an experimental framework what we saw in the previous observational findings: when citizens learned Bush's position, his supporters tended to adopt his view and his opponents rejected it.

8.4 The Perils of Cross-Sectional Research

The finding that people followed—they adopted their preferred politicians' policy positions when they learned them—is interesting in its own right, but it also helps explain why cross-sectional research often finds evidence of policy judgments while panel analyses do not. By cross-sectional, I mean studies that measure policy views and votes in the same survey, so at the same time. My analyses imply that such studies may sometimes get the story backward, interpreting correlations as evidence of policy voting when those correlations reflect the opposite—citizens following parties or candidates on policy. Media priming studies on policy issues seem especially vulnerable to this problem of finding the opposite of what is actually happening. In this section I test a prediction that follows from these findings. If citizens' tendency to follow after learning politicians' positions is what causes the conventional test of media priming to be misleading, then it should cause that test to be especially misleading when restricted to the learners. That is, the conventional test should find strong evidence of citizens increasingly judging politicians on policy issues once they learn the politician's positions, when what is really happening is just the opposite.

To test this prediction, I conduct what might be called the conventional test of learning effects; that is, I replicate the conventional priming test shown in chapter 3's figure 3.4, but only among those who learned the positions and, of course, only in those cases where I can measure this learning. To remind the reader, the key difference between the conventional test and those used elsewhere in this book is that it measures policy views and votes (or other outcome variable) at the same time: before the issue became prominent and then again afterward. The "after learning" issue weight is therefore estimated with policy views measured *after* learning has taken place. Since this learning led people to adopt their preferred party's or candidate's positions, their candidate/party preference will have already influenced their policy views at this point, and so this test should be biased by reverse causation. Indeed, figure 8.8 shows that it is: in every one of our cases, the conventional test finds that the learners were changing their votes (or some other outcome variable; I use the same variables here that I use in chapter 3) to reflect their policy views, even though we know from chapter 5 that no such effects occurred (compare figure 8.8 with figure 5.4).[19]

These findings highlight the severe inferential dangers researchers face when they measure citizens' policy views and their evaluations of politicians at the same time. Such studies may reach, not just the wrong conclusion, but the opposite of the right conclusion—and with impressive certainty. That is, researchers may conclude that citizens lead politicians when they actually follow.

8.5 Does Prior Persuasion Lead to Following?

The analyses in this chapter indicate that when people learn politicians' positions, they often follow them. Usually, though, between 40 and 50 percent of the panel survey respondents already know these positions (see table 5.1). These citizens, whom I call knowers, may not behave in the same way as the learners. In fact, they may be a different kind of voter. Since they care enough about the policy to learn politicians' positions

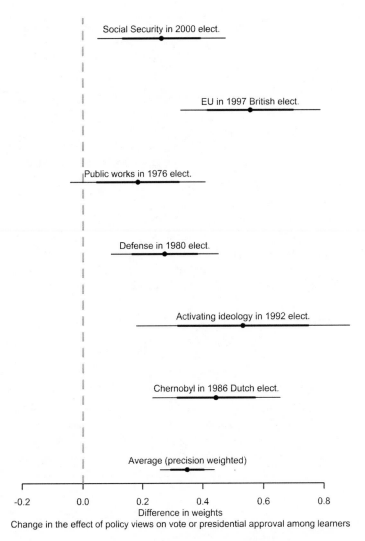

FIGURE 8.8. Given the tendency of learners to adopt their preferred parties' or candidates' positions, the conventional test should find learners appearing to judge politicians on policy issues, even when they are not actually doing so. Conventional test among learners (difference in issue weight = $\Omega_{ct} = f_{w3} - f_{w2}$, from equation 6 in the appendix) among learners. The appendix presents the least squares regression estimates (table 5). The thin and thick error bars show 90 percent and 68 percent confidence intervals, respectively.

before these issues become prominent, they may have developed their own view rather than adopted the view of whatever politicians they favor. On the other hand, they may be followers who happen to have learned and followed the politician's policy stance *before* their first interview in the panel survey, so I am unable to observe them following.

Which is it? Since I cannot exploit learning to determine whether these citizens are also following, I take another approach. I instead exploit prior changes in candidate or party support. For example, when citizens shift away from Gore and toward Bush during the 2000 campaign, do they later become supportive of Bush's proposal to invest Social Security funds?

To see whether they do I use the prior persuasion test. In chapter 4 I searched for policy and performance voting with this test, investigating whether persuasion on policy or on performance assessments between waves 1 and 2 leads to change in vote or presidential approval between waves 2 and 3. Here I employ the same test but look for evidence of the reverse process. That is, I test whether change in support for candidates or parties between waves 1 and 2 leads to change in policy views between waves 2 and 3.

As I noted in chapter 4, this test has advantages and disadvantages. Since I measure persuasion between prior waves, this test cannot get the story backward, an obvious advantage. Its main disadvantage, however, is that the effects of persuasion may occur too quickly to be captured by panel waves that often span months or years. In the ideology case, for example, a person who changes her level of approval for Bush between 1990 and 1991 would probably also have altered her ideology accordingly by 1991 (if she altered it at all). If she did, this test would miss the fact that she followed because it only looks for following afterward, between 1991 and 1992. It is therefore likely to be biased against finding evidence of following.

Since this test requires at least three interviews, I can only apply it to panel surveys with at least three waves. The cases I examine therefore include defense in the 1980 election, EU in the 1997 British election, public works in the 1976 election, activating ideology in the 1992 election, and unions in the 1948 election. (As in chapter 4, I control for the prior level and prior change on the lagged dependent variable; see equation 15 but with x and y reversed.)

Even with a test somewhat biased against finding evidence of following, I find strong evidence of citizens following. The left-hand side of figure 8.9 shows the estimates for all respondents. In every case we find that prior change in candidate or party support leads people to alter their policy views accordingly. When citizens became more favorable toward Bush early in the 2000 campaign, for instance, they later switched to support his policy of investing Social Security funds. The precision-

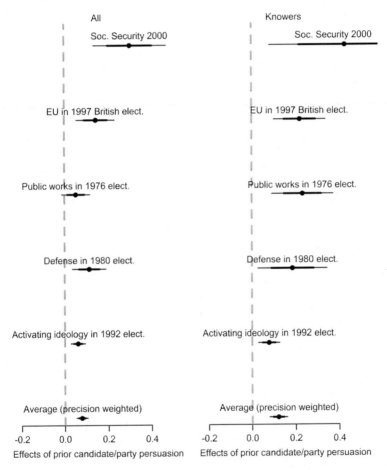

FIGURE 8.9. Summary of prior-persuasion test of candidate/party evaluations on policy views among all respondents and among learners. This figure shows that, when a person becomes more predisposed toward a candidate or party, he or she later shifts his policy positions in the direction of that candidate's or party's stances. (Ω_{x21}, see equation 15 but with x and y reversed). Ordinary least squares regression estimates with no additional controls. For the full model estimates, see the online appendix. The thin and thick error bars show 90 percent and 68 percent confidence intervals, respectively.

weighted average suggests that a voter who shifted the whole length of the party and candidate support scales between waves 1 and 2—for example, from strongly disapproving of Bush to strongly approving of him—would shift his or her support for Bush's policies by about 8 points on the 100-point scale between waves 2 and 3.

Moreover, the tendency to follow is pronounced among the knowers—those who already know the party or candidate stances. The right-hand side of figure 8.9 shows the result from estimating these effects only among the knowers. In every case this group's tendency to follow is stronger than the average tendency among all respondents—probably because the knowers know which way to bend their opinions. In the European integration case, for example, a knower who shifted from strongly favoring the Conservatives to strongly favoring Labour between 1995 and 1996 would be expected to increase his or her support for European integration by about 20 points on the 100-point scale between 1996 and 1997. Since this test is probably conservative, this estimate may represent a lower bound, suggesting that the true effect is larger. The knowers, it turns out, appear to be following just like the learners.

8.6 Informed Cueing or Blind Following?

We have seen that citizens tended to follow politicians, not only when they learn the politicians' positions, but even when they already knew those positions. This finding may look unflattering for democracy, but there are less troubling interpretations. For example, people may follow a party or candidate on a specific policy because they see the party or candidate as sharing their broader policy outlook—their ideology. Rather than following blindly, they may be taking cues from sources they trust.

A considerable body of scholarship supports this interpretation (Levendusky 2010; Lupia 1994; Lupia and McCubbins 1998; Mondak 1993). John Zaller's (1992) study of public opinion formation, for example, finds that public opinion largely follows elite opinion but does not do so blindly. Instead, people adopt the views of elites who share their policy predispositions, such as their overall ideology or their tendency toward hawkish or dovish defense policies. Consider, for example, President Ronald Reagan's support for the Contra guerrillas in Nicaragua. When promilitary and anticommunist elites endorsed Reagan's policy, defense hawks among the public listened. When they heard Colonel Oliver North, for instance, defiantly testifying in favor of the policy, they followed because they shared North's hawkish sensibility (Zaller 1992, 128–32). In contrast, those with a dovish predisposition rejected these messages.

Although the evidence in this book does not settle the question of whether citizens are following blindly or cue taking, several of my findings are inconsistent with the more flattering view and suggest that, at least for a share of the public, the tendency to follow looks worrisomely blind. In particular I find people following politicians, not just on policy views but also on predispositions. That is, people are following politicians on the same variables they are supposed to be using to determine for themselves which politicians to follow. European integration in the 1997 British election is an example. The survey question in this case asked not about a particular policy but about a general view of British sovereignty versus European government, with the choices ranging from "unite fully with the European Community" to "Britain should do all it can to protect its independence from the European Community." Even though this question arguably captures a general predisposition rather than a specific policy view, people followed their preferred party. Probably the most troubling example is the ideology case. Of all the cases I examine, that one involves the most general political predisposition. Yet people followed on this as well. I show this for the 1992 election (see figure 8.4), but I have replicated the result for the 2008 election, using the ANES panel, and for the 1976 election, using the 1976 Patterson panel. In other words, instead of saying, "I am conservative and the Republican Party is conservative, so I'll go along with Republican policy," people seem to be saying, "I support the Republican Party and it is conservative, so I'll be a conservative."

Besides the finding that citizens followed on predispositions, at least two other findings seem inconsistent with the informed cue-taking view. The first involves political knowledge. People who know little about politics, as measured by basic questions about government, are less likely to know which party or candidate shares their broader ideology. Nevertheless, they follow when they learn their preferred politicians' policy view on a particular issue at rates similar to, or higher than, politically knowledgeable people, who probably do know their preferred politicians' policy view. Figure 8.10 shows this result. On the left-hand side, it shows the estimates of learning-induced following, just as figure 8.4 does, but now only for individuals with below-the-median scores on general political

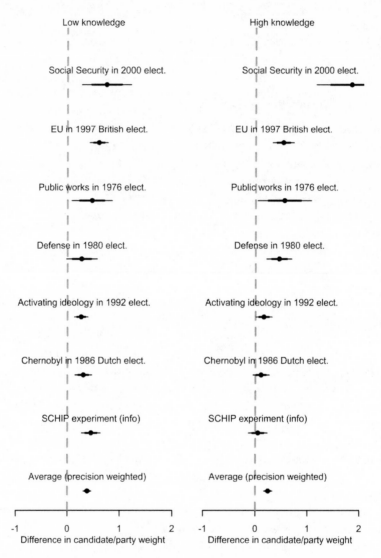

FIGURE 8.10. Do people follow parties or candidates on policy, even when they know relatively little about politics? This figure shows the estimates of learning-induced following of one's preferred party or candidate among those with below-the-median and above-the-median general political knowledge. It summarizes the results by showing only the difference statistic, that is, the increased importance of prior candidate or party support on *change* in policy views from before to after people learned—the same statistic shown at the bottom right of figure 8.3. Three-wave test of learning and adopting your candidate's position by knowledge (difference in candidate/party weights on policy views = $\Omega_{3wt} = f_{w2} - f_{w1}$, see equation 19 in the appendix). Ordinary least squares regression estimates. See the online appendix for the full results and the coding of the political knowledge scales. The thin and thick error bars show 90 percent and 68 percent confidence intervals, respectively.

knowledge. On the right-hand side, it shows these estimates for those with above-the-median scores. Despite some variability from case to case, the overall pattern indicates slightly more following among low-knowledge citizens than among high-knowledge citizens.[20] People appear to follow when they learn positions, even when they know relatively little about politics.

Of course, general political ignorance does not imply ignorance of a particular candidate's ideology. Those low-knowledge individuals who do follow may know their preferred candidate's ideology despite their generally low knowledge. Fortunately, four of the panel surveys, including the SCHIP experiment, asked respondents about the candidates' general ideology, allowing for a precise test. We find that citizens who were ignorant of the candidates' ideologies nevertheless followed at about the same or even a higher rate. Figure 8.11 shows this result for the four cases.[21] The left-hand side of figure 8.11 presents estimates of learning-induced opinion change (the same as that shown in figure 8.4), but only among those who were able to place the Democratic presidential candidate to the left of the Republican on the ideological scales. The right-hand side shows estimates of learning-induced opinion change for people who could not. These people either failed to place one or both candidates on the scale at all or else placed the Republican to the left of the Democrat. In three of the four tests, the tendency to follow is more pronounced among those who could not place the Democrat to the left of the Republican on the ideology scale. Carter backers in 1976, for instance, became more supportive of Carter's view on public works job programs, even though they could not place Carter to the ideological left of Ford.

The average effect for those who do not know the ideological positions (in all four surveys) is about 0.80, which is large. It indicates that a shift from strong opposition to strong support for a conservative candidate would lead a learner to become about 80 points more conservative on the policy (on the 100-point scales) than they otherwise would have been. For citizens who know the overall ideologies, the average shift is only about 20 points.[22]

I can also examine this question with the prior persuasion test. Above, I showed that when people changed their views of the parties or candidates, they changed their policy views accordingly. Are they also likely to do so even when they are unaware of parties' or candidates' overall ideologies? For example, will a Bush supporter who doesn't even know

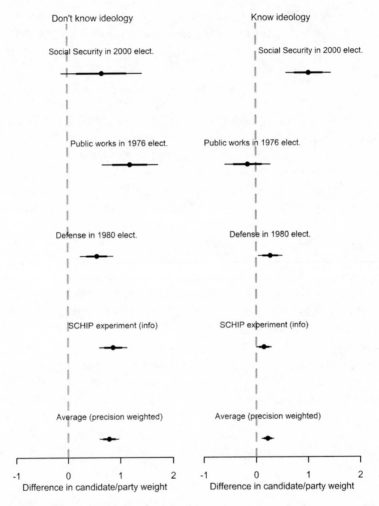

FIGURE 8.11. Do people follow candidates even when they remain ignorant of the candidates' overall ideological orientation? For the four surveys that asked about perceptions of the candidates' ideology, this figure shows that people followed as much or more when they could not place the Democrat to the left of the Republican. It summarizes the results by showing only the difference statistic, that is, the increased importance of prior candidate or party support on *change* in policy views from before to after people learned—the same statistic shown at the bottom right of figure 8.3. Three-wave test of learning and adopting your candidate's position by knowledge of ideology (difference in candidate/party weights on policy views = $\Omega_{3wi} = f_{w2} - f_{w1}$, see equation 19 in the appendix). Ordinary least squares regression estimates. See the online appendix for the full results and the coding of the political knowledge scales. The thin and thick error bars show 90 percent and 68 percent confidence intervals, respectively.

whether Bush is to the right or the left of Gore nevertheless change his own policy views to go along with those of Bush? Since following requires knowledge of politicians' stances on the particular policy issues—regardless of whether citizens do or do not have a sense for politicians' broader ideology—I test for following among knowers and learners; that is, among those who already knew or just learned the positions. Consistent with the results above, I find persuasion-induced following among those who are ignorant of the candidates' ideologies. The effects are large and statistically significant in all three cases. I show these findings in the online appendix.

These findings imply that, at least for some citizens, following can be worrisomely blind. It is worth considering, however, an alternative explanation. Rather than directly cueing off politicians, people may instead be accepting arguments from them. They may be adopting Gore's opposition to investing Social Security funds, for instance, not because they learned Gore's view (not having known it before), but because they heard Gore make compelling arguments against this policy. One piece of evidence against this interpretation is the surprising degree to which people followed when they learned the candidate or party positions. The sheer magnitude of these effects (see figure 8.4), combined with the utter absence of such effects among nonlearners, implies that learning the positions on its own drives this tendency.[23] The SCHIP experiment also supports this conclusion. It only finds an increased tendency to adopt or reject Bush's position in accordance with one's view of Bush among those who were randomly assigned to receive cues about Bush's and the Democrats' positions (info treatment). When these cues were not conveyed (no info treatment), people did not exhibit this tendency (see figure 8.7). By holding everything else constant, including potentially persuasive arguments,[24] this experiment bolsters the view that people can directly cue off politicians' positions—reasoned arguments for those positions by politicians or other elites aren't necessary.

Several of this chapter's findings therefore imply that a considerable share of the public exhibits a rather crude form of following. They did not just follow politicians on policy. They also appeared to follow politicians on basic political predispositions such as ideology. Furthermore, they followed the views of politicians even when they were ignorant about those politicians' broader policy outlooks, they followed even when they did not know much about politics in general, and they followed candidates as well as parties.

8.7 Following on Performance?

Do people also follow on performance issues? Although previous studies have found they do, I find little such evidence.[25] I have conducted this chapter's prior persuasion test on the performance-issue cases examined earlier in this book. (I do not, however, conduct the learning tests on performance-related issues, as there are no "positions" to learn. Everyone wants a good economy and honest and competent politicians.) With only a few exceptions, these fail to find following. The estimates are often in the correct direction, but small and not statistically significant (see the online appendix). To an extent, these results support the findings in chapters 2 and 3 that performance issues matter. Although people appear to follow on policy, they lead on performance.

8.8 Conclusion

In the policy-voting view of democracy, the public leads politicians on policy, and while politicians may help inform the public, they ultimately follow the public. As this book has revealed, however, a careful examination finds little evidence of this pattern. Instead, politicians lead and the public follows. We have seen this happening in case after case in this chapter. The tendency to follow is particularly evident among citizens who learned politicians' positions between their interviews. When supporters of George W. Bush learned, for example, that he opposed expanding a children's health care program (SCHIP), they too became opposed to the expansion. The tendency to follow even emerges for overall ideology. When citizens who supported a Republican president but whose own ideologies were to the left learned that the Republican Party was on the ideological right, they didn't shift against the Republican president—they shifted their own reported ideology to the right. The tendency to follow also emerges when people change their evaluations of candidates or parties. For example, between 1995 and 1996, British citizens became more favorable toward the Labour Party, and between 1996 and 1997 they became more favorable toward its policy of supporting integration with Europe. At least according to the evidence in this chapter, democracy appears to be inverted. Instead of politicians following the public will, the public appears to follow the will of politicians.

This chapter highlights the perils of cross-sectional research designs, especially when studying issue voting. When researchers measure policy views concurrently with vote choice or with party and candidate evaluations, they may reach erroneous conclusions (see especially figure 8.8). Although they interpret their findings as policy views influencing votes, the cases I examine suggest that the effects often go in the other direction. In the case of media priming on policy issues, I find that increased campaign and media attention to an issue creates the appearance of priming—the appearance that issues matter—through a two-part process. First, it informs some citizens about the parties' or candidates' positions on an issue. Second, these newly informed citizens often adopt their preferred party's or candidate's position as their own. Thus this process creates the appearance that issues matter (through priming) when they do not actually matter.

My results also shed light on a key question about cue taking: are citizens blindly following their tribe (or their candidate) or are they using a heuristic that more often than not leads them to policy views that reflect their interests? The finding that people took cues from candidates as much, or more, than they did from parties may imply that they are blindly following candidates who catch their fancy, rather than cueing off parties that represent their interests. Additionally, people who knew little about politics, as measured by basic questions about government, are less likely to know which party or candidate shares their outlook, yet they followed at rates identical to politically knowledgeable people, who probably did know. In several cases, the surveys asked respondents about the parties' or candidates' general ideologies, allowing for an even more specific test. Again, however, citizens who appeared ignorant of these broader stances nevertheless followed their parties or candidates at about the same rate.

Of course these results do not imply that citizens will always follow their party or candidate. On some policy issues, such as those involving race or social issues, many people may hold stable views (Converse 1964; Hillygus and Shields 2008; Mendelberg 2001; Valentino, Hutchings, and White 2002). They may therefore be unlikely to cue off their party or candidate. Even on difficult issues, such as investing Social Security funds, there must be a few people who hold their own views and would not simply follow even their favored candidate. Additionally, people may follow their party or candidate only because, even on the most prominent issues of the day, they rarely come across information about the issue in their everyday lives and lack incentives to seek out more information. A recent study suggests that when people are given unusually in-depth policy information and party cues, they rely more on the policy information than on party cues, though both matter (Bullock 2011). Finally, I do not find much evidence of changing views on performance assessments; citizens seem more firmly anchored to reality on that score.

CHAPTER NINE

Conclusion

Over the last two centuries, the reins of power in many countries have fallen into the hands of citizens. This book has examined how citizens use this power. Do they lead politicians by judging them on qualities relevant to performance in public office? In particular, do citizens base their judgments on candidates' policy stances and on candidates' performance-related characteristics? Or, rather than leading, do they follow? That is, do they adopt the views of parties or politicians whom they already prefer for other reasons?

Although these questions are basic, answering them is not. In fact, after years of research, we still lack clear answers. The problem, as I have explained, is observational equivalence: we know that views and votes correlate, but when they are measured at the same time—as is typically the case in political science studies—we cannot easily discern which is the cause and which is the effect. To overcome this problem, my analyses used panel surveys and experimental data to measure the proposed causes before measuring the effects. I then exploited major and minor political upheavals induced by wars, disasters, economic booms and busts, political campaigns, as well as experimental manipulations, to see if voters changed their judgments about politicians in accordance with their prior policy views or performance assessments. Much as earthquakes reveal otherwise hidden geological processes to geologists, these political upheavals helped us study the hard-to-observe role of policy and performance in voters' evaluations of parties and politicians. Specifically, these upheavals can cause three types of shifts in voters' thinking by (a) increasing the prominence of an issue (media priming), (b) changing voters' views about a policy or performance issue (persuasion), or (c) increasing voters' knowledge about politicians' policy positions (learning). If policy and performance matter to voters, these shifts in thinking should lead some of them to change their votes or candidate evaluations based on their prior policy views or performance-related assessments. Using panel surveys that spanned these upheavals, I investigated whether any of these three types of shifts ultimately led to such change. For example, when the Chernobyl reactor meltdown brought the issue of nuclear power to prominence in the 1986 Dutch election, did voters who already opposed nuclear power switch their votes to the antinuclear parties? When supporters of Al Gore later came to see him as dishonest during the course of the 2000 campaign, did they shift their votes to George W. Bush?

My analyses of these upheavals painted a mixed picture of voters' democratic choices. Confirming previous research, voters did appear to judge politicians on performance. When people thought the president excelled on a performance issue, such as Bill Clinton presiding over strong economic growth, they became more supportive of him as the economy became a prominent campaign issue (media priming). Likewise, when they were persuaded that George H. W. Bush had waged the Gulf War successfully, they later became more approving of his presidency (persuasion). On performance, therefore, citizens led.

My findings are different for policy. I found surprisingly little evidence that it carried much weight in voters' judgments. In the cases I analyzed, voters rarely shifted their votes to politicians who agreed with them. Even though the prominence of the issues often increased dramatically in these cases (media priming), the increases almost never led voters to place greater weight on those issues. Even though millions of voters learned about the candidates' stands (learning), this rarely altered voters' views of politicians. And even though campaigns and the news media (or other factors) persuaded many voters to shift their views on the issues (persuasion), this rarely led them to vote differently.

Instead of finding that policy issues influenced votes, I usually found the reverse: voters first decided to support a particular politician, then adopted that politician's policy views. When supporters of George W. Bush, for instance, learned that he opposed expanding a health-care-coverage program for children (SCHIP), they also became opposed to the expansion.

At least on policy, democracy therefore appears inverted. Not only did voters fail to lead politicians, but they instead followed politicians. Moreover, they followed politicians' positions on particular issues even when they knew little about those politicians' broader policy orientations.

9.1 Simple Judgments

The tests I have administered to citizens varied in difficulty. Some were hard; some were easy.

The tests on performance-related issues, shown in chapters 2 and 4, should have been easy, I argued, because a voter does not need to know particular politicians' positions on these issues (everyone desires better performance) and does not need to have his or her own well-developed views about a particular public policy. All the voter needs is a view about, for instance, the state of the economy. Since voters did pass these tests—that is, they did judge politicians on performance—we can at least say that they were not at the bottom of the spectrum of democratic expertise.

The policy-issue tests were harder. They required knowledge of politicians' positions on the particular policy and they required that voters hold views of their own about that policy. If voters had passed these tests, then we would view them as even more competent. For the most part, however, voters failed; that is, they rarely judged politicians on policy.

These performance and policy results tell us that citizens were neither at the bottom nor the top of the spectrum of democratic expertise. Chapter 5 refined this view. It administered a test easier than those on policy but harder than those on performance. It investigated whether learning about candidates' positions on policy led people to change their votes or their evaluations of presidents accordingly. It may be that policy judgments are rare because voters are often ignorant of politicians' policy stances, but when campaigns and the news media educate voters about these positions, it should be easier for voters to vote on policy. Did voters pass this easier test? They did not. Even when they had just learned candidates' positions on the most prominent issues in these elections, they did not vote on policy positions. These findings also imply that lack of knowledge about candidates' positions is not a central barrier to policy voting. Instead, lack of strong views about public policy appears to be the more important barrier.

Chapters 6 and 7 further refined our view of voters, indicating that they can handle policy issues under certain circumstances. Both chapters presented case studies of extraordinary events that raised the prominence of policy issues to unusual heights. In the case discussed in chapter 6, the Chernobyl nuclear reactor meltdown took place three weeks before Election Day in the Netherlands, where the incumbent parties' support for nuclear power was already an issue. In the case discussed in chapter 7, the Iranian hostage crisis and the Soviet invasion of Afghanistan induced overwhelming support for greater defense spending in the United States, just as an incumbent president with a dovish history began his reelection bid. If policy issues ever do matter, they should have mattered in these cases; these should have been easy tests of voters' ability to vote according to policy. In fact, I found little evidence in either case that voters ultimately judged politicians on their policy stances.

Instead, these case studies suggested an important wrinkle. Incumbents facing widespread public concern on issues that disadvantaged them responded strategically, adopting policy stances that mollified the public, thus ensuring that voters did not cast their ballots on those particular issues. Unlike all the other cases in this book, in which rival politicians maintain opposing views, the incumbents in these cases changed their positions so as to converge on their opponents' more popular views. In the Netherlands, the incumbent parties shifted from supporting nuclear power to opposing it—just one week after the Chernobyl disaster and two weeks before Election Day. In the United States, President Carter, despite some back and forth, ultimately shifted from a defense dove to a defense hawk. In both cases I found that the public learned about and accepted these dramatic shifts. Although any conclusions must be tentative, voters apparently failed to vote on either policy issue, not because they lacked interest or knowledge, but because the incumbents with unpopular policy positions changed their positions. These case studies added nuance to our view of voters. Most of the time voters apparently failed to judge politicians on policy—at least during campaigns. At times, however, public policy did interest the masses. In these unusual cases, politicians appeared to follow voters.

9.2 The Absence of Policy Voting

Of the book's findings, the absence of policy voting is probably the most important for our view of voters and democracy. Researchers are so used to finding correlations between policy views and votes that this absence will surprise many and will no doubt be met with skepticism. To a degree, I share this skepticism, but I also ask: what other real-world evidence do we have that these correlations are causal? What other evidence do we have that is not vulnerable to reverse causation?

Before discussing the implications of the policy findings, it's worth noting that some conceptions of democracy are perfectly consistent with a lack of policy voting. In fact, many people—including the Founding Fathers—have argued that voters should vote, not on policy, but on performance-related characteristics such as character.

Nevertheless, if policy voting is as rare as these analyses suggest, one can readily see unsettling ramifications. Most importantly, if voters rarely vote on policy, politicians may feel little constraint on the policies they pursue. Michael Alvarez and Jonathan Nagler (1998) summarize the consequences of voters' focus on the economy and their inattention to policy issues:

> The dominance of economic perceptions over issues has interesting normative implications for politics. The retrospective model of voting has suggested that voters reward or punish incumbents for economic performance and that this is a good thing since economic performance is observable and tangible. However, if incumbents have little control over short-term economic performance, voters are choosing candidates essentially at random. This suggests candidates have tremendous freedom to shirk in the policy areas over which they do exert considerable influence. . . . Thus, when voters use retrospective evaluations of national economic performance as their primary criteria in presidential elections, they might be losing their ability to ensure that they eventually achieve the noneconomic policy outcomes they desire. (p. 1362)

To a degree, economic voting will constrain incumbents' policy choices. Pursuing policies that retard growth will hurt their reelection bids, while policies that boost growth will help. Outside of these policies, however, politicians may indeed have considerable freedom. Of course, the economy is only one performance issue, but others, such as honesty, seem even less likely to constrain politicians on policy.

If politicians do have this leeway, what should we expect? One possibility is that politicians will cater to interest groups who aid their reelection bids. The financial donations and volunteer time these groups provide may cost politicians little and aid them considerably on Election

Day. And since politicians may lack control over the one thing the voters seem to judge them on—economic performance—these interest groups may provide insurance against voter retribution in poor economic times. But interest groups often don't reflect public opinion and, since they tend to be policy extremists (Puglisi and Snyder 2011; Schattschneider 1960), they may foster polarization among politicians.

Although I found little evidence that voters judged politicians on policy, my results do not rule out a crude form of policy voting suggested by aggregate-level analysis (Erikson, MacKuen, and Stimson 2002; Stimson, MacKuen, and Erikson 1995). The US public, according to this research, may not have much in the way of specific policy views, but it has a policy "mood." Sometimes it wants more government, sometimes less. When the mood shifts toward larger government, Democrats tend to win office. When the mood shifts toward small government, Republicans tend to win.[1] Although the evidence for this cruder form of policy voting is compelling, it is nevertheless based on relatively short time series (fifteen presidential elections). Currently, panel surveys lack the questions necessary to vet these important findings at the individual level.

It is also possible that while voters may not directly vote on policy, they may nonetheless end up selecting the right politicians in the aggregate. This would have to occur indirectly. For example, by heeding cues from interest groups, elites, or the news media—entities that often do have policy views—voters may act as if they had made these same policy judgments themselves.[2] Indeed, previous work may indicate that in the aggregate, democracy does manage—somewhat indirectly—to select national political leaders with policy and performance advantages. For instance, some presidential candidates perceived as holding extreme views, such as Barry Goldwater and George McGovern, have fared poorly (although others, such as Ronald Reagan, have been successful).[3]

9.3 Limitations

In assessing democracy's shortcomings, this book has several limitations worth noting. Given that we can't run experiments directly on issue voting—we can't randomly assign people's policy views, at least not on meaningful and salient issues—studies on issue voting will never be fully experimental. The data I examine are therefore primarily observational (as opposed to experimental). As with all observational studies, we must therefore worry about alternative explanations. Aspects of the research design used in this book, however, render it hard to generate alternative explanations for several reasons. First, the panel nature of the data rules out many—but not all—alternative explanations by design because we are holding the person constant.[4] Second, I replicate the main findings in many cases across several countries, which further limits the set of plausible alternative explanations. Finally, the policy findings (citizens follow rather than lead) replicate in an experiment, where I manipulate issue salience and knowledge of politicians' positions.

Probably the most important limitation concerns the generalizability of the findings. Since I test for issue and performance judgments among people who experience one of the three shifts—priming, learning, or persuasion—my results only apply to the kinds of people who experience these shifts. But they may not be an entirely representative sample of the public. In particular, they may be unrepresentative of those who care deeply about policy (e.g., Lee 2002)—people who may rarely experience any of these three shifts because they may already know the politicians' positions and may be unlikely to change their own well-developed views. Consequently, my tests may miss issue voting among a part of the population more likely to engage in it.

How severe is this problem? How much issue voting did I miss because of it? The honest answer is that we do not know. Since political scientists can only test for issue voting through shifts like these, our inferences are always limited to those who experience them.[5] Several findings, however, have suggested that we are not missing much. In particular, the one shift not vulnerable to this concern occurs when voters learn not about politicians' or parties' long-standing positions but about recently changed positions. Especially in the rare cases when parties alter their original positions during the course of a campaign—sometimes even swapping positions with the opposing party—people who care deeply about the policy have something new to learn and should tend to alter their support for particular parties. The panels I examined span two such shifts: the Labour and Conservative Parties swapping positions on European integration in the early 1990s and President Jimmy Carter briefly retreating in the 1980 campaign from his otherwise hawkish defense policy. In these cases I did find issue voting, though the effects were limited to relatively small segments of the population, indicating that the number of people who cared deeply about these policies was not large.

Since studying voters' reactions to position changes is especially revealing, I would ideally have examined more than just these two cases. In the United States, the Democratic and Republican Parties swapped positions on civil rights in the 1960s (Carmines and Stimson 1989). The two parties have also taken a similar position (or no clear position at all) on an issue for a time and then adopted different positions. For example, both parties generally supported greater defense spending in the early part of the Cold War but diverged in the late 1960s. Neither party took a strong stand on abortion until the 1980s and 1990s, when they took opposite stands (Adams 1997). Nor did they differ much in general ideology in the late 1960s and early 1970s, but they began to diverge considerably in the 1970s (McCarty, Poole, and Rosenthal 2006). Although time-series studies do indeed suggest that voters change parties based on the parties' changing positions on these issues (e.g., Carmines and Stimson 1989), we cannot know for sure without panel data (and even then, inferences can be tricky). Unfortunately, we have almost no panel surveys spanning these shifts.

One exception is the Youth-Parent Socialization Panel Study (Jennings et al. 2005; Jennings and Niemi 1981), which interviewed high school seniors in 1965 and reinterviewed them in 1973, 1982, and 1997, thus spanning the divergence of the Republican and Democratic Parties on general ideology and on abortion in particular. According to analysis of this panel, people's own ideology and abortion views, measured in earlier waves, appear to influence changes in their party affiliations between later waves.[6] The influence, however, appears to be moderate in size, especially when averaged across respondents (Achen and Bartels 2006). Analysis of this panel also reveals considerable evidence of voters following rather than leading politicians on the issue of abortion. For example, almost 60 percent of 1982 male prolife Democrats had become prochoice by 1997, while almost 40 percent of 1982 female prolife Democrats had done so (Achen and Bartels 2006).[7] Another exception is the Terman Longitudinal Study (1922–82), which spans the two parties' swapping of positions on civil rights. Analysis of this study reveals suggestive evidence that individuals' prior views about African Americans did indeed influence later changes in their political ideology (Sears and Funk 1999).

These few findings indicate that the concern about generalizability is real; my analyses were undoubtedly missing some policy voting among people who care so deeply about policies that they were unlikely to exhibit any of the three shifts. They also imply, however, that the concern is probably limited. The number of such people seems small. Future research using long-term panels may shed light on how small (or how large).[8]

Longer-term panels would also help address another limitation of my analyses. Since the panels I examined span just months or, at most, a few years, I can only test for short-term effects. If a policy takes years to influence votes, my analyses would miss that influence. I can therefore only say that policy usually matters little for major-party voting in the short term.

Another potential limitation is that I may miss policy voting if many citizens are primarily single-issue voters, which researchers call the "issue public" hypothesis (Converse 1964; Krosnick 1990; Hutchings 2003). In this case, tests on any one issue, such as those I have conducted, will likely miss policy voting because many people are voting on other issues. Unfortunately, we do not know whether few or many citizens are single-issue voters. As this book has tried to make clear, studying issue voting is hard. Several facts, however, seem inconsistent with the "issue public" hypothesis. In particular, people's knowledge of politics tends to be relatively general as opposed to issue specific (Zaller 1985). A person who knows about abortion policy, for example, is also likely to know about environmental policy. The importance of performance issues also seems inconsistent with a single-issue view. People do not focus on one policy issue to such a degree that they ignore performance issues, such as the economy, so why assume that they ignore other policy issues? All told, it seems unlikely that single-issue voting is widespread, thus masking policy voting in my analysis, but more research is needed.[9]

Studies on issue voting, including this one, probably also misjudge its extent because of measurement problems. Assessing the public's potentially complex policy views with survey questions is tricky and often yields noisy measures. This noise likely leads researchers to underestimate the importance of voters' policy views. Some studies have tried to measure policy views more reliably—for example, by using improved question formatting or by creating scales of multiple policy items—and indeed have found stronger associations between policy views and votes (Ansolabehere, Rodden, and Snyder 2008; Krosnick and Berent 1993; Miller and Shanks 1996; Shanks, Strand, and Carmines 2003). Although my own options are constrained by using large panel studies that have already been conducted by others, I have tried to address this measurement problem where I could. I have replicated the policy-voting analysis (chapters 3 and 5) with attitudes averaged across multiple prior years (for example, using average European integration views from 1994, 1995, 1996 instead of just those from 1996), which should substantially reduce random measurement error, yet I found similar results. I have also used multi-item scales where possible; I measured ideology with a three-item scale and measured learning about British parties switching positions on European integration with an eight-item scale. Overall, the results suggested that noisy measures did not account for the absence of evidence for policy voting.[10] Nonetheless, I would have more confidence in my findings if I could have measured policy views in every case with multi-item scales.[11]

Another limitation is that this book assesses only a few of democracy's many components. For example, I have tested whether voters use their own policy views and their own assessments of candidate performance to judge politicians, but not whether their judgments are wise or foolish. My finding that voters do use their own performance assessments to judge politicians on performance is therefore normatively reassuring, but only up to a point. Democracy could fail in many other ways. Voters' perceptions of a politician's performance do not always reflect reality, such as Republicans believing that the deficit worsened under President Bill Clinton or Democrats believing that unemployment rose under President Ronald Reagan (Bartels 2002a; Bartels 2008; Gaines et al. 2008; Shani 2006). I also did not examine whether politicians pursue the policies they espouse during campaigns. These are important questions, but outside the scope of this book.

Finally, it is worth noting the paucity of panel cases. Although I examined a wide range of issues, several important categories were left out. In particular, no panel spans an increase in the prominence of attitudes about policy related to race, immigrants, or other social groups, which are key issues in the United States and other countries. I also lack panel data on many types of performance-related issues, such as corruption. Future research will, I expect, more firmly conclude that such issues do influence at least some voters—the question will be, "how many?"

9.4 Additional Implications and Outstanding Questions

Importance of Performance Issues

Despite these limitations, this book contributes to research on democracy by overcoming the problem of observational equivalence. Most studies measure people's policy views or performance assessments concurrently with their votes or candidate evaluations and therefore cannot discern whether, when views and votes appear to be correlated, views are causing votes or votes are causing views. By overcoming observational equivalence, I am also able to shed light on other long-standing questions.

First, the findings provide further evidence of the importance of performance-related issues, such as the economy. Although politicians, journalists, and scholars often interpret elections ideologically, a growing body of evidence suggests that it is the economy and other performance domains, not ideology, that largely explain election outcomes. My results support this view.

Moreover, findings not compromised by reverse causation help us understand why, in particular, the economy matters. Although most scholars assume that citizens directly judge incumbents on the economy, we lacked conclusive evidence. We know that the economy affects elections and we know that people's economic perceptions correlate with their votes, but studies continue to raise doubts that citizens' judgments of the economy explain their votes (e.g., Evans and Pickup 2010). The American public, my findings indicated, does directly judge presidents on the economy. The key result here is that citizens' earlier perceptions of the national economy shaped later changes in their approval of the president.

Neutralizing Issues: Politicians' Ability to Switch Sides

Although this book mostly focuses on voters, its findings also have something important to say about candidates. Theories about elections often assume that candidates can change their stances on policy issues—for example, by adopting the position of the median voter (Downs 1957)—but we have surprisingly little evidence confirming that they can benefit from doing so (though see Tavits 2007; Tomz and Van Houweling 2010). We know that politicians often fail to converge to the median voter's position, which could mean that shifting positions is difficult.[12] We also know that parties generally shift their positions in response to movement in public opinion (Adams et al. 2004; Adams et al. 2006; Carrubba 2001; Erikson, MacKuen, and Stimson 2002; Ezrow et al. 2007; Hobolt and Klemmensen 2008; Steenbergen, Edwards, and de Vries 2007), but that doesn't mean they succeed in changing perceptions of their positions, nor does it mean they necessarily benefit.[13]

Chapters 6 and 7 presented evidence on the basic question of whether candidates can neutralize issues by changing public perceptions of their policy positions. Both chapters' findings supported the view that candidates can indeed do so. Chapter 6 tested Prime Minister Lubbers's ability to shift public perceptions of his parties' position on nuclear power in the 1986 Dutch election. Chapter 7 examined President Carter's attempt to fend off charges that he was weak on national defense during the 1980 election. In both cases the incumbents adopted more popular policy positions in the midst of campaigns. In both cases, the public learned about and apparently believed this midstream repositioning. For example, almost 60 percent of Dutch respondents shifted their perceptions of Lubbers's party's position on nuclear power, seeing it as more opposed (see figure 6.8).[14] They did so even though Lubbers and his party had strongly supported nuclear power for years.

In fact, voters shifted their perceptions so quickly in these cases that their behavior raised concerns. Had they forgotten about past stances too quickly? Did their willingness to accept such short-term repositioning constitute a failure to hold politicians accountable?

Although these findings are intriguing, it's important to note that Lubbers's and Carter's switches may have been exceptional. In the wake of major crises, the public may have granted these politicians greater leeway to change sides than it would otherwise have done. The broader implications for elections are therefore unclear. Nevertheless, their apparently successful position shifts suggest that big sudden shifts are possible—a finding with implications for policy voting, as I discuss below.

Why Performance More Than Policy?

These findings on candidate strategy may help address another outstanding question: why do performance issues appear to matter more often than policy issues do? In chapter 1, I noted one explanation—that performance issues are cognitively easier for voters. Policy issues require knowledge of politicians' positions on the particular policy, and they require that voters hold views of their own about that policy. These are formidable barriers. Across the policy issues examined in this book, I typically found that only about 50 percent of voters could correctly place the major candidates or parties to the right or left of each other—a relatively easy task.

There are, of course, other explanations for why performance issues appear to matter more often than policy issues do. Voters may have failed to judge politicians on policy, not because policy issues are too hard, but because politicians can more readily neutralize policy issues through several strategies, including shifting to positions that are more popular. On performance issues, however, they cannot easily do so. When Bob Dole sought to unseat Bill Clinton in the 1996 election, for example, he tried to neutralize the issue of the economy—a performance issue—by convincing the public that the economy was weak, but he failed. In contrast, when Lubbers faced reelection in the immediate aftermath of the Chernobyl nuclear disaster, he quickly changed his party's position on nuclear power—a policy issue—and apparently neutralized the issue. If politicians can change stances, neutralizing potentially damaging issues in advance of elections, policy voting should be rare—a prediction straight from Anthony Downs (1957). If politicians have a harder time neutralizing performance issues—for example, by convincing citizens that the economy is better than they think—voting on these issues should be more common.[15] So performance issues may matter more often in part because of the strategic difficulty they pose to politicians—it's harder to wriggle out of them.

One draws different conclusions about democracy depending on which (if either) of these explanations—voters' cognitive difficulties or candidates' policy repositionings—accounts for the absence of policy voting. If policy fails to matter because voters find the issues too hard, even when an issue creates a national crisis, then we should worry about democracy. If, however, policy fails to matter because politicians usually adopt popular policy views, then this "failure" may in fact indicate that democracy works, forcing politicians to "take at" least some heed of what the public wants.

Is either explanation right? Evidence for the cognitive account is limited because we cannot systematically measure the easiness of issues. Evidence on politicians' ability to neutralize issues is also limited, as I have already discussed. Most likely, both explanations are at play: policy issues probably matter when voters find issues easy to understand and candidates find them hard to neutralize. In what resembles a conspiracy, these two factors may work together to limit the influence of policy issues on votes. Most of the time, most voters lack strong policy views, ensuring that issues do not matter and that politicians are, at best, weakly bound

by their constituents' views. When voters do develop strong views, however, politicians are more likely to adopt popular positions, ensuring that
these strong views do not lead voters to change their votes. I discuss this
interpretation's implications for democracy at the end of the conclusion.

There is another explanation involving candidate strategy that may
explain the absence of policy voting—one that is less flattering for democracy. Instead of neutralizing issues by adopting the policies voters prefer, candidates may neutralize them by confusing voters. In the
United States we know that candidates from both parties tend to advertise on the same set of issues (Sides 2006). By obfuscating their own position (Page 1978; Shepsle 1972) and by raising doubts about their opponents' positions, candidates may undermine voters' confidence in their
own views and in their perceptions of the candidates' positions. Without
the resources or the incentives to sort through this barrage, voters may
just end up not voting on policy issues. In the 2000 campaign, for example, Gore strategists believed they had neutralized any advantage Bush
might have garnered from his popular Social Security proposal by raising doubts in supporters' minds about its financial feasibility (Jamieson
and Waldman 2001, 173). Although candidates try to do this on both policy and performance issues, they may be less successful on performance
issues, which are simpler and more tangible for voters.

One final explanation also deserves mention. Performance issues may
matter more than policy issues because voters see performance as more
fundamental to a politician's qualifications. Voters may want to ensure
first and foremost that a politician is honest and competent and will therefore only vote on policy differences among rival candidates when they are
satisfied on performance. Future research can explore this possibility.

Media Priming

This book's findings also have implications for research on media priming. The experiments on agenda setting and media priming conducted
by Shanto Iyengar, Donald Kinder, and their collaborators had a pro-
found effect on the fields of political science and political communications (Iyengar and Kinder 1987; Iyengar et al. 1984). Before their publications research had generally failed to produce much evidence of
campaign effects or media effects (Graber 1993; Patterson and McClure
1976). To a degree, these experiments revived the study of those effects.

They not only found evidence of the influence of campaigns and the media but also raised concerns about that influence, suggesting that voters are vulnerable to manipulation through media priming. The studies also had implications for candidate strategy, suggesting that candidates should avoid debating issues with opponents and stick to stressing issues favorable to themselves (Simon 2002).

The Iyengar and Kinder studies were about performance issues, but other researchers extended the findings to policy issues. This book's results confirm Iyengar and Kinder's findings on performance but contradict subsequent studies on policy issues. From one perspective, this is good news for democracy, since voters may not be vulnerable to manipulation through priming on policy, and candidates may not be strongly motivated to avoid policy debates. From a broader perspective, however, these findings seem less reassuring because they suggest that voters rarely consider policy issues in the first place—they are not so much immune to manipulation as indifferent to the issues.

One explanation for why I failed to find media priming on policy issues is that the competitive context of campaigns may mitigate their agenda-setting power. In a series of experiments on framing effects, Dennis Chong and James Druckman (2007) find that weaker arguments are less likely to influence opinions when they compete with stronger ones. Since most of the cases I analyzed take place during campaigns—the exception being the panel experiment on SCHIP—the competitive environment may have led voters to focus more on performance issues, if voters see them as more important.

The finding that campaigns primed the issue of the economy is also consistent with several other studies (Bartels 1992; Bartels 2006; Stevenson and Vavreck 2000). For example, Lynn Vavreck (2009) concludes that the economy matters in presidential elections, but *how* it matters depends on the particular campaign. She finds that candidates for whom the current state of the economy is an advantage are more likely to win their elections if they run what she calls a clarifying campaign—one in which they emphasize the state of the economy. Such candidates won in every presidential election she examines (1952–2000), with the sole exception of Ford's post-Watergate 1976 campaign. Of the five candidates who (according to Vavreck) should have but did not run a clarifying campaign, three lost: Richard Nixon in 1960, Hubert Humphrey in 1968, and Al Gore in 2000.

The Role of Campaigns: Fundamentals

Andrew Gelman and Gary King (1993) conclude that campaigns and the news media fulfill their most important role in democracy by enlightening voters, giving them the information they need about what the authors call "fundamentals," such as the economy or politicians' ideologies. Voters do their part, Gelman and King find, by incorporating this new information into their voting decisions.

According to my findings, Gelman and King are right about campaigns—they do inform voters about candidates' positions, fulfilling their role in democracy. At least on ideology, however, they are wrong about the more important question: whether this learning influences voters. Although many voters do learn about parties' and candidates' ideologies, voters apparently do little with this information. As I discussed in chapter 8, Gelman and King (1993) seem to have been misled on this point by reverse causation.

This book therefore paints a strange picture of campaigns. They inform certain voters about candidates' policy positions, but these seem to be the very voters who do not use what they have learned. Voters who do use such information because they care about the issues don't need campaigns to provide it; they already know the candidates' positions. Such findings suggest, in turn, that providing voters with more information about candidate positions will not improve the choices made in a democracy.

The Rationalizing Public

On many of the policies I examined, voters did not generally lead their politicians, but rather followed them. That is, instead of selecting candidates based on their policy views, voters appeared to adopt the policy views of their preferred party or candidate. The findings therefore broadly confirm Zaller's (1992) conclusions about elite-driven public opinion.

I also found that the tendency to follow politicians can have a simple mechanism: learning. When people learn the positions of parties or candidates, they adopt the position of their preferred party or candidate. Although some research has noted this behavior (Abramowitz 1978; Cohen 2003), its extent appears to have been underappreciated. Across the various issues I analyze, merely learning the position of one's candidate

(or party) increased the likelihood of shifting toward that position by between 20 and 90 points (on 100-point scales)—large effects. Additionally, several findings suggested that the tendency to follow politicians
more closely resembles blind following than a rational heuristic. I found
that voters will follow a candidate on a particular issue even when they
know little about that candidate's overall ideology.

Polarization

One of the most striking trends in recent US politics is the growing
polarization among partisans, including elites (McCarty, Poole, and
Rosenthal 2006) and voters (Abramowitz and Saunders 1998; Layman
and Carsey 2002). Studies have produced conflicting evidence on who is
behind the polarization. Is it the politicians or the voters? My findings
support the elite-driven view, such as Matthew Levendusky's (2009) conclusion that almost twice as many voters have changed their ideology to
match their party identification as have changed their party identification to match their ideology.

This book's findings also help us understand why partisans are becoming more polarized on ideology and policy. As party elites polarize, two mechanisms seem to be at work. First, the parties' positions will
become clearer. Consequently, voters will increasingly learn their own
parties' positions and increasingly follow.[16] Second, the more individuals like their own candidate or party, the more they follow. As polarization increases among politicians, voters seem increasingly predisposed
toward the candidates of their own party, at least according to their reported vote choices (Bartels 2000). They may therefore increasingly follow those candidates' policy positions.

Research Design: Studying Issue Voting

Political scientists have long suspected that causation goes both ways: a
voter's policy views not only influence his or her support for particular
candidates but also are themselves influenced by his or her support for
particular candidates. Nevertheless, researchers continue to infer from
mere policy-vote associations that policy views cause votes. The same
is true for performance and character assessments. Often these associations are dressed up with fancy statistical techniques, but they are never-

the less just associations. When it comes to issue voting, even our field's top journals continue to commit the sin of assuming that correlation implies causation—an embarrassing failure of the peer review process.

To help solve the problem, researchers have increasingly turned to panel surveys and to experiments embedded in panel surveys, as I have done in this book. Although panel surveys are no panacea, they do at least allow a cause—such as policy views—to be measured well before an effect—such as vote choice or candidate evaluation. The SCHIP study is one example of an experiment embedded in a panel, but there are many others (e.g., Chong and Druckman 2010; Mitchell 2011). In the past, embedding experiments in panel surveys was costly. Getting participants to return to the lab or recontacting interviewees by phone was and still is expensive and time consuming. With the advent of subject recruitment through online labor markets, however, embedding experiments in panel surveys is now cheap and easy (Berinsky, Huber, and Lenz 2011).

Panel studies also solve another problem. When conducting experimental studies, researchers must be careful about the questions they ask participants immediately before administering experimental treatments. Since most people pay little attention to politics, the questions we ask may influence the salience of issues for them. For example, asking participants about their racial attitudes probably makes race salient. When conducting a media priming study about race, a researcher would then want to avoid asking about race just before administering the treatment and control conditions. With experiments embedded in panels, researchers can avoid this problem by measuring the relevant attitudes days or weeks before administering treatments, as Tali Mendelberg (2001) does with a racial priming experiment. By measuring baseline attitudes in wave 1 and then administering experimental stimuli in wave 2, scholars also minimize concerns about participants guessing the study's hypothesis, which could lead them to alter their own behavior.

Besides measuring relevant attitudes pretreatment, researchers also need to be careful about the information in their experimental stimuli (Berinsky and Kinder 2006). The treatments in media priming studies usually convey facts about the issue being primed, and they convey these facts to participants who generally pay little attention to politics. So an experiment intended to test the effect of a change of salience may inadvertently be testing the effect of new information as well. Especially when the treatments inform participants that an issue is political or instruct participants about the positions of the candidates or parties, they can do much more than just raise the salience of an issue. Even studies with subtle priming stimuli, such as a candidate ad about crime that shows an ambiguously African American character, could still convey information about that candidate's stance, implying that he or she will be tough on African Americans. To avoid this, lab studies on media priming can be designed so that only the prominence of issues varies between treatment groups, not information about policy.

It's probably too much to hope that this book will reduce the number of studies that infer causation from correlation, as that provides an easy path to statistical significance ($p < 0.05$). A focus on causation, however, would probably speed up the generation of knowledge.

Why Do Candidates Campaign on Policy?

I note one final outstanding question: if campaigns generally fail to change votes through priming, learning, or persuasion on policy issues, why do they keep trying? There are many explanations. Candidates who do not campaign on policy proposals are often criticized by the media for lacking a policy agenda. So they may focus on policy merely to avoid being labeled as "substanceless." Politicians may also stress policy, not to change votes, but to keep the loyalty of their core supporters—the ones who really do care about policy and who also may go undetected by this book's analyses. Such supporters may not only provide reliable votes, but may also volunteer and donate. Another explanation is that politicians campaign on policy, not to prime the issues, but to alter their public images (Druckman, Jacobs, and Ostermeier 2004; Jacobs and Shapiro 1994). For example, as support for President Richard M. Nixon declined in national polls, his speeches began to mention his foreign policy more frequently, which he thought would convey the strength of his character (Druckman, Jacobs, and Ostermeier 2004). Politicians may also, of course, stress policy because they are true believers.

Since some policy stances undoubtedly could change the votes of many voters—such as a proposal to release all violent criminals from prison—the more important question may be why politicians campaign on policy issues that apparently fail to capture the public's interest. For example, why did the Conservative Party choose to campaign on British integration with Europe? This is just not the most gripping of issues, yet the Conservative Party campaigned on it in the 1997 election and again in the 2001 election, losing both times. The same holds for the proposal to invest Social Security funds in the 2000 election. Although a majority of the public favored the idea, it's hard to imagine such a proposal swaying millions of votes. How did the Bush campaign end up campaigning on it? Why did the Gore campaign respond?

There are many explanations, but I speculate on one that reflects positively on democracy and so provides a satisfying end to this book. Compelling issues, such as nuclear power after Chernobyl or defense spending after the Soviet invasion of Afghanistan, may generally be quickly neutralized by candidate repositioning. Consequently, candidates end up campaigning on issues that don't matter much to voters. For example, if George W. Bush had found a popular policy proposal on an issue that voters really did care about—one that would have easily won him the election in 2000—Al Gore's campaign would likely have adopted it, neutralizing the issue. No longer having a winning issue, Bush would have dropped it. By process of elimination, he ended up campaigning on investing Social Security funds in the stock market.[17] This process of elimination may generally rid campaigns of issues that could give them large advantages and so explain why candidates seem to run on less-than-compelling issues. Candidates, I'm sure, pine to campaign on welfare queens, communism, terrorism—policy issues that might capture voters' attention—but their opponents rarely let them.

This speculative interpretation has counterintuitive implications for how we view democracy, implying that politics is not about what it appears to be about. By this account, voters fail to lead on policies about which they care little—the ones on which candidates end up campaigning—but do lead on policies about which they do care—the ones on which candidates say little because they converge. In functioning democracies, therefore, politics will always appear to be about somewhat trivial policy issues, even though it is not.

My hunch is that this view of campaigns is overly optimistic. There are many issues that voters should care about, but apparently do not—George W. Bush's 2001 and 2003 tax cuts come to mind (Bartels 2005). There are also factors that voters do care about, but probably shouldn't—rum punch or a candidate's looks. Moreover, the evidence that candidate repositioning neutralizes issues is quite thin. Of the ten policy-issue cases I examined, only the 1986 Chernobyl case and the 1980 defense-spending case indicate such behavior. It is easy to point to anecdotes of successful repositioning—such as Barack Obama's about-face on offshore drilling in the 2008 election and Harry Truman's shift on communists in government before the 1948 election—but hard to find systematic studies.

9.5 Summing Up

This book has attempted to answer fundamental questions about voting behavior in democracies. For scholars who see democracy primarily as periodic referenda on the incumbent rather than as expressions of the public will on government policy (Riker 1982; Schumpeter 1942), my results are reassuring. Democratic elections, according to these results, are more referenda on performance issues than on policy issues. By rewarding politicians for performance, democracy may therefore succeed in selecting competent leaders over incompetent ones. Moreover, by throwing out leaders whose policies have led to bad outcomes, voters are likely having some influence on politicians' policy choices.[18]

For scholars who see democracy as fundamentally about voters expressing their views on policy (Dahl 1956; Pennock 1979), my findings are disappointing. In fact, democracy seems inverted. Instead of politicians following voters on policy, voters appear to follow politicians. Moreover, they appear to do so blindly, following politicians on particular policies even when they do not know those politicians' ideologies. Politicians may therefore have considerable freedom in the policies they choose.

Appendix

In this appendix I present the statistical models I use throughout this book. I define the tests of priming, persuasion, and learning, showing how they relate to a utility model of vote choice or candidate evaluations. Finally, I present the full estimates for the main results of the chapters. In the online appendix, I also show the full estimates for some analyses that cannot fit into this appendix, such as those for chapter 7, and also for secondary analyses and robustness checks.[1] Replication code and data are available from the author.

Simplified Utility Model

To test whether citizens are judging politicians on policy- or performance-related assessments, I would of course like to adopt a statistical model that we know to be true, that is, one that accurately captures citizens' decision making. As this book shows, however, we are a long way from understanding citizens' decisions well enough to know what this model looks like. Given our ignorance, I study these judgments with a relatively simple model and then show that findings hold with other plausible models.

Following Enelow and Hinich (1984), I define a voter's utility for each candidate (or party) based on one policy issue as

(1) $$U_{ij} = -\beta(x_i - P_j)^2,$$

where x_i is the policy position for voter i, P_j is the position of candidate (or party) j, and β represents an issue weight. In this model, a voter's utility increases with her proximity to a candidate ($x_i - P_j$) and with the weight she places on the issue (β). With multiple issues, utility is summed across issues. Squaring the distance between the voter and the candidate assumes what are called quadratic preferences—an assumption that may or may not be reasonable (Berinsky and Lewis 2007; Jackson 1991). Squaring also ensures that the distance increases with movement away from the candidate on either side. This model ignores the performance (or valence) dimension, which I add later.

When choosing among candidates, citizens vote for the one with the highest utility, I assume. When deciding between a Republican and a Democrat on one issue, for example, an individual prefers the Republican when he or she receives more utility from the Republican than from the Democrat:

(2) $$U_{iR} > U_{iD} = -\beta(x_i - P_R)^2 > -\beta(x_i - P_D)^2.$$

This is the basic model of utility assumed in most research, but again we don't know whether it describes citizens' choices (Lewis and King 2000).

Researchers encounter several problems when they attempt to estimate this model. Some citizens, evidence suggests, project their own positions onto candidates they already prefer or use party labels to guess at positions (Brody and Page 1972; Conover and Feldman 1982; Markus and Converse 1979; RePass 1971). That is, x_i may influence P_R and P_D. This tendency could lead researchers to overestimate the degree to which an issue influences votes, that is, to overestimate β. Since social scientists strive to be conservative about causal inferences, I drop issue distances from the analysis—at least for the main results (incorporating issue distances leaves the findings unchanged). Without issue distances, the model simplifies to

(3) $$y_i = f(\beta x_i)$$

where f represents a function linking policy position to utility and, to further simplify, y_i represents a vote choice between two candidates, but it can also represent an assessment of a single politician, such as a candidate evaluation or presidential approval. This model assumes that citizens behave as if they place candidates at the ends of issue scales, which is obviously not always the case. Of course, dropping candidate positions does not solve the problem of reverse causation, that is, y_i causing x_i. Despite this problem (and others), this model has several attractive features. Besides not being vulnerable to projection, its functional form is appropriate for policy issues and performance (or valence) issues. That is, x_i can represent a policy issue, such as defense spending, or a performance issue, such as the economy.

General Notes

Before formally describing the tests and presenting the least squares estimates, I make several general remarks about terminology and analysis.

Panel wave notation. The panel surveys I analyze usually have three or more interviews with each individual, which researchers refer to as waves. I denote these with the subscripts $w1$, $w2$, and $w3$, respectively. This notation style is nonstandard, but easier for less experienced readers than the more typical t and $t - 1$.

In the cases with at least three waves, the political earthquakes occur between the second two waves, that is, $w2$ and $w3$, so I test for priming, persuasion, and learning between these latter two waves. In the 1992 economy case, for example, the economy became prominent between the 1991 and 1992 interviews, so I test whether the issue weight on the economy increases between these waves. The 1991 wave provides a baseline (or pretreatment) estimate of the issue weight, while the 1992 wave provides the posttreatment estimate. I therefore label the three waves of the ANES panel $w1$ for 1990, $w2$ for 1991, and $w3$ for 1992. In the cases with two waves, I label them $w1$ and $w2$, respectively.

Constructing partial residual scatterplots. I present partial residual scatterplots throughout the book. I explain why I do so in chapter 2, but briefly they allow me to correct for bias from regression to the mean when showing data, that is, they account for the coefficient on the lagged dependent variable often being far below 1.0. I would much prefer to present even rawer data in the scatterplots, but bias from regression to the mean can be large and works against finding effects. Since much of the book finds null effects for policy issues, I must avoid as far as possible using a method biased toward finding null effects. Given that my use of control variables is minimal because of the null effects (see the next paragraph), the partial residual scatterplots generally reflect minimal correction from other variables. To create the partial residual scatterplots, I use the regression models presented here or, in a few cases, in the online appendix. I generate residuals by setting the coefficient on the relevant explanatory variable from these models (the x axis variable in the scatterplots) to zero, predicting the outcome variable, and then subtracting these predictions from the outcome (the relevant explanatory variable is also residualized). To bin responses for the figures, I then round this partial residual to the nearest tenths (e.g., 0.1, 0.2). Since I set the coefficient on the key explanatory variable to zero, the mean of the partial residuals is sometimes different from zero. Especially in cases with large overall shifts on the outcome variable, such as presidential approval of Bush between 1991 and 1992, I shift the mean of the residual scatterplots to show the shift. The best-fit lines in the scatterplots show the coefficient from the model, which does not necessarily best fit the points in the scatterplots because of bining (though it's always close).

Philosophy on control variables. With control variables, I take the most conservative approach in all cases. By control variable, I mean party identification, other policy views or performance assessments, etc., not lagged dependent variables. For all the analyses, I have estimated the statistical models without these control variables and with them. In almost all cases, control variables do not change findings—in part because panel analyses, to a degree, hold constant other variables by design. When I present results, I exclude controls in cases where I fail to find any effects, which is primarily in policy issue tests. I do so to reassure the reader that I have not searched for a particular set of control variables that yield a null result (because of chance or because a control operates as an intervening variable). When I do find effects, however, I present analyses with a large number of controls, which should reassure readers that effects are not the result of omitted control variables. Of course, including these controls raises concerns about specification searches. Rest assured, the effects I do find, which are mostly for performance issues, survive with and without controls. An earlier version of this manuscript presented results without control variables and with control variables. Although I prefer this presentation style—it reassures readers about omitted variables and specification searches—it entailed too much repetition. The analyses I've now excluded are available from the author. Although I present null findings without control variables, I make an exception for party identification and control for it when it is available, measuring it in a prior wave when possible.

Missing values. In the few cases where I do include control variables, I impute missing values on all control variables with demographics using

STATA's impute command (Version 10.1), which uses linear regression. The results are essentially the same with listwise deletion instead of imputation. I do not impute missing values on the lagged dependent variables or on the key explanatory variables.

Chapter 2 and 3: Media Priming

This section explains the tests of media priming used in chapters 2 and 3. I start with a definition of media priming.

Definition of media priming. According to the utility model (equation 3), media priming occurs when (1) the prominence of an issue in the news media or campaign messages increases and as a result (2) the absolute value of the issue weight, β, increases.

Conventional Test of Priming

As I describe in the introductory chapter, most research on issue voting, including research on priming, is associational, even if conducted as part of an experiment (policy views and performance assessments are never randomly assigned). Not only is it associational, but it is also vulnerable to bias from reverse causation because policy views or performance assessments are usually measured at the same time as the outcome variable, usually vote choice or candidate evaluations.

I call the approach often used for priming the conventional test. To estimate the pretreatment issue weight, β, researchers assume a model based on the simplified utility model I describe above:

(4) $$y_{w2} = b_{w2}x_{w2} + u_{w2}$$

The issue weight, b_{w2}, captures the importance of the issue, x, before it becomes prominent. In the 1992 economy case, for instance, x represents the economy and b_{w2} represents how well citizens' views about the issue predict their judgments about Bush. Here, u represents the random noise (with mean zero) that pervades judgments about people. To simplify the presentation, I drop the i subscript, exclude control variables, and assume a linear model with a continuous outcome variable.

Next, researchers estimate the issue weight after the issue becomes prominent, b_{w3}:

(5) $$y_{w3} = b_{w3}x_{w3} + u_{w3},$$

where the subscript $w3$ indicates that the opinion is measured after the election or after changes in political communications. Finally, researchers test for priming by testing whether the issue weight increases between waves 2 and 3:

(6) $$\Delta_{ct} = b_{w3} - b_{w2}.$$

If the absolute value of Δ_{ct} is greater than zero, researchers infer that citizens' policy views or performance assessments, for example, economic perceptions, became more predictive of views about politicians, for example, presidential approval. In other words, they conclude that citizens increasingly came to judge the president on the economy. I refer to the conventional test of priming with the subscript ct. In these models, and those below, I estimate Δ_{ct} by stacking the data and including an indicator variable for the posttreatment wave (Post) as well as an interaction between this indicator and issue attitudes, x, and this indicator and other control variables.

The problem with the conventional test is that it may get the story backward. As I show in chapter 8, citizens' views about issues, for example, their views about Social Security policy, x_{w3}, are often a consequence, not a cause, of their feelings about politicians, y_{w3}. For example, as investing Social Security funds became a prominent issue in the 2000 campaign, people increasingly adopted the policy view of the candidate they *already* preferred, either Bush or Gore, whom they apparently preferred for reasons other than Social Security policy. That is, if they liked Bush, they adopted his proposal to invest Social Security taxes in the stock market; if they liked Gore, they adopted Gore's position becoming opposed. This behavior causes the conventional test to find that citizens increasingly judged the president based on their economic perceptions, even though they did not. This is only one of many potential biases in this estimate of priming. Elsewhere, I formalize these biases (Lenz 2006).

Three-Wave Test of Priming: Overcoming Observational Equivalence

There is no perfect approach to priming. Since we cannot randomly assign people's policy views and performance assessments, testing for priming is difficult. The instability of these attitudes over time compounds the difficulty. The approach I take attempts to reduce bias from reverse causation.

I call the main test I use the three-wave test of priming. It differs from the conventional test in two ways. Most importantly, it measures policy views or performance assessments in a prior wave; that is, it measures the cause before the effect, eliminating bias from reverse causation. Second, it models change in prior votes or candidate evaluations (y) by including what researchers call the lagged dependent variable. By modeling change it addresses problems that can arise when measuring variables in prior panel waves. Specifically, without controlling for lagged vote or candidate evaluations, regression to the mean on these variables can bias issue-weight estimates downward because prior vote or candidate evaluations are often moderately or even strongly correlated with prior issue attitudes. For a discussion of this problem, see Finkel (1995). I stress, however, that the results in this book are not dependent on this particular model.

To present the three-wave test, let's return to the simplified utility model (equation 3):

$$y_i = f(\beta x_i)$$

Adding survey waves to the notation, dropping the i subscript, and, most importantly, differencing waves 3 and 2 produces

(7) $$y_{w3} - y_{w2} = f(b_{w3}x_{w3}) - f(b_{w2}x_{w2})$$

In this specification, b_{w3} captures the effect of change in x between waves 2 and 3. Since reverse causation can strongly influence x_{w3} (see chapter 8) and so upwardly bias b_{w3}, we cannot use it to estimate the effect of issue attitudes, and so I drop it from the model, a decision that can also be justified on other grounds (e.g., views are stable). Of course, dropping it introduces other potential biases, but these are comparatively less troublesome (see the discussion on the "time lag problem" in chapter 2). As I discuss at length in chapters 2 and 3, the main advantage of panel data is that we can measure policy views pretreatment (that is, in a prior wave), allowing us to measure the cause before the effect. By dropping b_{w3}, the effect of issue views is now only estimated with prior views, that is, b_{w2}. Rearranging terms, the model behind the three-wave test, as well as other tests I use in this book, is,

(8) $y_{w3} = f(b_{w2}x_{w2}) + y_{w2}$

This model examines how well prior policy views or retrospective assessments, x, influence change in vote choice or candidate evaluations, y.

For the three wave test of priming, I first estimate the issue weight before the issue becomes prominent, $\tilde{b}_{w1}$, as follows:

(9) $y_{w2} = \tilde{b}_{w1}x_{w1} + \tilde{\rho}_{w1}y_{w1} + \tilde{u}_{w2}$

After estimating the pretreatment issue weight, I then estimate the post-treatment issue weight, $\tilde{b}_{w2}$:

(10) $y_{w3} = \tilde{b}_{w2}x_{w2} + \tilde{\rho}_{w2}y_{w2} + \tilde{u}_{w3}$

Finally, I test for priming by testing whether the absolute value of the issue weight increases between waves 2 and 3:

(11) $\Delta_{3wt} = \tilde{b}_{w2} - \tilde{b}_{w1}$

I refer to the three-wave test of priming with the subscript $3wt$. It tests whether prior policy views or performance assessments better explain change in the outcome variable after the issue becomes prominent compared to before.[2] This test resembles the Granger causal test (Granger 1969), but in a difference-in-differences framework.

An increase in the estimated issue weight $\tilde{b}$, it is important to note, is merely a prediction of priming, not necessarily priming itself. If priming does occur (that is, the underlying weight β increases), we should expect the estimated weight $\tilde{b}$ to increase in absolute value, but there are other reasons $\tilde{b}$ might increase unrelated to priming. Learning candidates' positions or learning about changes in candidates' positions could increase $\tilde{b}$ (for a discussion of a related point, see Fiorina, Abrams, and Pope [2006, 183–86]), as could increases in certainty about these positions (Alvarez 1997) and increases in certainty about performance assessments, such as becoming more sure that the economy is performing poorly. Chapter 5 explains this for learning. To summarize, an individual cannot apply her desired weight on an issue, which is represented by β, unless she has some sense for the candidates' stances on the issue. When she learns these stances, she is able to apply the desired weight, which will lead to an increase in the estimated issue weight $\tilde{b}$ even though no priming has occurred (her desired issue weight β remained the same). For the most part, the source of increases in $\tilde{b}$, whether priming or other, is not important for my purposes. My primary focus is on using issue-weight increases—whether from priming, learning, or increases in certainty—to detect evidence of policy or performance-related judgments. I do, however, separate out the effects of learning candidates' positions, as I discuss below.

Two-Wave Priming Test

When I lack three waves of interviews, I rely on what I call the two-wave test for priming. With this test, I estimate the wave I (pretreatment) issue-weight as in the conventional test:

$$(12) \qquad\qquad y_{w1} = b'_{w1}x_{w1} + u'_{w1}.$$

I then estimate the wave 2 (posttreatment) issue weight with a similar equation as the conventional test except that I substitute wave 2 policy views (which could be biased by reverse causation) with wave I policy views:

$$(13) \qquad\qquad y_{w2} = b'_{w2}x_{w1} + u'_{w2}.$$

Finally, I test for priming by testing whether the issue weight increases:

$$(14) \qquad\qquad \Delta_{2wt} = b'_{w2} - b'_{w1}.$$

I refer to the two-wave test with the subscript $2wt$. This test is less ideal than the three-wave test because the pretreatment and posttreatment models differ.

Chapter 2 Estimates: Priming Performance-Related Assessments

Before discussing each chapter's estimates, I explain coding decisions and control variables. For chapter 2, controls for all three cases are standard ANES variables, including the moral traditionalism scale, which combines questions on feelings toward new lifestyles/mores, views on the world changing, views on tolerance, and views on traditional fam-

Three-wave test of media priming on performance issues (difference in issue weight $= \Delta_{3wt} = \tilde{b}_{w2} - \tilde{b}_{w1}$, see equation 11). To estimate the difference in issue weight, these data are stacked, include an indicator for wave 3 (Post), and interactions between this indicator and the other variables. Variables coded so that higher values are in the expected direction relative to the dependent variable and recoded to vary from 0 to 1.

	(1)	(2)	(3)	(4)
	Econ 96	Econ96	Econ 80	Econ 80
DV	Apprv Clinton	Apprv Clinton	Apprv Carter	Apprv Carter
Post indicator	0.17*	0.18*	0.025	−0.16*
	(0.053)	(0.066)	(0.033)	(0.079)
Prior Economic	−0.059	−0.045	0.028	0.033
assessments ($\tilde{b}_{w1}$)	(0.062)	(0.061)	(0.061)	(0.060)
Post*Prior Economic	0.16*	0.17*	0.12	0.12
assessments (Δ_{3wt})	(0.082)	(0.082)	(0.086)	(0.086)
Prior DV ($\tilde{\rho}_{w1}$)	0.56*	0.47*	0.47*	0.48*
	(0.065)	(0.066)	(0.032)	(0.032)
Post*Prior DV	−0.11	−0.082	0.13*	0.13*
	(0.077)	(0.078)	(0.047)	(0.047)
Prior Party ID	0.32*	0.25*	0.18*	0.17*
	(0.048)	(0.049)	(0.034)	(0.035)
Post*Prior Party ID	0.0077	−0.058	0.051	0.072
	(0.065)	(0.069)	(0.047)	(0.050)
Prior Abortion		0.13*		
		(0.038)		
---*Post		−0.096*		
		(0.053)		
Prior Minority aid		0.094*		
		(0.050)		
---*Post		−0.0089		
		(0.073)		
Prior Jobs		0.021		
		(0.051)		
---*Post		0.025		
		(0.075)		
Prior Gov. serv.		0.097*		−0.015
		(0.059)		(0.047)
---*Post		0.060		0.047
		(0.082)		(0.066)
Prior Ideology		0.15*		−0.10
		(0.070)		(0.061)
---*Post		0.081		0.13
		(0.10)		(0.087)
Prior Defense				−0.033
				(0.051)
---*Post				0.11
				(0.071)
Constant	0.012	−0.16*	−0.017*	0.077
	(0.040)	(0.049)	(0.025)	(0.056)
n	1090	1090	1204	1204
R^2	0.426	0.462	0.430	0.434
SER	0.30	0.29	0.26	0.26

Note: Ordinary least squares regression estimates with standard errors in parentheses. * $p < 0.1$

ily ties. In the 1996 Clinton case, presidential approval is unavailable in 1992, so I use the Clinton thermometer instead. In the 1992 case I average economic perceptions for 1990 and 1991, except when I examine the effect of these perceptions by levels of 1991 presidential approval (to address floor effects).

Table 1 presents the estimates of priming the economy for chapter 2's figures 2.8, 2.11, and 2.12. The estimates for the 1992 case are presented in chapter 2 itself. As noted earlier, I estimate Δ_{3wt} by stacking the data and including an indicator variable for the posttreatment wave (Post), which is wave 3 in these cases, as well as an interaction between this indicator and issue attitudes, x, and this indicator and other control variables.

Chapter 3 Estimates: Priming Policy Views

Table 2 presents the estimates for chapter 3's figure 3.4, which shows the conventional test of priming. Table 3 does so for figure 3.5, which shows the three-wave test of priming. Table 4 does so for figure 3.6, which shows the two-wave test of priming across all the policy issue cases. Figure 3.7 is from estimates in table 8, which is primarily used for the findings in chapter 5. Table 5 presents estimates from the conventional test among individuals who already know the candidates' or parties' positions (the table also shows the estimates for other knowledge and learning groups). I refer to table 5's results in chapter 3 and in other chapters. In these tables, I estimate Δ_{3wt} by stacking the data and including an indicator variable for the posttreatment wave (Post), which is wave 2 in the two-wave cases and wave 3 in the three-wave cases, as well as an interaction between this indicator and issue attitudes, x, and this indicator and other control variables.

The number of observations varies across tables 2 to 5 because the tests vary in the number of waves they require. When I constrain the samples to those required by all three tests, the findings remain the same. In the Social Security case, the survey only asked a small subset of respondents about their views on Social Security in the postelection interview. Since the conventional test requires posttreatment policy views, I therefore use late October interviews as wave 3, instead of the postelection wave. In the defense, Bush, and 9/11 case, the phone interviews used in the 2000 ANES collapsed the usual 7-point defense spending scale into

APPENDIX TABLE 2. **Estimates for chapter 3's figure 3.4.**

Conventional test of media priming on policy issues (difference in issue weight $= \Delta_{zi} = b_{w3} - b_{w2}$; see equation 6). According to this test, citizens increasingly judge politicians on policy issues as these issues became prominent (priming). This test, however, measures policy views posttreatment, rendering it vulnerable to bias from reverse causation. To estimate the difference in issue weight, these data are stacked, include an indicator for wave 3 (Post), and interactions between this indicator and the other variables. Variables coded so that higher values are in the expected direction relative to the dependent variable and recoded to vary from 0 to 1.

VARIABLES	(1)	(2)	(3)	(4)	(5)	(6)	(7)	(8)	(9)
	Soc Sec '00	Unions '48	EU '97	Pub Works '76	Def '80	ActivIdeo '92	Chernobyl '86	Trade '88	Def & 9/11
DV	Vote Bush	Vote Truman	Vote Labour	Vote Carter	Therm Reagan	Apprv Bush	VoteInc Parties	Vote Cons	Therm Bush
Post indicator	−0.037	−0.066	−0.063*	−0.039	0.0013	−0.48*	0.070*	−0.0042	−0.23*
	(0.043)	(0.058)	(0.036)	(0.042)	(0.056)	(0.048)	(0.030)	(0.051)	(0.030)
Issue (b_{w2})	0.089*	0.18*	0.39*	0.17*	0.18*	0.41*	0.37*	0.58*	0.15
	(0.035)	(0.064)	(0.046)	(0.052)	(0.044)	(0.058)	(0.036)	(0.031)	(0.030)
Post*Issue (Δ_{zi})	0.15*	0.11	0.098	0.11	0.11*	0.29*	0.071	0.081	0.19*
	(0.049)	(0.091)	(0.066)	(0.076)	(0.064)	(0.090)	(0.056)	(0.056)	(0.047)
Prior Party ID	0.95*	0.48*		0.83*	−0.24*	0.31*	0.82*	0.12	0.37*
	(0.044)	(0.038)		(0.053)	(0.030)	(0.030)	(0.037)	(0.080)	(0.024)
Post*Prior Party ID	−0.12*	0.078		−0.031	−0.062	−0.0056	−0.021	0.024	0.21*
	(0.064)	(0.053)		(0.073)	(0.043)	(0.044)	(0.052)	(0.11)	(0.035)
Constant	−0.019	−0.051	0.46*	0.025	0.52*	0.34*	−0.077*	0.19*	0.30*
	(0.032)	(0.041)	(0.025)	(0.030)	(0.039)	(0.033)	(0.022)	(0.036)	(0.021)
n	958	1154	1694	781	1066	1930	1570	1022	1420
R^2	0.540	0.290	0.095	0.508	0.203	0.366	0.547	0.475	0.462
SER	0.34	0.35	0.46	0.35	0.23	0.31	0.34	0.35	0.22

Note: Ordinary least squares regression estimates with standard errors in parentheses. * $p < 0.1$.

APPENDIX TABLE 3. **Estimates for chapter 3's figure 3.5.**

Three-wave test of media priming on policy issues (difference in issue weight $= \Delta_{3wt} = \tilde{b}_{w2} - \tilde{b}_{w1}$, see equation 11). Although the conventional test finds priming in every one of these cases, when we test with policy views measured in a prior wave, we fail to find priming. To estimate the difference in issue weight, these data are stacked, include an indicator for wave 3 (Post), and interactions between this indicator and the other variables. Variables coded so that higher values are in the expected direction relative to the dependent variable and recoded to vary from 0 to 1

	(1)	(2)	(3)	(4)	(5)	(6)
	Soc Sec '00	Unions '48	EU '97	Pub Works '76	Def '80	ActivIdeo '92
DV	Vote Bush	Vote Truman	Vote Labour	Vote Carter	Therm Reagan	Apprv Bush
Post indicator	0.049	0.036	0.0058	0.18*	−0.12*	−0.28*
	(0.031)	(0.045)	(0.017)	(0.052)	(0.050)	(0.045)
Prior Issue ($\tilde{b}_{w2}$)	0.045*	0.13*	0.027	0.038	0.13*	0.35*
	(0.025)	(0.049)	(0.019)	(0.055)	(0.037)	(0.059)
Post*Prior issue (Δ_{3wt})	−0.033	−0.065	−0.0069	0.028	−0.027	−0.24*
	(0.035)	(0.074)	(0.027)	(0.075)	(0.051)	(0.081)
Prior DV ($\tilde{b}_{w1}$)	0.71*	0.65*	0.94*	0.68*	0.50*	0.47*
	(0.036)	(0.037)	(0.014)	(0.089)	(0.034)	(0.028)
Post*Prior DV	−0.00058	0.17*	−0.000092	−0.071	0.15*	−0.075*
	(0.051)	(0.048)	(0.020)	(0.10)	(0.051)	(0.041)
Prior Party ID	0.31*	0.25*		0.68*	−0.14*	0.12*
	(0.046)	(0.036)		(0.056)	(0.026)	(0.031)
Post*Prior Party ID	−0.036	−0.091*		−0.34*	0.010	0.14*
	(0.065)	(0.051)		(0.086)	(0.037)	(0.043)
Constant	−0.044*	−0.060*	0.021*	−0.18*	0.31*	0.20*
	(0.022)	(0.029)	(0.012)	(0.043)	(0.036)	(0.032)
n	836	1044	1412	616	1008	1880
R^2	0.804	0.650	0.879	0.629	0.484	0.466
SER	0.22	0.28	0.17	0.30	0.18	0.28

Note: Ordinary least squares regression estimates with standard errors in parentheses. $* \; p < 0.1$.

APPENDIX TABLE 4. **Estimates for chapter 3's figure 3.6.**

Two-wave test of media priming on policy issues (difference in issue weight $= \Delta_{2wt} = b'_{w2} - b'_{w1}$, see equation 14). As with the three-wave test, this test fails to find that citizens were increasingly judging politicians on policy issues as these issues became prominent. To estimate the difference in issue weight, these data are stacked, include an indicator for wave 3 (Post), and interactions between this indicator and the other variables. Variables coded so that higher values are in the expected direction relative to the dependent variable and recoded to vary from 0 to 1.

	(1)	(2)	(3)	(4)	(5)	(6)	(7)	(8)	(9)
	Soc Sec '00	Unions '48	EU '97	Pub Works '76	Def '80	ActivIdeo '92	Chernobyl '86	Trade '88	Def & 9/11
DV	Vote Bush	Vote Truman	Vote Labour	Vote Carter	Therm Reagan	ApprvBush	Vote Inc Parties	Vote Cons	Therm Bush
Post indicator	0.015	0.0058	−0.017	−0.013	0.0047	−0.31*	0.051*	0.046	0.028
	(0.040)	(0.066)	(0.036)	(0.043)	(0.049)	(0.047)	(0.031)	(0.054)	(0.027)
Issue (b'_{w1})	0.13*	0.32*	0.39*	0.17*	0.28*	0.41*	0.37*	0.58*	0.13*
	(0.032)	(0.073)	(0.047)	(0.052)	(0.040)	(0.060)	(0.036)	(0.044)	(0.029)
Post*Prior Issue	−0.022	0.0018	0.0095	0.0066	−0.0094	−0.10	−0.017	−0.024	0.13*
(Δ_{2wt})	(0.046)	(0.046)	(0.066)	(0.074)	(0.057)	(0.084)	(0.084)	(0.062)	(0.041)
Prior Party ID	0.98*	0.58*		0.83*	−0.25*	0.31*	0.82*	0.12	0.39*
	(0.041)	(0.042)		(0.053)	(0.029)	(0.031)	(0.037)	(0.085)	(0.021)
Post*Prior	−0.025	0.055		0.017	−0.041	0.078*	−0.028	0.062	−0.028
	(0.057)	(0.060)		(0.073)	(0.040)	(0.044)	(0.053)	(0.12)	(0.030)
Party ID			0.46*			0.34*	−0.077*	0.19*	0.30*
			(0.025)			(0.034)	(0.022)	(0.038)	(0.019)
Constant	−0.040	−0.15*		0.025	0.54*				
	(0.028)	(0.046)		(0.031)	(0.034)				
n	934	1062	1694	781	1082	1930	1570	1022	1716
R^2	0.619	0.331	0.079	0.499	0.221	0.341	0.543	0.415	0.381
SER	0.31	0.38	0.47	0.35	0.22	0.31	0.34	0.37	0.21

Note: Ordinary least squares regression estimates with standard errors in parentheses. * $p < 0.1$.

APPENDIX TABLE 5. **Conventional test of media priming on policy issues among the knowers and other groups (difference in issue weight = $\Delta_{ci} = b_{w3} - b_{w2}$, see equation 6).**

These estimates are mentioned in Chapter 3, but the results are not shown in a figure. To estimate the difference in issue weight, these data are stacked, include an indicator for wave 3 (Post), and interactions between this indicator and the other variables. Variables coded so that higher values are in the expected direction relative to the dependent variable and recoded to vary from 0 to 1.

	(1)	(2)	(3)	(4)	(5)	(6)
	SocSec '00	EU '97	PubWorks '76	Def '80	ActivIdeo '92	Chernobyl '86
DV	Vote Bush	Vote Labour	Vote Carter	Therm Reagan	Apprv Bush	Vote Inc Parties
Post indicator	0.030	0.18*	0.0089	0.32	−0.46*	0.14*
	(0.22)	(0.10)	(0.17)	(0.21)	(0.20)	(0.078)
Issue*Knowers	0.23*	0.86*	0.49*	0.53*	0.60*	0.52*
	(0.086)	(0.064)	(0.090)	(0.094)	(0.096)	(0.057)
--*Post (Δ_{ci})	0.21*	0.031	−0.054	0.11	0.31*	0.087
	(0.12)	(0.092)	(0.13)	(0.14)	(0.14)	(0.086)
Issue*Learners	−0.095	0.13	0.10	0.11	0.22	0.19*
	(0.093)	(0.10)	(0.094)	(0.075)	(0.14)	(0.082)
--*Post (Δ_{ci})	0.26*	0.56*	0.18	0.27*	0.53*	0.44*
	(0.13)	(0.14)	(0.14)	(0.11)	(0.21)	(0.13)
Issue*Never learners	−0.20	−0.21*	−0.18*	−0.027	0.089	0.28*
	(0.13)	(0.095)	(0.096)	(0.071)	(0.12)	(0.069)
--*Post (Δ_{ci})	0.23	0.036	0.38*	0.062	0.049	−0.17
	(0.18)	(0.14)	(0.14)	(0.10)	(0.19)	(0.11)
Issue*Forgetters	0.17	0.53*	0.31	0.49*	0.21	0.40*
	(0.15)	(0.13)	(0.27)	(0.19)	(0.19)	(0.089)
--*Post (Δ_{ci})	0.0027	−0.39*	−0.43	−0.28	0.18	−0.054
	(0.24)	(0.19)	(0.36)	(0.26)	(0.35)	(0.13)
Party ID*Knowers	0.80*	−0.29*	0.64*	−0.31*	0.30*	0.66*
	(0.12)	(0.084)	(0.095)	(0.066)	(0.051)	(0.057)
--*Post	−0.25	−0.21*	0.020	0.035	−0.031	0.040
	(0.16)	(0.12)	(0.13)	(0.095)	(0.073)	(0.079)

(continued)

APPENDIX TABLE 5. (Continued)

DV	(1) SocSec '00 Vote Bush	(2) EU '97 Vote Labour	(3) Pub Works '76 Vote Carter	(4) Def '80 Therm Reagan	(5) ActivIdeo '92 Apprv Bush	(6) Chernobyl '86 Vote Inc Parties
Party ID*Learners	1.00*		0.76*	-0.25*	0.48*	0.96*
	(0.11)		(0.096)	(0.051)	(0.071)	(0.088)
--*Post	-0.014		0.034	0.036	-0.18*	-0.21
	(0.16)		(0.14)	(0.074)	(0.10)	(0.13)
Party ID*Never learners	0.83*	0.39*	0.82*	-0.16*	0.20*	0.83*
	(0.17)	(0.086)	(0.095)	(0.047)	(0.061)	(0.081)
--*Post	0.22	-0.21*	-0.051	-0.11*	0.13	-0.035
	(0.24)	(0.12)	(0.13)	(0.067)	(0.087)	(0.12)
Party ID*Forgetters	0.82*		0.73*	-0.20*	0.19*	0.81*
	(0.23)		(0.24)	(0.11)	(0.096)	(0.090)
--*Post	-0.032		0.34	-0.28*	0.045	-0.0018
	(0.32)		(0.30)	(0.15)	(0.14)	(0.12)
Knowers	0.056		-0.16	-0.033	-0.37*	-0.018
	(0.16)		(0.12)	(0.18)	(0.14)	(0.062)
Learners	0.21	0.083	0.055	0.25	-0.20	0.038
	(0.17)	(0.088)	(0.13)	(0.17)	(0.15)	(0.080)
Never learners	0.33*		0.26*	0.32*	0.076	0.12
	(0.19)		(0.13)	(0.17)	(0.15)	(0.079)
Post*Knowers	-0.049		0.030	-0.36	0.0011	-0.088
	(0.24)		(0.18)	(0.25)	(0.21)	(0.087)
Post*Learners	-0.21	-0.43*	-0.14	-0.48*	-0.072	-0.14
	(0.25)	(0.12)	(0.19)	(0.23)	(0.24)	(0.11)
Post*Never learners	-0.34		-0.17	-0.25	0.017	0.019
	(0.28)		(0.19)	(0.23)	(0.23)	(0.11)
Constant	-0.066	0.44*	0.031	0.31*	0.57*	-0.091*
	(0.14)	(0.074)	(0.12)	(0.16)	(0.13)	(0.055)
n	494	1694	781	1066	1930	1570
R^2	0.532	0.229	0.547	0.257	0.393	0.572
SER	0.35	0.43	0.34	0.23	0.30	0.33

Note: Ordinary least squares regression estimates with standard errors in parentheses. * $p < 0.1$.

5 points. In the European integration case, the panel only asked subsets of respondents the party identification question in 1995 and 1996, so I do not include a control for party identification. I have tried including the party likability scale and the results remain the same.

Chapter 4: Prior Persuasion Test

The second shift I exploit in people's thinking is persuasion. While priming is about changes in the issue weight, β, persuasion is about changes in policy views or performance assessments, that is, changes in x. If individuals judge politicians on these issues, such changes should, all else equal, change individuals' votes or candidate evaluations, as is apparent in the utility model above.

Definition of the effect of persuasion. According to the simplified utility model (equation 3), I define the effect of policy or performance persuasion as follows: when individuals *change* their views on policy or performance issues, x, they *change* their support for politicians, y, bringing it in line with their new policy views or performance assessments.

Testing for the effects of persuasion is more difficult than testing for priming. With priming, I measure people's policy and performance issues in a prior interview, which rules out the possibility that people are following instead of leading. With persuasion, I cannot simply measure attitudes in a prior interview because these attitudes are changing. To surmount this problem, I test for persuasion in cases where studies interviewed people at least three times. I examine whether persuasion between the first two interviews leads to changes in support for politicians between the second and third waves (using an approach that shares similarities with Sekhon [2004]).

To test whether persuasion between waves 1 and 2 changes votes between waves 2 and 3, I use the prior persuasion test, which uses the following model:

$$(15) \quad y_{w3} = \Delta_{x21}(x_{w2} - x_{w1}) + b_{w1}x_{w1} + \Delta_{y21}(y_{w2} - y_{w1}) + \rho_{w1}y_{w1} + u_{w3}$$

The variables here are the same as those above, that is, y is vote choice or candidate evaluations and x is policy views or performance-related assessments, such as honesty in the Gore case. The key test is whether prior changes in policy views or performance assessments, $x_{w2} - x_{w1}$, lead to changes in vote or candidate evaluations, y_{w3}. If they do, Δ_{x21} will be different from zero.[3] If it is, we can be more confident that policy views or performance assessments matter. We can be more confident because the approach is likely conservative and cannot get the story backward. If views or assessments change further between waves 2 and 3, which they undoubtedly do, it will likely make detecting the effects of persuasion even harder, rendering this test even more conservative.

Ideally, I would use a difference-in-differences approach as I do with the other tests while jointly testing for the effect of prior persuasion, priming, and learning. Unfortunately, this would require at least four waves, which I lack in all but a few cases. Consequently, the persuasion effects I find for performance issues could reflect priming.

Chapter 4 Estimates: Effects of Policy and Performance Persuasion

Table 6 presents estimates for figure 4.5, which tests whether prior persuasion on policy issues leads to later change in vote or candidate evaluations. Table 7 does the same for figure 4.6, which tests whether prior persuasion on performance-related issues leads to later change in vote or candidate evaluations.

As I explain in chapter 4, these models control for the prior level and prior change on a continuous measure of candidate and party support (candidate/party support). This variable is Bush minus Gore favorability ratings in the Social Security case (asked on a 100-point scale), Labour minus Conservative likeability in the European integration case, Carter minus Ford likeability in the public works case, Carter minus Reagan thermometer in the 1980 defense case, Bush thermometer in the 1992 Activating Ideology/Economy/Gulf War cases, Clinton thermometer in the 1996 economy case, and McCain minus Obama thermometer in the Palin case.

Since I find effects on performance issues (table 7), I control for additional variables. The moral traditionalism scale combines questions on feelings toward new lifestyles/mores, views on the world changing, views on tolerance, and views on traditional family ties. In the 1992 panel, ideology is the three-item index (7-point ideology, feeling toward liberals, and feeling toward conservatives). In the other panels, it is just the 7-point scale.

APPENDIX TABLE 6. **Estimates for figure 4.5.**

Prior persuasion test on policy issues (Δ_{21}, see equation 15). No persuasion effects on policy issues. Variables coded so that higher values are in the expected direction relative to the dependent variable and recoded to vary from 0 to 1, except for the persuasion variables (w2-w1) which vary from -1 to 1.

	(1)	(2)	(3)	(4)	(5)	(6)
	Soc Sec '00	Unions '48	EU '97	Pub Works '76	Def '80	Activ Ideo '92
DV w3	Vote Bush	Vote Truman	Vote Labour	Vote Carter	Apprv Carter	Apprv Bush
Issue w2−w1 (Δ_{21})	0.0024	0.069	0.0021	0.048	0.027	0.0083
	(0.037)	(0.052)	(0.021)	(0.056)	(0.053)	(0.067)
Issue w1	−0.010	0.060	0.015	0.080	0.099*	0.12*
	(0.027)	(0.048)	(0.020)	(0.053)	(0.050)	(0.070)
DV w2−w1	0.47*	0.79*	0.48*	0.56*	0.52*	0.18*
	(0.056)	(0.031)	(0.038)	(0.053)	(0.040)	(0.048)
DV w1	0.67*	0.84*	0.86*	0.78*	0.73*	0.32*
	(0.048)	(0.032)	(0.030)	(0.085)	(0.040)	(0.056)
Party ID w2−w1	0.027			0.26*	0.11*	0.044
	(0.081)			(0.100)	(0.061)	(0.055)
Party ID w1	0.21*	0.15*		0.32*	0.17*	0.24*
	(0.054)	(0.030)		(0.062)	(0.035)	(0.034)
Cand./Party supp. w2−w1	0.13		0.098*	0.036	−0.22*	0.11*
	(0.086)		(0.057)	(0.069)	(0.067)	(0.067)
Cand./Party supp. w1	0.25*		0.19*		−0.12*	0.28*
	(0.075)		(0.049)		(0.065)	(0.079)
Constant	−0.070*	−0.023	−0.044*	−0.081*	−0.021	−0.18*
	(0.029)	(0.028)	(0.016)	(0.043)	(0.061)	(0.040)
n	418	522	706	308	488	940
R^2	0.802	0.779	0.904	0.715	0.583	0.366
SER	0.22	0.22	0.15	0.27	0.23	0.29

Note: Ordinary least squares regression estimates with standard errors in parentheses. * $p < 0.1$.

Prior persuasion test on performance-related issues (Δ_{x21}, see equation 15). For the 1996 case, DV w1 and DV w2-w1 are missing because Clinton was not president in w1 (1992). Variables coded so that higher values are in the expected direction relative to the dependent variable and recoded to vary from 0 to 1, except for the persuasion variables (w2-w1) which vary from -1 to 1.

	(1)	(2)	(3)	(4)	(5)
	Econ '80	Econ '92	Econ '96	Palin '08	Gulf War '92
DV w3	Therm Reagan	Apprv Bush	Apprv Clinton	Vote McCain	Apprv Carter
Issue w2−w1 (Δ_{x21})	0.11*	0.12*	0.11*	0.036*	0.052
	(0.066)	(0.046)	(0.048)	(0.020)	(0.039)
Issue w1	0.13*	0.26*	0.073	−0.00055	0.12*
	(0.078)	(0.057)	(0.069)	(0.020)	(0.052)
DV w2−w1	0.46*	0.13*		0.67*	0.12*
	(0.044)	(0.049)		(0.019)	(0.049)
DV w1	0.65*	0.27*		0.86*	0.26*
	(0.047)	(0.061)		(0.015)	(0.062)
Party ID w2-w1	0.10	0.046		0.094*	0.021
	(0.064)	(0.054)		(0.028)	(0.055)
Party ID w1	0.15*	0.23*		0.087*	0.22*
	(0.039)	(0.034)		(0.017)	(0.034)
Cand./Party supp. w2−w1	−0.40*	0.061	0.58*	−0.016	0.067
	(0.094)	(0.067)	(0.068)	(0.032)	(0.069)
Cand./Party supp. w1	−0.29*	0.24*	0.70*	−0.055*	0.23*
	(0.092)	(0.080)	(0.075)	(0.028)	(0.082)
Ideology w2−w1	0.075	−0.017	0.16*	0.024	−0.042
	(0.074)	(0.065)	(0.077)	(0.020)	(0.067)
Ideology w1	0.11	0.021	0.22*	0.048*	0.027
	(0.072)	(0.074)	(0.077)	(0.025)	(0.075)
Defense w2−w1	0.064	0.097*	0.039		0.091*
	(0.057)	(0.045)	(0.056)		(0.046)
Defense w1	0.11*	0.15*	0.049		0.15*
	(0.053)	(0.051)	(0.063)		(0.052)
Gov. services w2−w1		0.091	0.088*		0.087
		(0.067)	(0.053)		(0.069)
Gov. services w1	0.010	0.12*	0.11*		0.13*
	(0.048)	(0.073)	(0.067)		(0.075)
Gulf War app. w2−w1		0.052			
		(0.038)			
Gulf War app. w1		0.12*			
		(0.051)			
Foreign aff. app. w2−w1		−0.0034			−0.00034
		(0.035)			(0.035)
Foreign aff. app. w1		−0.12*			−0.11*
		(0.047)			(0.048)
Moral trad. scale w2−w1		0.045			0.042
		(0.051)			(0.052)
DV w2			0.15*		
			(0.045)		
Abortion w2−w1			0.043		
			(0.047)		
Abortion w1			0.041		
			(0.036)		

APPENDIX TABLE 7. (*Continued*)

DV w3	(1) Econ '80 Therm Reagan	(2) Econ '92 Apprv Bush	(3) Econ '96 Apprv Clinton	(4) Palin '08 Vote McCain	(5) Gulf War '92 Apprv Carter
Minority aid w2−w1			0.13* (0.053)		
Minority aid w1			0.0024 (0.054)		
Jobs w2−w1			−0.0018 (0.051)		
Jobs w1			0.082 (0.061)		
Economy w2−w1				0.041 (0.028)	0.11* (0.047)
Economy w1				0.051 (0.033)	0.26* (0.058)
Econ. policy scale w2−w1				0.0013 (0.018)	
Econ. policy scale w1				−0.013 (0.022)	
Gay marriage w2−w1				−0.0062 (0.012)	
Gay marriage w1				−0.023 (0.016)	
Biden w2−w1				−0.021 (0.020)	
Biden w1				−0.020 (0.019)	
Constant	0.013 (0.078)	−0.30* (0.050)	−0.12* (0.064)	0.052 (0.032)	−0.30* (0.051)
n	447	957	555	1870	928
R^2	0.594	0.392	0.576	0.909	0.387
SER	0.22	0.28	0.26	0.15	0.28

Note: Ordinary least squares regression estimates with standard errors in parentheses. * $p < 0.1$.

In the Sarah Palin case, the economic policy scale combines questions on taxes on the wealthy, universal health care, and increased prescription drug benefits for senior citizens. Some control variables in this case were not asked in September 2008 (wave 1), but were asked in January or June 2008. For the table, I code these control variables as wave 1, even though they were asked in January or June. The January control variables include the economic policy scale, respondents' views on the economy, and their feelings about legalizing gay marriage. The only June control variable is the 7-point ideology scale. All wave 2 control variables are from October.

In the vote choice cases, I exclude individuals who fail to report a major party vote (or vote intent) in any of the three waves. Although this could potentially influence the results by selecting individuals who have strong partisan affiliations, or have already made up their minds for other reasons (and so more likely to form a vote intent early), two findings indicate that this is not a problem. First, a few of the cases use presidential approval or candidate thermometers instead of vote, yielding the same findings as the vote choice cases. Second, when I code nonvoters in waves 1 and 2 to 0.5 (instead of to missing) or use more continuous outcome variables, such as candidate thermometers, the same patterns emerge. The only exception is with the unions in the 1948 election case. Among individuals who lack a major party vote intent in June or October, prior persuasion on unions better predicts later change in vote. Further analysis, however, suggests that this is largely a result of an outlier— one individual who shifts from being a strong union supporter to being a strong union opponent.

Chapter 5: Learning Politicians' Positions

Effect of Learning Politicians' Positions

The final shift in people's thinking I exploit is learning about politicians' positions. Much of the public remains unaware of candidates' and parties' positions, even on the most prominent issues of the day. In terms of the utility model, the positions of the candidates (or parties), P_j, is just blank when people are entirely unaware of these. Even if they care deeply about an issue, citizens cannot place weight on it, that is, they cannot apply their desired β, unless they have some sense for these positions. When individuals learn these positions, however, they can place their desired weight on the issue and shift their vote or support for politicians accordingly.

Definition of learning and the effect of learning. Measuring learning is difficult because people report perceptions of politicians' positions even when they appear to have no sense for those positions (e.g., they place them on the wrong sides of each other). To get around this problem, I define learning and knowledge about the candidates' (parties') positions with a relatively easy test: whether respondents place politicians on the right side of each other, such as placing the Democratic candidate to the left of the Republican. More precisely, I define learning as a transition from failing to place the candidates (parties) or failing to place them correctly relative to each other in wave 2, to correctly placing them in wave 3. I break respondents into four categories for the sake of completeness: those who (1) *knew before*, that is, correctly placed the parties before and after the issue becomes prominent; (2) *learned from*, that is, incorrectly placed or failed to place the candidates (parties), but both correctly afterward; (3) *never learned*, that is, incorrectly placed or failed to place the candidates (parties) before and after; and finally (4) *forgot*, that is, correctly placed them before but incorrectly placed or failed to place them afterward. As I discuss in chapter 3, the candidates or parties take reasonably clear and distinct positions in all the cases I examine with the exception of the Chernobyl case and defense in the 1980 US election cases. Except for those two cases, to which I devote entire chapters, determining which side of each other the parties or candidates are on is relatively straightforward.

According to the simplified utility model (equation 3), I define the effect of learning as follows: when individuals learn according to the definition above, they apply their preexisting β and change their support for politicians, y, accordingly. This definition leads to a prediction: learning positions should increase the absolute value of b, from zero to the issue-weight people intended to apply, β. Priming and learning thus make similar predictions: increases in the absolute value of b. With learning positions, it is important to note, the underlying issue weight β does not change, only whether people apply the weight.

Three-Wave and Two-Wave Tests of Learning Effects

Since priming and learning lead to the same prediction, an increase in the absolute value of y, I use the same test for learning as for priming, either the three-wave or two-wave test. With learning, however, I apply this test among those who learn the candidates' position between waves 2 and 3. I do so by including interactions with indicator variables for learning and the other knowledge categories. These interactions provide estimates of the change in issue weights for each category, that is, separate estimates of $\Delta_{3wt} = \tilde{b}_{w2} - \tilde{b}_{w1}$ for the learners, those who knew before, and so on. They therefore allow me to test whether, as predicted, the issue weight does increase among individuals who learn.

Chapter 5 Estimates: The Effect of Learning Policy Positions

Table 8 presents the estimates for Chapter 5's figure 5.4, which tests whether learning the candidates' or parties' positions leads people to change their votes or candidate evaluations accordingly. In cases with three waves, it presents the three-wave test. In the cases with two waves, it presents the two-wave test.

Chapter 6: Chernobyl

The partial residual scatterplots in this chapter are estimated with equation 16 and confirm the two-wave tests findings presented in chapters 3, 5, and 8. Since the Chernobyl case only has two waves, I cannot use the prior-persuasion test from chapter 4, which requires three, and instead test for persuasion with only two waves, using the following equation:

(16) $y_{w2} = \Delta_{21}(x_{w2} - x_{w1}) + b_{w1}x_{w1} + \rho_{w1}y_{w1} + u_{w2}.$

Where y is vote choice and x represents attitudes about nuclear power. This test is likely biased in favor of finding persuasion effects because of reverse causation, but I show the results anyway because, even with this bias, I still find no evidence that persuasion on nuclear power influences vote change.

For the most-important-issue figure, I code an issue as mentioned if respondents listed it as one of the five possible responses (var014– var018). I code the various issues as follows: 19 and 21 for nuclear power, 12 for nuclear arms, 74 for unemployment, and 15 for deficit.

Chapter 7: Defense Spending

The partial residual scatterplots and results presented in chapter 7 are based on many statistical models. Unlike the models of other chapters, they are not easily combined into one or two tables. I therefore present them in the online appendix, where I show the models behind these figures and additional specifications.

APPENDIX TABLE 8. **Estimates for chapter 5's figure 5.4.**

Does learning about candidates' and parties' positions change votes? Two-wave and three-wave tests of learning effects find no increase in the importance of these issues among individuals who learn these positions. (For the two-wave test, the difference in issue weight = $\Delta_{2wt} = b'_{w2} - b'_{w1}$ from equation 6. For the three-wave test, the figure shows $\Delta_{3wt} = \bar{b}_{w2} - \bar{b}_{w1}$ from equation 11.) To estimate the difference in issue weight, these data are stacked, include an indicator for wave 3 (Post), and interactions between this indicator and the other variables. Variables coded so that higher values are in the expected direction relative to the dependent variable and recoded to vary from 0 to 1.

	(1)	(2)	(3)	(4)	(5)	(6)
	Soc Sec '00	EU '97	Pub Works '76	Def '80	ActivIdeo '92	Chernobyl '86
DV	Vote Bush	Vote Labour	Vote Carter	Therm Reagan	Apprv Bush	Vote Inc Parties
Post indicator	−0.023	−0.015	0.38*	0.060	−0.50*	0.11
	(0.18)	(0.049)	(0.22)	(0.16)	(0.18)	(0.078)
Prior Issue*Knowers	0.081	0.045	0.22*	0.23*	0.41*	0.52*
	(0.060)	(0.035)	(0.094)	(0.065)	(0.092)	(0.057)
--*Post (Δ_{3wt})	−0.049	−0.024	−0.11	−0.051	−0.070	0.035
	(0.089)	(0.050)	(0.14)	(0.097)	(0.13)	(0.081)
Prior Issue*Learners	−0.060	0.049	−0.032	0.0017	0.17	0.19*
	(0.066)	(0.044)	(0.099)	(0.086)	(0.16)	(0.082)
--*Post (Δ_{3wt})	0.11	−0.062	0.029	0.023	−0.067	0.031
	(0.096)	(0.063)	(0.14)	(0.11)	(0.21)	(0.12)
Prior Issue*Never learners	0.016	−0.031	−0.14	0.0076	0.18	0.28*
	(0.090)	(0.039)	(0.11)	(0.058)	(0.13)	(0.070)
--*Post (Δ_{3wt})	0.19	0.019	0.23	0.093	−0.43*	−0.18*
	(0.13)	(0.058)	(0.15)	(0.081)	(0.17)	(0.098)
Prior Issue*Forgetters	0.069	−0.058	−0.21	0.34*	0.015	0.40*
	(0.13)	(0.059)	(0.26)	(0.13)	(0.18)	(0.090)
--*Post (Δ_{3wt})	−0.037	0.078	0.21	−0.48*	−0.056	0.067
	(0.18)	(0.082)	(0.42)	(0.17)	(0.25)	(0.13)
Party ID*Knowers	0.035	−0.10*	0.67*	−0.14*	0.13*	0.66*
	(0.10)	(0.041)	(0.093)	(0.052)	(0.051)	(0.058)
--*Post	−0.021	0.021	−0.64*	0.010	0.14*	−0.040
	(0.14)	(0.055)	(0.15)	(0.074)	(0.073)	(0.081)

(continued)

APPENDIX TABLE 8. (*Continued*)

	(1)	(2)	(3)	(4)	(5)	(6)
	Soc Sec '00	EU '97	Pub Works '76	Def '80	ActivIdeo '92	Chernobyl '86
DV	Vote Bush	Vote Labour	Vote Carter	Therm Reagan	Apprv Bush	Vote Inc Parties
Party ID*Learners	0.40*	−0.098*	0.66*	−0.14*	0.25*	0.96*
	(0.13)	(0.046)	(0.10)	(0.050)	(0.075)	(0.088)
---*Post	0.18	0.051	−0.13	0.097	−0.066	−0.0061
	(0.18)	(0.061)	(0.16)	(0.072)	(0.11)	(0.13)
Party ID*Never learners	−0.073	0.011	0.66*	−0.15*	0.067	0.83*
	(0.15)	(0.051)	(0.11)	(0.040)	(0.057)	(0.082)
---*Post	0.40		−0.19	−0.036	0.21*	−0.040
	(0.23)		(0.16)	(0.057)	(0.082)	(0.12)
Party ID*Forgetters	0.49*		0.51*	−0.12	0.068	0.81*
	(0.18)		(0.21)	(0.087)	(0.097)	(0.091)
---*Post	0.030	−0.0034	−0.51	−0.0089	0.073	−0.12
	(0.27)	(0.072)	(0.43)	(0.13)	(0.13)	(0.13)
Prior DV*Knowers	0.90*	0.96*	0.45*	0.60*	0.52*	
	(0.077)	(0.025)	(0.13)	(0.061)	(0.043)	
---*Post	0.014	0.010	0.39*	0.073	−0.20*	
	(0.11)	(0.035)	(0.16)	(0.095)	(0.063)	
Prior DV*Learners	0.56*	0.92*	0.74*	0.46*	0.44*	
	(0.095)	(0.028)	(0.18)	(0.064)	(0.062)	
---*Post	−0.089	0.013	−0.32	0.29*	0.00038	
	(0.14)	(0.039)	(0.20)	(0.096)	(0.095)	
Prior DV*Never learners	0.92*	0.87*	0.59*	0.42*	0.39*	
	(0.100)	(0.033)	(0.19)	(0.062)	(0.052)	
---*Post	−0.21	0.0068	−0.10	0.11	−0.015	
	(0.15)	(0.046)	(0.21)	(0.091)	(0.079)	
Prior DV*Forgetters	0.46*	0.91*	1.64*	0.33*	0.42*	
	(0.12)	(0.041)	(0.41)	(0.11)	(0.091)	

	(1)	(2)	(3)	(4)	(5)	(6)
--*Post	0.029	−0.036	−0.64	0.34*	0.097	−0.018
	(0.19)	(0.061)	(0.49)	(0.17)	(0.14)	(0.062)
Knowers	0.0084		0.17	−0.090	−0.40*	0.038
	(0.15)		(0.18)	(0.13)	(0.12)	(0.081)
Learners	0.16		0.23	0.18	−0.24	0.12
	(0.15)		(0.20)	(0.15)	(0.15)	(0.079)
Never learners	0.054		0.40*	0.21	−0.075	−0.082
	(0.17)		(0.21)	(0.14)	(0.14)	(0.088)
Post*Knowers	0.048		−0.15	−0.11	0.24	−0.12
	(0.20)		(0.23)	(0.18)	(0.19)	(0.11)
Post*Learners	−0.15		−0.23	−0.32*	0.19	0.035
	(0.21)		(0.24)	(0.19)	(0.21)	(0.11)
Post*Never learners	−0.17		−0.35	−0.23	0.24	
	(0.23)		(0.26)	(0.18)	(0.21)	
Constant	−0.048	0.098*	−0.38*	0.25*	0.50*	−0.091*
	(0.14)	(0.037)	(0.18)	(0.12)	(0.12)	(0.055)
n	448	1412	616	1008	1880	1570
R^2	0.775	0.881	0.655	0.507	0.485	0.569
SER	0.24	0.17	0.30	0.18	0.28	0.33

Note: Ordinary least squares regression estimates with standard errors in parentheses. * $p < 0.1$.

Chapter 8: Following

To examine whether people follow, rather than lead, I simply reverse the three-wave test, that is, reverse x and y. I first establish a baseline by estimating the weight people place on their candidate or party evaluations when changing their policy views. With tests of priming and learning, I denote this weight with b_{w1}. For the reverse weight, I use f_{w1}. For the baseline period, I estimate

(17) $$x_{w2} = f_{w1}y_{w1} + \rho_{w1}y_{w1} + u_{w2}$$

After estimating the pretreatment issue weight, I then estimate the post-treatment candidate/party weight, f_{w1}:

(18) $$x_{w3} = f_{w2}y_{w2} + \rho_{w2}y_{w2} + u_{w3}$$

Finally, I test for priming by testing whether the absolute value of the issue weight increases:

(19) $$\Omega_{3wt} = f_{w2} - f_{w1}$$

I estimate Ω_{3wt} by stacking the data and including an indicator variable for the posttreatment wave, Post, as well as an interaction between this indicator and issue attitudes, x, and this indicator and other control variables. For the one case where I can measure learning and for which there are only two waves (Chernobyl), I use the two-wave test, which follows the logic of the two-wave test of priming or learning effects, but again with x and y reversed. For the prior-persuasion tests, I control for the prior level and prior change on the lagged dependent variable; see equation 15 but with x and y reversed.

Chapter 8 Estimates

Table 9 presents the estimates for "All" in figures 8.1 and 8.3. Table 10 presents the estimates for chapter 8's figure 8.4, which shows the three-wave test of following. The remaining models from this chapter are shown in the online appendix.

APPENDIX TABLE 9. **Three-wave test of adopting your preferred parties' or candidates' positions without knowing/learning interactions.**

Estimates from the first column are used for "All'" in chapter 8's figure 8.3. Three-wave test of learning and adopting your candidate's position (difference in candidate/party weight $= \Omega_{3wt} = f_{w2} - f_{w1}$, see equation 19). To estimate the difference in candidate/party weight, these data are stacked, include an indicator for wave 3 (Post), and interactions between this indicator and the other variables. For the Chernobyl case, I must use the two-wave test, so the lagged dependent variable coefficients are not estimated. Variables coded so that higher values are in the expected direction relative to the dependent variable and recoded to vary from 0 to 1.

VARIABLES	(1)	(2)	(3)	(4)	(5)	(6)
DV	Soc Sec '00	EU '97	Pub Works '76	Def '80	ActivIdeo '92	Chernobyl '86
	Soc Sec	EU	Pub Works	Defense	Ideology	Nuc Power
Post indicator	-0.20*	-0.011	0.017	0.11*	0.017	-0.10*
	(0.051)	(0.026)	(0.044)	(0.043)	(0.023)	(0.020)
Prior Cand./Party supp.	0.22*	0.095*	0.15*	0.16*	0.062*	0.39*
	(0.057)	(0.028)	(0.063)	(0.044)	(0.019)	(0.020)
Post*Prior Cand./Party supp. ($\Omega_{3w1or2wt}$)	0.36*	0.12*	0.054	0.0065	0.072*	-0.073*
	(0.082)	(0.040)	(0.085)	(0.061)	(0.027)	(0.029)
Prior issue	0.69*	0.62*	0.65*	0.67*	0.62*	
	(0.031)	(0.021)	(0.037)	(0.035)	(0.027)	
Post*Prior issue	-0.14*	-0.080*	-0.051	-0.098*	-0.18*	
	(0.045)	(0.030)	(0.053)	(0.049)	(0.037)	
Constant	0.11*	0.092*	0.10*	0.13*	0.19*	0.22*
	(0.036)	(0.019)	(0.033)	(0.032)	(0.016)	(0.014)
n	1102	2766	844	1004	1970	1636
R^2	0.506	0.395	0.459	0.434	0.376	0.297
SER	0.34	0.26	0.26	0.18	0.13	0.29

Note: Ordinary least squares regression estimates with standard errors in parentheses. * $p < 0.1$.

APPENDIX TABLE 10. **Estimates for chapter 8's figure 8.4.**

Three-wave test of learning and adopting your candidate's position (difference in candidate/party weight = $\Omega_{3wt} = f_{w2} - f_{w1}$, see equation 19). To estimate the difference in candidate/party weight, these data are stacked, include an indicator for wave 3 (Post), and interactions between this indicator and the other variables. For the Chernobyl case, I must use the two-wave test, so the lagged dependent variable coefficients are not estimated. Variables coded so that higher values are in the expected direction relative to the dependent variable and recoded to vary from 0 to 1.

	(1)	(2)	(3)	(4)	(5)	(6)
	SocSec '00	EU '97	PubWorks '76	Def '80	ActivIdeo '92	Chernobyl '86
DV	SocSec	EU	PubWorks	Defense	Ideology	NucPower
Post indicator	0.42	0.32*	0.31*	0.20	0.070	−0.028
	(0.26)	(0.089)	(0.16)	(0.15)	(0.082)	(0.050)
Prior Cand/Party*Knowers	0.42*	0.20*	0.32*	0.31*	0.12*	0.53*
	(0.12)	(0.043)	(0.095)	(0.077)	(0.028)	(0.031)
---*Post	0.31*	0.031	−0.066	−0.21*	0.024	−0.13*
	(0.18)	(0.062)	(0.14)	(0.11)	(0.039)	(0.044)
Prior Cand/Party*Learners	0.22	−0.11*	−0.073	0.088	−0.044	0.17*
	(0.16)	(0.056)	(0.14)	(0.085)	(0.043)	(0.049)
---*Post	0.97*	0.57*	0.44*	0.33*	0.22*	0.21*
	(0.23)	(0.080)	(0.18)	(0.11)	(0.060)	(0.069)
Prior Cand/Party*Never learners	0.031	−0.15*	−0.19	0.032	−0.039	0.25*
	(0.23)	(0.056)	(0.13)	(0.077)	(0.035)	(0.043)
---*Post	−0.27	0.083	0.15	−0.13	0.010	−0.069
	(0.32)	(0.082)	(0.17)	(0.11)	(0.049)	(0.061)
Prior Cand/Party*Forgetters	0.40	0.38*	0.43*	0.19	0.068	0.50*
	(0.28)	(0.091)	(0.21)	(0.14)	(0.056)	(0.050)
---*Post	−0.29	−0.51*	−0.46	0.12	−0.017	−0.20*
	(0.42)	(0.14)	(0.32)	(0.19)	(0.087)	(0.071)
Prior Issue*Knowers	0.65*	0.70*	0.72*	0.67*	0.74*	
	(0.074)	(0.034)	(0.056)	(0.059)	(0.036)	
---*Post	−0.17	−0.058	−0.097	0.062	−0.11*	
	(0.11)	(0.049)	(0.087)	(0.085)	(0.051)	

	(1)	(2)	(3)	(4)	(5)	(6)
Prior Issue*Learners	0.60*	0.42*	0.57*	0.62*	0.47*	
	(0.081)	(0.046)	(0.076)	(0.080)	(0.067)	
--*Post	-0.16	0.00027	-0.011	-0.33*	-0.25*	
	(0.12)	(0.066)	(0.11)	(0.11)	(0.089)	
Prior Issue*Never learners	0.70*	0.45*	0.58*	0.61*	0.34*	
	(0.11)	(0.042)	(0.075)	(0.056)	(0.060)	
--*Post	-0.17	-0.019	0.0068	-0.033	-0.11	
	(0.15)	(0.061)	(0.11)	(0.079)	(0.079)	
Prior Issue*Forgetters	0.70*	0.51*	0.41*	0.86*	0.35*	
	(0.14)	(0.068)	(0.12)	(0.12)	(0.082)	
--*Post	-0.11	-0.16	0.14	-0.33*	-0.19*	
	(0.20)	(0.098)	(0.19)	(0.16)	(0.11)	
Knowers	0.058	0.049	-0.0039	0.12	-0.25*	0.033
	(0.20)	(0.070)	(0.12)	(0.12)	(0.058)	(0.040)
Learners	0.30	0.28*	0.27*	0.27*	-0.030	0.17*
	(0.21)	(0.076)	(0.12)	(0.13)	(0.067)	(0.050)
Never learners	0.29	0.26*	0.32*	0.28*	0.076	0.14*
	(0.23)	(0.078)	(0.13)	(0.12)	(0.067)	(0.049)
Post*Knowers	-0.54*	-0.31*	-0.20	-0.099	-0.064	-0.049
	(0.28)	(0.095)	(0.17)	(0.16)	(0.087)	(0.057)
Post*Learners	-1.09*	-0.58*	-0.56*	-0.091	-0.080	-0.19*
	(0.30)	(0.10)	(0.18)	(0.17)	(0.100)	(0.071)
Post*Never learners	-0.32	-0.30*	-0.38*	-0.057	-0.043	-0.11
	(0.33)	(0.11)	(0.19)	(0.16)	(0.098)	(0.070)
Constant	-0.072	-0.014	-0.0011	-0.059	0.34*	0.15*
	(0.18)	(0.065)	(0.11)	(0.11)	(0.055)	(0.036)
n	566	2766	844	1004	1970	1636
R^2	0.528	0.451	0.488	0.468	0.439	0.331
SER	0.34	0.25	0.26	0.17	0.13	0.29

Note: Ordinary least squares regression estimates with standard errors in parentheses. * $p < 0.1$.

The number of observations increases in these tables over those in previous chapters because they use candidate/party support as the dependent variable instead of vote, and so do not lose respondents who fail to report a vote intent or choice. Candidate/party support is Bush minus Gore thermometer in the Social Security case, Labour minus Conservative likeability in the European integration case, Carter minus Ford likeability in the public works case, Carter minus Reagan thermometer in the 1980 defense case, Bush thermometer in the 1992 Activating Ideology case, and incumbent party identification versus opposition party identification in the Chernobyl case. As I note in the chapter, the results are similar, though slightly attenuated, when I use vote instead of candidate evaluations.

SCHIP Expansion Experiment

The results of the State Children's Health Insurance Program (SCHIP) experiment are presented throughout the book. Here I briefly summarize the methods used to analyze the experiment and review the findings. I reinterviewed 2007 Cooperative Congressional Election Study (CCES) participants and attempted to prime and induce learning effects on the issue of SCHIP expansion where the outcome is approval of President George W. Bush. Following the design of previous studies, the treatment group read two short news stories about proposals to expand SCHIP and two stories on other issues, which the control group also read. The study contains two methodological improvements over most previous priming studies. First, I measure policy views (in this case, support for SCHIP expansion) before and after the treatment (about six months before as part of the 2007 CCES). Second, I eliminate the alternative of learning effects by, in one condition, not conveying information about politicians' positions. I do so by administering two priming treatment conditions. In the no info condition, participants read stories about SCHIP that contain no information about Bush's or the parties' positions on this issue. In the info condition, participants read identical stories, except that I change the language slightly so that the stories convey these positions, mimicking the treatments in many priming studies, which often unintentionally convey this information.

To measure attitudes about SCHIP, I use the 5-point, CCES question about support for SCHIP expansion (see chapter 3). I create a scale from the responses that varies between 0 and 1, with 1 indicating definite opposition. To assess learning about Bush's position on this issue, the survey asked, "Is President Bush for or against this proposal?" Respondents could reply "yes," "no," or "don't know." To measure Bush approval, I use the standard presidential approval question in the CCES.

To summarize, respondents were first interviewed in late 2007 (wave 1) and asked about their Bush approval and their attitudes about SCHIP expansion. About six months later, they were reinterviewed (wave 2). Their reinterview began with the priming treatments or the control condition, followed (in order but separated by filler items) by questions about Bush approval, respondents' attitudes about SCHIP expansion, and whether Bush supports SCHIP expansion. Of course, respondents may have learned about Bush's SCHIP position from the news media between interviews. If they did, it should make finding effects harder, since the info condition can inform fewer people about the positions.

As expected, the info condition induced learning about Bush's position on SCHIP expansion. In the control group, only 45 percent of respondents correctly reported that Bush opposed SCHIP expansion. In the info condition, this rises to 62 percent, a 17 percentage point increase ($p < 0.001$). As expected, no significant learning occurred in the no info condition.

Testing Media Priming and Learning Effects with Two-Wave Experiments

To test for media priming and learning effects in the experiment, I estimate the equations for the three-wave test, but substitute the control group for the baseline estimate. I estimate the issue weight in the control group, $\tilde{b}_{cw1}$, as follows:

$$(20) \qquad y_{cw2} = \tilde{b}_{cw1} x_{cw1} + \tilde{\rho}_{cw1} y_{cw1} + \tilde{u}_{cw2}.$$

I estimate the issue weight in each treatment group, $\tilde{b}_{tw1}$ with the same equation:

$$(21) \qquad y_{tw2} = \tilde{b}_{tw1} x_{tw1} + \tilde{\rho}_{tw1} y_{tw1} + \tilde{u}_{tw2}.$$

Finally, the experimental tests for priming or learning effects assess the absolute value of the issue weight increases:

$$\text{(22)} \qquad \Delta_{exp} = \tilde{b}_{tw1} - \tilde{b}_{cw1}.$$

Instead of comparing the issue weight after the issue becomes prominent to before it becomes prominent, this test compares the issue weights in the treatment group and the control group. Since it controls for the lagged dependent variable, it is a model of change in y, which is in this case presidential approval. I denote the test of priming that compares the no info condition to the control group with $\Delta_{exp:p}$. I denote the test combining learning and priming, which compares the info condition to the control group, with $\Delta_{exp:pr+lr}$. I estimate these by stacking the data and including an indicator variable for the posttreatment wave, Post, as well as an interaction between this indicator and SCHIP views, x, and this indicator and the lagged dependent variable.

Testing for Following with Two-Wave Experiments

To test whether the experimental treatments induce following, I conduct the same tests as in chapter 8 but again substitute a control group for the baseline. I estimate the effect of presidential approval on change in SCHIP attitudes in the control group with this equation:

$$\text{(23)} \qquad x_{cw2} = \tilde{f}_{cw1} y_{cw1} + \tilde{\rho}_{cw1} x_{cw1} + \tilde{u}_{cw2}.$$

I estimate the same equation in each of the treatment groups:

$$\text{(24)} \qquad x_{tw2} = \tilde{f}_{tw1} y_{tw1} + \tilde{\rho}_{tw1} x_{tw1} + \tilde{u}_{tw2}.$$

Finally, I test for following with the absolute value of

$$\text{(25)} \qquad \Omega_{exp} = \tilde{f}_{tw1} - \tilde{f}_{cw1}.$$

Since it controls for the lagged dependent variable, it is a model of change in x, which is SCHIP views. I denote the test of following due only to increased salience, which compares the no info condition to the control group, with $\Omega_{exp:pr}$. I denote the test combining learning and salience, which compares the info condition to the control group, with $\Omega_{exp:pr+lr}$.

SCHIP Results

Table 11 summarizes the results from the SCHIP experiment. I first test for priming using the conventional test, where Bush approval and SCHIP views are measured both pretreatment and posttreatment (equation 6, with indicator variables and interactions for the treatment conditions). Since SCHIP views are measured in wave 2, this test is potentially biased because people may change their SCHIP views in response to the treatment. Based on the panel findings presented throughout this book, the conventional test should find the appearance of priming only in the info condition because only here are individuals learning Bush's position and then, as a result, adopting or rejecting his position depending on whether they like him. We would not expect to find the appearance of priming in the no info condition because no learning occurs. The results show precisely this pattern. The conventional (but potentially biased) test of priming finds priming only in the info condition. In this condition, SCHIP attitudes became more predictive of Bush approval ($\Delta_{expct:pr+lr} = 0.15$, see the interaction between wave 2 SCHIP views and the info condition indicator variable). No significant priming effect occurs in the no info condition ($\Delta_{expct:pr+lr} = 0.07$). Thus, when the priming treatment conveyed information about Bush's and the Democrats' positions on SCHIP expansion, we find the appearance of priming, but when we take away this information, the apparent priming effect vanishes. This is exactly what I find using observational data in the panel cases.

The second step in confirming the panel findings is to test whether conveying this information creates the appearance of priming because (1) media priming actually occurs and respondents are changing their Bush approval to match their SCHIP attitude or because, as in the panel data, (2) they are changing their SCHIP views to better match their Bush approval (following). Instead of measuring SCHIP attitudes posttreatment (wave 2), I measure them six months earlier (wave 1), following Equation 22. I model wave 2 Bush approval as a function of treatment indicator variables (info or no info), wave 1 SCHIP attitudes, wave 1 Bush approval (so that the analysis examines change while accounting for regression to the mean), and the interactions. As shown in column 2, the priming finding in the conventional test vanishes when we use wave 1 SCHIP attitudes instead of wave 2 SCHIP attitudes. This suggests that the appearance of priming in the conventional test arises

APPENDIX TABLE 11. **SCHIP expansion experiment. All variables coded to vary between 0 and 1.**

	Conventional tests		Prior opinion tests		Following tests
	Priming and learning		Priming and learning		
	See equation 6		See equation 22		See equation 25
	(1)		(2)		(3)
	Wave 2 Bush approval		Wave 2 Bush approval		Wave 2 SCHIP views
Info condition	-0.06	Info condition	-0.04		-0.04
	(0.05)		(0.03)		(0.05)
No info condition	-0.07	No info condition	-0.04		0.01
	(0.05)		(0.03)		(0.05)
Wave 2 SCHIP views	0.34*	Wave 1 SCHIP views	0.08*		0.70*
	(0.06)		(0.04)		(0.07)
--*Info condition	0.15* ($\Delta_{expc:pr+b}$)	--*Info condition	0.06 ($\Delta_{expp:pr+b}$)		-0.20*
	(0.03)		(0.06)		(0.10)
--*No info cond.	0.07 ($\Delta_{expc:pr}$)	--*No info cond.	0.12* ($\Delta_{expp:pr}$)		-0.09
	(0.08)		(0.07)		(0.10)
		Wave 1 Bush approval	0.78*		0.14*
			(0.05)		(0.08)
		--*Info condition	-0.04		0.24* ($\Omega_{exp:pr+b}$)
			(0.07)		(0.11)
		--*No info cond.	-0.12		-0.03 ($\Omega_{exp:pr}$)
			(0.08)		(0.12)
n	446		446		446
R^2	0.246		0.710		0.523
SER	0.255		0.199		0.305

Note: Ordinary least squares regression estimates with standard errors in parentheses. * $p < 0.1$.

because people were changing their wave 2 SCHIP attitudes in response to the treatment.

To further explore this possibility, column 3 uses the same model but replaces the dependent variable, Bush approval at wave 2, with SCHIP attitudes wave 2 (equation 25). As implied by the results in columns 1 and 2, this column shows that individuals in the info condition were changing their SCHIP attitudes between wave 1 and wave 2 to reflect their views about Bush: the interaction between info condition and Bush approval at wave 1 is large and highly statistically significant, suggesting considerable issue opinion change. To get a sense for the magnitude of this effect, consider a pro-Bush individual in the info condition with an anti-Bush individual in the control condition. The pro-Bush individual will on average shift against SCHIP expansion by about 0.24 on the 1-point SCHIP scale.

In sum, this experiment confirms the panel findings. It suggests that campaign and media attention can lead to the appearance of media priming (without actually causing priming) by informing individuals about the candidates' or parties' positions, leading individuals to adopt their candidate's or party's position as their own.

(There is one noteworthy anomaly in this table. Although we fail to find a priming effect in the no info condition using SCHIP attitudes at wave 2 [the coefficient is 0.07 in column 1], a small but significant priming effect emerges when we use SCHIP attitudes at wave 1 [the coefficient is 0.12 in column 2]. In the real world, campaigns and the news media convey information about politicians' positions. So the no info condition is unusual and the implications of his results are unclear.)

The SCHIP experiment was part of a larger study that also attempted to induce effects on two other issues: warrantless wiretapping and the economy. On warrantless wiretaps, the experiment failed to induce a priming effect, a learning effect, or lead individuals to adopt or reject Bush's position (depending on whether they approved or disapproved of Bush). The failure to find these effects probably stems from a failure of the info treatment to induce learning on this issue. Despite pretesting that suggested otherwise, the percent correctly saying that Bush supports such wiretaps was already high in the control group, above 80 percent. This may constitute a ceiling. On the economy, the experiment also fails to induce a priming effect or lead people to shift their perceptions of the economy in line with their support for Bush. The absence of either effect may stem from Bush approval and perceptions of the econ-

omy being strongly related in the control group (a one-to-one relationship), making either effect unlikely. I did not include an info treatment
for the economy because everyone presumably knows Bush would prefer
a better economy.

The full study sample size was about a thousand. I exclude individuals who on average read the news stories, answered the question about it,
and moved on to the next page in less than five seconds per story (about
10 percent). An examination of the means across the conditions in the
survey indicates successful randomization. One anomaly, however, is
worth noting: wave 1 (2007 CCES) attitudes about SCHIP correlates
more strongly in the SCHIP treatment groups than in the control group.
While this may bias conventional test estimates, it seems unlikely to bias
the two-wave test estimates.

Notes

Chapter 1

1. *Federalist Papers*, no. 68.

2. George Gallup was so confident about a Truman loss that he stopped polling in mid-October and the *Chicago Daily Tribune* went to press, before the results were in, with its infamous headline, "Dewey Defeats Truman" (McCullough 1993).

3. The survey interviewed a representative sample of adults in Elmira, New York, on as many as four occasions in 1948. These results are from the October interviews, which asked about union support and vote intent. For union support, respondents could choose one of four statements, ranging from the strongly prounion, "Labor unions in this country are doing a fine job," to the strongly antiunion, "This country would be better off without any labor unions at all," with the other two statements falling in between.

4. In a statistical study of post–World War II campaigns, Bartels (1992) concludes that robust economic growth, Truman's spending advantage, and the consistent tendency of underdogs to gain ground can together account for Truman's comeback.

5. Many studies have documented this tendency to adopt views consistent with one's preferred party or candidate (Abramowitz 1978; Bartels 2002a; Bartels 2002b; Campbell et al. 1960; Carsey and Layman 2006; Druckman 2001; Gerber and Jackson 1993; Jacoby 1988; Miller 1999; Prior 2007; Rahn, Krosnick, and Breuning 1994; Zaller 1994). They have done so with policy views, such as on the legality of abortion (Carsey and Layman 2006). They have also done so with performance assessments, such as perceptions of the national economy (Bartels 2002a). Researchers use several terms to describe this behavior, including *projection* (Iyengar and Kinder 1987), *persuasion* (Brody and Page 1972), *rationalization* (Jacoby 1988), and *cue taking* (Kuklinski and Hurley 1994). The

tendency of people to adopt policy and performance views consistent with their party or candidate is strong. In fact, as I show in chapter 8, it is strong enough to produce the pattern in figure 1.2.

6. Although these tools provide important insights into issue voting (e.g., Brader 2006; Tomz and Van Houweling 2008; Tomz and Van Houweling 2009), and I use experiments in this book, directly applying experimental methods to real-world policy voting is difficult. Fully experimental designs require randomly assigning individuals to policy views—for example, assigning some to hold a liberal opinion on an issue and some to a conservative opinion—and then observing their votes. Obviously, this is not easy. Instead, most experimental studies manipulate some other variable and then observe respondents' policy views and performance assessments, sometimes doing so posttreatment, which leaves the results frustratingly open to alternative explanations. Researchers have also attempted to sort out what is causing what with structural equation estimation (Franklin and Jackson 1983; Jackson 1975; Margolis 1977; Markus and Converse 1979; Page and Jones 1979). As Achen and Bartels (2004b) write, however, "Those attempts mostly served to underline the extent to which the conclusions drawn from such analyses rested on fragile and apparently untestable statistical assumptions."

7. More recent examples include Shanks, Strand, and Carmines (2003) and Hutchings (2003).

8. The authors of *The American Voter* allow for exceptions when people hold strong issue positions out of step with those of their party (Campbell et al. 1960, 135).

9. The debate about issue voting was more prominent in the 1970s (cf. Brody and Page 1972; Margolis 1977; Markus and Converse 1979), but is no more settled today. In a recent example, Abramson, Aldrich, and Rohde (2003) argue that policy issues failed to influence vote choice in the 2002 congressional elections, while Shanks, Strand, and Carmines (2003) find that such issues had a substantial effect.

10. Several recent studies have examined these questions with panels (Carsey and Layman 2006; Goren 2005; Levendusky 2009).

11. Besides focusing on causal inference, I also attempt to address several other thorny methodological issues that bedevil the study of issue voting. To reduce concerns about random measurement error in voters' substantive views (Ansolabehere, Rodden, and Snyder 2008), I average policy views and performance assessments across multiple prior panel interviews or across multiple indicators. When showing results, I address concerns about bias from specification search by noting both bivariate and multivariate findings. Finally, to render the analyses more accessible and informative, I present most findings graphically and show as much data as I can.

12. Only about 40 percent placed both the candidates and the parties correctly; that is, placed Barack Obama as more prochoice than John McCain and placed the Democratic Party as more prochoice than the Republican Party. The percentages were similar in 2004.

13. Consider another example from the 1948 election. Besides disagreeing about government policy toward unions, Truman and Dewey also took opposing positions on price controls, used to stem rampant inflation. Truman supported such controls, while Dewey opposed them. According to Lazarsfeld and his colleagues, Truman's and Dewey's differences on these two issues were "reasonably straightforward and clear" and were "crucial issues in the campaign, much discussed in the communication media" (Berelson, Lazarsfeld, and McPhee 1954, 227–28). Nonetheless, their survey found a pervasive ignorance: only 16 percent knew both candidates' positions on both issues.

14. Researchers refer to such comparatively simple issues as "easy issues" (Carmines and Stimson 1989; Converse 1964; Sniderman, Brody, and Tetlock 1991). According to Carmines and Stimson (1980), three qualities characterize easy issues: they are symbolic rather than technical, they are more likely to deal with policy ends than with means, and they have been on the political agenda for a long time.

15. Following research in psychology (Taylor and Fiske 1978), studies on media priming usually assume that cognitive accessibility mediates priming effects (Iyengar and Kinder 1987; Iyengar et al. 1984; Kinder and Sanders 1996; Mendelberg 2001; Price and Tewksbury 1997; Valentino 1999), an assumption that is supported for racial attitudes (Valentino, Hutchings, and White 2002). The evidence is ambiguous, however, and some work supports other mechanisms such as importance and applicability (Althaus and Kim 2006; Miller and Krosnick 2000; Nelson, Clawson, and Oxley 1997). It's important to note that priming, as political scientists use the term, is not necessarily the same as the psychological concept of priming.

16. To my knowledge, no experiment measuring policy views pretreatment has found media priming using vote or candidate evaluation as the dependent variable—though experiments have done so with policy views as the dependent variable (Mendelberg 2001; Nelson and Kinder 1996). A handful of observational studies measuring policy views pretreatment do find priming with vote or candidate evaluation as the dependent variable (Bartels 2006; Ladd 2007); I discuss these studies in chapter 3. Media priming studies on performance (as opposed to policy) issues have found priming with pretreatment measures, including priming in experiments (Iyenger and Kinder 1986) and in an observational study (Druckman and Holmes 2004).

17. This is measured by having survey respondents place the two parties on a 7-point ideology scale (see chapter 5).

Chapter 2

1. Numerous books provide accounts of this election (Germond and Witcover 1993; Goldman 1994; Loevy 1995; Matalin and Carville 1995) and at least two academic articles study it systematically (Alvarez and Nagler 1995; Hetherington 1996).

2. More generally, citizens come to see (or report seeing) politicians they already prefer as more intelligent, more competent, and more honest (Bartels 2002b; Goren 2002).

3. In fact, some individual-level studies find no evidence that economic perceptions have an effect on political choices (e.g., Erikson 2004; Evans and Pickup 2010).

4. This panel also spans the Gulf crisis. Although Bush's handling of this crisis is also a performance issue, I do not test for priming in the Gulf War case for two reasons: we lack the two prior interview waves necessary to apply my approach (see below) and we lack stable perceptions of Bush's performance on this issue in the aggregate. Unlike the economy during 1990–92, when attitudes are consistently negative, approval of Bush's handling of the Gulf crisis changes markedly. In the panel, approval of Bush's Gulf crisis handling rises from 58 prewar to 80 postwar (coded on a 100-point scale). Given this change, testing for priming based on prewar crisis evaluations may bias this test against finding priming. This attitude change, however, provides an opportunity to study persuasion effects, which I do in chapter 4.

5. When the attitudinal control variables I describe later are added, the issue-weight increase remains similar in size, 0.22, and highly statistically significant.

6. The list is available from the author.

7. This test also suffers from other problems. For example, increased certainty about performance assessments or increased certainty about candidates' positions on policy issues could bias it (Alvarez 1997). In the appendix I discuss some of the other effects this test could capture.

8. Adding these variables leaves the estimate essentially unchanged. Without controls, the difference in issue weights is 0.22, SE = 0.07, $p < 0.003$, $n = 956$.

9. Several books provide accounts of this election (Thomas 1997; Woodward 1996).

10. Source: http://www.movingimage.us/cg96/ad911.htm. Accessed January 24, 2009.

11. As noted above, I rescale presidential approval responses throughout this book to a 100-point scale.

12. The results are similar without these control variables. As I noted earlier, the only control variable that changes the results is the lagged dependent variable (Prior DV).

13. The uneven intervals could bias this test in favor of finding priming because the interval in the baseline is longer.

14. Moreover, when making judgments on performance, citizens may often rely on crude measures, focusing not on the incumbent's actual influence on the outcome but on the outcome itself. Voters may have judged Bush not on his policies' effects on the economy but on the economy itself. If citizens evaluate incumbent performance on such crude but readily available information, a much greater percentage of the public may hold sufficiently strong attitudes on performance issues so as to judge politicians on these issues.

15. The estimates of this difference include control variables. For a formal definition of this test and the full model results, see the appendix.

16. See Raudenbush and Bryk (2002, 40).

17. The results are also consistent with one of the few other priming studies that measures economic perceptions in a prior wave. Analyzing campaigns between 1980 and 2000, Bartels (2006) finds evidence consistent with the priming of economic perceptions. Several studies reach similar conclusions with aggregate-level data. Examining eleven postwar presidential campaigns, for instance, Bartels (1992, 265) finds that the incumbent party gains or loses an average of about 1.6 percent of the vote between June and November for every 1 percent change in real income. Research from other countries suggests similar findings. Using a sample of thirteen democracies, one study found that the longer the campaign, the greater the correspondence between vote choice and economic measures (Stevenson and Vavreck 2000). Examining the 2006 Mexican presidential election, Austin Hart (2011) finds that campaign ads prime economic perceptions in Mexican elections.

18. Hetherington (1996) finds another form of manipulation in the 1992 election. Citizens who reported greater media exposure tended to see the economy as worse than it probably was.

19. Although they may not be the best judges of performance (Achen and Bartels 2004a; Achen and Bartels 2004b; Healy and Malhotra 2009), it is nevertheless reassuring that performance matters.

Chapter 3

1. I present evidence on learning in chapter 5.

2. Johnston et al. break news segments into statements that are typically of one sentence in length, by one source, about one candidate, and about one topic.

3. I use Reinterview Panel A. The dates of interviews are as follows: Wave 1: July 21–30 and August 4–13. Wave 2: August 4–13 and August 18–27. Wave 3: November 11–December 7. The panel also contains an October 18–31 wave, a

period during which this issue became increasingly prominent. The results hold when I treat this wave as wave 3.

4. Showing that I can replicate the original cross-sectional finding in the panel is also reassuring.

5. It uses estimates from a linear probability model that regresses vote on attitudes about investing Social Security funds. I adopt a linear probability model to facilitate comparisons with the other cases in this book (probit yields similar results).

6. The p value is: $p < 0.05$. This increase also holds when using the same controls as Johnston et al. (2004).

7. Of course, this doesn't, in itself, mean Social Security is becoming THE issue on which candidates are judged, only that it is becoming AN issue on which candidates are judged.

8. I show the equations for this test in the appendix. See equation 11. I control only for party identification, though the same findings emerge with additional control variables. For these results with additional controls, I use the same ones as Johnston et al. (2004) with some exceptions.

9. I present key results in the text and robustness checks (using different variables, coding rules, and so on) in an online appendix at http://www.press.u chicago.edu/books/lenz.

10. Lazarsfeld and his colleagues do not test for priming with the conventional test but instead use an approach that relies on responses to open-ended questions. For a critique of their approach, see the online appendix.

11. It also asked three other questions about New Deal policies, including about opposition to large corporations, support for Taft-Hartley, and support for price controls. I checked for effects on all of these questions but found none. I also considered creating a scale but found little correlation between responses, none reaching even 0.2. The lack of effects here may simply reflect the weakness of these questions.

12. Neither author uses the term *priming*, but both imply that the increasing salience or prominence of this issue caused policy-driven vote change, for example, "the impact of attitudes towards European integration would . . . exhibit increasing strength, with voters against integration becoming increasingly more likely to vote Conservative" (Andersen 2003, 615).

13. The dates of interview were January 22–February 25, June 4–July 13, September 2–October 1, and November 5–November 25. For ease of presentation, I refer to these panel waves as January, June, September, and postelection throughout the book.

14. Research on activating fundamentals springs from an important finding in scholarship on American politics: presidential election outcomes are predictable. Using variables such as the economy and partisanship—fundamentals— researchers can accurately forecast presidential election outcomes (e.g., Hibbs

2000). Despite this predictability, polls conducted during campaigns exhibit variability. Based on this discrepancy, Gelman and King (1993) ask, "Why are American presidential election campaign polls so variable when votes are so predictable?" The answer, they argue, is that campaigns prime or activate these fundamentals. Early in campaigns, polls are variable because the fundamentals remain latent. By Election Day, however, the campaign has provided citizens with information about fundamentals and likely prompted voters to consider them, thereby making the election result predictable. In support of this hypothesis, Gelman and King show that income, race, and self-reported ideology become more associated with vote choice over the course of the 1988 presidential election campaign. These findings suggest that citizens weigh these issues more heavily at the end of the campaign, indicating that campaigns prime or activate fundamentals.

15. As revealed in American National Election Studies (Zaller 2004).

16. The results are essentially unchanged with just the 7-point scale. The 1992 election study asked the ideology questions only in the preelection wave of the 1992 survey, which interviewed individuals in September and October of that year.

17. I thank Erik Voeten for bringing this case to my attention.

18. On changes in public opinion after 9/11, see also Kinder and Kam (2009).

19. In 2006, SCHIP ensured more than seven million children (CBO 2007). In reauthorizing the SCHIP program in 2007, both houses of Congress approved measures that would expand its coverage. President Bush vetoed the expansion, expressing the concern it would crowd out private insurance (Abramowitz 2007). The House of Representatives fell just short (273–156) of the two-thirds majority required to override the president's veto. Congress again passed a reauthorization that expanded coverage, while addressing some of Bush's concerns. Bush vetoed this new measure in December of 2007, saying it was essentially identical to earlier legislation (CNN 2007). Finally, in late December, Congress passed and Bush signed a temporary reauthorization, lasting just over a year, giving Congress and Bush more time to reach a compromise.

20. A few studies have found priming with policy views measured before the stimulus (Mendelberg 2001; Nelson and Kinder 1996; Sears and Funk 1999), but they have done so only when the dependent variable is another issue attitude, such as priming views about racial groups when assessing attitudes about government aid to the poor. I am not aware of any priming findings where the dependent variable is vote choice or candidate preference, except for the observational studies by Ladd (2007), which I discuss in this chapter, Bartels (2006), and Druckman (2004). At least one experimental study fails to find priming with prior views and a policy outcome (Berger, Meredith, and Wheeler 2008).

21. For the experimental case, I model Bush approval in the treatment and control groups as a function of posttreatment SCHIP attitudes. For the 9/11 case, I compare the 2000 coefficient on defense spending with the 2004 coefficient, in-

stead of 2002, because the 2002 ANES lacks the defense spending scale. In the cases with three waves, I use waves 2 and 3 for this test, though the results look similar if I use wave 1 instead of wave 2. For more details, see the appendix.

22. As I discuss later, in the panels that asked respondents to place the parties or candidates on the policy issues, I could use proximity measures instead of entering policy views directly into the equations. Switching to proximity measures, however, does not change the findings.

23. The large drop in the activating ideology case occurs almost entirely among respondents who I call "never learners"—those who failed to place either the Democratic or Republican Parties on the ideology scale or, if they did place them, put the Democratic Party to the right of the Republican Party. Believe it or not, these people make up about 26 percent of the sample.

24. For the experimental case, I model Bush approval in the treatment and control groups as a function of pretreatment SCHIP attitudes. See the appendix for details.

25. Of course, as I discuss later in this chapter, those who know the positions might be resistant to priming because they already care about the issue.

26. Using alternative measures, such as placing the parties on the right side of the midpoint, yield similar results. The activating-ideology-position questions asked about the Democratic and Republican Parties. For more details on coding, see chapter 5.

27. These findings deepen the mystery of why the conventional test finds priming in the full sample, but tests using prior policy views do not. I investigate this question in chapter 8.

28. We could also potentially use the panel to measure changes in issue salience at the individual level. If issue-weight increases tend to occur only when the salience of an issue increases, this would support priming. Unfortunately, survey-based measures of issue salience or issue importance have proved problematic and generally fail to correspond with issue weights (Niemi and Bartels 1985; Grynaviski and Corrigan 2006; but see Krosnick 1988). These questions also sometimes confuse being a problem with being important (Wlezien 2005).

29. For a formal presentation of this and other biases particular to this test, see Lenz (2006). Another potential source of conservative bias is that the post-DV is sometimes measured after Election Day and after the priming event. Measurement error in the issue attitude variables also probably biases this test against finding priming.

30. As measured by the correlation between waves, views about the economy appear to be somewhat less stable than views on policy, making the downward bias larger in the economy cases. See the online appendix for details.

31. I instrument all variables, including the lagged dependent variable, with variables from two waves prior. I can therefore only apply this test to the three-wave cases.

32. A fifth reason is that the estimates suggest that prior policy views did matter before the issues became prominent in four of the six three-wave cases (that is, $\tilde{b}_{w1} > 0$, though not much greater than zero, see the appendix), indicating that this test is not hopelessly biased against effects. Why not consider the positive issue weights on prior policy views (i.e., $\tilde{b}_{w1} = \tilde{b}_{w2} > 0$) as evidence that policy views matter? First, because these issue weights generally fall to zero with additional controls. Second, even if they do not fall to zero, uncontrolled or poorly controlled variables could explain them. To help rule out such confounding factors, the approach I take is to search for issue-weight increases that coincide with increases in prominence.

33. Research on proximity and directional models also potentially suffers from bias because of citizens adopting their preferred candidate's or party's position. Chapter 8 shows that this bias can be severe.

34. For these tests I calculate proximity two ways: with respondents' placements of parties and candidates and, to avoid concerns about projection, with mean placements of parties or candidates.

35. Omitting control variables as I do in the main results could induce a conservative bias if these omitted variables were "deprimed." When someone decides for whom to vote, he presumably considers a number of issues. The weights he places on these various considerations, whether partisan identification or the candidates' hair colors, must sum to one. Since priming involves placing more weight on one consideration, it necessarily involves placing less weight on others. In the Truman case, if an individual places more weight on New Deal issues, he must then place less on international issues, for example, or on his partisan identification. If these considerations are orthogonal to the issue being primed, these issue-tradeoffs should pose no problem for inferences. If they correlate, however, the declining coefficients on these omitted variables could bias estimates of priming downward.

36. Of the three-wave cases, the only vote choice case where we lack continuous outcome measures is unions in the 1948 election. In the other three cases, which are Social Security, European integration, and public works, the (precision weighted) average priming effect on continuous outcome measures is close to zero and precisely estimated (0.013, SE = 0.008).

37. Although not among those who already know the politicians' and parties' positions.

Chapter 4

1. Additional analyses I conducted found no evidence of media priming, but that's not surprising.

2. In one exception, Johnston et al. (1992) find that the leadership debate in

the 1988 Canadian election persuaded many individuals to oppose free trade with the United States, leading them to support the candidate (Liberal Party) who opposed free trade. Researchers have also examined politicians' tendency to change their own policy decisions in response to aggregate change (persuasion) in the public's views about a policy (Bartels 1991; Erikson, MacKuen, and Stimson 2002; Page and Shapiro 1992; Stimson, MacKuen, and Erikson 1995).

3. These data are from the 2000 Annenberg Election Study, Multi-Reinterview Panel A. The exact dates of the interviews are as follows. Wave 1: August 4–13 and August 18–27. Wave 2: October 18–31. Wave 3: November 11–December 7.

4. This approach shares some similarities with Sekhon (2004).

5. The results are similar with probit models.

6. For a discussion of the few policy items asked in the Elmira study, see chapter 3. About 23 percent of panel respondents become more supportive of unions between June and October, about 67 percent maintain the same level of support, and the remaining 10 percent become less supportive.

7. In cases with more than two waves before the issue became prominent in the campaign, I examine persuasion in the two waves before the postelection wave.

8. As noted in chapter 2, I do not test for priming in the Gulf War case for two reasons: we lack the two prior waves necessary to apply the three-wave test and we lack stable perceptions of Bush's performance on this issue. Unlike the economy during 1990 and 1992, when attitudes are consistently negative, approval of Bush's handling of the Gulf crisis changes markedly, as I have already noted. Given this change and given the ceiling on the approval measure (only a 5-point scale), testing for priming based on prewar evaluations probably biases this test against finding priming.

9. Some of this change is likely noise. For example, many interview respondents may have never thought about a particular issue before and make up their responses on the fly. In successive interview waves, different considerations will pop into their heads, giving researchers a misleading impression that they are changing their views. This is what we call random noise. There can also be nonrandom noise. For example, between interviews, a respondent might have started listening to conservative talk radio or watching liberal-minded TV shows. This change in media exposure could shift the respondent's views and even his or her vote. Since the researcher doesn't know what lies behind the change in views, it will look like noise, but in truth it's not random. Meanwhile, some of the observed change in views is real. Unfortunately, we can't distinguish between the real change and the noise. To the degree that the noise is truly random, it will probably work against finding any effects.

10. In cases where the outcome variable is vote choice, I also control for prior level and prior change on the more continuous candidate or party evaluations, such as comparative feeling thermometers, as I did in the honesty case. Control-

ling for these continuous measures may better capture overall trends toward or away from candidates compared to the binary vote measures.

Chapter 5

1. This 60 percent is probably inflated by guessing. The source is the ANES 2008 Time Series Study. The survey question was phrased as follows: "There is much concern about the rapid rise in medical and hospital costs. Some people feel there should be a government insurance plan which would cover all medical and hospital expenses for everyone. Suppose these people are at one end of a scale, at point 1. Others feel that all medical expenses should be paid by individuals through private insurance plans like Blue Cross or other company paid plans. Suppose these people are at the other end, at point 7. And, of course, some other people have opinions somewhere in between, at points 2, 3, 4, 5, or 6." I code individuals as having correct perceptions if they place Obama at a lower point on the scale than McCain.

2. There are, of course, exceptions (Abramowitz 1978; Alvarez 1997; Jenkins 2002; Johnston, Hagen, and Jamieson 2004; Sekhon 2004). Researchers have also experimentally studied the effects of learning on policy views (e.g., Berinsky 2007; Gilens 2001), but my focus is on vote and candidate evaluations.

3. Although the parties sometimes muddled their messages, their positions were clear to knowledgeable respondents. Among the top 10 percent in terms of factual knowledge in the British Election Panel Study ($n = 139$), more than 75 percent placed Labour as more pro-EU than Conservatives in 1992 and almost 90 percent did so in 1997.

4. I use this relative measure, as opposed to an absolute measure, because it is probably less sensitive to individual differences in responses to these scales. Using nonrelative measures yields similar though slightly weaker results.

5. It does so only for the learners, though the results are identical in the other three groups (as we would expect in light of the chapter 3 findings).

6. I code incorrect placements as either placing the parties or candidates on the wrong side of each other or both the same as each other or for failing to place either or both parties or candidates. The exceptions include the Social Security and SCHIP cases, which lack multipoint scales and ask only whether the politicians support or oppose a particular policy. In these cases I code knowledge as correctly reporting the politicians' positions. In the Social Security case, this means reporting that Bush supports investing Social Security funds in the stock market and Gore opposes it. In the SCHIP case, this means reporting that Bush opposes expanding SCHIP coverage. I also use a nonrelative measure in the 1980 case. Given that the priming effect only appears to emerge for Reagan

and given that Carter worked vigorously to appear as a defense hawk during this period (see chapter 7), I measure learning and knowledge based only on perceptions of Reagan, coding a correct perception as placing him at either of the top 2 points of the 7-point defense spending scale. (Using a measure based on relative perceptions of Reagan and Carter produces similar results.)

7. I only present the results in this chapter for learners, but we know from chapter 3 that there are no issue-weight increases either in the full sample or among knowers. Among those who never learned, the issue weights tend to be close to zero and do not change. Among forgetters, the issue weights tend to decrease. Results for all four groups are shown in the appendix.

8. For the list of two-wave and three-wave cases, see chapter 3.

9. In this experiment, as I note in the next chapter, Republicans were more likely than Democrats to learn about Bush's opposition to SCHIP expansion, probably because many more Republicans than Democrats started out with the mistaken notion that Bush supported it.

10. I have confirmed this surprising finding for ideology in two other panel studies with the questions necessary to replicate it: the Patterson (1980) panel study of the 1976 US election and the ANES 2008–9 Panel Study. In both I find the same pattern. Many people learned the candidates' ideologies—they became able to place the Democrat to the left of the Republican by the end of the campaign—but they failed to act on this newly acquired knowledge.

11. In a review of the literature on attitude strength, Joanne Miller and David Peterson (2004, 862) write, "Different substantive conclusions about the role of attitude strength, as either a mediator or moderator of observed relationships, could be reached depending on which attribute [of attitude strength] one chooses to measure" (see also Krosnick et al. 1993).

12. As noted above, I can check this possibility only in the cases with multipoint candidate-position scales, which excludes the Social Security and SCHIP experiment cases.

13. I instrument all variables, including the lagged dependent variable, with variables from a prior wave. I can only apply this test to the three-wave cases.

14. It's also worth noting that the "after learning" issue-weight estimates are small and not statistically different from zero in these cases as well ($b'_{w2} = 0$ in equation 13 and $\tilde{b}_{w2} = 0$ in equation 10). The "after learning" issue weights are also small and not statistically different from zero in the two-wave cases when I control for the lagged dependent variable.

15. Repeating these analyses using party support scales or multinomial logit produces similar results.

16. In fact, the learning effects I find below only appear with the eight-item index. When I use the single European integration question used above, I find no evidence that learning matters. In case it changed the earlier learning findings, I also replicated the tests for learning effects between 1996 and 1997, pre-

sented earlier in this chapter, using this 1992 index, but again found no evidence of effects.

17. In coding learners I thus exclude those who failed to place one or both parties correctly in 1992. Including these individuals (as I do in the cases above) produces similar though somewhat weaker findings. The 1992 wave asked only half of respondents about their perceptions of the parties' positions. I exclude from the analysis those who were not asked these questions.

Chapter 6

1. The following statistics and accounts of the campaign are from the English-language articles cited below, especially a longer article from the *Economist* (Economist 1986). Several scholars have written in English on this election and on Dutch politics in the 1980s (Brug 2001; Daalder and Irwin 1989; Eijk, Irwin, and Niemöller 1986; Gladdish 1986; Gladdish 1991; Whitten and Palmer 1996).

2. For comparison, about 36 percent correctly place all four parties relative to each other.

3. With a few exceptions (e.g., Mendelberg 2001; Simon 2002), research on campaigns and media priming has ignored the strategic behavior of political actors.

4. In fact, it only interviewed fourteen people in the week between news of Chernobyl and Lubbers's attempt to switch sides.

5. This is a highly significant difference ($p < 0.001$, $n = 1,356$) even with only forty-eight interviews post-Chernobyl in the preelection survey. None of the other issues showed statistically significant changes between pre-Chernobyl and post-Chernobyl (but preelection) interviews. Since those interviewed post-Chernobyl may be a nonrandom selection of the sample, I also tried controlling for vote intent and a host of demographic variables, but the results remained unchanged.

6. Since some respondents failed to notice Lubbers's shift, we might be able to test whether the issue of nuclear power had the potential to hurt Lubbers by examining whether these respondents, who still saw Lubbers as pronuclear, turned against his coalition. This test might reveal whether the issue had the potential to hurt Lubbers had he failed to shift positions. I conducted several analyses to search for such a pattern, but found no evidence that nuclear power hurt Lubbers's coalition among those who missed the shift and still considered him as pronuclear as he had always been. Although an intriguing result, it probably arises because the kinds of people who missed Lubbers's shift were probably the kinds of people who did not care enough about the issue of nuclear power to base their votes on it.

7. Other European countries did not hold national elections immediately fol-

lowing Chernobyl and did not change their nuclear power policies as radically as did the Dutch. When Germany held regional elections not long after Chernobyl, the incumbents faced protests and calls to cut back on nuclear power but resisted major policy change.

Chapter 7

1. The data for 1976 come from the Patterson panel described in chapter 3, which is not from a national sample. Unfortunately, I have not been able to find a national survey before 1980 that asked about Carter's position on defense, which in itself suggests that the issue was much less prominent than it became in 1980.

2. This positive relationship is highly statistically significant in least squares regression models with and without control variables. The controls include party identification, attitudes about government spending and services, perceptions of the national economy, and attitudes about reducing unemployment versus reducing inflation (all measured in January; see the appendix for details). I use these controls throughout the chapter, measured in a prior wave whenever possible. A similar pattern holds for Carter approval.

3. Alternatively, Carter's efforts may have convinced his supporters to become hawks. Unfortunately, we cannot tell which took place because we lack panel data before January 1980.

4. For an alternative view, see Posen and Van Evera (1980).

5. This group also includes those who initially saw him as a dove but then failed to place him in June.

6. To measure this knowledge in the September wave, I code placing Carter as more dovish than Reagan as the correct perception. This is arguably the more appropriate comparison in September, when citizens were presumably comparing these two candidates. The same result holds, however, if I instead use a midpoint or below placement for Carter in the September wave.

7. Although these individuals could still have learned that Carter was more dovish than they had previously thought or become more certain about his dovishness.

8. Another alternative explanation is that Republicans, who tend to be pro-defense, may have lowered their approval of Carter between January and June, not because of Carter's retreat, but because of other factors, such as the poor national economy. As they came to dislike Carter, Republicans may have projected the dovish defense position they disliked onto him, creating the appearance of learning. The evidence, however, appears inconsistent with this projection alternative. Among those who saw Carter as a hawk in January, respondents' own defense-spending attitudes failed to predict changes in perceptions of Carter on defense. That is, those who were defense-spending hawks in January were no

more likely to shift their perception of Carter on defense to the dovish side of the scale than were respondents who were doves.

9. A caveat is that we cannot exclude from the learners those who failed to retain their learning, as we did for the analysis between January and June, because the fourth wave lacks questions about defense spending.

10. At http://www.gallup.com/poll/110548/Gallup-Presidential-Election-Trial Heat-Trends-19362004.aspx#2, accessed November 18, 2011.

11. If we include non-major-candidate voters from the September wave, support for Carter actually rose slightly between the September and postelection waves.

Chapter 8

1. We can observe the sequence of his views because he is interviewed multiple times. With only one interview, which is all researchers usually have, we could not distinguish policy adopting from policy voting. They would look the same.

2. These include cross-sectional studies (Bartels 2002a; Bartels 2002b; Berelson, Lazarsfeld, and McPhee 1954; Campbell et al. 1960; Zaller 1992), instrumental variables studies (Gabel and Scheve 2007; Gerber and Jackson 1993; Jacoby 1988), experimental studies (Bullock 2011; Cohen 2003; Druckman 2001; Kam 2005; Prior 2007), and panel studies (Abramowitz 1978; Achen and Bartels 2006; Carsey and Layman 2006; Ladd and Lenz 2008; Lenz 2009; Miller 1999; Rahn, Krosnick, and Breuning 1994; Zaller 1994). Researchers have also examined the effect of party cues in shaping candidate evaluations, conducting both experimental studies (Bullock 2011; Malhotra and Kuo 2008; Rahn 1993) and observational studies (Ansolabehere et al. 2006; Schaffner, Streb, and Wright 2001).

3. Researchers more often use cue taking to describe how people rely on cues to align their votes with their policy preferences (Popkin 1991; Sniderman, Brody, and Tetlock 1991). For example, Brady and Sniderman (1985) contend that people can use the likability of social groups, such as blacks and whites, to infer where these groups stand on policy.

4. Another explanation is that a desire to seem consistent may give rise to following, especially in the social context of a survey interview (Berinsky 2004; Paulhus 1984). Reducing "cognitive dissonance" (Festinger 1957) could also motivate this behavior.

5. Using vote choice instead of comparative approval ratings yields a similar finding, but a less eye-pleasing figure.

6. Since I am interested in the total effect of candidate support on changes in policy views, I do not control for party identification or other variables that might

influence views about the candidates, though substituting support of a particular party for support of a particular candidate yields similar findings.

7. The exact dates of the interviews are as follows. Wave 1: July 21–30 and August 4–13. Wave 2: August 4–13 and August 18–27. Wave 3: October 18–31. In previous chapters, I used the postelection wave as wave 3. In this case, unfortunately, the postelection wave asked only a small number of respondents about investing Social Security funds, resulting in a sample size of only about 220. Since I did not need to measure investing attitudes in wave 3 for priming or learning tests (because I always measure policy attitudes in prior waves), this posed no problem in the previous chapters. In this chapter, however, investing attitudes are the dependent variable, so I use the October interviews as wave 3 to increase the sample size. The findings do hold up if I use the postelection wave as wave 3, despite the small sample size.

8. About 5 percent appear to forget. These percentages differ slightly from those in the previous chapter (see table 5.1) because I am using the October wave, rather than the postelection wave, as wave 3 (see the previous endnote).

9. The estimates in the appendix show these effects for the two other knowledge groups—the never learners and the forgetters. We would not expect to find increased following among these groups and the estimates do not show any.

10. The decrease in effect size probably arises because strong supporters are more likely to follow than are weak supporters. Since the vote choice codes strong and weak supporters to the same value—for example, Republican vote—it underestimates the size of the effect between strong Democrat and strong Republicans.

11. As noted in chapter 3, I use vote whenever possible as the outcome variable, since vote is what we most care about in elections, but the absence of priming or learning effects holds when I use the same continuous measures.

12. As shown in the appendix, three of the cases have slightly negative baseline effects among the learners (f_{w1} from equation 19), which range from -0.044 in this case to -0.11 in the EU case. These negative baseline estimates may exaggerate the effect of learning, though never by more than 0.11. My motivation for using the three-wave test throughout this book is to establish a baseline, which is almost always positive among knowers and learners in other analyses.

13. In the appendix, I show that this pattern shows up for the whole sample in three of the six cases.

14. In two cases, public works jobs and defense, I can measure learning about both the candidates' and the parties' positions. When I switch to party positions in these two cases (using the same relative placement measure) and use party identification as the explanatory variable, I find effects similar to those in figure 8.4; that is, prior party identification has a surprisingly large and statistically significant effect on later policy views among those who learned the parties' positions. Among those who learned both the parties' and the candidates'

positions—forty-four people in the public works case and fifty-seven people in the defense case—party position mattered more than candidate position to the former but less to the latter (and it is statistically significant in both despite the small samples).

15. People may find candidates to be more or less reliable cue givers than parties for a variety of reasons. They may find parties more reliable because they know more about them than they do about candidates or because candidates can shift positions more quickly than can parties. Alternatively, they may find parties less reliable than candidates because parties are often made up of fractious coalitions.

16. Political science priming studies are not fully experimental because policy views are not randomly assigned. Likewise, this analysis is also not fully experimental because Bush approval, the key explanatory variable, is not randomly assigned, though it is observed six months before the experiment.

17. The 2007 interviews (wave 1) are from the Cooperative Congressional Election Study (Ansolabehere 2007). The 2008 reinterviews (wave 2) began with the priming treatment or the control condition, followed (in order but separated by filler items) by questions about (1) Bush approval, (2) respondents' attitudes about SCHIP expansion, and (3) whether Bush supports SCHIP expansion.

18. Put differently, this figure captures the intent-to-treat effect. Although the sample size is small, we can estimate the treatment effect on the treated with an instrumental variables (IV) estimator. To do so I look at the direct effect of knowing Bush's position on SCHIP views by party identification (rather than the effect of Bush approval on SCHIP views). Since the effect of the info treatment on knowledge of Bush's position (first stage) is considerably stronger for Republicans, this analysis only yields significant effects for Republicans. Instrumenting knowledge with an indicator for the info treatment yields an IV estimate for Republicans of 0.27 (SE = 0.17). This estimate implies that learning about Bush's position leads Republicans to shift toward Bush's view by about 27 points on the 100-point SCHIP expansion scale, a large effect given that Republicans already generally opposed expansion.

19. Although the estimates in the figures above strongly suggest that learning and adopting one's candidate's or party's position accounts fully for the appearance of priming in the conventional test, I do not show that here. In most of these cases, I have estimated the contribution for each knowledge category—knowers, learners, and so on—which is a function of the percentage of the sample that falls into each category and the change in the issue weight for that category according to the conventional test. These estimates suggest that over 90 percent of the conventional test's findings arise from the learners or partial learners.

20. The precision-weighted average is 0.38 for low knowledge and 0.24 for high knowledge, a difference that is statistically significant ($p < 0.03$).

21. I code respondents as knowing the candidates' ideological positions if

they place the liberal candidate to the left of the conservative candidate. If the surveys asked for candidate and party placements, I code respondents as knowing only if they correctly place the parties relative to each other and the candidates relative to each other. See the online appendix for details. This approach generally categorizes between 60 and 70 percent of respondents as knowing the ideologies.

22. More precisely, the precision-weighted average is 0.22 (SE = 0.07) for people who know the ideologies and 0.78 (SE = 0.11) for those who do not, a difference that is statistically significant at conventional levels ($p < 0.01$).

23. For compelling arguments to have produced effects this size, learning the positions and being exposed to those arguments would have to have been highly correlated.

24. In both the info and no info conditions, the participants read stories that indicate the arguments for and against expanding SCHIP.

25. For example, studies consistently find an association between party identification and candidate performance evaluations or assessments of the national economy (e.g., Gerber and Huber 2010).

Chapter 9

1. These studies on mood avoid problems with reverse causation by measuring aggregate public mood in the previous period.

2. A large theoretical and empirical literature investigates heuristics in politics (Althaus 2003; Austen-Smith and Banks 1996; Brady and Sniderman 1985; Iyengar 1990; Kuklinski and Quirk 2000; Lau and Redlawsk 2001; Lau and Redlawsk 2006; Lupia 1994; Meirowitz 2002; Popkin 1991; Sniderman 1993; Sniderman, Brody, and Tetlock 1991; Sniderman et al. 1986).

3. E.g., Zaller (2004). Aggregate-level evidence from subnational races is also consistent with some policy-based voting, though not a lot (Ansolabehere, Snyder, and Stewart 2001; Canes-Wrone, Brady, and Cogan 2002; Clinton 2008; Erikson, Wright, and McIver 1993; Gerber and Lewis 2004; Jacobson 1993; Poole and Rosenthal 1997).

4. For a discussion, see Gerber, Huber, and Washington (2010).

5. That is, we can only estimate what are called local treatment effects.

6. An earlier version of this manuscript included analysis of this panel in chapter 3. Since the other cases I analyze occur during campaigns and span just months or years, while this panel spans decades, I excluded it.

7. In contrast, only about 25 percent of male and female 1982 Republicans converted to prochoice views. Achen and Bartels's (2006) analysis excludes Catholics.

8. Given that only about 45 percent of respondents typically know the candi-

date or party positions on an issue (see table 5.1), the percent who care deeply about policy is almost certainly below that number.

9. The broader implications for democracy may not be that different even if most voters really do care about only one or two policies, since such a distribution of voters' concerns may still grant politicians considerable leeway on policy.

10. Although the multi-item-scale findings are often interpreted as supporting policy voting, their findings are nevertheless merely correlations—however strong—and so are vulnerable to the same reverse-causation problem that I discuss throughout this book. Instead of better capturing an underlying policy opinion, the multi-item scales could therefore be capturing people's tendency to follow their preferred party. If so, these scales may predominately contain variation from following and may even throw out (through averaging) information about people's policy preferences that are not driven by following.

11. Merrill Shanks and his collaborators have been collecting precisely this kind of data with their Public Agendas and Citizen Engagement Survey (PACES).

12. There are, of course, other explanations for the lack of convergence. A large theoretical literature explores when candidates should converge (Alesina 1988; Calvert 1985; Kollman, Miller, and Page 1992).

13. We also know that politicians "trespass," frequently discussing issues that seem to advantage their opponents (Sides 2006; Sigelman and Buell 2004). They may do so, as Anthony Downs explains, to appear more moderate: "Each party casts some policies to the other's territory in order to convince voters that its net position is near them" (1957, 135). For example, George W. Bush's support for education reform in the 2000 election may have made him seem moderate.

14. Only 16 percent shifted in the opposite direction; that is, came to see his party as more supportive of nuclear power.

15. Politicians can also try to lay blame elsewhere for poor performance. An alleged example of the latter is Jacksonian Democrats' avoiding blame for the credit crunch that followed the Bank War (President Jackson's dismantling of the Bank of the United States by removing federal deposits). According to one historical account, the public blamed the bank president, Nicholas Biddle, not Jackson or his party, and so did not punish Jackson's party in the 1834 midterm election (Brands 2006). More generally, Mark Kayser and Michael Peress (2011) find that voters do not punish incumbents for weak economies that result in global downturns, suggesting that incumbents may be able to lay blame elsewhere under certain conditions.

16. In concluding remarks about the cause of partisan polarization among citizens, Laura Stoker and Kent Jennings (2008) ask, "Are those cues sent primarily through election campaigns and the positions taken by major, national-level candidates?" My findings confirm that this is indeed a route to polarization. Future research could assess the influence of learning from campaigns on polar-

ization by examining whether citizens' knowledge of the parties' positions has increased along with their polarization on ideology and policy and whether variation in this knowledge explains variation in this polarization.

17. Continuing the logic of this account, had Bush's investing proposal swayed numerous voters, Gore probably would have buried the lockbox and endorsed the investing proposal. If he had, the issue probably would have vanished. Likewise, had Conservative Party appeals on European integration begun to erode Tony Blair's lead in the 1997 UK campaign, he might have shifted to the Conservative's popular position. William Riker (1996) called this the Dispersion Principle.

18. A large theoretical literature examines moral hazards, adverse selection, and retrospective voting (e.g., Ferejohn 1986; Banks and Sundaram 1993; Fearon 1999).

Appendix

1. The online appendix is available at http://www.press.uchicago.edu/books/lenz.

2. Ideally, I would measure changes in salience across the panel and interact this with issue attitudes. If issue-weight increases tend to occur only when the salience of an issue increases, this would support priming. Unfortunately, survey-based measures of issue salience or issue importance have proved problematic and generally fail to correspond with issue weights (Grynaviski and Corrigan 2006; Niemi and Bartels 1985), though see Krosnick (1988). Instead, I assume that any increase in issue weights between the pretreatment and posttreatment waves, not accounted for by learning, arises from priming. This is far from perfect. In particular, increases in certainty about the candidates' positions (Alvarez 1997) or about a performance issue could lead to increases in the issue weights. However, since I rarely find increases in issue weights (except with performance issues), these are potential, not actual problems. A possible problem with this test occurs if ρ is close to, or greater than, one, in which case, a constant $\tilde{b} > 0$ could imply a priming effect.

3. This is equivalent to estimating the following model:

$$y_{w2} = b_2 x_{w2} + b_{w1} x_{w1} + \rho_2 (y_{w2} - y_{w1}) + \rho_{w1} y_{w1} + u_{w1}, \text{ in which case } b = \Delta_{x21}.$$

References

Abramowitz, Alan I. 1978. "Impact of a Presidential Debate on Voter Rationality." *American Journal of Political Science* 22 (3): 680–90.

——. 1984. "National Issues, Strategic Politicians, and Voting-Behavior in the 1980 and 1982 Congressional Elections." *American Journal of Political Science* 28 (4): 710–21.

Abramowitz, Alan I., and Kyle. L. Saunders. 1998. "Ideological Realignment in the U.S. Electorate." *Journal of Politics* 60 (3): 634–52.

Abramowitz, Michael. 2007. "Bush Vetoes Children's Health Insurance Plan." *Washington Post*, October 3.

Abramson, Paul R., John H. Aldrich, and David W. Rohde. 2003. *Change and Continuity in the 2000 and 2002 Elections*. Washington, DC: CQ Press.

Achen, Christopher H., and Larry M. Bartels. 2004a. "Blind Retrospection: Electoral Responses to Drought, Flu, and Shark Attacks." Manuscript. Princeton University.

——. 2004b. "Musical Chairs: Pocketbook Voting and the Limits of Democratic Accountability." Manuscript. Princeton University.

——. 2006. "It Feels Like We're Thinking: The Rationalizing Voter and Electoral Democracy." Manuscript. Princeton University.

Adams, Gary D. 1997. "Abortion: Evidence of an Issue Evolution." *American Journal of Political Science* 41 (3): 718–37.

Adams, James, Michael Clark, Lawrence Ezrow, and Garrett Glasgow. 2004. "Understanding Change and Stability in Party Ideologies: Do Parties Respond to Public Opinion or to Past Election Results?" *British Journal of Political Science* 34 (4): 589–610.

——. 2006. "Are Niche Parties Fundamentally Different from Mainstream Parties? The Causes and the Electoral Consequences of Western European Parties' Policy Shifts, 1976–1998." *American Journal of Political Science* 50 (3): 513–29.

Alesina, Alberto. 1988. "Credibility and Policy Convergence in a Two-Party System with Rational Voters." *American Economic Review* 78 (4): 796–805.

Althaus, Scott L. 2003. *Collective Preferences in Democratic Politics: Opinion Surveys and the Will of the People.* New York: Cambridge University Press.

Althaus, Scott L., and Young Mie Kim. 2006. "Priming Effects in Complex Information Environments: Reassessing the Impact of News Discourse on Presidential Approval." *Journal of Politics* 68 (4): 960–76.

Alvarez, R. Michael. 1997. *Information and Elections,* Michigan Studies in Political Analysis. Ann Arbor: University of Michigan Press.

Alvarez, R. Michael, and Jonathan Nagler. 1995. "Economics, Issues, and the Perot Candidacy: Voter Choice in the 1992 Presidential Election." *American Journal of Political Science* 39 (3): 714–44.

——. 1998. "Economics, Entitlements, and Social Issues: Voter Choice in the 1996 Presidential Election." *American Journal of Political Science* 42 (4): 1349–63.

Andersen, Robert. 2003. "Do Newspapers Enlightened Preferences? Personal Ideology, Party Choice, and the Electoral Cycle: The United Kingdom, 1992–1997." *Canadian Journal of Political Science* 36 (3): 601–19.

Andersen, Robert, James Tilley, and Anthony F. Heath. 2005. "Political Knowledge and Enlightened Preferences: Party Choice through the Electoral Cycle." *British Journal of Political Science* 35 (2): 285–302.

Anderson, Harry. 1986. "The Politics of Chernobyl." *Newsweek*, June 2, 35.

Andrews, Robert M. 1980. "Carter Rejects Reagan Criticism; Kennedy Wraps Both." *Associated Press*, April 10.

Ansolabehere, Stephen (PI). 2007. "CCES Common Content, 2007," http://hdl .handle.net/1902.1/14078 V3 [Version].

Ansolabehere, Stephen, Shigeo Hirano, James M. Snyder, and Michiko Ueda. 2006. "Party and Incumbency Cues in Voting: Are They Substitutes?" *Quarterly Journal of Political Science* 1 (2): 119–37.

Ansolabehere, Stephen, and Shanto Iyengar. 1995. *Going Negative: How Attack Ads Shrink and Polarize the Electorate.* New York: Free Press.

Ansolabehere, Stephen, Jonathan Rodden, and James M. Snyder. 2008. "The Strength of Issues: Using Multiple Measures to Gauge Preference Stability, Ideological Constraint, and Issue Voting." *American Political Science Review* 102 (2): 215–32.

Ansolabehere, Stephen, James M. Snyder, and Charles Stewart. 2001. "Candidate Positioning in U.S. House Elections." *American Journal of Political Science* 45 (1): 136–59.

Austen-Smith, David, and Jeffrey S. Banks. 1996. "Information Aggregation, Rationality, and the Condorcet Jury Theorem." *American Political Science Review* 90 (1): 34–45.

Bafumi, Joseph, Andrew Gelman, and David K. Park. 2004. "What Does 'Do Campaigns Matter?' Mean?" Manuscript.

Banks, Jeffrey S., and Rangaragan K. Sundaram. 1993. "Moral Hazard and Adverse Selection in a Model of Repeated Elections." In *Political Economy: Institutions, Competition, and Representation*, edited by William A. Barnett, Norman Schofield, and Melvin Hinich, 295–311. New York: Cambridge University Press.

Bartels, Larry M. 1988. *Presidential Primaries and the Dynamics of Public Choice*. Princeton, NJ: Princeton University Press.

———. 1991. "Constituency Opinion and Congressional Policy Making—The Reagan Defense Buildup." *American Political Science Review* 85 (2): 456–74.

———. 1992. "The Impact of Electioneering in the United States." In *Electioneering: A Comparative Study of Continuity and Change*, edited by David Butler and Austin Ranney, 244–51. New York: Oxford University Press.

———. 1994. "The American Public's Defense Spending Preferences in the Post-Cold-War Era." *Public Opinion Quarterly* 58 (4): 479–508.

———. 2000. "Partisanship and Voting Behavior, 1952–1996." *American Journal of Political Science* 44 (1): 35–50.

———. 2002a. "Beyond the Running Tally: Partisan Bias in Political Perceptions." *Political Behavior* 24 (2): 117–50.

———. 2002b. "The Impact of Candidate Traits in American Presidential Elections." In *Leaders' Personalities and the Outcomes of Democratic Elections*, edited by Anthony King, 44–70. Oxford: Oxford University Press.

———. 2005. "Homer Gets a Tax Cut: Inequality and Public Policy in the American Mind." *Perspectives on Politics* 3 (1): 15–31.

———. 2006. "Priming and Persuasion in Presidential Campaigns." In *Capturing Campaign Effects*, edited by Richard Johnston and Henry E. Brady. Ann Arbor: University of Michigan Press.

———. 2008. *Unequal Democracy: The Political Economy of the New Gilded Age*. Princeton, NJ: Princeton University Press.

Belknap, George, and Angus Campbell. 1951. "Political Party Identification and Attitudes toward Foreign Policy." *Public Opinion Quarterly* 15 (4): 601–23.

Berelson, Bernard, Paul F. Lazarsfeld, and William N. McPhee. 1954. *Voting: A Study of Opinion Formation and Presidential Campaigns*. Chicago: University of Chicago Press.

Berger, Jonah, Marc Meredith, and S. Christian Wheeler. 2008. "Contextual Priming: Where People Vote Affects How They Vote." *Proceedings of the National Academy of Sciences* 105 (26): 8846–49.

Berinsky, Adam J. 2004. *Silent Voices: Public Opinion and Political Participation in America*. Princeton, NJ: Princeton University Press.

———. 2007. "Assuming the Costs of War: Events, Elites, and American Public Support for Military Conflict." *Journal of Politics* 69 (4): 975–97.

———. 2009. *In Time of War: Understanding American Public Opinion from World War II to Iraq*. Chicago: University of Chicago Press.

Berinsky, Adam J., Gregory A. Huber, and Gabriel S. Lenz. 2011. "Using Mechanical Turk as a Subject Recruitment Tool for Experimental Research." Manuscript. Massachusetts Institute of Technology.

Berinsky, Adam J., and Donald R. Kinder. 2006. "Making Sense of Issues through Media Frames: Understanding the Kosovo Crisis." *Journal of Politics* 68 (3): 640–56.

Berinsky, Adam J., and Jeffrey B. Lewis. 2007. "An Estimate of Risk Aversion in the U.S. Electorate." *Quarterly Journal of Political Science* 2 (2): 139–54.

Brader, Ted. 2006. *Campaigning for Hearts and Minds: How Emotional Appeals in Political Ads Work*. Chicago: University of Chicago Press.

Brady, Henry E., and Paul M. Sniderman. 1985. "Attitude Attribution—A Group Basis for Political Reasoning." *American Political Science Review* 79 (4): 1061–78.

Brands, Henry W. 2006. *Andrew Jackson: His Life and Times*. New York: Anchor Books.

Brians, Craig L., and Martin P. Wattenberg. 1996. "Campaign Issue Knowledge and Salience: Comparing Reception from TV Commercials, TV News, and Newspapers." *American Journal of Political Science* 40: 172–93.

Brody, Richard A., and Benjamin I. Page. 1972. "Comment—Assessment of Policy Voting." *American Political Science Review* 66 (2): 450–58.

Brown, Colin. 1997. "Major Pledges to Halt EU Reform." *The Independent*, April 22.

Brown, Derek. 1986a. "Chernobyl Boost for Labour in Dutch Election: Political Effects of the Soviet Nuclear Accident." *Guardian* (London), May 19.

———. 1986b. "Lubbers' Juggernaut Steamrolls Dutch Election." *Guardian* (London), May 23.

Brug, Wouter van der. 2001. "Perceptions, Opinions, and Party Preferences in the Face of a Real World Event: Chernobyl as a Natural Experiment in Political Psychology." *Journal of Theoretical Politics* 13 (1): 53–80.

Bullock, John G. 2011. "Party Cues and Policy Information in Informed Electorates." *American Political Science Review* 105 (3): 496–515.

Burt, Richard. 1980. "Carter, under Pressure of Crises, Tests New Foreign-Policy Goals." *New York Times*, January 9, A1, A8.

Butler, David, and Dennis Kavanagh. 1997. *The British General Election of 1997*. New York: St. Martin's Press.

Calvert, Randall L. 1985. "Robustness of the Multidimensional Voting Model: Candidate Motivations, Uncertainty, and Convergence." *American Journal of Political Science* 29: 69–95.

Cameron, Charles, and Nolan McCarty. 2004. "Models of Vetoes and Veto Bargaining." *Annual Review of Political Science* 7 (1): 409–35.

Campbell, Angus, Philip E. Converse, Warren E. Miller, and Donald E. Stokes. 1960. *The American Voter*. Chicago: University Of Chicago Press.

Canes-Wrone, Brandice, David W. Brady, and John F. Cogan. 2002. "Out of Step, Out of Office: Electoral Accountability and House Members' Voting." *American Political Science Review* 96 (1): 127–40.

Carmines, Edward G., and James H. Kuklinski. 1990. "Incentives, Opportunities, and the Logic of Public Opinion in American Political Representation." In *Information and Democratic Processes*, edited by John A. Ferejohn and James H. Kuklinski, 421. Urbana: University of Illinois Press.

Carmines, Edward G., and James A. Stimson. 1980. "The Two Faces of Issue Voting." *American Political Science Review* 74 (1): 89–91.

———. 1989. *Issue Evolution: Race and the Transformation of American Politics*. Princeton, NJ: Princeton University Press.

Carrubba, Clifford J. 2001. "The Electoral Connection in European Union Politics." *Journal of Politics* 63 (1): 141–58.

Carsey, Thomas M., and Geoffrey C. Layman. 2006. "Changing Sides or Changing Minds? Party Identification and Policy Preferences in the American Electorate." *American Journal of Political Science* 50 (2): 464–77.

CBO. 2007. "The State Children's Health Insurance Program." Accessed June 6, 2011. http://www.cbo.gov/ftpdocs/80xx/doc8092/05-10-SCHIP.pdf.

Chong, Dennis, and James N. Druckman. 2007. "Framing Public Opinion in Competitive Democracies." *American Political Science Review* 101 (4): 637–55.

———. 2010. "Dynamic Public Opinion: Communication Effects over Time." *American Political Science Review* 104 (4): 663–80.

Citrin, Jack, Donald P. Green, Christopher Muste, and Cara Wong. 1997. "Public Opinion toward Immigration Reform: The Role of Economic Motivations." *Journal of Politics* 59 (3): 858–81.

Clinton, Joshua D. 2008. "Representation in Congress: Constituents and Roll Calls in the 106th House." *Journal of Politics* 68 (2): 397–409.

CNN. 2007. "President Bush Vetoes Child Health Bill Again." December 13. Accessed November 11, 2008. http://articles.cnn.com/2007-12-12/politics/bush .schip_1_veto-message-schip-health-insurance-program?_s=PM:POLITICS.

Cobb, Michael D., and James H. Kuklinski. 1997. "Changing Minds: Political Arguments and Political Persuasion." *American Journal of Political Science* 41 (1): 88–121.

Cohen, Geoffrey L. 2003. "Party over Policy: The Dominating Impact of Group Influence on Political Beliefs." *Journal of Personality and Social Psychology* 85 (5): 808–22.

Conover, Pamela J., and Stanley Feldman. 1982. "Projection and the Perception of Candidates' Issue Positions." *Political Research Quarterly* 35 (2): 228–44.

Converse, Philip E. 1964. "The Nature of Belief Systems in Mass Publics." In *Ideology and Discontent*, edited by David E. Apter. New York: Free Press.

———. 1975. "Public Opinion and Voting Behavior." In *Handbook of Political*

Science, edited by Fred I. Greenstein and Nelson W. Polsby. Reading, MA: Addison-Wesley.

Daalder, Hans, and Galen A. Irwin. 1989. *Politics in the Netherlands: How Much Change?* London: Frank Cass.

Dahl, Robert Alan. 1956. *A Preface to Democratic Theory.* Chicago: University of Chicago Press.

Delli Carpini, Michael X., and Scott Keeter. 1996. *What Americans Know about Politics and Why It Matters.* New Haven, CT: Yale University Press.

Dover, E. D. 1998. *The Presidential Election of 1996: Clinton's Incumbency and Television.* Westport, CT: Greenwood Publishing Group.

Downs, Anthony. 1957. *An Economic Theory of Democracy.* New York: Harper.

Druckman, James N. 2001. "Using Credible Advice to Overcome Framing Effects." *Journal of Law, Economics, and Organization* 17 (1): 62–82.

Druckman, James N., and Justin W. Holmes. 2004. "Does Presidential Rhetoric Matter? Priming and Presidential Approval." *Presidential Studies Quarterly* 34 (4): 755–78.

Druckman, James N., Lawrence R. Jacobs, and Eric Ostermeier. 2004. "Candidate Strategies to Prime Issues and Image." *Journal of Politics* 66 (4): 1180–202.

Duch, Raymond M., and Randolph T. Stevenson. 2008. *The Economic Vote: How Political and Economic Institutions Condition Election Results.* New York: Cambridge University Press.

Economist. 1986. "Which Way Will the Wind Blow Holland?" May 17, 45.

Eijk, Cees van der, Galen Irwin, and Kees Niemöller. 1986. "The Dutch Parliamentary Election of May 1986." *Electoral Studies* 5 (3): 289–96.

Enelow, James M., and Melvin J. Hinich. 1984. *The Spatial Theory of Voting: An Introduction.* New York: Cambridge University Press.

Erikson, Robert S. 1989. "Economic Conditions and the Presidential Vote." *American Political Science Review* 83 (2): 567–73.

———. 2004. "Macro vs. Micro-Level Perspectives on Economic Voting: Is the Micro-Level Evidence Endogenously Induced?" Manuscript. Columbia University.

Erikson, Robert S., Michael MacKuen, and James A. Stimson. 2002. *The Macro Polity.* New York: Cambridge University Press.

Erikson, Robert S., Gerald C. Wright, and John P. McIver. 1993. *State House Democracy: Public Opinion and Policy in the American States.* New York: Cambridge University Press.

Espo, David. 1980. "Kennedy Compares Carter to Reagan." *Associated Press*, May 30.

Evans, Geoffrey. 1998. "Euroscepticism and Conservative Electoral Support:

How an Asset Became a Liability." *British Journal of Political Science* 28 (4): 573–90.

———. 1999. "Europe: A New Electoral Cleavage?" In *Critical Elections: British Parties and Voters in Long-Term Perspective*, edited by Geoffrey Evans and Pippa Norris, 207–22. Thousand Oaks, CA: Sage Publications.

Evans, Geoffrey, and Mark Pickup. 2010. "Reversing the Causal Arrow: The Political Conditioning of Economic Perceptions in the 2000–2004 U.S. Presidential Election Cycle." *Journal of Politics* 72 (4): 1236–51.

Evans, Rowland, and Robert Novak. 1980. "The Other Face of Carter's Defense Policy." *Washington Post*, August 27, A15.

Ezrow, Lawrence, Catherine de Vries, Marco Steenbergen, and Erica Edwards. 2007. "Dynamic Representation versus Dynamic Correspondence: Do Parties Respond to the Mean Voter Position or to Their Supporters?" Paper read at the Annual Meeting of the Midwest Political Science Association, Chicago.

Fearon, James. 1999. "Electoral Accountability and the Control of Politicians: Selecting Good Types versus Sanctioning Poor Performance." In *Democracy, Accountability, and Representation*, edited by Susan C. Stokes, Adam Przeworski, and Bernard Manin, 55–96. New York: Cambridge University Press.

Ferejohn, John. 1986. "Incumbent Performance and Electoral Control." *Public Choice* 50 (1): 5–25.

Festinger, Leon A. 1957. *A Theory of Cognitive Dissonance*. Evanstan, IL: Row and Peterson.

Finkel, Steven E. 1995. *Causal Analysis with Panel Data*. Thousand Oaks, CA: Sage Publications.

Finkel, Steven E., and John G. Geer. 1998. "A Spot Check: Casting Doubt on the Demobilizing Effect of Attack Advertising." *American Journal of Political Science* 42 (2): 573–95.

Fiorina, Morris P. 1981. *Retrospective Voting in American National Elections*. New Haven, CT: Yale University Press.

Fiorina, Morris P., Samuel J. Abrams, and Jeremy Pope. 2006. *Culture War? The Myth of a Polarized America*. 2nd ed. New York: Pearson Longman.

Fowler, Anthony, and Michele Margolis. 2011. "The Political Consequences of Uninformed Voters." Massachusetts Institute of Technology.

Franklin, Charles H., and John E. Jackson. 1983. "The Dynamics of Party Identification." *American Political Science Review* 77 (4): 957–73.

Freedland, Jonathan, and Michael White. 1997. "Major Launches Bitter Attack on Blair." *Guardian*, April 30, 12.

Gabel, Matthew, and Kenneth Scheve. 2007. "Estimating the Effect of Elite Communications on Public Opinion Using Instrumental Variables." *American Journal of Political Science* 51 (4): 1013–28.

Gaines, Brian J., James H. Kuklinski, Paul J. Quirk, Buddy Peyton, and Jays Verkuilen. 2008. "Same Facts, Different Interpretations: Partisan Motivation and Opinion on Iraq." *Journal of Politics* 69 (4): 957–74.

Gelman, Andrew, and Gary King. 1993. "Why Are American Presidential Election Campaign Polls So Variable When Votes Are So Predictable?" *British Journal of Political Science* 23 (4): 409–51.

Gerber, Alan S., and Gregory A. Huber. 2009. "Partisanship and Economic Behavior: Do Partisan Differences in Economic Forecasts Predict Real Economic Behavior?" *American Political Science Review* 103 (3): 407–26.

———. 2010. "Partisanship, Political Control, and Economic Assessments." *American Journal of Political Science* 54 (1): 153–73.

Gerber, Alan S., Gregory A. Huber, and Ebonya Washington. 2010. "Party Affiliation, Partisanship, and Political Beliefs: A Field Experiment." *American Political Science Review* 104 (4): 720–44.

Gerber, Elisabeth R., and John E. Jackson. 1993. "Endogenous Preferences and the Study of Institutions." *American Political Science Review* 87 (3): 639–56.

Gerber, Elisabeth R., and Jeffrey B. Lewis. 2004. "Beyond the Median: Voter Preferences, District Heterogeneity, and Political Representation." *Journal of Political Economy* 112 (6): 1364–83.

Germond, Jack W., and Jules Witcover. 1993. *Mad as Hell: Revolt at the Ballot Box, 1992.* New York: Warner Books.

Gilens, Martin. 2001. "Political Ignorance and Collective Policy Preferences." *American Political Science Review* 95 (2): 379–96.

Gladdish, Ken. 1986. "The Dutch Political Parties and the May 1986 Elections." *Government and Opposition* 21 (3): 317–37.

———. 1991. *Governing from the Centre: Politics and Policy-Making in the Netherlands.* London: Hurst.

Goldman, Peter Louis. 1994. *Quest for the Presidency, 1992.* College Station: Texas A&M University Press.

Goren, Paul. 2002. "Character Weakness, Partisan Bias, and Presidential Evaluation." *American Journal of Political Science* 46 (3): 627–41.

———. 2005. "Party Identification and Core Political Values." *American Journal of Political Science* 49 (4): 882–97.

Graber, Doris A. 1993. *Mass Media and American Politics.* 4th ed. Washington, DC: CQ Press.

Granger, Clive W. J. 1969. "Investigating Causal Relationships by Econometric Models and Cross Spectral Methods." *Econometrica* 37 (3): 424–38.

Green, Donald P., Bradley Palmquist, and Eric Schickler. 2002. *Partisan Hearts and Minds: Political Parties and the Social Identities of Voters.* New Haven, CT: Yale University Press.

Greenfield, Jeff. 1982. *The Real Campaign: How the Media Missed the Story of the 1980 Campaign.* New York: Summit Books.

Groseclose, Tim, and Nolan McCarty. 2001. "The Politics of Blame: Bargaining before an Audience." *American Journal of Political Science* 45 (1): 100–119.

Grynaviski, Jeffery D., and Bryce E. Corrigan. 2006. "Specification Issues in Proximity Models of Candidate Evaluation (with Issue Importance)." *Political Analysis* 14 (4): 393–420.

Guardian. 1997. "Wake Up to the Facts (Ad)." April 26, 28.

Hart, Austin. 2011. "Why Economic Messages Matter: The Campaign and the Economic Vote." Manuscript. University of Texas at Austin.

Healy, Andrew J., Neil A. Malhotra, and Cecilia H. Mo. 2010. "Irrelevant Events Affect Voters' Evaluations of Government Performance." *Proceedings of the National Academy of Sciences* 107 (28): 12506–11.

Healy, Andrew, and Neil Malhotra. 2009. "Myopic Voters and Natural Disaster Policy." *American Political Science Review* 103 (3): 387–406.

Hershey, Marjorie Randon. 2001. "The Campaign and the Media." In *The Election of 2000*, edited by Gerald M. Pomper, 46–72. New York: Seven Bridges Press.

Hetherington, Marc J. 1996. "The Media's Role in Forming Voters' National Economic Evaluations in 1992." *American Journal of Political Science* 40 (2): 372–95.

Hibbs, Douglas A. 1987. *The American Political Economy: Macroeconomics and Electoral Politics*. Cambridge, MA: Harvard University Press.

———. 2000. "Bread and Peace Voting in U.S. Presidential Elections." *Public Choice* 104 (1–2): 149–80.

Hillygus, D. Sunshine, and Todd Shields. 2008. *The Persuadable Voter: Wedge Issues in Political Campaigns*. Princeton, NJ: Princeton University Press.

Hobolt, Sara B., and Robert Klemmensen. 2008. "One for All, All for One: Issue Competition in Party Leader Rhetoric." Paper read at the Annual Meeting of the Midwest Political Science Association, Chicago.

Hume, David. 1888. *A Treatise of Human Nature*. Oxford: Clarendon Press.

Hurwitz, Jon, and Mark Peffley. 2005. "Playing the Race Card in the Post–Willie Horton Era." *Public Opinion Quarterly* 69 (1): 99–112.

Hutchings, Vincent L. 2003. *Public Opinion and Democratic Accountability*. Princeton, NJ: Princeton University Press.

Hyman, Herbert H., and Eleanor Singer. 1968. *Readings in Reference Group Theory and Research*. New York: Free Press.

Iyengar, Shanto. 1990. "Shortcuts to Political Knowledge: The Role of Selective Attention and Accessibility." In *Information and Democratic Processes*, edited by John A. Ferejohn and James H. Kuklinski, 160–85. Urbana: University of Illinois Press.

Iyengar, Shanto, and Donald R. Kinder. 1987. *News That Matters: Television and American Opinion*. Chicago: University of Chicago Press.

Iyengar, Shanto, Donald R. Kinder, Mark D. Peters, and Jon A. Krosnick. 1984.

"The Evening News and Presidential Evaluations." *Journal of Personality and Social Psychology* 46 (4): 778–87.

Jackson, John E. 1975. "Issues, Party Choices, and Presidential Votes." *American Journal of Political Science* 19 (2): 161–85.

———. 1991. "Estimation of Models with Variable Coefficients." *Political Analysis* 3 (1): 27–50.

Jacobs, Lawrence R., and Robert Y. Shapiro. 1994. "Issues, Candidate Image, and Priming: The Use of Private Polls in Kennedy's 1960 Presidential Campaign." *American Political Science Review* 88 (3): 527–40.

Jacobson, Gary C. 1989. "Strategic Politicians and the Dynamics of United States House Elections, 1946–86." *American Political Science Review* 83 (3): 773–93.

———. 1993. "Deficit-Cutting Politics and Congressional Elections." *Political Science Quarterly* 108 (3): 375–402.

Jacoby, William G. 1988. "The Impact of Party Identification on Issue Attitudes." *American Journal of Political Science* 32 (3): 643–61.

Jamieson, Kathleen Hall. 1996. *Packaging the Presidency: A History and Criticism of Presidential Campaign Advertising.* 3rd ed. New York: Oxford University Press.

Jamieson, Kathleen Hall, and Paul Waldman. 2001. *Electing the President, 2000: The Insiders' View.* Philadelphia: University of Pennsylvania Press.

Jenkins, Richard W. 2002. "How Campaigns Matter in Canada: Priming and Learning as Explanations for the Reform Party's 1993 Campaign Success." *Canadian Journal of Political Science* 35 (2): 383–408.

Jennings, M. Kent, Gregory B. Markus, Richard G. Niemi, and Laura Stoker. 2005. "Youth-Parent Socialization Panel Study, 1965–1997: Four Waves Combined." http://dx.doi.org/10.3886/ICPSR04037.

Jennings, M. Kent, and Richard G. Niemi. 1981. *Generations and Politics: A Panel Study of Young Adults and Their Parents.* Princeton, NJ: Princeton University Press.

Johnston, Richard, Andre Blais, Henry E. Brady, and Jean Crête. 1992. *Letting the People Decide: Dynamics of a Canadian Election.* Stanford, CA: Stanford University Press.

Johnston, Richard, Michael Gray Hagen, and Kathleen Hall Jamieson. 2004. *The 2000 Presidential Election and the Foundations of Party Politics.* New York: Cambridge University Press.

Johnston, Richard, and Emily Thorson. 2009. "Coalitions in Presidential Campaigns, 2000–2008: Structure and Dynamics." Manuscript. University of British Columbia.

Kaiser, Robert G. 1980. "Draft Platform Reflects Carter's Shift on Positions." *Washington Post*, June 22, A2.

Kam, Cindy. D. 2005. "Who Toes the Party Line? Cues, Values, and Individual Differences." *Political Behavior* 27 (2): 163–82.

Kaufman, Burton I., and Scott Kaufman. 2006. *The Presidency of James Earl Carter, Jr.* 2nd ed. Lawrence: University Press of Kansas.

Kayser, Mark Andreas, and Michael Peress. 2011. "Benchmarking across Borders: Electoral Accountability and the Necessity of Comparison." Manuscript. University of Rochester.

Kelleher, Christine A., and Jennifer Wolak. 2006. "Priming Presidential Approval: The Conditionality of Issue Effects." *Political Behavior* 28 (3): 193–210.

Kenski, Kate, and Natalie J. Stroud. 2005. "Who Watches Presidential Debates? A Comparative Analysis of Presidential Debate Viewing in 2000 and 2004." *American Behavioral Scientist* 49 (2): 213–28.

Kiewiet, D. Roderick. 1983. *Macroeconomics and Micropolitics: The Electoral Effects of Economic Issues.* Chicago: University of Chicago Press.

Kinder, Donald R., and Cindy D. Kam. 2009. *Us against Them: Ethnocentric Foundations of American Opinion.* Chicago: University of Chicago Press.

Kinder, Donald R., and Lynn M. Sanders. 1996. *Divided by Color.* Chicago: University of Chicago Press.

Kollman, Ken, John H. Miller, and Scott E. Page. 1992. "Adaptive Parties in Spatial Elections." *American Political Science Review* 86 (4): 929–37.

Kramer, Gerald H. 1971. "Short-Term Fluctuations in U.S. Voting Behavior, 1896–1964." *American Political Science Review* 65 (1): 131–43.

———. 1983. "The Ecological Fallacy Revisited: Aggregate-versus Individual-Level Findings on Economic and Elections, and Sociotropic Voting." *American Political Science Review* 77 (1): 92–111.

Krosnick, Jon A. 1988. "The Role of Attitude Importance in Social Evaluation: A Study of Policy Preferences, Presidential Candidate Evaluations, and Voting Behavior." *Journal of Personality and Social Psychology* 55 (2): 196–210.

———. 1990. "Government Policy and Citizen Passion: A Study of Issue Publics in Contemporary America." *Political Behavior* 12 (1): 59–92.

Krosnick, Jon A., and Matthew K. Berent. 1993. "Comparisons of Party Identification and Policy Preferences: The Impact of Survey Question Format." *American Journal of Political Science* 37 (3): 941–64.

Krosnick, Jon A., David S. Boninger, Yao C. Chuang, Matthew K. Berent, and C. G. Carnot. 1993. "Attitude Strength: One Construct or Many Related Constructs?" *Journal of Personality and Social Psychology* 65 (6): 1132–51.

Krosnick, Jon A., and Laura Brannon. 1993. "The Impact of the Gulf War on the Ingredients of Presidential Evaluations: Multidimensional Effects of Political Involvement." *American Political Science Review* 87 (4): 963–75.

Kuklinski, James H., and Norman L. Hurley. 1994. "On Hearing and Interpreting Political Messages: A Cautionary Tale of Citizen Cue-Taking." *Journal of Politics* 56 (3): 729–51.

Kuklinski, James H., and Paul J. Quirk. 2000. "Reconsidering the Rational Public: Cognition, Heuristics, and Mass Opinion." In *Elements of Reason: Cognition, Choice, and the Bounds of Rationality*, edited by Arthur Lupia and Mathew Daniel McCubbins, 153–82. New York: Cambridge University Press.

Labunski, Richard E. 2006. *James Madison and the Struggle for the Bill of Rights*, Pivotal Moments in American History. New York: Oxford University Press.

Ladd, Jonathan McDonald. 2007. "Predispositions and Public Support for the President during the War on Terrorism." *Public Opinion Quarterly* 71 (4): 511–38.

Ladd, Jonathan McDonald, and Gabriel S. Lenz. 2008. "Reassessing the Role of Anxiety in Vote Choice." *Political Psychology* 29 (2): 275–96.

Lang, Kurt, and Gladys Engel Lang. 1966. "The Mass Media and Voting." In *Reader in Public Opinion and Communication*, edited by Bernard Berelson and Morris Janowitz, ix, 788. New York: Free Press.

Lau, Richard R., and David P. Redlawsk. 2001. "Advantages and Disadvantages of Cognitive Heuristics in Political Decision Making." *American Journal of Political Science* 45 (4): 951–71.

———. 2006. *How Voters Decide: Information Processing during Election Campaigns*. New York: Cambridge University Press.

Layman, Geoffrey C., and Thomas M. Carsey. 2002. "Party Polarization and 'Conflict Extension' in the American Electorate." *American Journal of Political Science* 46 (4): 786–802.

Lee, Taeku. 2002. *Mobilizing Public Opinion: Black Insurgency and Racial Attitudes in the Civil Rights Era*, Studies in Communication, Media, and Public Opinion. Chicago: University of Chicago Press.

Lenz, Gabriel S. 2006. "What Politics Is About: Reevaluating the Evidence for the Priming Hypothesis." PhD diss., Princeton University.

———. 2009. "Learning and Opinion Change, Not Priming: Reconsidering the Priming Hypothesis." *American Journal of Political Science* 53 (4): 821–37.

Levendusky, Matthew. 2009. *The Partisan Sort: How Liberals Became Democrats and Conservatives Became Republicans*. Chicago: University of Chicago Press.

———. 2010. "Clearer Cues, More Consistent Voters: A Benefit of Elite Polarization." *Political Behavior* 32 (1): 111–31.

Lewis, Jeffrey B., and Gary King. 2000. "No Evidence on Directional vs. Proximity Voting." *Political Analysis* 8 (1): 21–33.

Lippmann, Walter. 1927. *The Phantom Public*. New York: Macmillan.

Loevy, Robert D. 1995. *The Flawed Path to the Presidency, 1992: Unfairness and*

Inequality in the Presidential Selection Process. Albany: State University of New York Press.

Lupia, Arthur. 1994. "Shortcuts versus Encyclopedias: Information and Voting Behavior in California Insurance Reform Elections." *American Political Science Review* 88 (1): 63–76.

———. 1995. "Who Can Persuade? A Formal Theory, a Survey Experiment, and Implications for Democracy." Paper read at the Annual Meeting of the Midwest Political Science Association, Chicago.

Lupia, Arthur, and Mathew D. McCubbins. 1998. *The Democratic Dilemma: Can Citizens Learn What They Really Need to Know?* New York: Cambridge University Press.

Macdonald, S. E., G. Rabinowitz, and O. Listhaug. 1998. "On Attempting to Rehabilitate the Proximity Model: Sometimes the Patient Just Can't Be Helped." *Journal of Politics* 60 (3): 653–90.

Mackie, Diane M., and Joel Cooper. 1984. "Attitude Polarization: Effects of Group Membership." *Journal of Personality and Social Psychology* 46 (3): 575–85.

Malhotra, Neil, and Alexander G. Kuo. 2008. "Attributing Blame: The Public's Response to Hurricane Katrina." *Journal of Politics* 70 (1): 120–35.

Margolis, Michael. 1977. "From Confusion to Confusion: Issues and the American Voter (1956–1972)." *American Political Science Review* 71 (1): 31–43.

Markus, Gregory B. 1988. "The Impact of Personal and National Economic Conditions on the Presidential Vote: A Pooled Cross-Sectional Analysis." *American Journal of Political Science* 32 (1): 137–54.

Markus, Gregory B., and Philip E. Converse. 1979. "Dynamic Simultaneous Equation Model of Electoral Choice." *American Political Science Review* 73 (4): 1055–70.

Matalin, Mary, and James Carville. 1995. *All's Fair: Love, War, and Running for President.* New York: Simon and Schuster.

McCain, John, and Mark Salter. 2002. *Worth the Fighting For: A Memoir.* New York: Random House.

McCarty, Nolan M., Keith T. Poole, and Howard Rosenthal. 2006. *Polarized America: The Dance of Ideology and Unequal Riches.* Cambridge, MA: MIT Press.

McCullough, David. 1993. *Truman.* New York: Simon and Schuster.

McLeod, Don. 1980. "Bush Wraps Carter, Reagan on War Talk." *Associated Press,* March 1.

Meirowitz, Adam. 2002. "Informative Voting and Condorcet Jury Theorems with a Continuum of Types." *Social Choice and Welfare* 19 (1): 219–36.

Mendelberg, Tali. 2001. *The Race Card: Campaign Strategy, Implicit Messages, and the Norm of Equality.* Princeton, NJ: Princeton University Press.

Miller, Joanne M., and Jon A. Krosnick. 2000. "News Media Impact on the Ingredients of Presidential Evaluations: Political Knowledgeable Citizens Are Guided by a Trusted Source." *American Journal of Political Science* 44 (2): 295–309.

Miller, Joanne M., and David A. M. Peterson. 2004. "Theoretical and Empirical Implications of Attitude Strength." *Journal of Politics* 66 (3): 847–67.

Miller, Warren E. 1976. "The Cross-National Use of Party Identification as a Stimulus to Political Inquiry." In *Party Identification and Beyond*, edited by Ian Budge, Ivor Crewe, and Dennis Farley, 21–32. New York: Wiley.

———. 1999. "Temporal Order and Causal Inference." *Political Analysis* 8 (2): 119–42.

Miller, Warren E., and Teresa E. Levitin. 1976. *Leadership and Change: The New Politics and the American Electorate*. Cambridge, MA: Winthrop Publishers.

Miller, Warren E., and J. Merrill Shanks. 1982. "Policy Directions and Presidential Leadership: Alternative Interpretations of the 1980 Presidential Election." *British Journal of Political Science* 12 (3): 299–356.

———. 1996. *The New American Voter*. Cambridge, MA: Harvard University Press.

Mitchell, Dona Gene. 2011. "It's about Time: The Dynamics of Information Processing in Political Campaigns." Manuscript. University of Nebraska.

Mondak, Jeffery J. 1993. "Source Cues and Policy Approval: The Cognitive Dynamics of Public Support for the Reagan Agenda." *American Journal of Political Science* 37 (1): 186–212.

Morris, Kenneth E. 1997. *Jimmy Carter, American Moralist*. Athens: University of Georgia Press.

Mutz, Diana C. 1992. "Mass Media and the Depoliticization of Personal Experience." *American Journal of Political Science* 36 (2): 483–508.

Nagourney, Adam. 1996. "Dole Asserts Data on Economy Shows Recession Is Near." *New York Times*, October 31.

Nelson, Jack. 1980. "New Bomber to Give U.S. Military Edge, Brown Says." *Los Angeles Times*, September 5, A1.

Nelson, Thomas E., Rosalee A. Clawson, and Zoe M. Oxley. 1997. "Media Framing of a Civil Liberties Conflict and Its Effect on Tolerance." *American Political Science Review* 91: 567–83.

Nelson, Thomas E., and Donald R. Kinder. 1996. "Issue Frames and Group-Centrism in American Public Opinion." *Journal of Politics* 58 (4): 1055–78.

Niemi, Richard G., and Larry M. Bartels. 1985. "New Measures of Issue Salience—An Evaluation." *Journal of Politics* 47 (4): 1212–20.

Norris, Pippa. 1998. "The Battle for the Campaign Agenda." In *New Labour Triumphs: Britain at the Polls*, edited by Anthony King, 113–44. Chatham, NJ: Chatham House Publishers.

Page, Benjamin I. 1978. *Choices and Echoes in Presidential Elections: Rational Man and Electoral Democracy.* Chicago: University of Chicago Press.

Page, Benjamin I., and Calvin C. Jones. 1979. "Reciprocal Effects of Policy Preferences, Party Loyalties, and the Vote." *American Political Science Review* 73 (4): 1071–89.

Page, Benjamin I., and Robert Y. Shapiro. 1992. *The Rational Public: Fifty Years of Trends in Americans' Policy Preferences.* Chicago: University of Chicago Press.

Patterson, Thomas E. 1980. *The Mass Media Election: How Americans Choose Their President.* New York: Praeger.

Patterson, Thomas E., and Robert D. McClure. 1976. *The Unseeing Eye: The Myth of Television Power in National Politics.* New York: Putnam.

Paulhus, Delroy L. 1984. "Two-Component Models of Socially Desirable Responding." *Journal of Personality and Social Psychology* 46 (3): 598–609.

Pennock, J. Roland. 1979. *Democratic Political Theory.* Princeton, NJ: Princeton University Press.

Petrocik, John R. 1996. "Issue Ownership in Presidential Elections, with a 1980 Case Study." *American Journal of Political Science* 40 (30): 825–50.

Poole, Keith T., and Howard Rosenthal. 1997. *Congress: A Political-Economic History of Roll Call Voting.* New York: Oxford University Press.

Popkin, Samuel L. 1991. *The Reasoning Voter: Communication and Persuasion in Presidential Campaigns.* Chicago: University of Chicago Press.

Posen, Barry R., and Stephen W. Van Evera. 1980. "Overarming and Underwhelming." *Foreign Policy* 40: 99–118.

Price, Vincent, and David Tewksbury. 1997. "News Values and Public Opinion: A Theoretical Account of Media Priming and Framing." In *Progress in Communication Sciences*, vol. 13, edited by G. A. Barnett and F. J. Boster, 173–212. Greenwich, CT: Ablex.

Prior, Markus. 2007. "Is Partisan Bias in Perceptions of Objective Conditions Real? The Effect of an Accuracy Incentive on the Stated Beliefs of Partisans." Manuscript. Princeton University.

Puglisi, Riccardo, and James M. Snyder. 2011. "The Balanced US Press." Manuscript. Harvard University.

Rabinowitz, George, and Stuart E. Macdonald. 1989. "A Directional Theory of Issue Voting." *American Political Science Review* 83 (1): 93–121.

Rahn, Wendy M. 1993. "The Role of Partisan Stereotypes in Information Processing about Political Candidates." *American Journal of Political Science* 37 (2): 472–96.

Rahn, Wendy M., Jon A. Krosnick, and Marijke Breuning. 1994. "Rationalization and Derivation Processes in Survey Studies of Political Candidate Evaluation." *American Journal of Political Science* 38 (3): 582–600.

Raudenbush, Stephen W., and Anthony S. Bryk. 2002. *Hierarchical Linear Mod-*

els: Applications and Data Analysis Methods, Advanced Quantitative Techniques in the Social Sciences, 1. Thousand Oaks, CA: Sage Publications.

Raun, Laura. 1986a. "Dutch Balk at Lubbers' Austerity Policies." *Financial Times* (London), May 19, 3.

———. 1986b. "Dutch Farmers May Sue Moscow." *Financial Times* (London), May 13, 3.

RePass, David E. 1971. "Issue Salience and Party Choice." *American Political Science Review* 65 (2): 389–400.

Rhodes, Richard. 2007. *Arsenals of Folly: The Making of the Nuclear Arms Race*. New York: Alfred A. Knopf.

Riker, William H. 1982. *Liberalism against Populism: A Confrontation between the Theory of Democracy and the Theory of Social Choice*. San Francisco: W. H. Freeman.

———. 1996. *The Strategy of Rhetoric: Campaigning for the American Constitution*. New Haven, CT: Yale University Press.

Roberts, Steven V. 1980. "Reagan, in Chicago Speech, Urges Big Increases in Military Spending." *New York Times*, March 18, B8.

Ropeik, David, and George Gray. 2002. *Risk: A Practical Guide for Deciding What's Really Safe and What's Dangerous in the World around You*. Boston: Houghton Mifflin.

Schaffner, Brian F., Matthew Streb, and Gerald Wright. 2001. "Teams without Uniforms: The Nonpartisan Ballot in State and Local Elections." *Political Research Quarterly* 54 (1): 7–30.

Schattschneider, Elmer E. 1960. *The Semisovereign People: A Realist's View of Democracy in America*. Hinsdale, IL: Dryden Press.

Schuil, Roberts. 1986. "Sunny Outlook for Lubbers Suddenly Clouded by Poison of Chernobyl." *The Times* (London), May 19.

Schumpeter, Joseph Alois. 1942. *Capitalism, Socialism, and Democracy*. New York: Harper.

Sears, David O., and Carolyn L. Funk. 1999. "Evidence of the Long-Term Persistence of Adults' Political Predispositions." *Journal of Politics* 61 (1): 1–28.

Sears, David O., and Richard R. Lau. 1983. "Inducing Apparently Self-Interested Political Preferences." *American Journal of Political Science* 27 (2): 223–52.

Sekhon, Jasjeet S. 2004. "The Varying Role of Voter Information across Democratic Societies." Manuscript. University of California, Berkeley.

Shani, Daniel. 2006. "Knowing Your Colors: Can Knowledge Correct for Partisan Bias in Political Perceptions?" Manuscript. Princeton University.

Shanks, Merrill, Douglas Strand, and Edward Carmines. 2003. "Policy-Related Issues in the 2002 Election." Paper read at Annual Meeting of the American Political Science Association, Philadelphia.

Shaw, Gaylord. 1980. "New Bomber to Give U.S. Military Edge, Brown Says." *Los Angeles Times*, August 23, A1.

Sheafer, T., and G. Weimann. 2005. "Agenda Building, Agenda Setting, Priming, Individual Voting Intentions, and the Aggregate Results: An Analysis of Four Israeli Elections." *Journal of Communication* 55 (2): 347–65.

Shepsle, Kenneth A. 1972. "The Strategy of Ambiguity: Uncertainty and Electoral Competition." *American Political Science Review* 66 (2): 555–68.

Sides, John. 2006. "The Origins of Campaign Agendas." *British Journal of Political Science* 36 (3): 407–36.

Sigelman, Lee, and E. H. Buell. 2004. "Avoidance or Engagement? Issue Convergence in U.S. Presidential Campaigns, 1960–2000." *American Journal of Political Science* 48 (4): 650–61.

Simon, Adam F. 2002. *The Winning Message: Candidate Behavior, Campaign Discourse, and Democracy.* New York: Cambridge University Press.

Smith, Terence. 1980. "Carter's Plans for Arms Rise." *New York Times,* December 14, A7.

Sniderman, Paul M. 1993. "The New Look in Public Opinion Research." In *Political Science: The State of the Discipline II,* edited by Ada Finifter, 219–45. Washington, DC: American Political Science Association.

Sniderman, Paul M., Richard A. Brody, and Philip Tetlock. 1991. *Reasoning and Choice: Explorations in Political Psychology.* New York: Cambridge University Press.

Sniderman, Paul M., Michael G. Hagen, Philip E. Tetlock, and Henry E. Brady. 1986. "Reasoning Chains: Causal Models of Policy Reasoning in Mass Publics." *British Journal of Political Science* 16 (4): 405–30.

Steele, Jonathan. 1986. "Dutch to Shelve N-Plants: Halt in Nuclear Plant Plans Could Signal an End of Expansion Programme." *Guardian* (London), May 8.

Steenbergen, Marco R., Erica E. Edwards, and Catherine E. de Vries. 2007. "Who's Cueing Whom? Mass-Elite Linkages and the Future of European Integration." *European Union Politics* 8 (1): 13–35.

Stevenson, Randolph T., and Lynn Vavreck. 2000. "Does Campaign Length Matter? Testing for Cross-National Effects." *British Journal of Political Science* 30 (2): 217–35.

Stimson, James A., Michael B. MacKuen, and Robert S. Erikson. 1995. "Dynamic Representation." *American Political Science Review* 89 (3): 543–65.

Stoker, Laura, and M. Kent Jennings. 2008. "Of Time and the Development of Partisan Polarization." *American Journal of Political Science* 52 (3): 619–35.

Tavits, Margit. 2007. "Principle vs. Pragmatism: Policy Shifts and Political Competition." *American Journal of Political Science* 51 (1): 151–65.

Taylor, Shelley E., and Susan T. Fiske. 1978. "Salience, Attention, and Attribution: Top of the Head Phenomena." *Advances in Experimental Social Psychology* 11: 249–88.

Tesler, Michael. 2011. "Priming Predispositions and Projecting Policy Positions:

An Account of When Political Communications Cause Priming or Projection." Manuscript. University of California, Los Angeles.

Thomas, Evan, ed. 1997. *Back from the Dead: How Clinton Survived the Republican Revolution*. New York: Atlantic Monthly Press.

Todorov, Alexander, Anesu N. Mandisodza, Amir Goren, and Crystal C. Hall. 2005. "Inferences of Competence from Faces Predict Election Outcomes." *Science* 308 (5728): 1623–26.

Tomz, Michael, and Robert P. Van Houweling. 2008. "Candidate Positioning and Voter Choice." *American Political Science Review* 102 (03): 303–18.

———. 2009. "The Electoral Implications of Candidate Ambiguity." *American Political Science Review* 103 (01): 83–98.

———. 2010. "Candidate Repositioning." Manuscript. University of California, Berkeley.

Toner, Robin. 1992. "Under the Dome: The Overview; Bush Promises Across-the-Board Tax Cut and an Economic Revival in a Second Term." *New York Times*, August 21, A1.

Trenaman, Joseph, and Denis McQuail. 1961. *Television and the Political Image: A Study of the Impact of Television on the 1959 General Election*. London: Methuen.

U.S. News & World Report. 1986. "An Aftershock Hits the Politics of Western Europe." June 2, 33.

Valentino, Nicholas A. 1999. "Crime News and the Priming of Racial Attitudes during Evaluations of the President." *Public Opinion Quarterly* 63 (3): 293–320.

Valentino, Nicholas A., Vincent L. Hutchings, and Ismail K. White. 2002. "Cues That Matter." *American Political Science Review* 96 (1): 75–90.

Vavreck, Lynn. 2009. *The Message Matters: The Economy and Presidential Campaigns*. Princeton, NJ: Princeton University Press.

Weisman, Steven R. 1980a. "Carter and Reagan 'Debate' in Ohio, Six Blocks Apart." *New York Times*, May 30, A1, B6.

———. 1980b. "The President and Congress Are Certain to Clash Again." *New York Times*, June 15, E4.

Westholm, Anders. 1997. "Distance versus Direction: The Illusory Defeat of the Proximity Theory of Electoral Choice." *American Political Science Review* 91 (4): 865–83.

Whitten, Guy D., and Harvey D. Palmer. 1996. "Heightening Comparativists' Concern for Model Choice: Voting Behavior in Great Britain and the Netherlands." *American Journal of Political Science* 40 (1): 231–60.

Wicker, Tom. 1980a. "Carter's Spending Games." *New York Times*, April 22, A23.

———. 1980b. "Jimmy Carter's Chickens." *New York Times*, September 14, E21.

Wilcox, Nathaniel, and Christopher Wlezien. 1993. "The Contamination of Responses to Survey Items: Economic Perceptions and Political Judgments." *Political Analysis* 5 (1): 181–213.

Wilson, George C. 1980a. "Carter to Support New U.S. Bomber." *Washington Post*, August 14, A1.

———. 1980b. "Carter: Shifting, Shoring up Position on Defense." *Washington Post*, August 19, A1, A4.

———. 1980c. "Joint Chiefs of Staff Break with Carter on Budget Planning for Defense Needs." *Washington Post*, May 30, A1, A16.

———. 1980d. "Navy's Shipbuilding May Shrink." *Washington Post*, August 9, A1.

———. 1980e. "Pentagon Budget Is Stretched Out." *Washington Post*, March 15, A13.

———. 1980f. "President, Brown Attack House Defense Additions." *Washington Post*, May 23, A1.

Wines, Michael. 1992. "The 1992 Campaign: The Republicans; Bush Says Economy Is Not as Bad as People Think." *New York Times*, September 22, A25.

Wlezien, Christopher. 2005. "On the Salience of Political Issues: The Problem with 'Most Important Problem.'" *Electoral Studies* 24 (4): 555–79.

Woodward, Bob. 1996. *The Choice: How Clinton Won*. New York: Simon and Schuster.

Yekev, Gary. 1986. "Landslide Win in Dutch Vote." *Christian Science Monitor*, May 23, 13.

Zaller, John. 1985. "Analysis of Information Items in the 1985 ANES Pilot Study." In *ANES Pilot Study Report, No. 002261*.

———. 1992. *The Nature and Origins of Mass Opinion*. New York: Cambridge University Press.

———. 1994. "Politics as Usual: The Rise and Fall of Candidate Perot." Manuscript. University of California, Los Angeles.

———. 2004. "Floating Voters in U.S. Presidential Elections, 1948–2000." In *Studies in Public Opinion: Attitudes, Nonattitudes, Measurement Error, and Change*, edited by Willem E. Saris and Paul M. Sniderman, 166–212. Princeton, NJ: Princeton University Press.

Index

Page numbers in italics refer to illustrations.

Huber, Gregory A., 22, 31, 232
Hume, David, 8
Humphrey, Hubert, 229
Hurley, Norman L., 89
Hurwitz, Jon, 20, 87
Hussein, Saddam, 98
Hutchings, Vincent L., 106, 213, 223
Hyman, Herbert H., 186

ideology in 1992 election, 7, 66–67, 97, 204;
and learning, 117–18; media priming of
overall ideology, 13; and voter following, 195–96, 207
ideology scale, 254, 277n17
informed cueing, 206–11
instrumental variables, 83, 121
interest groups, 219–20
"invisible bomber," 170
Iranian hostage crisis, 17, 65, 151, *154*, 156,
218
Irwin, Galen A., 68, 126, 128, 141, 143, 145
issue distances, 121, 238
"issue public" hypothesis, 223
issue voting, 1, 86, 122; among informed
voters, 221; performance issue voting,
49–52
issue voting studies, limitations and questions, 3–7, 231–33; associational research, 241; assumption that correlation implies causation, 6, 232, 233;
difficulty of using experimental methods, 276n6; experiments on agenda
setting and media priming, 228–29;
importance of performance issues,
224–25; information in experimental
stimuli, 232–33; measurement problems, 223–24; polarization, 231; politicians' ability to switch sides, 225–26;
primarily observational data on, 220–
21; rationalizing public, 230–31; role of
campaigns, 230; why candidates campaign on policy, 233–34; why performance more than policy, 226–28. *See
also* methodological issues
issue weights, *80*, 239, 241–42, 244, 282n28,
283n32, 294n2; changes in after increased prominence of issue, 26–28, 27,
74; and conventional test, 30; degree of
uncertainty, 35; of the economy, change
in 1980, 1992, and 1996 elections, 50–

52, *51*; of the economy, change in 1991
and 1992 surveys, 35; of the economy,
increase in before election of 1980, 48–
49; effect of media priming on economy
in evaluation of Bush in 1992, 29–30;
and media priming, 25–26, 216; positive, 114; of Social Security in 2000
election, correlation of with voting behavior, 58, *59*; three-wave test of comparison of two issue weights, 33–34
Iyengar, Shanto, 11, 15, 52, 89, 109, 228, 229

Jackson, Andrew, 293n15
Jackson, John E., 238
Jacksonian Democrats, 293n15
Jacobs, Lawrence R., 233
Jacobson, Gary C., 49
Jamieson, Kathleen Hall, 9, 45, 54, 57, 58,
65, 87, 88, 90, 176, 228
Japanese attack on Pearl Harbor, 155
Jennings, M. Kent, 222, 293n16
Johnston, Richard, 9, 57, 58, 68, 88, 90, 100,
280n8, 283n2

Kaiser, Robert G., 169
Kaufman, Burton I., 151
Kaufman, Scott, 151
Kavanagh, Dennis, 63, 110, 111
Kayser, Mark Andreas, 293n15
Keeter, Scott, 10
Kelleher, Christine A., 52
Kennedy, Edward, 45, 157, 163
Kenski, Kate, 64
Kiewiet, D. Roderick, 11, 21
Kinder, Donald R., 11, 52, 89, 228, 229, 232
King, Gary, 16, 52, 66, 83, 109, 125, 230,
238, 280n14
knowers, 70, *80*, 85, 105, 117–18, *118*, 134–
35, 136, 202, 206, 211, 286n7
Kohl, Helmut, 64
Kramer, Gerald H., 11, 21, 31
Krosnick, Jon A., 9, 98, 223
Kuklinski, James H., 89
Kuwait, Iraq invasion of, 98

Labour Party, Great Britain, 111, 221
Labour (PvdA), Netherlands, 126, 128,
142, 143
Labunski, Richard E., 1
Ladd, Jonathan McDonald, 69, 281n20

media priming (*continued*)
1980, 1992, and 1996 elections using
three-wave test, 50, *51*; of economy in
1996 campaign, three-wave test of, 43,
44; of economy in 1980 election, three-
wave test of, 45, 47–49, *48*; of economy
in 1992 election, three-wave test of, *32*,
33, 34, *36*, *38*; of economy in 1996 election, *41*, 41–42; effect on issue weight of
economy in evaluation of Bush, 1992,
29–30; and European Union integration as issue in British election of 1997,
63–64; failure of on nuclear power issue in 1986 Dutch election, 130, 132,
134, *135*; of Gore's dishonesty in 2000
election, 89; and importance of prior
assessments of economy as economy
becomes a more prominent campaign
issue, 50; and increased salience of an
issue, 12, 13; and issue weights, 25–26,
216; of labor union views, and 1948
Truman victory, 13; may lack power to
affect elections for policy issues, 86;
and misleading results of studies on
policy issues, 201–2; of overall ideology in 1992 presidential election, 13;
of performance issues, 245–47, 277n16;
and policy views, 247–53, 277n16; and
potential for voter manipulation, 52;
of Reagan's campaign emphasis on defense spending and Carter's battle with
Congress over the issue, 163; reverse
causation gives rise to appearance of,
186, 201–2; three-wave test of on policy issues, 55–56, 74–76, *75*, 242–45,
247, *249*; three-wave test of Social Security issue in 2000 election, 57–62, *60*,
61; two-wave test of on policy issues,
76–77, *78*, 247, *250*; and voter weighing
of economy when judging incumbent
president, 24
Mendelberg, Tali, 20, 87, 213, 232
Meredith, Marc, 281n20
methodological issues, 276n11; causation
from correlation, mistaken assumption of, 6, 232, 233; coding of learning
and knowledge, 285n6, 287n17, 291n21;
cross-sectional research, 185, 201–2,
213; directional models, 283n33; floor
and ceiling effects, 39; ideology scale,

254, 277n17; information in experimental stimuli, 232; instrumental variables,
83, 121; lagged dependent variable, 243,
278n12; multi-item scales, 224, 293n10;
open-ended questions, 280n10; placebo
test, 95; precision-weighted averages,
50, 74, 81, 103; proximity models, 83–
84, 282n22, 283n33, 283n34; regression
to the mean, 38–39, 179, 239, 243; structural equation modeling, 7, 276n6. *See
also* observational equivalence; partial
residual scatterplots; reverse causation
Mexican presidential election, 2006,
279n17
Miller, Joanne, 286n11
Miller, Warren E., 65, 168, 186, 223
missing values, 240–41
Mitchell, Dona Gene, 232
Mo, Cecilia H., 7
Mondak, Jeffrey J., 89, 186, 206
Mondale, Walter, 161
moral traditionalism scale, 245, 247, 254
Morris, Kenneth E., 151
Mulroney, Brian, 68
multi-item scales, 224, 293n10
Mutz, Diana C., 52
MX nuclear missile, 169

Nagler, Jonathan, 42–43, 219
Nagourney, Adam, 42
National Annenberg Election Study, 54,
57, 59, 60, 61, 91, 93, 94, 184, 188, 189,
191, 192, 284n3
NATO forces, 183
Nelson, Jack, 170
Netherlands: ban on outdoor grazing of
dairy cows after Chernobyl, 129; Christian Democrats (CDA), 126, 129, 142,
143, *144*; election results, 1982 and
1986, *142*; Labour (PvdA), Netherlands, 126, 128, 142, 143; Liberals
(VVD), 126, 129, 142; political parties before the 1986 election, *129*; polling forecasts and actual election results
for number of seats each party holds in
parliament, 1982 and 1986, *142*; Social
Liberals (D66), 126
Netherlands, nuclear power issue in 1986
election, 17, 67–68, 71, 77, 82, 117, 193,
218, 287n6; change in policy views but